The New Woman as Librarian

The Career of Adelaide Hasse

Clare Beck

The Scarecrow Press, Inc.
Lanham, Maryland • Toronto • Plymouth, UK
2006

SCARECROW PRESS, INC.

Published in the United States of America
by Scarecrow Press, Inc.
A wholly owned subsidiary of
The Rowman & Littlefield Publishing Group, Inc.
4501 Forbes Boulevard, Suite 200, Lanham, Maryland 20706
www.scarecrowpress.com

Estover Road
Plymouth PL6 7PY
United Kingdom

British Library Cataloguing in Publication Information Available

Library of Congress Cataloging-in-Publication Data
Beck, Clare.
  The new woman as librarian : the career of Adelaide Hasse / Clare Beck.
    p. cm.
  Includes bibliographical references and index.
  ISBN-13: 978-0-8108-5106-1 (pbk. : alk. paper)
  ISBN-10: 0-8108-5106-7 (pbk. : alk. paper)
  1. Hasse, Adelaide Rosalia, 1868–1953. 2. Women librarians–United States–
Biography. 3. Documents librarians–United States–Biography. 4. Government
publications–United States–Bibliography–Methodology–History. I. Title.
Z720.H35B43 2006
020.92–dc22   2006001892

♾™ The paper used in this publication meets the minimum requirements of
American National Standard for Information Sciences — Permanence of
Paper for Printed Library Materials, ANSI/NISO Z39.48-1992.
Manufactured in the United States of America.

Contents

Preface

This account of the life and career of Adelaide Hasse follows a conventional chronological structure. Some incidents appear in more than one chapter, in order to discuss them in different contexts. The prologue introduces persons and themes that will have a major part in the narrative, while the epilogue discusses Hasse's reputation and its place in the historiography of American libraries.

The nature of biography is such that almost every sentence might cite a reference. Mindful of the *Chicago Manual of Style*'s warning to minimize the clutter of notes, I have tried to simplify and consolidate references as much as possible, while still providing sufficient information. In many cases, several references have been combined in a single note at the end of the paragraph, as long as it seemed clear which source went with which quotation. There are numerous references to contemporary periodicals, particularly brief items in *Library Journal (LJ)* that may not have unique titles, such as editorials, letters, or reports on new publications or personnel changes; these are cited by date and page only. Conference proceedings in LJ or the *ALA Bulletin* usually are referenced as the proceedings issue and pages. Newspaper articles or editorials are cited only by date, with the headlines sometimes mentioned in the text. Annual reports of libraries or government agencies have been cited in a standard form, "[year] Annual Report," rather than giving the exact title, which may be long and variable. The annual report of New York Public Library (NYPL) was issued in two editions, as a separate and in the NYPL *Bulletin*; I used whichever was conveniently at hand and have not distinguished between them in the notes, which cite "NYPL [year] Annual Report"; usually the references are to Hasse's readily identifiable divisional reports.

The largest portion of the book deals with Hasse's twenty-one years at New York Public Library, which has been more written about than most American libraries. Background information was drawn from multiple sources. The library's annual reports, the extensive coverage in *Library Journal*, the official histories by Harry Lydenberg and Phyllis Dain, the biographies of John Shaw Billings, Catherine Shanley's dissertation on the Library Employees Union, and the memoir of Keyes Metcalf all are rich mines of information on an organization with a particularly complex history. As a key participant in the events recounted, Metcalf is quoted extensively, although, as the reader will learn, he is a notably unreliable narrator. Shanley is the essential source on the union and related issues. Phyllis Dain's *The New York Public Library: A History of Its Founding and Early Years* (New York: NYPL, 1972) provides a lucid overview of the library in the Billings era.

Hasse had a wide acquaintance, requiring mention of many of her contemporaries. Unless otherwise cited, biographical information is from standard references. For librarians, this is usually the *Dictionary of American Library Biography*, supplemented by *Who's Who in Library Service* (1933) and *Library Journal*. For those outside the library world, sources include *Who Was Who in America*, *National Cyclopedia of American Biography*, *Dictionary of American Biography*, and *Cyclopedia of American Biography*.

Hasse was acutely attuned to the spirit of her times, and events often had a dramatic impact on her life, requiring an account of the times as inseparable from the life. That context is drawn both from contemporary periodicals and from the vast historical literature of the sixty years beginning around 1890. Three invaluable studies were constant companions and guides: Mark Sullivan's five-volume *Our Times: The United States, 1900-1925* (New York: Scribner's, 1928-35), a contemporary journalist's lively account of America at the beginning of the twentieth century; David Kennedy's *Over Here: The First World War and American Society* (New York: Oxford University Press, 1980), a masterful history of the Progressive Era's collision with World War I; and Nell Irvin Painter's *Standing at Armageddon: The United States, 1877-1919* (New York: Norton, 1987).

Hasse's biography could not have been written without the collections of her papers in the NYPL Archives and the Library of Congress. Each has distinctive characteristics:

The papers at the Library of Congress (cited as AH-LC) are a small collection of what was left at her death and donated by her nephew. They are essential for tracing her career after she left New York but also contain materials going back to its beginning in 1889; in using these, I often mention them as something Hasse had kept all her life, in an indication of their apparent special significance to her. The LC collection also contains some family letters but little that provides insight into Hasse's personal life. There is no correspondence with two women especially close to her, Tessa Kelso and Tilloah Squires, and little about her adopted son.

In NYPL's Record Group (RG) 7, the Economics Division records, there are four boxes of the office files Hasse left behind in 1918 (cited as AH-NY). These were kept to be searched for evidence against her; apparently they were put in a box at some point and never discarded, eventually surfacing as an invaluable picture of details of her work. In addition to the letters she received, her replies are often included. Unfortunately, the papers have not been organized, and using them is like delving into a very cluttered attic. Box 3 is the most useful for the range of subjects and correspondents, while Box 2 contains her extensive correspondence with Henry Gardner about the state documents index, and Box 1 is mostly about collection building and reference service. Box 4 contains only a few items, and there also is an indecipherable letter book.

Also in RG 7 is the fascinating Adelaide R. Hasse Case box (cited as AH-CB), believed to be the papers collected by the administration as evidence against her. These are well organized by period and subject, but they make puzzling reading, because so many of them don't show anything bad about Hasse, and by current standards, most would not be appropriate evidence against an employee. There are no explanatory notes, but with long immersion in the attitudes of the director, Edwin Anderson, I surmised a subtext of resentment towards Hasse for such offenses as corresponding with the rebellious John Cotton Dana, expressing mildly feminist views, receiving praise from prominent library users, and criticizing the culture of public libraries. In citing these papers, I have often mentioned their provenance in the file of evidence against Hasse, because their use gives them added significance in the story.

Abbreviations

AH	Adelaide Hasse
AH-CB	Adelaide R. Hasse Case box, RG 7, Economics Division, New York Public Library Archives
AH-LC	Adelaide Hasse papers, Manuscript Division, Library of Congress
AH-NY	Adelaide Hasse papers, RG 7, Economics Division, New York Public Library Archives
ALA	American Library Association
DALB	*Dictionary of American Library Biography*
GPO	U.S. Government Printing Office
LAPL	Los Angeles Public Library
LC	Library of Congress
LEU	Library Employees Union
LJ	*Library Journal*
NYPL	New York Public Library
PL	*Public Libraries*
SL	*Special Libraries*
SLA	Special Libraries Association

Acknowledgments

This biography of Adelaide Hasse was undertaken at the suggestion of Norman Horrocks of Scarecrow Press. His interest in library history and biography is especially valuable for its rarity in a profession that too often lacks awareness of its past.

I am especially grateful for the help of several admirers of Adelaide Hasse. Her great-grandniece, Ariel Fielding, shared materials in her possession and her own well-informed perceptions about Hasse and the women of her era, as well as providing constant interest and encouragement. David Laughlin most helpfully shared his reasearch, and Thomas Duszack was generous with encouragement and support.

Many librarians and archivists helped my research and thinking about Adelaide Hasse. At New York Public Library, Bob Sink pointed me to archival records that answered various questions. Susan McGrath and Sarah Chilton of the Brookings Institution located essential materials in their archives. Kim Walters of the Braun Research Library, Southwest Museum, Nancy MacKechnie of the Vassar College Archives, and Julio Hernandex-Delgado and Maggie Desgranges of the Hunter College Archives were prompt in retrieving and sending copies of material in their collections, as were staff of the American Library Association Archives in the University of Illinois Library, the University of Pennsylvania Library, the New Mexico State Museum, and the Gelman Library of George Washington University. Staff of the National Archives in Washington and College Park, at the Franklin D. Roosevelt Presidential Library, and at the Federal Civilian Personnel Records Center provided invaluable help in locating items requested from their national treasure trove. Mary Redmond provided both a friend's interest and help in tracking down some obscure references to New York State Library publications. Jane Rubens shared her home on several of my expeditions to New York. Margaret Mouzon, Lorna Peterson, Bernadine Abbott Hoduski, Patricia Belier, the late Lois Mills, Helen Wilkinson, and the late Nelly Doll offered encouragement and useful insights.

Grateful acknowledgment is made to the New York Public Library, Astor, Lenox, and Tilden Foundation, for permission to quote from papers in the library's archives and in the Richard Rogers Bowker papers, Manuscripts and Archives Division, and to the Manuscripts and Special Collections Library, Columbia University, for permission to quote from the Melvil Dewey papers.

A German scholar, Peter Burger, shared his understanding of the German background of the Hasse family. My brother Justin Beck helped with research on a California lawsuit, and my nephew Brian Beck checked references in the Dewey papers while a student at Columbia. Julie Berebitsky shared her knowledge of adoption by single career women early in the twentieth century.

My interest in investigating the career of Adelaide Hasse began with a serendipitous encounter with Laurel Grotzinger's article on Hasse in the *ALA World Encyclopedia of Library and Information Services*. I am grateful to Dr. Grotzinger for her research in the lives of women librarians and the lucid writing that aroused my curiosity, as well as her encouragement of my further research. With hindsight, I see the hazards of attempting a biography of a woman whose career not only lasted sixty years but also encompassed the major professional issues of her time; while I wish I could have spent another ten years exploring many questions, my hope is that others will pursue further discoveries out of the same curiosity with which I followed in the footsteps of Laurel Grotzinger. On this journey of discovery, I greatly benefited from the friendship of another pioneer in the history of women librarians, Suzanne Hildenbrand, who shared her insights on library history and prodded me to write when I wanted to go on and on with the research. Both of these scholars have made unique contributions to study of the history of women in libraries, and this book would not have been written without their pathfinding.

Prologue

American Library Association, 1891

When the American Library Association held its annual conference in October 1891, the meeting was on the West Coast for the first time in ALA's fifteen-year history. The choice of San Francisco was meant to be an inclusive symbol of the national nature of the library movement and its association, which had been founded and largely dominated by those from the Northeast.

The attendance was not large, only eighty, as few eastern librarians made the transcontinental journey, but a dedicated group of association leaders had traveled together, making the long train trip part of the conference networking, "knitting together with golden threads," as Richard Bowker of *Library Journal* put it, the bonds of a profession that was sure it was reinventing itself in America.[1] For California librarians, it was a rare opportunity to attend a national conference and meet the leaders in their developing field. For one young newcomer in particular, it was the beginning of decades of professional activity in a career of unusual length and prominence.

Adelaide Hasse was only twenty-three and had been employed by the Los Angeles Public Library for just two years, but her energy and ability had already made her the "first assistant" to the librarian, Tessa Kelso. She had come with Kelso to join the discussions about the perennial topics of such meetings: standardization, public support, relations with the schools, and the best methods of improving access to libraries by cataloging, classifying, shelving, binding, and building design. In his presidential address, Samuel Green spoke of the fundamental task of serving people and pointed to the progress made in meeting the pragmatic test of usefulness, ranging from the spread of public libraries in cities and towns to the development of the largest medical library in the world by Dr. John Shaw Billings, a name that would have special meaning for Adelaide Hasse.

Among those in attendance were others who would figure in Hasse's career. There was John Cotton Dana of the Denver Public Library, an iconoclast who would be an ally and inspiration. Richard Bowker, editor and publisher of *Li-*

brary Journal and longtime chair of ALA's Public Documents Committee, would be an ambivalent observer, often praising Hasse's work but publicly attacking her at a time of crisis. Azariah Root of Oberlin College would indirectly play a key role in her life by bringing into library work his brother-in-law Keyes Metcalf, who would be Hasse's cleverest enemy. Colonel W. H. Lowdermilk, a Washington book dealer who specialized in government publications, would be of crucial help in advancing her career.

Also present were such prominent women librarians as Mary Eileen Ahern, Caroline Hewins, and Mary Wright Plummer, all of whom Hasse would know well in the coming years. There were almost as many women as men librarians at the meeting, and although there had not yet been a woman president of the association, the women members served on committees and participated in discussions, and the conference would elect Hewins the first woman vice-president. All the talk in the press of the "New Woman"—independent, educated, ambitious—seemed to be reality among librarians. For Hasse, already inspired by Tessa Kelso, such visible evidence of the opportunities for women in library work was an added spur to her growing ambition.

Indeed, *Library Journal* had just published Caroline Hewins' thoughts on women librarians, warning those who expected short hours and undemanding work, "There are no easy places in a library where a girl can play 'lady.'"[2] The work was physically and intellectually demanding, eight or ten hours a day, including most evenings, and the successful woman would need "perfect health, a quick, alert mind, ability to adapt herself to all kinds of people, the power of analysis and comparison, a good memory, a knowledge of languages—the more the better—familiarity with books of reference, and habits of system and order." This could have been a description of Adelaide Hasse, and certainly it expressed her view that libraries required more than a ladylike fondness for genteel literature. Hewins had written originally for her local newspaper, explaining library work to the community, just as Tessa Kelso, a former journalist, encouraged publicity for their efforts in Los Angeles.

The Californians had ample opportunity to get acquainted with the eastern librarians, for along with the sessions where papers were read and business conducted, there was a whirl of expeditions and social events, to the point that the conference was criticized for doing little work. The visiting librarians took the street railway to Golden Gate Park, Sutro Heights, and the Cliff House, where the millionaire bibliophile Adolph Sutro entertained them. There was a boat trip round San Francisco Bay and a special train to the new Stanford University, where they were addressed by the president and entertained by Senator and Mrs. Stanford. In the evenings, there were titillating tours of the dark, crowded warrens of Chinatown. One afternoon they crossed the bay to Oakland and Berkeley, where President Kellogg welcomed them to the small, dusty campus of the University of California. Just a month earlier, the university had received its first gift from a philanthropist who would be a major force in its development, when Phoebe Hearst gave money for the first scholarships for women, to go to those of "high character and noble aims."[3]

There was an elegant closing banquet in the white and gold splendor of the Palace Hotel, where the courses included canapés de caviar, filet de boeuf à la

Richelieu, asparagus with hollandaise sauce, petits fours, fruit, cheese, and even champagne toasts, accompanied by many speakers and much inspiration. President Kellogg came from his unimpressive campus in Berkeley to predict that the local universities, Stanford and the University of California, would be as Harvard and Yale or Oxford and Cambridge in the great progress of the coming twentieth century. A representative of the city spoke also of progress and the vital role of librarians in organizing and retrieving information, proclaiming, "There is no employment so important in the economy of the present civilization as that of the librarian."

For Hasse, there was personal significance in the speech of the president-elect, Dr. K. A. Linderfelt of the Milwaukee Public Library. She had been born and raised in the distinctively German American culture of Milwaukee and would always be proud of her ancestry and the progressive values of her native state. Amid the usual banalities about the beauty and prosperity of his city, Linderfelt proclaimed that while it might be unusual in San Francisco to see ladies present at a hotel banquet, "what men can do in Milwaukee, women can do." The accuracy of his assertion would be demonstrated six months later, when Linderfelt was charged with embezzlement and replaced as Milwaukee librarian by a woman, Theresa West, who later would be ALA's first woman president.

The banquet did not end Hasse's encounter with the eastern librarians, who returned home by way of a leisurely trip down the coast that included a stop in Los Angeles. Their visit was vividly reported to the readers of *Library Journal* by Mary Eileen Ahern:

> To say the entertainment . . . was in the hands of Miss Kelso and her able assistant Miss Hasse, declares at once its high order. A very elegant and cordial reception . . . was held in the evening in the handsome rooms of the public library, where youth, beauty, and intellect bade a hearty welcome to this vigorous city. A late hour found the party wending the way back to the Westminster [hotel],—the gentlemen with ghosts of bright eyes and silvery voices keeping company with their reluctantly returning steps, and the young ladies wishing Tempus wouldn't fugit. . . . Next morning, Miss K. with her able co-adjutants were at the hotel at an early hour, and the librarians were taken around to see the city. Down the wide avenues the party wended its way, each carriage with some fair or brave resident in it, to point out the places of interest or beauty, or even to give a tip on the price of corner lots. The wonderful stories of wealth and progress, where just a few years ago "the rank thistle nodded in the wind," were amazing.

After only two years in the field, working in the small, remote city of Los Angeles, Hasse now had met the leaders of the library movement and been praised in the pages of their professional journal. That was a heady experience, but equally important was her exposure to a topic that had frustrated the association at meeting after meeting for most of its existence, the problems of government publications.

At the end of its first century, the United States Government could point to many achievements, but a coherent information policy was not among them. Starting as a new form of government in the new capital city of a new country, the federal government had dealt more or less effectively with enormous challenges, necessarily improvising and compromising, without established institutions or traditions of public administration. There was no national library (though the Library of Congress partially played the role), no national archives, no national gazette of government announcements, no central statistical agency, and no complete catalog or index of government publications. The tripartite nature of the government complicated efforts to develop policy, with many publications issued three times: the original agency issuance, another edition in the numbered series of congressional documents, and then again within the thick bound volumes of another numbered congressional series (the "serial set"). The Government Printing Office was in the legislative branch, while the Superintendent of Documents office, which struggled to achieve bibliographic control of government publications, was in the executive branch as a subdivision of the Interior Department. There was a well intentioned effort to make public documents widely available by distribution to depository libraries, but the designated libraries found this a mixed blessing, as a deluge of documents arrived without guidance or support for organizing and maintaining them.

ALA's 1891 discussion began at the first session with the report of the Public Documents Committee. Chairman Richard Bowker, the publisher with wide experience in both business and reform movements, spoke of his efforts to lobby Congress for "better and more equitable distribution to libraries of the public documents." A congressional committee was inquiring into the issues, and Superintendent of Documents John G. Ames had presented his views, shared by ALA, on the need for a more systematic approach to government printing. The Public Documents Committee hoped to testify as well.

A minority report from J. P. Dunn, state librarian of Indiana, dissented from Bowker's hopeful view. He had visited the committee with the intention of testifying but had been brusquely dismissed by the chairman, Senator Manderson, "who has not the slightest comprehension of this subject from the library standpoint." Dunn bluntly expressed what would often be a quiet complaint among librarians, that congressional attention focussed erratically on cutting costs more than on real efficiency, with no understanding of the needs of libraries and little sense of government information policy. As for the agencies, they had no consistent policy or practice in distributing their publications, with some "laboring under the delusion that they exist by divine grace, and whether the public is served or not served, it is to their eternal glory." Dunn called for action by librarians to get the attention of their local newspapers and members of Congress.

This was discreetly reinforced by the reading of a letter from Superintendent of Documents Ames, who urged ALA to appoint a "strong committee," able to present its views to congressional committees and backed up by libraries' communications to their representatives in Washington. He also noted the need for a comprehensive index of the publications of all government agencies.

On Bowker's motion, President Green appointed a special committee of Bowker, Lowdermilk, and Hewins to report to the conference on public documents. Lowdermilk immediately launched into a litany of the problems: lack of codification of printing laws, delays in distribution to depository libraries, the bewildering nature of the congressional series, the lack of a proper index. He was careful, however, to express confidence in the good intentions of Congress if fully informed on the issues. President Green added assurances that Senator Manderson was a friend of libraries and that ALA had "made a real advance" and was "acting on the right line." Bowker repeated his hope of progress, "as the public is beginning to understand the value of having government publications at hand for consultation."

At the last session, Bowker presented the special report on public documents that identified the essential elements of a "satisfactory system of government issues" sought by ALA: standardized formats and issuance; complete distribution to depository libraries by a central office; and comprehensive indexing, planned in "full consultation with the best bibliographical authorities." The accompanying resolutions spoke sharply of the "present lack of system . . . great waste . . . an entire confusion as to arrangement, indexing and binding" and offered ALA's assistance in "promoting better methods." The report and resolutions were unanimously adopted, and the standing Committee on Public Documents was referred back to its continuing task of negotiating with Congress. It would be four more years before major legislation passed in the form of the Printing Act of 1895, which would give new direction to the distribution and bibliographic control of public documents. It also would give Adelaide Hasse a unique opportunity at a crucial point in her career.

Earlier in the conference, public documents also had been discussed in a paper on their cataloging and classification in the San Francisco public library. A few months previously, *Library Journal* had published a similar piece on the classification and organization of documents as a special collection in a university library.[4] Both writers emphasized the problems documents presented for libraries, particularly their issuance in complicated series that included diverse subjects. The special aspects of government publications would be on Adelaide Hasse's mind back in Los Angeles as she organized her library's documents, and they would become the focus of a career that would last for sixty hectic, sometimes stormy years dedicated to improving public access to government information.

Notes

1. All references to the conference are from the proceedings, *Library Journal* 16 (Dec. 1891). Prior to the establishment of the *ALA Bulletin* in 1908, conference proceedings were published as an issue of LJ.

2. Caroline Hewins, "Library Work for Women," LJ 16 (June 1891): 273-74.

3. Judith Robinson, *The Hearsts: An American Dynasty* (New York: Avon Books, 1991), 263.

4. W. A. Merrill, "Cataloging of Public Documents," LJ 16 (April 1891): 107.

PART I

BEGINNINGS

Chapter 1

Origins, 1868-1889

Adelaide Hasse was born into an America forever changed by the Civil War. With the slavery problem finally settled, the northern states dominant, and the federal government strengthened, the United States hurtled ahead on a course of expansion and development. By the end of its first century, the nation would be transformed from the original thirteen small agrarian states to a dynamic economic power, its vast area linked by new means of transportation and communication. The pace of change brought enormous turmoil, making great demands on government as it developed along with the country.

The year of Adelaide Hasse's birth, 1868, was typical of the tumultuous postwar period, but it acquired special significance for American women when Congress' passage of the Fourteenth Amendment for the first time limited a constitutional right to "male citizens." In so explicitly denying them the right to vote, Congress shocked American women into awareness that civil rights would not be readily granted by a beneficent male power structure but would have to be fought for over many long, hard years; the National Woman Suffrage Association was founded the next year. To the educated, reform-minded women of the North, expecting recognition for their work in the antislavery movement and the war effort, it was painful to realize that newly emancipated, illiterate black field hands had a constitutional right to vote so long as they were men, while no women were guaranteed that fundamental right of citizenship. Five years later, the Supreme Court ruled that women had no constitutional right to enter the professions, deciding against Myra Bradwell's suit to obtain a license to practice law. In a concurring opinion, one justice claimed that divine law limited women to the private, domestic sphere.

Rejection as women became an impetus to seek change as women, in women's organizations, women's colleges, and women's professions. American women organized for social change, from small local clubs to the large organizations that linked them across the nation: the General Federation of Women's Clubs, the suffrage movement (split into two organizations for much of the period), and the largest and most dynamic, the Women's Christian Temperance

Union, founded in 1874 to fight the destructive power of liquor but soon allied with suffrage and other groups seeking reforms. Denied the vote, women developed their own organizations and leaders to influence civic affairs. Denied entrance to many occupations, they expanded their niches in teaching and health care and entered new fields like public libraries and social work. Increasingly, they pursued higher education, in women's colleges, mostly female normal (teachers') colleges, and the new coeducational state universities. It would be the era of the New Woman, and for Adelaide Hasse and many women of her generation, there would be unprecedented opportunities and painful limitations in their search for a new way of life. Their aspirations were immortalized in another notable event of 1868, the publication of Louisa May Alcott's *Little Women*, with its rebellious heroine Jo March, whose "ambition was to do something very splendid; what it was she had no idea . . . but left it to time to tell her; and meanwhile found her greatest affliction in the fact that she couldn't read, run, and ride as much as she liked. A quick temper, sharp tongue, and restless spirit were always getting her into scrapes, and her life was a series of ups and downs."

Adelaide was also shaped by the atmosphere of her native city. Milwaukee was known as the center of the successful immigrant culture of German Americans, with a civic life richer than that of most midwestern cities. Hasse's ancestry was German on both sides, all her grandparents having come from Germany.

Her mother, Adelaide Trentlage, was born in 1848, the eldest child of J. G. Trentlage, who had immigrated in 1842 at the age of eighteen, perhaps with the common motive of avoiding military service, as a biographical note mentions that he had the experience of being drafted in both Germany and the United States. After a period of traveling, he settled in New York City, where he married Elise Perkin. They soon moved to Milwaukee, where he clerked in stores until opening his own hardware store in 1871. He may have been delayed in starting his business by having to pay a substitute when he was drafted in the Civil War, despite being almost forty and a father. Trentlage enjoyed moderate success, with the size of his store growing steadily over time, and was able to support his family of seven children in a "pleasant residence" on First Avenue.[1]

Her father's side of the family was more intellectual. The Hasses were an established family with a tradition of highly educated civil servants, pastors, and professors in the German kingdom of Saxony.[2] Her great-grandfather was a mine inspector in Freiberg, a mining center near Dresden. The area had been known for its silver and lead mines for centuries, and Freiberg was the administrative center of the kingdom's mines and site of a mining school renowned for its faculty, laboratories, and library. Her grandfather, Carl Edward Hasse, had a university education and a career as a lawyer, judge, and actuary in the Freiberg area, but in the 1840s he decided to emigrate to America with his wife Rosalie Thiele, a merchant's daughter, and their son Hermann.[3] With characteristic Hasse thoroughness, he prepared so carefully that he was able to publish a book of directions for Germans interested in going to Wisconsin and Iowa in 1841, four years before the Hasse family made the journey to Wisconsin.[4]

Carl Edward seems to have had political motives for leaving his homeland and career in middle age. His granddaughter Adelaide later identified him as a

"Forty-Eighter," one of the idealistic liberals who rebelled against the autocratic governments of Europe in 1848: "My father's father collected his belongings after the revolution of 1848, and, collecting himself, he obeyed his government's orders to leave Germany, and came to the United States."[5] This does not match the arrival date, 1845, given in two biographical dictionaries, which not only specify the date but also mention that Adelaide's father, born in 1836, well remembered the long trip when he was nine years old. Many immigrants in the period considered themselves Forty-Eighters regardless of the exact year of departure. Tensions were rising in Saxony in the early 1840s, as the middle class pressed for reforms, such as freedom of the press and public judicial proceedings. In 1845, a crisis developed with the appointment of a reactionary government and an incident of troops firing on demonstrators. Whether Carl Edward was ordered to leave, as his granddaughter wrote, or found himself unable or unwilling to work in the legal system under the circumstances, the Hasse family departed for Wisconsin.

In any event, the Hasses were spiritually Forty-Eighters, part of a group that was something of an elite among German Americans and made a special impact on Milwaukee. As Carl Schurz, a Forty-Eighter who became a leading American reformer, recalled the "German Athens of America":

> Milwaukee . . . had received rather more than its proportional share of the German immigration of 1848. The city had possessed a strong German element before,—good-natured, quiet, law-abiding, order-loving, and industrious citizens. . . . But the 'Forty-Eighters' brought something like a wave of spring sunshine into that life. They were mostly high-spirited young people, inspired by fresh ideals which they had failed to realize in the old world, but hoped to realize here; ready to enter upon any activity they might be capable of; and eager not only to make that activity profitable but also to render life merry and beautiful; and . . . full of enthusiasm for the great American Republic which was to be their home and the home of their children . . . all went to work with a cheerful purpose to make the best of everything. They at once proceeded to enliven society with artistic enterprises. . . . It is also true that, in a few instances, the vivacity of this spirit ran into attempts to realize questionable or extravagant theories. But, on the whole, the inspiration proved itself exhilaratingly healthy, not only in the social, but soon also in the political sense.[6]

Carl Edward took up farming near Milwaukee and was sufficiently active in civic affairs to be elected to two terms in the state legislature, in 1852 and 1859. His son Hermann attended public schools and a private classical academy. At twenty, he began the study of medicine, but finding the medical college in St. Louis not up to German standards, he returned to Europe in 1857 for several years of study at the universities in Leipzig (where he had relatives), Prague, and Wurzburg. Back in Milwaukee just as the Civil War began, he enlisted in the Union Army, serving as a surgeon with Wisconsin infantry in the Army of the Cumberland through four hard years of war in the South. Afterward he began medical practice and soon was courting Adelaide Trentlage, who was only eighteen when they married on February 3, 1867. Their firstborn, Adelaide Rosalie, arrived the following year, on September 13, 1868.

Adelaide's first few years were somewhat unsettled as her parents moved to DeSoto, Missouri, where Hermann's parents and younger brother had relocated. The area near St. Louis was popular with German immigrants and even had lead mines reminiscent of Saxony. After Carl Edward's death in 1872, Hermann returned to Milwaukee, where he practiced medicine and raised a growing family in a brick house on Grove Street. Adelaide was followed by three more daughters, Elsa (later known as Elsbeth), Hilda, and Jessie, and a son, Carl. She also had two maternal aunts close in age; a childhood friend recalled playing with Lillie Trentlage and Addie Hasse, with her "long 'titian' tinted braids."[7] Her parents were sociable and active in the community; Dr. Hasse was a Mason, a member of the GAR (the influential veterans' organization), and several times the elected county physician. He also found time for a scientific hobby, the study of lichens, on which he became a recognized authority. Dr. Hasse particularly enjoyed reading accounts of explorations, an interest his daughter shared and would make the subject of one of her first published bibliographies. At some point, Adelaide also developed what would be a lifelong interest in a distant connection who was an early career woman, the eighteenth-century diva Faustina Bordoni, wife of the composer Johann Adolf Hasse. Family life was full of books, music, and laughter; the only surviving picture of Adelaide as a child shows her leaning on a stack of books.[8]

The Hasses remained in Milwaukee until Adelaide was seventeen, so whatever education she received took place there. The nature of her education is unclear, as, perhaps uncomfortable about a lack of formal educational credentials, she tended to be vague on the subject. Her entry in *Who Was Who in America* says she studied in public schools and with private tutors, but other sources say she was educated entirely by tutors at home, and a 1915 interview quoted her as saying she "never went to school a day in her life."[9] Given the energy and drive that were Adelaide's most noted qualities, she may have been so precocious or so restless that education at home seemed preferable to her parents. An education that was partly or entirely at home with tutors would have contributed to a sense of being special, unwilling to settle for a conventional life.

In 1885, the family was uprooted by a move to Little Rock, Arkansas, in search of a more healthful climate. Two years later, they moved again, to Southern California, then booming with the completion of the Santa Fe Railroad. Los Angeles still had traces of frontier rawness, and its real estate bubble was about to burst, but the region had an idyllic climate that attracted affluent health seekers, making it a popular refuge for upper-class easterners in search of a new way of life. Among them was Charlotte Perkins Gilman, recovering from the breakdown described in *The Yellow Wallpaper*, who recalled a paradise of sunlight and clear air, with a glorious profusion of fruit and flowers. Adelaide Hasse later remembered an "unusual community. . . . Vastly more isolated than at present, its population was largely composed of families accustomed to an environment of culture and attainment."

Dr. Hasse obtained appointment as chief physician of the home for disabled veterans, responsible for the operation of its hospital. The complex, home to a rapidly growing population of veterans, was located on a plateau surrounded by ranch land, a few miles inland from the seaside village of Santa Monica. The family was provided a house on the spacious grounds, and the younger children were soon busy with school, exploring the countryside, and learning about the often eccentric residents of the institution.[10]

Adelaide, however, felt that she had landed at "the world's end" in this remote spot between mountains and the Pacific. Entering adulthood, she needed a sense of purpose, but her options were limited. Taller than average at five feet eight inches and unusually energetic, she threw herself into the bicycling craze that gave women freedom and strength, to the alarm of those who wondered if God intended women to ride bicycles. At a time when not only was the frame heavy but the wheels weighed more than sixty pounds, she won the title "Champion Fast Lady Bicycle Rider of Los Angeles."[11] Sports could not satisfy the need for work that stimulated her mind, however. College was drawing bright young women from cultivated families, despite warnings that it would damage their health and marital prospects, but higher education was just beginning in Southern California, and the local teachers' college was unlikely to appeal to the Hasses. Her parents may have been unwilling to send her away to college, or perhaps, with four younger children at home, Adelaide felt obliged to support herself. A college degree was not the common credential it would become over the next century, and she was confident that she was well educated. Apparently preferring to ignore what became an awkward subject, she never explained her lack of higher education. Writing about training for library work in the 1890s, she acknowledged that a college degree was preferred for admittance to Melvil Dewey's school in New York and was generally desirable, but it was not a practical requirement in less populous regions, where "a completed high school course or its equivalent" was sufficient. The public librarian must have "a good general education," she said, but it was unrealistic to require a college degree in places like Los Angeles.[12]

In the long run, her lack of higher education was problematic, as college degrees became more widespread and practically universal in the higher levels of her field. It also may have affected her in less tangible ways, leading to insecurity behind her confident and outspoken style. She would base her career on her energy and capacity for work, and the absence of education credentials may have intensified her temperamental need to work harder and longer than anyone else, to take on large projects involving exhausting attention to detail. She would tend also to make sweeping statements and call for change to solve fundamental problems, often in rather baroque rhetoric, while her more conventionally educated contemporaries tended to focus on limited issues, discussed in standard expository prose. To her many admirers, she would seem an inspiring visionary, always ready to challenge the conventional wisdom, but others would react with resentment and distrust.

Whatever the reasons, the bright and energetic Addie Hasse did not go to college, and just when she was in need of an occupation, an opportunity appeared, one that would give her not just a job but a career that became a consuming lifelong mission.

Notes

1. *History of Milwaukee, Wisconsin* (Chicago: Western Historical Co., 1881), 1307.

2. Peter Burger, e-mail on the background of the Hasse family, Oct. 1997.

3. Information on Hermann Hasse and his parents from *National Cyclopedia of American Biography,* 16:167-68, and J. M. Guinn, *Historical and Biographical Record of Southern California* (Chicago: Chapman, 1902), 384, 387.

4. C. E. Hasse, *Childerung des Wisconsingebietes in Nordeamerika* (Grimma: Comtoirs, 1841).

5. Adelaide Hasse, *The Compensations of Librarianship* (privately printed, 1919), 3.

6. Carl Schurz, *Reminiscences* (New York: McClure, 1907-08), 2:44-46.

7. Imogene Martin to AH, 18 Jan. 1910, AH-NY.

8. A charming picture of Hasse family life is provided by AH's sister, Elsbeth [Elsa] Andrae, *The Dear Old Boys in Blue: Memories of the Early Days of the Veterans Administration Center, Los Angeles* (San Francisco: Reynard Press, 1948); picture of AH as a child, AH-LC.

9. Statements that she did not attend school: *Woman's Who's Who of America,* 371; AH federal employment file, U.S. National Archives and Records Administration, Civilian Personnel Records, St. Louis; *New York Evening Mail,* 17 Sept. 1915.

10. Andrae, *Dear Old Boys; New York Times,* 31 Jan. 1897.

11. "Miss Adelaide R. Hasse," *New York Times Illustrated Magazine* (17 June 1897): 15.

12. Adelaide Hasse, "The Training of Library Employes II," LJ 20 (July 1895): 239.

Chapter 2

Los Angeles Public Library, 1889-1895

In the summer of 1889, Hasse heard that the Los Angeles Public Library was seeking staff for its new quarters in the city hall. Despite lack of experience, she bravely decided to apply. Her parents could hardly object to employment that was seen as safe and suitable for a well-read young lady. The librarian, Miss Tessa Kelso, was a woman, and library work seemed a promising field for women. It didn't pay well, but that kept men from competing for most of the jobs, and it made use of middle-class women's education and cultural interests, while seemingly less stressful than teaching or nursing. There was a tendency to see it as a refuge for the delicate or routine clerical work for the politically connected, but such assumptions were unlikely to persist in the presence of Tessa Kelso, whose ideas and personality would influence Hasse profoundly.

Kelso was only five years older than Hasse and would become her lifelong friend. The two women were similar in their energy and ambition, but Kelso had led a far more adventurous life as a journalist, coming alone to California from her native Ohio. A woman of great vitality and originality, Kelso was the antithesis of the image of the librarian as delicate, reserved, and genteel. Cheerfully unconventional, Kelso smoked, wore her hair cut short, went hatless, and never hesitated to express her opinions, "witty, vehement, and to the point."[1] She was not always consistent in those opinions, but perhaps exuberant inconsistency was part of being a Californian, boldly in search of a new way of life. Kelso was careful, however, not to go seriously beyond the bounds of propriety, and she was welcome among the high-minded women who were busily organizing women's clubs and congresses in Southern California. The civic leader Caroline Severance made Kelso an honorary member of her influential Friday Morning Club and served one term on the library board (1891-92), the only woman member in its first two decades. Kelso also was active in the Southern California Historical Society, and she was a pioneer in historic preservation who deserves credit for starting the movement to save the California mission

churches, recruiting first local women and then the writer and polymath Charles
Lummis to what became the California Landmarks Club. This worthy effort
added to the doubts about Kelso in some circles, however, since the preservation
of historic Catholic churches was not popular with the Protestant clergy.[2]

Kelso would always insist that the effective librarian should be active and
visible in the community, even to the point of spending half her working hours
outside the library. Charles Lummis, a character even more colorful than Kelso,
gave her high praise, describing her publicly as a "woman of extraordinary business ability, quenchless energy, and great executive force" and privately as the
"best man" ever to hold the job.[3] Clever, worldly like men like Lummis appreciated Kelso and were drawn to the library. As Hasse recalled, "There was ever
an atmosphere of open house about the library, an atmosphere of its being notably a citizens' habitat where distinguished guests from across the divide were always brought as a matter of course."[4] The popular journalist and poet Eugene
Field spent much of the winter of 1892-93 in Kelso's office, complaining about
the cold and teasing the staff, and Hamlin Garland, the rising realist writer about
the hardships of farms and factories, was recruited to address the library club she
established.

Kelso had good rapport with the library board, especially the chairman,
George Dobinson, a lawyer, Shakespeare scholar, and talented amateur actor, and
Frank Howard, a spirited talker and litigator who was an early leader of the local
bar.[5] She had won over the board in applying for the position of librarian when
she brushed aside her lack of experience with the confident assertion that she
could hire people who knew about the technical aspects of library work. She
knew libraries as a constant user since childhood and a member of the American
Library Association since reporting on its 1886 conference, but it was no more
necessary for a head librarian to be an expert cataloger, she told the board, than
for a newspaper editor to be an expert typesetter. Her idea of the position as an
executive, not a technician, was in tune with the board's desire for someone
businesslike with organizational ability. This usually meant a man, but the
members were highly satisfied with Kelso and soon reported that the new librarian showed "a capacity and intelligence which make her remarkably fitted for the
important position she occupies."[6]

Kelso's vibrant personality, her warm interest in others, those "twinkling,
snapping blue eyes," would attract friends and admirers all her life. Such free
spirits also attract animosity, however, especially if they are women "with the
habit of going unerringly to the heart of a situation" and quick to offer
"vigorous denunciation or approval."[7] Kelso would be involved in controversies
and subject to fierce attacks, but she never backed down and was quite capable
of counterattacking, even against men in positions of authority. For the young
Adelaide Hasse, Kelso was such a complete mentor and model that it is difficult
to imagine her career apart from her experience in Los Angeles.

~ ~ ~

On August 28, 1889, Kelso notified Hasse that she had been appointed an
"attendant" at $40 per month for three months' probation and should report im-

mediately to prepare for the new library's opening on September 2.[8] There were four women attendants who would work with the librarian and her first assistant Jessie Gavitt. From a state of uncertainty, Hasse suddenly found herself in an exciting and purposeful situation, with the newly established board, recently hired librarian, and expanded facilities and funds offering opportunities to develop the library according to modern concepts. The library had just moved into the third floor of the handsome new Romanesque Revival city hall, overlooking the bustling town of fifty thousand, its population down from the peak of the real estate boom but still almost five times that of 1880. The collection consisted of only six thousand books, but the board and Kelso were determined to expand both the collection and the library's role in the community.

A revision of the city charter had given the library a degree of independence from city government, with its own board, albeit appointed by the mayor. The charter also made provision for library funds that could be as much as five cents of every hundred dollars of tax revenue. This was subject to appropriation by the city council, however, and by 1891 the library board already was complaining of crippling funding cuts, though this didn't prevent the growth of the staff and collection. That the new charter provisions had not insulated the library from the city's stormy politics became evident in 1890, when an alternative library board ran in the city elections and sued to replace the appointed board.[9] The courts rejected the claim, but the controversy gave Kelso warning that there were political forces contending for control of the library and her job.

Kelso was quick to recognize Hasse's ability. In December, her appointment was confirmed and her salary increased to $50.[10] A few months later, Hasse was raised to the rank of first assistant; her salary would increase substantially over the next few years as her responsibilities continuously expanded. Her predecessor, Jessie Gavitt, had long experience in the library, having served as librarian from 1884 until the establishment of the board in 1889 and then continued for a year as first assistant. For Kelso, there were advantages to a new assistant even younger and less experienced than she was: Hasse was no threat to her authority, had no attachment to past practices, and was not widely acquainted in the city. Hasse later said that she had been promoted because her excellent health enabled her to work long hours, but her achievements over the next few years showed that it was her energy and enthusiasm for organizing every aspect of the library that Kelso appreciated and encouraged. By 1894, the board commended her for having "developed a remarkable faculty for library work" as a "most efficient and faithful" second to Kelso.[11]

Soon "Addie Hasse" of the 1889 annual report became the more business-like "Adelaide R. Hasse." Distinguishing her attitude from the image of the lady librarian who loved genteel reading, Hasse later described her work with Kelso: "It was not the books we cared for, but the best part of the work, having them arranged in the best possible way for the convenience of the public."[12] That would be a constant theme in Hasse's career, to establish herself as businesslike, an organizer of large projects, above all *efficient,* the quality most valued, if not always clearly defined, by Americans at the turn of the twentieth century. And always her goal would be to make the library's materials accessible to users.

Her position with the board secure and Hasse appointed second in command, Kelso left in the summer of 1890 on a tour of libraries from northern California to Ohio, aimed particularly at learning about trends in cataloging and branch libraries. She returned unimpressed with the prevailing faith in branches as a convenience and cataloging as a kind of pseudoscience. Branch libraries she dismissed as "universally cumbersome and expensive, repeating and emphasizing the faults of the central institution." Not that she didn't recognize the needs that branches aimed to meet; her analysis showed that most LAPL users lived near either the library or the trolley lines, but her preferred solutions were to work closely with the schools and develop delivery points in remote neighborhoods, rather than take on the cost and complications of branches to reach more residents.

As for cataloging, Kelso was dismissive of the "undue prominence given to catalogs . . . when . . . a catalog at its best is an unreliable, misleading, uninteresting, and minor influence . . . forced into the place of intelligent human guides."[13] Kelso always would be skeptical about the conventional wisdom, but here she verged on heresy in questioning an article of faith of American librarianship. A visiting English librarian was amused by the "over-pretentiousness of a somewhat boastful patriotism" with which librarians explained the superiority of American library methods, as though he had never heard of such things: "Over and over again did I receive lucid and lengthy explanations of . . . dictionary catalogs, the use of card-charging systems, the extraordinary novelty of card catalogs, and generally of every feature of library work." With their pride in efficiency and standardization, he warned, American librarians didn't seem to realize the "danger of originality being stifled, all future work becoming purely mechanical, thus reducing every department of library work to a dead level of mediocre uniformity."[14] Hasse and Kelso could not have missed his comments, which appeared on the same page in *Library Journal* as a report on Hasse's library training class, and they must have had a good laugh at the picture of librarians earnestly explaining the superiority of their catalogs. Kelso's objection to the prevailing faith in cataloging didn't mean that she opposed a catalog for the library; her annual reports made it clear that cataloging was important, but she gave equal emphasis to providing checklists, bibliographies, and well-trained reference staff to help locate information. As for Hasse, the report of her training class shows that the students were expected to have thorough knowledge of cataloging history and theory, but she shared Kelso's reservations, and throughout her career she would be acutely, sometimes outspokenly, aware of the limitations of library cataloging.

Together Kelso and Hasse set out to develop what Hasse later described as "one of the livest, most progressive libraries I have known."[15] Expanding the book collection was a priority; it grew to forty-two thousand in six years. But Kelso had a much broader vision of making the library useful to the community. She immediately pressed the board to make it truly a "free public library" by removing the borrower's fee, which was reduced in 1889 and eliminated in 1891, encouraging a hundredfold increase in card holders to twenty thousand. She also called for open stacks, an innovation only approved after her departure. Sunday hours were added, and the magazines were allowed to circulate, which *Library Journal* found highly unusual but admirable as a way to encourage "higher grade reading" than that of the "confirmed novel-devourer" who so worried librarians of the period.[16] She created new special collections and services: sheet music and scores that circulated, an art collection supported by the Friday Morning Club; a clippings service of current information for businessmen, coordinated with the Chamber of Commerce; government depository status and an organized collection of federal and state government documents; cooperation with the public schools, taking over the school libraries in 1892, and with the state university's extension service; a newsletter, the *Library Bulletin;* a local history collection; and a California subject index.

With all this expansion, Kelso was careful to emphasize efficiency. She developed statistics for every department and featured them in her annual reports to show that library work involved far more than the obvious "taking in and giving out of books," a point particularly praised by *Library Journal.*[17] She made a point of keeping operating expenses low in relation to book expenditures, determined to avoid the tendency "that as libraries grow . . . expenditures for books steadily decrease and administrative expenses increase" as a proportion of the budget.[18] Controlling costs also meant keeping down staff pay. Kelso knew that the library needed more resources and the women who worked there needed better pay, but she also understood the importance of establishing her effectiveness as an executive who would be respected by the business establishment.

Though Kelso was not inclined to accept the pieties of other librarians, she was an enthusiastic networker who lobbied for holding the 1891 ALA conference in San Francisco. It was a great opportunity to meet librarians from the East, and, always encouraging staff development, she took her two chief assistants, Hasse and Estelle Haines, to the convention, where they would see their work as part of a national movement of recognized importance. They also saw their boss elected to the ALA Council, a tribute to a California woman who had been a librarian only a short time. Entertaining the touring ALA leaders in Los Angeles was a further opportunity to socialize with prominent people in both the profession and the city, with the added benefit of praise in *Library Journal.*

Ever alert to the value of publicity, Kelso sent copies of her annual reports and other library publications to *Library Journal,* where they were quoted and praised, thus creating more opportunities for networking as librarians all over the country requested copies. Not one to be intimidated by ALA's reputation as a bastion of proper New Englanders, Kelso was eager to be involved in ALA issues. In 1892, she wrote to LJ to protest the proposed ALA women's section, arguing for equality, not separate spheres.[19] The next year, she travelled to Chicago where the world's fair was the site of both an ALA exhibit and the ALA annual conference, as well as the World Congress of Librarians, which was intended to be an international gathering of the movement. Kelso presented papers at both meetings and was a vigorous participant in discussions, arguing for open stacks and even daring to differ with the great Melvil Dewey.

Inspired by their experience with the ALA conference in October 1891, Kelso and Hasse founded the Southern California Library Club, which held its first meeting that December. The program focused on the library, with Kelso speaking on its history and the aims of the club, followed by Estelle Haines' report on bibliographical aids to book selection. The next meeting was on classification, followed by a program on "Public Libraries in Relation to University Extension," where Hasse spoke on the history of the extension movement and urged the potential of libraries as "laboratories of the movement," where classes might meet and be guided to relevant reading. The topic drew teachers from the high school and the normal college, whose interest encouraged the club to take on broader literary and educational topics.[20]

At the December 1892 club meeting, Kelso, in her iconoclastic mode, remarked that she opposed segregating children's books, because "a book written for children which will not stand the test of interest of older people is not a proper book for any child to read." No one was reported to have questioned that assertion, which Kelso continued to make over the years, apparently in reaction to the insipid nature of much of what was written for children; she would repeatedly criticize children's literature and children's services at ALA conferences. In 1894, Hasse told the readers of *Library Journal* that LAPL policy was "unalterably opposed to segregation of children from adults in our library."[21] This would soon cause them problems, but Kelso and Hasse would always be wary of too sentimental a view of children's services, another way of putting women in a separate sphere linked to the maternal instinct, while setting libraries apart from the real world as mere recreation for women and children. In questioning the importance of both children's service and cataloging, however, Kelso was challenging the basic structure of librarianship as a feminized profession in which women could claim professional status by conforming to gender stereotypes. Children's service was linked to woman's essentially maternal nature, while strict rule-based cataloging was suitable work for women, assumed to be good at details but not intelligent enough to exercise much judgment.[22] Such attitudes might seem pragmatic to most women librarians, who were glad to have respectable jobs, but Kelso could see the danger that gender roles would limit opportunities for personal and professional development.

Later that month, there were three special club meetings to hear talks on American literature by Hamlin Garland, the writer known for bleak realism and Populist sympathies. Garland had gained recognition by writing for the progressive journal *The Arena*, and he probably encouraged Kelso to publish her thoughts on public libraries, which appeared there the following May and were excerpted in *Library Journal*.[23] Kelso combined skepticism and idealism in an assertion of the "highest value of the public library . . . its power to add to the fast-diminishing store of human pleasure, to be a means of overcoming the intemperance of work." She pointed to the movement of population from rural villages to large, crowded cities that lacked opportunities for either recreation or intellectual development, both of which could be provided by libraries. This point was missed by those who worried "that a library offered a loafing place for all the idlers in a city; but if the library did no more than become the recognized loafing-centre of a city, its existence on that basis would be warranted." Librarians had themselves "assisted the misunderstanding by constantly deprecating the reading of fiction or any literature that might be read for amusement," thus furnishing "a weapon to be used against the support of public libraries." In a country that made work a religion and cast special scorn on "loafers," while regarding pleasure and amusement with Puritan uneasiness, these were daring ideas. Kelso inverted a stereotype to make her point, telling *Arena*'s readers that there was nothing wrong with libraries serving women who read novels and men without jobs. She strewed controversies throughout her paper, expressing doubts about the "undue prominence given to catalogs," the tendency to separate books from people with closed stacks, the growth of administrative expenses, and the proliferation of "cumbersome and expensive" branches. Long before any federal government support for library programs, she pointed to the absence of national policy on libraries reflected in the indifference of the Bureau of Education and the lack of innovation in the Library of Congress, which "has never, in any way, fulfilled its mission as a national library to the country at large." The desirability of national coordination of access to information through libraries would be a theme of Kelso's at ALA conferences for years to come.

While Kelso stirred controversy, Hasse focused her energy on library work. Later in her career, she would amplify her mentor's criticisms, but in the early years, she was discreet and devoted herself to the day-to-day operation of the library, which had ten attendants by 1891 and sixteen in 1892, and to several large projects, including developing a library training school and organizing the library's government documents. She also spent six weeks in Santa Barbara organizing its public library and was invited to do the same in Pasadena, Riverside, Santa Monica, and at the local normal college, indications of her reputation in the region. She directed staff or students in variously classifying, cataloging, and shelflisting local library collections ranging from twenty-five hundred to seven thousand volumes.

Hasse also became known nationally as she published in *Library Journal* and compiled widely disseminated bibliographies. Such opportunities were unusual for a young woman in her first job, and Hasse appreciated how fortunate she was to have the encouragement of Kelso, "who was quick to discern latent capacity and always most generous in making opportunity for its development."[24] By 1892, their rapport was such that they decided to live together; city directories for the next few years show them at the same addresses in the booming area of new apartment buildings around Broadway and Hill.

~ ~ ~

The library training class that Hasse designed and taught was authorized by the board in October 1891. Hasse was proud to proclaim it the first such class sponsored by an American public library and to point to the successful librarians it produced.[25] A similar program had begun at Pratt Institute in Brooklyn the year before, and others soon followed at Drexel Institute in Philadelphia, Armour Institute in Chicago, and the Denver Public Library, indicating growing recognition of the need for education for library work in more accessible settings than Dewey's school at the New York State Library in Albany. Kelso initiated the class to meet several needs: to provide a pool of trained, known potential employees; to circumvent the constant pressure to hire those with personal or political connections; and to expand the staff at low cost with students working for little or no pay as part of their training. Graduates were not guaranteed employment, but only graduates were eligible for any library appointment, an unusual requirement for an organization whose lowest rank (of nine) paid only $10 per month and whose highest-ranking staff had no formal training. Kelso was determined to develop a team in which everyone had a common educational base and was ready to be a full contributor from the first day on the job, with no one relying on patronage or family connections.[26]

Admission to the program required a high school diploma, good health, and examination by a committee to ascertain the applicant's adaptability, practicality, reading habits, and knowledge of culture and current events. Applicants were expected to be well educated and well read, though Hasse explained that a college degree was not a practical requirement in Los Angeles; she did acknowledge that her most intellectually lively class consisted of teachers and other college graduates. The class was specified to be for "young women," which may have been simply a recognition that men were unlikely to seek employment in an organization with an all female staff and a woman director, especially when all employees were required to start at the bottom and be promoted only by seniority (apparently further efforts to protect against political interference). Still, it strikes an inconsistent note in the same year as the letter in which Kelso opposed a separate ALA women's section with the assertion, "There is but one standard of management for a live business, and sex has nothing to do with that standard."[27]

The program Hasse organized consisted of two six-month courses that met three hours daily, the first ending with a long examination and a thesis, the second with an examination only. Much of the students' time was spent working in the library's various departments under the supervision of the staff. The board was concerned that the amount of staff time given to training must not outweigh the benefit of the students' unpaid labor, but Hasse was confident that the students encouraged alertness in the staff without being a burden. Those who passed the first exam with a grade above 85 were entitled to be paid $10 per month during the second course, but they had to work four hours a day—an hour of public contact at the circulation desk and three hours of cataloging.

The classes drew considerable interest, with twenty applicants for the first, but they were kept small, usually only six students admitted from two or three times as many applicants. Already showing her tendency to go full tilt into new projects, Hasse took on a second class four months after the first began, and a third class three months after that. A fourth class was postponed when none of the applicants qualified, and six to twelve months elapsed between the next three classes. Everyone on the staff shared in the training as students rotated weekly among departments in what Hasse described as "nothing more or less than the old-fashioned apprentice system." She thus provided what became a popular label for such library-based training, but her program was broader than the usual idea of apprenticeship; the students studied all aspects of library work, and much of their time was spent in class, learning such intellectual underpinnings as library types, organization, laws, and statistics. Hasse created a sophisticated combination of apprentice training and seminar that ranged from practical details to more theoretical aspects of library work. Learning about classification, for example, was not limited to the outlines of the Dewey Decimal and other systems. The students spent time shelving, to become "thoroughly familiar" with how classification actually worked in the library, but they also reviewed the classes as subject disciplines, learning the scope, authorities, leading periodicals and writers, current trends, and relations to other subjects. That Hasse could organize such a wide-ranging and rigorous program in only her third year as a librarian, with no formal training of her own, showed the extent to which she had been reading and thinking about the issues of library organization and management. By 1894, ALA's Committee on Library School and Training Classes approved her program as a "school of library economy" based on its "systematic curriculum, the number . . . who have completed it, the character of the instruction as indicated by the examination papers." The following year, Hasse wrote a detailed account of the school for *Library Journal*.

Hasse did not hesitate to fail half of the first two classes, showing the community that the library had high standards. By 1894, she could report that all the graduates had jobs (except one who married), most of them at LAPL. The program had succeeded in providing trained employees hired for their qualifications, not their connections. She and Kelso could take pride in establishing high standards for library employees while simultaneously expanding the staff at low cost. They may have been imprudent, however, to be so open in their intention to establish what was effectively a civil service system that would "eliminate everything that savors of personal or political influence." The reform-minded would appreciate their good intentions, but the men who valued such influence over jobs could be dangerous enemies to young women without political power.

~ ~ ~

At the same time that she was creating the training program, Hasse was organizing the library's collection of government publications, beginning what would be her life's work and a career model for generations of librarians. In her first annual report, Kelso had mentioned the need to organize the accumulation of thirteen hundred U.S. documents, "in which there is a rich fund of information." When LAPL became a depository in 1891, the issue became more pressing, and the report for the year commended Hasse's "excellent service in the notation and classification of Public Documents on an original plan to make their contents more easily available to the public."[28] The discussion of documents at the ALA conference intensified her awareness of the issues, but when Hasse looked back on her career, it was Kelso's guidance more than any intention of her own that steered her towards working with government publications:

> It was my first employer who aroused my interest in . . . specializing in government documents. She was so sympathetic in her efforts that, almost without being aware of having done so, somehow I had organized the collection of documents, not inconsiderable, . . . devised a classification for them, and had begun a checklist of them. . . . One day, away off in Los Angeles, there came a request from Washington, to allow the section of the checklist . . . to be published by the Dept. of Agriculture. . . . Had it not been for [Kelso's] constant interest . . . , I should never have ventured on these enterprises.[29]

This brief account was all Hasse had to say about how she became involved with public documents, nor did she explain the thinking behind the decisions she made in what would be a key event in the development of the concept of a separate collection of government publications classified by issuing agency.[30] Whether she and Kelso considered integrating the documents into the Dewey-classed book collection is unknown, but from their perspective at the time, there were many reasons for such a special collection:

For one thing, the collection was already "segregated," Hasse later said, but it is not clear that this was a policy.[31] As often happened in libraries, the documents may have been set aside pending decisions on how to deal with them. The simplest approach was to keep them separately arranged by agency and series. The idea of separate government documents collections with special classification was not unique to Hasse. In 1891, *Library Journal* had published papers on that type of organization in two other libraries. Both writers seem to have referred primarily to the serial set, which contained the most used documents, but special treatment of public documents was accepted as a general principle by American and British authorities of the time.

Secondly, most documents were issued in series, and ALA's 1891 resolution had urged that every government publication be assigned to a series. It obviously was easier to record the documents as numbers in series, rather than try to classify them individually by subject. Hasse would always be a dedicated collector who aimed to complete series, but she acknowledged that the libraries that didn't collect entire series were justified in classifying individual reports as part of their book collections.

At the time, subject classification in the Dewey Decimal or Library of Congress systems was not established as the American library consensus. The LC classification did not yet exist, and Cutter had encountered much resistance to combining letters and numbers in his "expansive" system, while Dewey's decimal classification was in use in only a third of libraries surveyed in 1893, with half using a local system. Since open shelves were uncommon, subject classification for browsing was not as desirable as it would become with the change to open stacks. What librarians wanted was a flexible system to free them from fixed shelf locations, but once that goal was accomplished, the advantages of one system over another were not obvious. What was evident was the intractable limitation that one volume could have only one location, regardless of classification; in consequence, librarians emphasized catalogs, which had multiple points of entry. For government documents in series, as most were, there was a practical advantage to keeping them together in series, which would grow only at the end, simplifying shelving and space planning.

Besides, the documents most likely to be collected by libraries did not necessarily lend themselves to subject classification. The Department of Agriculture series included many monographs that might be suitable for subject classification, but that would have meant taking them out of their series, only to be faced with the inadequacy of the decimal classification for agricultural subjects. Other series were even more problematic. What were the subjects of census reports, annual reports of agencies, or *Statutes at Large*? They were essential references for many subjects or had special uses, not comparable to subjects in the book collection. The congressional series was even less classifiable by subject. Each volume of the serial set, which was distributed to all depository libraries, typically included multiple congressional documents and reports, as well as reports from executive branch agencies. In their original issuance as individual documents, some could appropriately be classified by subject, but others were of interest primarily as part of the legislative process or other technical aspects of government operation.

Kelso and Hasse were especially concerned with providing knowledgeable assistance to users, and LAPL assistants were expected to keep up with current events, which often involved government. As Hasse thought about documents, she became convinced that effective reference work was integrally related to understanding the structure and functions of government. Keeping the documents as a special collection in the reference room encouraged the staff's awareness of government agencies and their publications as a source of information. Such special collections by form were not unusual at LAPL. Kelso encouraged collections of various nonbook materials with their own card file records. The documents collection in the reference room was readily available for varied uses and had more visibility there as a special service of a depository library.

There are no surviving records to explain Hasse's decisions or even to show just what her original classification was. The source that remains is her checklist of publications of the U.S. Department of Agriculture, which used an agency-based classification similar to what became known as the Documents Office or Superintendent of Documents Classification.[32] All of the agency's publications were identified by the mnemonic AG, with the bureaus and divisions assigned numbers which were further subdivided by series:

Secretary of Agriculture, Office:
    AG 2: (year)   Annual reports
    AG 21:   Monthly reports
    AG 22:   Special reports
Experiment Stations, Office:
    AG 35: (year)   Annual reports
    AG 351:   Experiment Station Record
    AG 352:   Bulletins

A striking aspect of this early version, at least to one familiar with the system's later development, was the lack of changes in class to reflect changes in government organization. An agency classification would involve splitting serials into different classes when reorganization moved the issuing offices, which some would see as a problem, but it was an issue Hasse either didn't consider or chose to ignore in the checklist. Her annotations show that she was fully aware that the Department of Agriculture had existed for twenty-one years as a section of the Patent Office before becoming a separate department in 1862 and a Cabinet-level department in 1889, but her classification included publications from 1841 to 1895 in one class, which was not correct in a system based on provenance. Perhaps she didn't see it as an issue worth spending time on when her goal was to develop a practical arrangement that library staff could apply easily

to the documents at hand. In compiling the checklist, she included older documents in order to provide a complete list of the agency's issuances, using annotations to clarify their history. Later, with considerable experience in collecting
documents, she became more concerned with how best to reflect changes in
provenance in the class notation. At the time, she saw the classification in her
checklist as "the result of practical experience . . . offered merely as a suggestion
to librarians who keep their files of Government publications apart from their
general collection of books," widely useful because "the notation may be applied
to the publications of every Department."[33]

Although Hasse would continue to believe in special treatment for government documents, she always said the choice was a practical matter for each library to decide. As she went on to develop large collections, she would argue
for agency-based collections with expert staff to get at the contents of documents
through reference service and bibliographies, but she never asserted that every library should use agency classification. She repeatedly said that small libraries
should not collect large numbers of documents and were justified in integrating
selected documents into their book collections. In the early years of her career,
she apparently was interested in developing classifications—she also created a
fiction authors "arrangement scheme expressed by numbers from 1-9999"— and
later she took pride in being known as the creator of the widely used documents
classification, but she did not publish her thinking on the subject. At an early
library club program on classification, Hasse confined herself to reading a paper
from the ALA conference proceedings which summed up the obvious: classification was inevitably imperfect and should be supplemented by bibliographies,
subject cataloging, and reference service, but it would be useful as open shelves
became more common.[34] Hasse's interest soon shifted more to bibliography, indexing, and cataloging. Classification was needed for shelving, but it did not
provide access to the content of publications as bibliography could. Bibliography then had a considerable mystique as a movement to make the nineteenth-
century explosion of information accessible to the developing scholarly disciplines, the professions, government officials, and a general public that was more
literate than at any time in history.

~   ~   ~

The checklist of Agriculture Department publications published in 1896 was
important to Hasse's career and has special significance as the early record of her
classification, but it was only one of several publications she produced at
LAPL. She learned early to turn her library projects into publications and to organize staff and students to prepare bibliographies under her direction. Her work
with agricultural documents led to a bibliography on California agriculture in
the LAPL *Bulletin* in November 1892, four years before publication of the Agriculture Department checklist. The training class was the subject of a series of
bylined articles in *Library Journal* in 1895, as well as an earlier unsigned piece
that prominently identified Hasse as being in charge of the class, and other library projects were reported in LJ under Hasse's name, starting with a brief account of her plan for a California subject index in 1892.[35]

Hasse used the fourth training class to compile a 148-page list of the fiction in the library, all 12,456 volumes in English, French, German, Spanish, and Italian with 113 pages of author entries, a subject index, and a short bibliography of criticism. When it was issued in March 1894, she distributed copies to the press and received considerable attention, both locally and nationally, with the result that the library's 1894 report proudly noted sales of 2596 copies. *Library Journal*'s review had high praise from Helen Haines, who found it deserving "the careful attention of librarians . . . not only for the admirable simplicity of its form, but for . . . innovations in the way of annotations and arrangement." Haines described the helpful notes, the list of "some of the best modern criticism, which is as a rule, absolutely unknown to the average novel reader," and the subject index, "admirably suggestive of what may be done in this direction." The list reflected "very high credit" on Hasse and could serve as a "working model" for other libraries, "one practical solution to the ever-present 'fiction problem,' in that they [lists] are a means by which novel-reading may be so guided and directed as to result in real benefit to the reader." Notice was not limited to LJ and the Los Angeles newspapers. "Even the *Nation,* that Nestor among critics, has deigned to give us a passing wink," Hasse reported happily to Henry Carr, sending five requested copies and apologies for an error he had pointed out, failure to continue authors' names at the head of the second column on the page. *The Nation* found the list useful for "the cultivation of taste" but noted that it was "cheaply printed" and contained two misspellings.[36]

With the fiction list completed, Hasse wrote a report for *Library Journal*, "The New Charging System at the Los Angeles Public Library," about the procedure she had developed to deal with the pressure of increased circulation. When a prominent eastern librarian commented that there was nothing new about the system, Hasse replied that it was new to Los Angeles (which was all the title indicated), and although it was "doubtless an old story to many," she had intended only to report on her library's system, which had since been adopted by several small libraries in the region.[37]

Kelso encouraged Hasse to follow her example in getting her name in print. In her letter to Henry Carr, Hasse reported that Kelso was at a women's congress in San Francisco, where the newspapers found her paper on public libraries as philanthropic institutions "rousing." Some library staff resented Kelso's constant activity outside the library, but Hasse would always be grateful for the encouragement that was so much a part of Kelso's style but was seldom heard from other head librarians. The more typical situation was described in LJ by the unidentified author of "The Anonymous Assistant":

> The library assistant . . . hides her light under the librarian's bushel. . . .
> Anonymity is the immemorial usage in library economy. . . . A dozen years
> of plodding those paths of library science which usage and custom make
> all but hopelessly obscure scarcely emboldens one to seek new fields or
> reap new honors. It is the silent subjugation of the assistant that restrains
> her from attaining her honest, appropriate level. . . . For example, there is
> the library which is especially noted for its bureau of information; and yet,
> although this work has been done by the same woman for the past 10 years,
> she remains anonymous both in and outside of her own city; her name is

not found in any of the library's annual reports. . . . Our best catalog of children's books bears upon its title-page, 'Prepared by the State Superintendent'; while nowhere within its pages is found the name of the real author—the superintendent's *assistant*—who devoted months of thought to its preparation. The compilation of one of our most noted and authoritative catalogs was carried on by a woman who received a word of acknowledgment, in the preface, from the librarian. What possible harm could have come from placing the name of the painstaking cataloger, in modest type, on the title-page? The advantage of such an omission is surely for the man or men at the head of the institution.[38]

Ironically, the sad tale of these unrecognized women toilers appeared immediately following one of Hasse's bylined series of reports on her training class. (Perhaps the placement is a clue that the author, identified only as an assistant who wasn't anonymous, was Hasse herself.) Early in her career, Hasse had the pleasure of seeing her name in print, fully credited for her achievements. Kelso promoted herself as the executive who directed the library, but she never took credit for Hasse's projects or required anonymity of her assistant. With such an unusual woman mentor, Hasse acquired the image of a rising star in her early twenties, frequently published and praised in the press, so that by the time she was in her thirties, Charles Lummis would describe her as "the most famous woman in library service in America today."[39] In a field where the resentment of the anonymous assistant was common, such public attention could be a mixed blessing, stirring envy even as it advanced Hasse's career. And in a period riven by conflict over just about everything, including the place of women, the successful self-promotion of women with the confidence of Kelso and Hasse was bound to rouse animosity. They might have the support of their board, but others, both inside and outside of the library, were not so pleased.

~   ~   ~

Despite the influx of affluent and cultivated easterners, Los Angeles had not shed its frontier roughness. Politics was hardball, and there was a general feistiness and enthusiasm for lawsuits. The role of women was much debated. California women were on the offensive, vigorously campaigning for the vote (narrowly defeated in 1896), quick to write indignant letters to newspapers that made sexist comments, and eagerly assembling in congresses to discuss issues and ideas, including the ways in which gender was shaped by society. In 1894, Kate Galpin challenged the status quo by running for Los Angeles Superintendent of Public Instruction to make the point that the law might bar women from voting but not from holding public office. The mood was just what Charlotte Perkins Gilman needed to reinvent herself as a feminist writer and lecturer, attacking the status quo in speeches to women's clubs and writing *The Yellow Wallpaper*, her classic account of a woman driven to suicidal despair by marriage, motherhood, and a "rest cure" that denied her any intellectual activity.

The newspapers carried on a continuous discussion of what was clearly a popular topic, woman's place, generally presented in terms of "the feminine woman" versus "the New Woman." Their tone was variously sensational, patronizing, hostile, or sympathetic, as they reported on the many women's clubs, lectures, and conferences, and discussed controversies like suffrage, dress reform, and the storm over Elizabeth Cady Stanton's *Woman's Bible*, all mixed with the usual advice about fashion, beauty, and husband hunting. There also were some lively opinion pieces by women writers, such as the flamboyant Tennessee Claflin Cook (sister of Victoria Woodhull) in the *Herald* on "The woman of the future. The slowness of her elevation to her true position. The continued oppression of one sex by the other." The *Times* matched it with "Women Bachelors," which claimed that "few of the great women of the world ever married," due to their tendency to "love men of small brains" and remain single from being "ashamed to ally themselves with men of intellect feebler than their own."[40]

Debates about women did not exist in a vacuum. They were a part of the volatile mix of extreme economic turmoil that began with a financial panic in the early summer of 1893 and developed into one of the worst depressions in American history. It was already a period of violent conflict between management and labor: the year before, Andrew Carnegie and Henry Clay Frick had ruthlessly broken the Homestead steelworkers' strike, and the following year President Cleveland would send troops to attack the Pullman strikers. Los Angeles might feel remote from the struggles in mines and factories, but as business failures created unemployment estimated at between two and three million nationally, California was not immune. By the fall, there were gangs of unemployed men calling themselves "industrial armies" and seizing trains to take them on their search for work. Support soared for the radical Populist Party. As the economy froze and voters turned to the Populists, politicians and businessmen were looking for scapegoats. Kelso seems not to have recognized that it was a hazardous time for a woman "executive" on the public payroll, especially one who preached the equality of the sexes and didn't hesitate to express unconventional opinions.

Kelso's first problem arose from a two-week trip to the American Library Association conference and the World Congress of Librarians in Chicago in July 1893. She delivered papers at both meetings, but the trip involved far more, for Chicago was the site of the World's Columbian Exposition, where ALA exhibited a model library that was vastly influential in the development of American public libraries. The ALA conference had its largest attendance ever as librarians from all over the country joined the throngs awed by the modern wonders displayed in the four hundred buildings of the fair's White City. The fair was also notable for its Woman's Building, which included an exhibit of seven thousand books written by women. For a librarian with high standards and a desire to bring the best modern ideas to her city, a visit to the fair was practically essential, and the board agreed she should not miss the opportunity to learn about the "latest and most advanced methods and systems."[41]

In September, Kelso made a routine request for a $200 travel reimbursement that had been approved by the library board. Under the 1889 charter, such approved expenditures were sent to the city auditor, who could object to all or part of the bill and return it to the board, which could overrule the auditor by voting approval a second time. This is what happened with Kelso's request, but when the board reapproved it, Auditor Fred Teale still refused to number and record it

for payment as required by the charter. When he persisted in refusing to comply
with her demands that he follow the charter procedure, Kelso sought a court order, filing an affidavit of the events leading to her request for a writ of mandate
from the Los Angeles Superior Court. After a trial, the court granted Kelso relief, but Teale still refused and instead appealed to the California Supreme
Court, keeping the matter tied up in litigation for over a year. Teale's lawyers,
C. H. McFarland and Albert Crutcher, made three specious arguments: (1) Kelso
could have gotten her payment from the city treasurer even if the auditor refused
to number and record it; (2) the demand was not properly itemized to show that
Kelso had been a delegate to the World Congress of Librarians; (3) the board
should not have made the appropriation in the first place, because "the benefits
to be derived by the taxpayers and patrons of the library from what might be
learned by a delegate to a congress of librarians are too remote, too speculative,
too chimerical to make the expenses of such a delegate a legal charge upon the
public funds." Eventually, the California Supreme Court would reject all three
arguments and affirm the lower court's order that the auditor accept the library
board's properly authorized expenditure.[42]

Kelso was represented by Frank Howard and Sheldon Borden, members of
the library board attacked by Teale's actions. In its 1893 report, the board complained of the attempt "by ignorant and prejudiced people to criticise in an entirely unwarrantable manner" its considered action.[43] Clearly it was an attack on
Kelso as well, accusing her of squandering the taxpayers' money on worthless
travel. At a time of economic crisis, she was put in the position of publicly demanding $200, an enormous sum to the desperate unemployed, for her trip to
the glittering world's fair. Though the auditor's case had no legal merit, and
Kelso was defending a worthy principle, she also was in a no-win situation
where her reasonable actions were fodder for demagoguery and resentment. By
1894, there was rumored to be "strong political influence averse to Miss Kelso's
continuance in office."[44] Since Kelso never wrote an account of her experience in
Los Angeles, there is no way to know if she tried to avoid further trouble, but
events suggest that she chose offense as the best defense. Probably she was determined not to be intimidated and concluded that she could not dissuade those
who wanted to replace her, since their real objective was power over the library's
jobs for patronage.

Early in 1894, several meetings of the library club were devoted to the subject of realism in fiction. "Where to draw the line in realism" drew an
"unusually large and responsive gathering."[45] The speakers had a relaxed attitude
towards what was acceptable in literature, but a clergyman warned that "what
was food to one mind was poison to another." The discussion may have alerted
Kelso's enemies to the menace of indecent books in the library.

In May, not inclined to cease travel to meetings, Kelso was off to San
Francisco to deliver her "rousing" paper at a women's congress. California
women's demand for the right to vote was intensifying, and there were rumors
of Kate Galpin's intention to run for office. The papers were full of the suffrage
issue and the New Woman. The economic situation showed no improvement,
and the "armies" of unemployed were marching on Washington to demand relief; Coxey's Army from Ohio was the most prominent, but there were others

from around the country, including Los Angeles. At the same time, the workers who built Pullman railroad cars went on strike in Chicago; when the railroad workers' union joined them in sympathy, rail traffic came to a halt, cutting off California agricultural produce from its markets in the East. Newspaper headlines shrieked of riots, culminating early in July when the president sent troops who fired on the strikers.

On top of the national turmoil, the Los Angeles political scene was agitated by jockeying for position in the December mayoral election and a movement to revise the charter. Much of this focused on the ever popular demands for reductions in the size and cost of government by cutting salaries and eliminating positions and boards. In March, there was a large meeting of the Citizens' League, "including some of the leading citizens and heaviest taxpayers," according to the *Herald,* where there were complaints that Los Angeles had unusually high taxes and large budgets.[46] Soon there were several committees proposing charter revisions, particularly drastic cuts in the salaries of city officials. By May, the city council's committee was proposing that the librarian's salary be cut to $1,500 from Kelso's $1,800, and, in apparent retaliation for the lawsuit, that "all demands on the library fund shall be subject to the approval of the Mayor and city council."[47] Kelso was not without friends, however, and supporters persuaded a joint committee of the Citizens' League and the Chamber of Commerce to support retention of the $1,800 salary.

Throughout 1894, the *Herald* was vehement in complaints about the "great array of officials and employees who are supported" by local government, which was accused of the usual waste and corruption.[48] The publishers, James Ayers and Joseph Lynch, claimed to have changed from a Democratic paper to an independent advocate of "great reforms and retrenchments."[49] "Whenever we discover an abuse in our local government," proclaimed the *Herald,* "we intend to denounce it and to keep on denouncing it till a remedy is effected."[50] The school board, alleged to be taking the schools into "a vortex of villainous political management," the assessor, the street superintendent, all came under attack in the *Herald,* as did its rising Republican rival, the *Los Angeles Times* and its publisher, Harrison Gray Otis, accused of seeking to be the "boss" of the city and county.[51] (Otis and his family would indeed become a major power in the region.) Despite its claim of independence, the *Herald* supported Democratic candidates and frequently attacked the "Republican ring" that controlled city government; its editor, Joseph Lynch, was remembered by Charles Lummis as an "ardent Democrat" (and a hard-drinking brawler).[52] The *Herald* made appeal to struggling workers with sympathy for the unemployed and assurances that eliminating city positions would free money for relief of the poor. The paper claimed that its attacks on government had greatly increased its circulation, although the prominence given to crime and sex scandals probably helped, as did its ridicule of the women's rights movement. Invoking an old misogynist theme, an editorial titled "Women on Top" informed "the clamorous women's rights women who are constantly inveighing against the tyrant man" that "the fair sex in Chicago is rapidly replacing men in a wide range of departments of industry."[53] That was just what its male readers feared.

Initially the *Herald* was respectful towards the library while turning its fire on other departments. It reported favorably on Hasse's fiction list and denounced a threat to the library's federal government depository status as a "great loss to the public." There was mild ridicule, along with acknowledgment that the library was heavily used, in a feature, "Some Library Characters, Queer Types to Be Found in the Reading Room," which pictured the library as a hangout for odd men, such as street preachers and "dissipated old men who pore over abstruse works," and silly women, "the fiction fiends . . . made up mainly of young girls . . . insatiate devourers of fiction and poetry of the point lace and diamond style, afternoon teas and lawn tennis frubbery" and the "old maids who . . . devote themselves . . . to works on women's suffrage."[54]

In June, the *Herald* headlined "Leads All American Cities, Some Interesting Facts about the Library" on a story about a board meeting at which Kelso made a special midyear report on the heavy use of the library and the need for more money. She explained that the library had a higher proportion of card holders to population than any other American city, but the pressure for "rigid economy" was reducing the availability of books and having a "perceptible effect upon the usefulness of the library." The financial pressure was partly due to a deficit from the previous year, but Kelso emphasized that the city's policy of keeping the library's appropriation below its maximum of five cents of every hundred dollars of revenue "seriously impairs its usefulness." She suggested a bulletin to library users asking them "to take steps to present the needs of the institution to the honorable council" that controlled the funds. Although technically only a suggestion to the board, this was reported in the press, effectively taking the issue of library funding to the public in a way that would not have endeared Kelso to the council members. Two weeks later, board chairman Dobinson appealed to the city council for $500 to purchase new books. The request was referred to committee when opposed by Francis Nickell, a Democrat from a Republican district and a favorite of the *Herald*. Nickell made no criticism of the library but argued that no money was available, other departments having expended the cash fund for the next sixty days.[55]

Then suddenly the *Herald* launched an all-out attack on Kelso and Dobinson. Under the headline "Plain Facts about the Library," it purported to analyze the usage and financial data to show that Kelso was overpaid and underworked as head of an organization overstaffed for work that consisted only of checking out books and supervising the reference and reading rooms, which could be done just as well by a "small and efficient" staff. Kelso was compared unfavorably with the girls "who do the greater portion of the work and receive the minimum pay," and her travel expenses were the object of sarcasm: "Absorbed in deep, abstruse problems, with reference to the ethics of bibliology to be sometime projected on the heads of sapient thinkers in some book congress in Chicago, San Francisco or Hong Kong (with expenses paid by the taxpayers), it is very rare, indeed, that Miss Kelso or her high-salaried assistants condescend to do anything in the way of doling out books to the library patrons." Urging the replacement of Dobinson with a "conscientious business man," the *Herald* expressed confidence that "the force of young lady employees could be reduced by one half." It also criticized the library for having its own janitor, instead of using the city hall janitors, and, in a vaguely sexual innuendo, complained about the "two 'private offices,' one of which . . . was much frequented by Mr. Dobinson," as if there were something sinister about the presence of the board chairman in a library office.[56]

When another paper defended the library, the *Herald* expanded on its complaints in "The Mismanaged Library," waxing even more vehement about the "injustice" to the "poorly paid workers." Some information seemed to have come from library staff resentful at their long hours (up to twelve-hour days) for $20 per month, with no paid sick leave, while Kelso was alleged to work nine to five for $150, with a month of paid vacation. In an appeal to its readers' feelings about a woman executive, the *Herald* piously proclaimed: "No one objects to the employment of young women in the library or the enlargement of woman's sphere of usefulness, but the taxpayers do object to supporting drones in this public hive while poorly paid girls do all of the work." It reiterated that Kelso had inflated the circulation figures to get more money and justify twenty employees, even though the Library of Congress needed only "half a dozen employees to handle the millions of volumes." (LC's pitifully small staff had been the subject of indignant editorial comment in *Library Journal*.) The editors may have been reminded of their recent praise for Hasse's fiction list, for she now was exempted from the criticism and described as "both competent and hardworking, as the new catalogue shows."[57]

Though unpleasant, these crude attacks didn't seem terribly damaging. Kelso's salary was less than those of other city officials, and she had been careful to keep expenses low and publish data on the work done in every department of the library. But the *Herald* had just been laying the groundwork for its real attack, a guaranteed circulation booster, the "Indescribable Revelation" of a "consummately obscene" French novel on the shelves of the library.[58] With the addition of a sex angle, the *Herald* went into a frenzy of titillating indignation.

The source of the commotion was *Le Cadet* by Jean Richepin, a popular and prolific contemporary French writer. It was a long and lurid tale involving, among many plot developments, a sensual young woman who had an affair with her brother-in-law before eventually retiring to a convent.[59] Although *Le Cadet* was the only indecent book it ever identified, the *Herald* claimed that "the shelves of the city library are covered with books that are not only not fit to be read but which are indescribably filthy . . . novels of such indescribable atrocity that human nature itself is violated." Much of the blame was placed on Dobinson, "whose moral standing is confessedly bad." Showing a connection with the maneuvering for the mayoral race, the *Herald* explained further: "Mr. Dobinson, a Republican who, by the favor of Mayor Rowan, is at the head of our board of library trustees, is, as everybody except possibly the mayor knows, a person utterly unfit to be intrusted with such a responsibility. Outside of a capricious favoritism shown to him by the mayor, he could not get three votes for any office in the city of Los Angeles."[60]

When board member Frank Howard wrote a vigorous response, the *Herald* refused to print his letter in full, on the grounds that it was not sufficiently polite, but then used it as an excuse for further fulminations. To Howard's point that the board as a whole, not just Dobinson, was answerable for the library, the paper insisted that "Dobinson personified the library management," while the other board members, men of "unsullied moral character," had only acquiesced in the "all pervading, all managing part" ascribed to Dobinson. As for Howard's explanation that the book had been acquired in a lot from a dealer to meet the demand for French fiction "suitable for a public library," and no one could be expected to examine every book in such a large shipment, making it "inevitable that an objectionable book should from time to time creep into a library," the *Herald* assured its readers that Howard was "still unaware of the unspeakably vile character of *Le Cadet* . . . or he would probably admit that no excuse was sufficient to pardon the fact that it has been on the shelves of the library, open to the perusal of any young boy or girl." The paper's indignation focused on the danger to youth, while admitting that some literary classics might be accused of obscenity and certainly censorship, especially of the press, could be hazardous to liberty. But in the case of a public library, "the idea of censorship is by no means offensive or objectionable," because it "has no reference to the suppression of thought or subjection of the mind, but has entire relation to the protections of ingenuous youth . . . and to the unequivocal rebuke . . . to salacious and corrupting writers."[61]

The emphasis on the danger to youth suggests that Kelso's views on children's reading had been noted with alarm in some quarters. Under the headline "Obscenity in the Library," the *Herald* reported that "pernicious literature in the public library with absolutely no restriction on its circulation among the growing youth of the city, the students in the public schools, has excited profound anxiety and regret among all good citizens who desire to have the children protected from contact with vile books." Translations of passages from the book had been shown to local clergymen and the French consul, all of whom were horrified by its presence in the library and availability to youth. The Reverend John Gray, who wanted such books publicly burned, said that he had observed "dozens of young girls . . . at perfect liberty to follow their own instincts of precocity in the selection of books. . . . [T]he consequences should be viewed with alarm by every parent." He understood that in other cities, "proper restrictions are placed on the issuance of books to boys and girls, and it is a matter of infinite and pressing importance that the same safeguard should be provided here." The Reverend William Knighten was appalled that such a book was "in circulation among the young people, poisoning and corrupting their minds, and its evil effects already cannot be estimated. . . . As citizens we should demand the complete quarantine of the library until it is fumigated and generally disinfected." Even the French vice-consul joined the chorus, condemning the book as "one of the vilest in the French language," one that should not be in the public library, "especially when a large proportion of the patrons are young boys and girls."[62]

The *Herald* followed with "Start by Getting Rid of Dobinson" and "Will the Directors Resign?" The latter mentioned that more criticism from the clergy would issue from the pulpits on Sunday. Two sermons were then printed in their entirety, both citing the Apostle Paul's preaching in Ephesus to such effect that the people made a bonfire of their books. "Cleanse the library by fire . . . the only sure way of ridding the community of bad books," cried J. W. Campbell of the First Methodist Church. His sermon did not mention Kelso by

name; she had warned him in advance that she could not be held personally responsible for the book's presence in the library, and both the indignant clergy
and the *Herald* seemed to avoid specific reference to her, perhaps because she
had shown herself capable of legal action. Campbell even said that no one employed in the library could be wholly blamed, since the real problem was the
community's tolerance for "this evil of a flooded market of superficial, weak and
wicked works upon which the youth of today feed their minds." After the sermon, however, Campbell prayed for Kelso, "Oh Lord, vouchsafe thy saving
grace to the librarian of the Los Angeles City Library and cleanse her of all sin
and make her a woman worthy of her office."[63]

Kelso had warned Campbell, and now she pounced, promptly suing him for
slander and asking $5,000 damages. She argued that the prayer implied that she
was a sinful and immoral woman, unfit for her office. She pointed out that public prayer for church members guilty of immoral conduct was Methodist practice, but she was not a member of the church, did not read French, and was not
responsible for censoring every book in the library. Such impeachment of her
character would disqualify her for her position in a library employing young
women and serving many girls.[64]

The lawsuit caused a sensation, of course, and was reported in papers across
the country. As *Library Journal* judiciously noted, it had significance beyond
library circles, because of clergymen "who misuse the forms of prayer," which
Campbell had taken to an extreme. The minister and his supporters argued that
he might as well be sued by President Cleveland, for whom he also had prayed,
but he hastily announced that he had "nothing but the best of thought" for
Kelso. The *Herald* claimed to be amused by her foolishness.[65]

Despite the ridicule and raised eyebrows, Kelso's lawsuit was a shrewd
counterattack to demagoguery that was spiraling out of control with the calls for
book burning. By suing the overwrought Campbell, she put the clergy and the
Herald on notice to be careful what they said about her. By moving the issue
into court, she put herself on an equal footing with her attacker, able to present
her case in an orderly, rational setting and invoke the protection of the law.
Since the court hearing would not be held for months, there was some calming
effect on a situation that was being used in the mayoral contest.

In going on the offense, however, Kelso did not solve her problem, and it
could be argued that she would have been wiser to hunker down and wait for the
storm to pass. Beyond her own assertive temperament and the advice of the lawyers on the library board, there was much in the spirit of the times to influence
her choice. As the suffrage struggle intensified, California women were increasingly determined to enter the public sphere. A month after Kelso filed suit, Kate
Galpin sought nomination to be the first woman to run for office in the state;
when the Republicans rejected her, the Democrats nominated her for Los Angeles school superintendent, gleefully accusing the Republicans of hypocrisy in
endorsing suffrage but refusing to nominate a woman candidate. As the most
visible woman holding public office in the region, Kelso may have felt a special
responsibility to defend herself. Litigation is an American tradition, of course,
and lawsuits among prominent men were not uncommon in Los Angeles. For
women, lacking economic and political power, litigation offered an opportunity

to seek redress (and revenge), most often in the then common breach-of-promise suits. The city had been entertained for several years in the 1880s by *Perkins v. Baldwin*, a teenage girl's lawsuit against the rich man who had seduced and abandoned her, and earlier in the year, the *Herald* itself had treated its readers to extensive front-page coverage of the Pollard-Breckenridge scandal, a suit against a member of Congress by his former mistress. Two years before, there had been much press attention to a legal imbroglio that began when Dr. Mary Dixon Jones sued the *Brooklyn Eagle* for attacks on her professional reputation as a surgeon.[66] Kelso's action also reflected the undercurrent of anticlericalism among women seeking emancipation, often opposed by the clergy. The following year, Elizabeth Cady Stanton powerfully attacked organized religion for its role in the subordination of women with her *Woman's Bible*, which caused a bitter split in the suffrage movement.

The *Herald* announced that it would continue its "crusade" and urged clergymen to persevere in "their noble efforts," but it took a milder tone, more amused than angry, and claimed that the public sympathized with Campbell, "a fine genial, kind-hearted gentleman" attacked by a shrewish woman. It printed a letter complaining about Kelso's travel and dismissing her as a mad woman who had "been led to do a very foolish thing by evil counselors, who are really the guilty parties." The congregations of the clergy who had attacked the library passed resolutions in support of Campbell, shamelessly calling for the "widest possible range of free speech" for the ministers who had urged book burning.[67] She may not have helped her ultimate prospects by fighting back, but Kelso did succeed in changing the atmosphere.

While taking aggressive action against Campbell, Kelso and the library board also made conciliatory gestures. At its September 5 meeting, the board received a report from Dobinson and Howard, the book committee, on their efforts to exercise an appropriate "duty of censorship." They acknowledged a responsibility to protect against "simply immoral" books, but it was a "very grave and much-disputed question how far library management can exercise parental discrimination over the reading of its patrons." They had been criticized for going too far in "ostracizing" works of Tolstoy, Zola, Helen Gardener, and others, but they could say that only one "unworthy book" had slipped past their vigilance in five years, and it was in French.[68] A few months later, the library's 1894 annual report included a section on children's reading that emphasized, "Great care is taken in the selection of books that are marked as suitable for young people." Kelso assured the community that the staff at the delivery desk tried to "direct and influence" young readers, and she also urged development of delivery stations in areas distant from the library, so that library books might "supplant . . . the iniquitous 'nickel novel' with its heroes of highwaymen and thieves."[69]

The court hearing was scheduled for December, and meanwhile the *Herald* had the charter revision and the election season to keep it busy. Kelso carried on as usual. In October, she read a paper, "The Public Library as a Means of Education," at the third annual Women's Parliament, where it "elicited a good deal of comment" among the mostly middle-class women meeting to discuss suffrage, dress reform, the differing socialization of boys and girls, and the most fundamental question: "Is home life women's sphere?"[70]

On December 3, Kelso's suit came before the probate court on a motion to dismiss Campbell's demurrer that as a clergyman he was immune to lawsuits for his public prayer. His attorney maintained that it was traditional in the Methodist Church to pray for public officials and, since no one was without sin, "ergo no one was without the pale of prayer." Kelso's junior counsel, W. G. Foley, argued that habits of religious denominations had no place in the principles of justice. The prayer for Kelso was "quite superfluous" and contained innuendoes that could not be explained away. Frank Howard then pointed to the statements in Campbell's sermon that magnified the objectionable nature of the prayer. He argued that a person's position affected whether remarks were slander, citing numerous authorities who held that statements that might not be slander of an individual could be actionable when directed against a public official to diminish public trust.[71]

On the same day, the voters elected a new Republican mayor, Frank Rader, who overwhelmingly defeated the Democrat endorsed by the *Herald*. Mayor Rader appointed an entirely new library board, ending the service of Kelso's supporters, Dobinson, Howard, and Borden. The new chairman, Major George Bonebrake, was a power in the business community, a bank president and leader of the effort that brought the Santa Fe Railroad to the city. He also was a lawyer, as were Henry O'Melveny, who would be a longtime leader of the California bar, and the politically ambitious Frank Flint, who soon would be U.S. Attorney for Southern California and then a U.S. senator. The other members were George Stewart and H. E. Storrs, a farmer. The city soon bubbled with rumors that Kelso would be replaced.

As Kelso entered a new year with two lawsuits pending and a possibly hostile new board, she must have found considerable irony in the position of the *Herald,* which had changed ownership and become her vocal supporter. The new publisher was a businessman, John Bradbury, who adopted a calmer tone with less indignation about the working man and more attention to the single tax movement, which appealed to both middle-class reformers and organized labor with a theory that tax and land reform would solve the terrible problems of poverty in industrialized economies. While the paper continued to devote much space to murders, sex scandals, and the marriages of American heiresses to titled Europeans, there was more material aimed at women's interests across the spectrum, from beauty aids to suffrage.

Late in March, the California Supreme Court issued its ruling in Kelso's favor in her suit against the city auditor. Ten days later, Judge Clark ruled in her favor in regard to Campbell's claim that his public prayer was privileged. The court held that no public prayer containing slander could be exempt from the legal consequences and no communication by a pastor to his congregation could be considered privileged by the relationship. That left the question of whether the prayer was slanderous still to be determined, but it did establish that Kelso's suit was not as absurd as her critics had claimed.[72]

Between the two court rulings, the new library board held its organizational meeting on March 25. Most of the time was given to the farewell address of Dobinson, who pointed with pride to the library's improved collection and efficient management, asserting that "in no department of the public service has greater real economy been practiced." He reminded the new board that the library had never received its full appropriation under the charter, operated with a sum that was insignificant compared to other departments of government, and maintained financial records that had been praised by the accountant who reviewed them. He noted that the salary expenditures covered long hours and low pay for everyone on the staff, including the librarian, who was paid less than the head of any comparable library. In an indication that patronage jobs were an unspoken issue, Dobinson gave particular attention to the library's employment system, recalling that when he took office six years earlier, the board encountered the "annoyance of being besieged at all hours by applicants and their friends who urged their claims for appointments." He urged that the system that had "worked so admirably" be continued, noting that the mayor had assured him that he was "in sympathy," so that he had "therefore no reason to doubt that you gentlemen will continue it also." Dobinson ended with thanks to the board members, especially Frank Howard's devoted service, and to the staff, especially "Miss Kelso and Miss Hasse for their able work and intelligent conduct of the details of their profession." This was followed a few days later by a *Times* editorial of unqualified praise for the library.[73]

The new board immediately showed its interest in the hiring system. Meeting four days after its first session, it spent much of the time learning about the system. Then, appropriately on April 1, the board met in a state of confusion that "rivaled a circus." It started auspiciously enough with approval of a resolution to continue Kelso's employment system. Then Henry O'Melveny offered a resolution that there be no changes in the library staff, except to fill vacancies, before the end of the fiscal year in ninety days. Since O'Melveny proved to be a Kelso supporter, this may have been meant to reassure her that she would not be summarily dismissed and to warn job seekers not to expect immediate openings. Instead of seeing it as a chance to either establish a working relationship with the new board or hunt for a new job, Kelso reacted to it as an insult that effectively put her on three months' probation after six successful years as head of the library. Telling the board that the resolution put her in a bad position, she offered her immediate resignation, and Hasse also resigned. This discombobulated the board, and three of the members complained that Kelso had forced the issue of her continuation. The board proceeded to pass O'Melveny's resolution, with only Bonebrake opposed, on the grounds that it did indeed put Kelso in an unpleasant position. Flint countered with a motion to accept the resignations, which only O'Melveny opposed, but the board then found itself in the awkward position of not being able to agree on a replacement. O'Melveny nominated Kelso to succeed herself, with a second by Stewart, who also nominated Mrs. Clara Fowler, the choice of Flint and Bonebrake. Storrs, who was reluctant to choose under the circumstances, nominated Professor Horace Brown. O'Melveny argued that Kelso had been an able administrator whose removal would set a bad precedent. Storrs said his favorable view of Kelso had changed when she forced the issue, but, knowing little of the library and nothing of Clara Fowler, he nominated a third candidate to give him the option of denying a majority to either woman. Three votes produced no decision, as Flint and Bonebrake voted for Fowler, Stewart and O'Melveny for Kelso, and Storrs stuck with his spoiler vote for Brown. Finally, Storrs suggested Kelso withdraw her resignation, which she did, and the board decided, over Flint's objection, to expunge the record of the whole matter. As the meeting ended, reported the *Herald*, "Miss Tessa Kelso looked happy while the board looked ill at ease." Flint told the *Herald* that he had accepted appointment with the intention of making the change in library management "the people desired."[74] Since the other members seemed less certain, it is unclear why Kelso was so quick to resign without waiting to see where she stood with a majority. She probably believed that her situation was impossible, given the hostility of Flint and Bonebrake, and so followed her instinct to take the offense towards demeaning treatment.

In its new incarnation as a Kelso supporter, the *Herald* editorialized "Keep Politics Out," urging the board to "promptly and unanimously re-elect the present librarian and her capable assistant." Alleging that "a certain city official has promised the place to someone else, and the promise must be kept, even if the library and the reading people of the city are to suffer inconvenience and the city itself to risk its reputation for intelligence in consequence," the paper advised the "several men who are not disposed to be made party to schemes of this sort" to "stand firm and keep the library out of politics."[75]

The next day, the board met again, and Flint called on the city attorney, who advised that public records could not be expunged but was reluctant to get involved in the question of Kelso's status. When Flint demanded that Kelso produce the minutes, she said she hadn't kept them, which led to dispute about who had moved and seconded what. Flint, "with a fiery eye," denounced the destruction of public records so furiously that O'Melveny inquired, "Is that in large capitals, Mr. Flint?" After some nervous jocularity about routine matters, Flint returned to his real object with a motion to reduce Kelso's and Hasse's salaries from $150 and $100, respectively, to $100 and $75, an insult obviously calculated to induce them to resign all over again. O'Melveny protested that their salaries should be not lowered but raised in reward for excellence, but the motion carried with the votes of Flint, Storrs, and Bonebrake. Despite Flint's concern for the public record, none of the three offered any explanation for such drastic action.[76]

The board then adjourned but was informally addressed by the superintendent of schools, who spoke feelingly of the teachers' and principals' distress at the board's action when "no city . . . had a better public library," one that worked effectively with the schools under Kelso's direction. This brought a fierce reproof from the intimidating Bonebrake, and the superintendent hastily departed. The meeting petered out with no further resignations, but the press reported that Kelso and Hasse were expected to take jobs elsewhere.

The *Herald,* now as sarcastic in defending Kelso as it had been in attacking her, sneered again at the board's misguided economy:

> It is always expected of new boards that they do something of this kind and
> if they show special discretion in striking at the pay of those who hold
> their positions by reason of brains and competency rather than through
> political influence, they are fairly safe from adverse criticism. But viewing
> it again strictly from the viewpoint of economy, the question arises

whether the board has gone far enough. . . . The librarian of Wayback, Indiana, is said to get only $30 a month and boards around with the members of the board. In Frogmore, Michigan, the librarian received only $24.50 a month, but is allowed to take in washing and thus increase her revenue a little. As a matter of fact, right here in cultivated Los Angeles, a number of people could be found who would not hesitate to accept the job at $40 a month, and at the free employment bureau two men have been heard to say they would take it for a dollar a day. Having started in to do the cheap act, it is to be hoped that the board will not turn aside from applying the principle through the whole business. Why pay $1.50 or $2.00 for the novels of Scott and Thackeray, when the literary performances of Smith and Jones may be had for 75 cents or $1? What is the sense of squandering $50 on a set of Shakespeare, when much larger books with a good deal more printing in them can be found at any second-hand store for half the money? Or, to carry the principle a little nearer home, why should Major Bonebrake pay $18.50 for a large oil painting for his front parlor when Mr. Flint can find a chromo just as good for $2.25?[77]

Three weeks later, when the board met on April 30, Kelso, Hasse, and Estelle Haines submitted their resignations. O'Melveny voted against accepting them, and Bonebrake mysteriously abstained, but the other members accepted the resignations. Stewart, who had seemed inclined to support Kelso, had been the recipient of anonymous letters, apparently from a library employee resentful of the librarian's outside activity:

Not that she is a desirable person for several reasons, for she is frequently away from the Library, attending Friday Morning Clubs. Making speeches, etc., popularizing herself at the expense of the "Taxpayers," for she is paid her salary when absent. This is not fair, not just. I don't see the public or the Library are benefitted [sic] by her gossip, or talk. Don't let her "coax" and don't let her "coerce" the Library Directors. . . . Miss Kelso wishes to be head and Chief above all.[78]

The board then engaged in what the *Herald* called "one of those charming comediettas for which [it] . . . has become famous," with the members nominating five different people for Kelso's position. After much confusion, Clara Fowler, a widow who worked in the county clerk's office, was chosen. Hasse's job went to Daisy Austin, whose father was reported to have withdrawn from the mayoral contest in exchange for the promise of a good library job for his daughter. In a violation of the employment system the board had voted to retain, neither woman had graduated from the training school, though Austin had attended the first half of the course.

Stewart's anonymous informant now protested that "those possessing talent and ability have been passed over by influence and favoritism." The letter writer seems to have been a graduate of the training school who worked in the library and seethed with resentment at the better pay and higher status of the librarian and the first assistant. Perhaps she also was behind the *Herald*'s attack on Kelso as overpaid—and perhaps even the discovery of the obscene French novel. As discussed in chapter 10, there is reason to suspect Bertha Pierce, a graduate of the first training class who was in the middle of the library's pay scale. Pierce was a literature cataloger who knew French, and later events would demonstrate her proclivity for secret accusations.

The press reported that Kelso's plans were undetermined, but Hasse had the satisfaction of announcing that she would leave for Washington to work at a much improved salary of $1,600 as librarian in the newly established office of the Superintendent of Documents in the Government Printing Office. Still it was a sad moment of loss as she told the *Herald* that she would have preferred to remain, "to have played chip for chip and met every move as it was made in this game." "But what is a person to do where expert politicians are opposed to a woman?" she sighed and "gazed wearily out the window."[79]

There was some consolation when *Library Journal* issued the "strongest condemnation" of the board's treatment of Kelso and Hasse, whose "skill and energy" were praised: "They were among the ablest library workers on the Pacific coast, and together they developed the Los Angeles Public Library from a condition of comparative insignificance into its present position as a medium of broad usefulness and educational force." This was effectively a eulogy for Kelso's career as a librarian, but for Hasse it was an encouraging sign when she read it in Washington. As she entered the next stage of her career, her merit had been recognized by an editorial that she believed had been written by Melvil Dewey himself. She sent thanks for his defense of the "politically oppressed," assuring him that her new job was "an opportunity to introduce and maintain good library methods, which I shall make every effort to take advantage of."[80]

As Hasse left Los Angeles, *Library Journal* was running her series on the LAPL training class, demonstrating her professional knowledge and values at the very time she was being replaced by a woman without qualifications. Hasse owed the support of LJ and her new opportunity in Washington to her publications and Kelso's promotion of their work; without this publicity and her contacts at the 1891 ALA meeting, she would have been just another of the many women library workers at the mercy of powerful men, and her misfortune in Los Angeles might barely have registered with leaders like Dewey and Bowker. Kelso's lessons about visibility would influence the rest of Hasse's career, as would her mentor's willingness to fight back when attacked. The values she absorbed in Los Angeles were summed up shortly before her departure by none other than the *Herald* in commentary on the New Woman by the popular singer Jessie Bartlett Davis:

I believe in the new woman most fully. I believe in her capacity, her ambition, and her success. . . . I respect and admire the woman who is not afraid to express her opinion, who is not afraid to strike out for herself no matter what difficulties are before her. The real "new woman" must and will succeed."[81]

Notes

1. Bernadette Soter, *The Light of Learning: An Illustrated History of the Los Angeles Public Library* (Los Angeles: Library Foundation of Los Angeles, 1993), 22; Marian Manley, "Tessa L. Kelso, August 13, 1933," LJ 58 (1 Oct. 1933): 800.

2. Historical Society of Southern California, *Annual Publication* (1891-94); Turbese Lummis Fiske, *Charles F. Lummis: The Man and His West* (Norman: University of Oklahoma Press, 1975), 87-88.

3. Charles Lummis, "Books in Harness," *Out West* (Sept. 1906): 209; Lummis Journals–The Week As Was . . . Dec. 6 to 12, 1891, Lummis papers, Braun Library, Southwest Museum, Los Angeles.

4. "Tessa Kelso, Librarian, 1889-1895" in LAPL 1936 Annual Report, 42.

5. Laura Cooley, "The Los Angeles Public Library," *Historical Society of Southern California Quarterly* 23 (March 1941): 16.

6. LAPL 1936 Annual Report, 40-41.

7. LAPL 1936 Annual Report, 40; Manley, "Kelso," 800.

8. Kelso to AH, 28 Aug. 1889, AH-LC.

9. LAPL 1891 Annual Report, 5-6, 9.

10. George Dobinson to AH, 3 Dec. 1889, AH-LC.

11. LAPL 1894 Annual Report, 6.

12. "Miss Adelaide R. Hasse," *New York Times Illustrated Magazine* (27 June 1897): 5

13. Tessa Kelso, "Some Economical Features of Public Libraries," LJ 18 (Nov. 1893): 473-74, reprinted from *Arena* 7 (May 1893): 709-13.

14. James Brown, "An Englishman on American Libraries," LJ 19 (March 1894): 90.

15. Adelaide Hasse, *The Compensations of Librarianship* (privately published, 1919), 3.

16. LJ 19 (Feb. 1894): 43.

17. Ibid., 42-43.

18. Kelso, "Economical Features," 473.

19. LJ 17 (Nov. 1892): 444.

20. LJ 17 (Jan. 1892): 25, (May 1892): 173, (July 1892): 246.

21. LJ 18 (Jan. 1893): 18-19; LJ 19 (Oct. 1894): 329.

22. The most influential study of sex roles in American libraries is Dee Garrison, *Apostles of Culture: The Public Librarian and American Society, 1876-1920* (New York: Free Press, 1979). For more recent discussion, see Roma Harris, *Librarianship: The Erosion of a Woman's Profession* (Norwood, NJ: Ablex, 1992); "Conference Report: Librarianship as a Women's Profession: Strategies of Empowerment," *Canadian Journal of Information Science* 17 (September 1992):1-43; Joanne Passett, *Cultural Crusaders: Women Librarians in the American West, 1900-1917* (Albuquerque: University of New Mexico Press, 1994); Suzanne Hildenbrand, ed., *Reclaiming the American Library Past: Writing the Women In* (Norwood, NJ: Ablex, 1996); Abigail Van Slyck, *Free to All: Carnegie Libraries and American Culture, 1890-1920* (Chicago: University of Chicago Press, 1995), 160-200; Christine L. Williams, *Still a Man's World: Men Who Do "Women's Work"* (Berkeley: University of California Press, 1995).

23. Kelso, "Economical Features," 473-74.

24. LAPL 1936 Annual Report, 43.

25. Hasse, *Compensations*, 4.

26. The training class was extensively documented in LJ and LAPL's *Bulletin* and annual reports. It evolved over the three years Hasse directed it, with the fullest information appearing near the end of her tenure. A table of the dates and enrollment is in LAPL 1894 Annual Report. This section draws primarily on *Los Angeles Public Library Training Class*, Announcement No. 1 (July 1893), AH-LC; "Los Angeles Public Library Training Class," LJ 19 (March 1894): 90-91; "The Library Schools and Training Classes of the United States," LJ 19 (Sept. 1894): 306-7; Tessa Kelso, "The Los Angeles Public Library Training Class," in U.S. Bureau of Education, *Report of the Commissioner of Education for the Year 1892-93* (Washington: GPO, 1895): 764-771; Adelaide Hasse, "The Training of Library Employes," pt. I, LJ 20 (June 1895): 202-3, pt. II, LJ 20 (July 1895): 239-41, pt. III, LJ 20 (August 1895): 272-73, pt. IV, LJ 20 (Sept. 1895): 303-5; Harriet Child Wadleigh, "The Los Angeles Public Library Training Class," LJ 23 (1898 conference proceedings): 69; Marion Horton, "The Los Angeles Library School," LJ 48 (15 Nov. 1923): 959. For an overview of library education in the 1890s, see Sarah Vann, *Training for Librarianship before 1923* (Chicago: ALA, 1961).

27. LJ 17 (Nov. 1892): 444.

28. LAPL 1889 Annual Report, 17; 1891 Annual Report, 8.

29. Hasse, *Compensations*, 3-4.

30. For an overview, see Gail K. Nelson and John V. Richardson Jr., "Adelaide Hasse and the Early History of the U.S. Superintendent of Documents Classification Scheme," *Government Publications Review* 13 (Jan.-Feb. 1986): 79-88.

31. Adelaide Hasse, "Building Up a Public Document Collection," LJ 31 (Sept. 1906): 661.

32. Adelaide Hasse, *List of Publications of the Agriculture Department from 1841 to June 30, 1895, Inclusive; Library Bulletin No. 9* (Washington: GPO, 1896).

33. Ibid., 5.

34. Adelaide Hasse, *Fiction (Authors') Arrangement Scheme Expressed by Numbers from 1-9999, Assigned to Each Letter of the Alphabet* (typescript for LAPL, ca. 1890), gift of AH to NYPL; W. E. Foster, "Classification from the Reader's Point of View," LJ 15 (1890 conference proceedings): 6-9.

35. LJ 17 (Sept. 1892): 373.

36. Helen Haines, review of *List of Novels and Tales in the English, French, German, and Spanish Languages*, LJ 19 (April 1894): 136-37; AH to Henry Carr, 10 May 1894, ALA Archives, University of Illinois; *The Nation* 58 (3 May 3 1894): 331.

37. Adelaide Hasse, "The New Charging System of the Los Angeles Public Library," LJ 19 (June 1894): 195-96; letter from Ellen Coe, LJ 19 (Sept. 1894): 288; AH reply, LJ 19 (Oct. 1894): 329.

38. "The Anonymous Assistant, by One Who Isn't," LJ 20 (July 1895): 241-42.

39. Lummis, "Books," 209.

40. *LA Herald*, 8 July 1894; *LA Times*, 2 Sept. 1894.

41. LAPL 1893 Annual Report, 6-7.

42. *Kelso v. Teale, City Auditor*, 106 Cal. 477 (1895).

43. LAPL 1893 Annual Report, 6-7.

44. LJ 20 (May 1895): 161.

45. LJ 19 (March 1894): 95.

46. *Herald*, 25 March 1894.

47. *Herald*, 19 May 1894.

48. *Herald*, 22 March 1894.

49. *Herald*, 13 Aug. 1894.

50. *Herald*, 26 Aug. 1894.

51. *Herald*, 3, 14 Sept. 1894.

52. Fiske, *Lummis*, 29-30.

53. *Herald*, 4 Aug. 1894. The classic discussion of this symbolism is Natalie Zemon Davis, "Woman on Top," in *Society and Culture in Early Modern France* (Stanford, CA: Stanford University Press, 1975), 124-51. In relation to the New Woman, see Carroll Smith Rosenberg, "The New Woman as Androgyne," in *Disorderly Conduct; Visions of Gender in Victorian America* (Oxford and New York: Oxford University Press, 1985), 286-88.

54. *Herald*, 13, 15, 23 March 1894.

55. *Herald*, 6, 16 June 1894.

56. *Herald*, 21 July 1894.

57. *Herald*, 8 Aug. 1894.

58. *Herald*, 13 Aug. 1894.

59. The only English-language book on Richepin, Howard Sutton's *Life and Work of Jean Richepin* (Geneva: Droz, 1961), says that *Le Cadet* shows "execrable taste" but still judges it to be among the best novels of the period.

60. *Herald*, 13 Aug. 1894.

61. Ibid.

62. Ibid.

63. *Herald*, 16, 17, 29 Aug. 1894.

64. LJ 19 (Oct. 1894): 340.

65. LJ 19 (Oct. 1894): 329; *Herald*, 26, 27 Aug. 1894.

66. Regina Morantz-Sanchez, *Conduct Unbecoming a Woman: Medicine on Trial in Turn-of-the-Century Brooklyn* (New York: Oxford University Press, 1999).

67. *Herald*, 26, 27 Aug., 1 Oct. 1894.

68. *LA Times*, 6 Sept. 1894. Helen Hamilton Gardener (1853-1925) was a prominent free-thinker and feminist lecturer and writer who appeared frequently in periodicals such as *The Arena*, of which she was an editor. She was especially known for her criticism of the expert opinion that women's brains were inferior to men's and for her lurid and very popular novel of a young woman's ruin by respectable men.

69. LAPL 1894 Annual Report, 32-33.

70. *LA Times*, 4 Oct. 1894.

71. *Herald*, 4 Dec. 1894.

72. *LA Times*, 23 March 1895; *Herald*, 2 April 1895; *New York Times*, 3 April 1895.

73. *Herald*, 26 March 1895; *LA Times*, 28 March 1895.

74. *Herald*, 2,3 April 1895.

75. *Herald*, 7 April 1895.

76. *Herald*, 9 April 1895; *LA Times*, 9 April 1895.

77. *Herald*, 10 April 1895.

78. *Herald*, 30 April 1895. The anonymous letters, in a scrapbook in the LAPL Rare Book Room, were quoted in an unpublished draft of Debra Gold Hansen, Karen Gracy, and Sheri Irvin, "At the Pleasure of the Board: Women Librarians and the Los Angeles Public Library, 1880-1905." In the final version published in *Libraries and Culture* 34 (Fall 1999): 311-46, the quotations had been removed.

79. *Herald*, 30 April 1895.

80. LJ 20 (May 1895): 161-62; AH to Dewey, 26 May 1895, Dewey papers, Rare Book and Manuscript Library, Columbia University.

81. *Herald*, 8 March 1895.

Chapter 3

Government Printing Office, 1895-1897

In her later recollection, Hasse was vague about how she came to be hired by the Government Printing Office (GPO), connecting it with her checklist of Agriculture Department publications, which was compiled in Los Angeles but not published until 1896. Closer to the event, she told a reporter that two people familiar with her documents cataloging work happened to recommend her to the new Superintendent of Documents, Francis Crandall. One was W. H. Lowdermilk, an antiquarian book dealer who specialized in government publications. He and Hasse probably met at the 1891 ALA conference and kept in touch about their mutual interest in documents. Lowdermilk had urged the Agriculture Department to hire her and publish her checklist, and he repeatedly advised Crandall of Hasse's "superior ability." When Crandall offered a job sight unseen, Lowdermilk assured her, "It was upon my statement that he wants you."[1] Presumably Hasse had expressed interest in work in Washington, as he would have been unlikely to make so much effort on his own initiative, but her lifelong habit was to claim that somehow she was "called" to her various jobs, in unsolicited recognition of her ability. This may have indicated awareness that ambition was unseemly in a woman librarian, or perhaps it reflected the messianic temperament that saw her career as a mission and a calling.

Crandall was in haste to hire a librarian to start gathering and organizing public documents in an office that had just been established by the Printing Act of 1895. On April 24, he wired Hasse, "LIBRARIANS PLACE OPEN. CAN YOU COME. IF SO WHEN AND ON WHAT TERMS." Two days later, he told her he could not wait long but "MAKE IT SIXTEEN HUNDRED AND JUNE 1 AND ITS A BARGAIN." Hasse promptly wired her acceptance, and Crandall fired off another message urging her to make haste.[2] Soon Los Angeles was far behind her as Hasse began work on the sixth floor of a building overlooking G Street. Aside from offices at the front, the rest of the vast floor space would hold the documents Hasse would collect and organize.

Once again, Hasse was getting in on the beginning of a new organization with an ambitious leader. It had been only four months since enactment of the legislation to reform and centralize the distribution of United States federal government documents in the new office of the Superintendent of Documents within the Government Printing Office. The Documents Office, as it was commonly known, was to supervise the sale and distribution of government publications, including the program of depository libraries that received shipments of documents free of charge with the obligation to make them available to the public. The office was to prepare and publish three major new bibliographic tools: a "comprehensive index" of federal government publications, a "consolidated index" of congressional documents to replace their hodgepodge of indexes, and a monthly catalog of new documents. The office also was assigned to acquire the older documents accumulated in government departments and retain two copies of every document published since the fifty-third Congress.

The law did not call for the establishment of a library, and Crandall's successor said that it was "unnecessary" and "never contemplated" by the author of the printing bill, who intended only a warehouse.[3] Crandall nevertheless saw a library and the position of librarian as implicit in the duties of his office (and perhaps also related to the lobbying by librarians for the reform of government publishing). He was determined to have qualified staff with professional expertise and civil service status, which was granted that summer. The appointment of Crandall, a newspaper editor from Buffalo, had been opposed by ALA, which preferred John G. Ames, Superintendent of Documents in the office's previous incarnation in the Interior Department. Ames had labored long on the bibliographic control of government publications and had worked with ALA on reform legislation, while Crandall was unknown and without library connections. By moving quickly to consult the library constituency and hire librarians, Crandall won approval, particularly from Richard Bowker, a key figure by virtue of his positions with *Library Journal* and the ALA Public Documents Committee. Soon LJ was purring about Crandall's "praiseworthy" performance and "sympathy" for the aims of librarians.[4]

Library Journal also suggested that the Documents Office be housed in the new building of the Library of Congress, which Bowker wanted officially established as the national library. Crandall's vision of the Documents Office library as a comprehensive collection of government documents, accompanied by sales, information services, publication of catalogs and indexes, and distribution to depository libraries, would have fit well into a national library, had one ever been designated.

Crandall went beyond the terms of the Printing Act to establish a library of government publications intended to serve several purposes. In his view, the requirement to keep two copies of every document since the fifty-third Congress implied a library, and it would be useful to include whatever earlier documents could be found, rather than have the law's arbitrary starting date limit the collection. As Crandall found his office deluged with requests for all sorts of government information, he became convinced of the need for a complete library, which he saw as the key to "unlock the treasures of public documents and make all their contents immediately and practically available."[5] The library organized on the shelves would be a guide to the contents of the thousands of duplicate copies stored in the three ranges of double-decker bins that took up much of the floor space, so that copies could be retrieved and distributed to those seeking information.

Hasse's first task was to gather the masses of documents that had accumulated haphazardly in government buildings, an experience she recalled with relish: "I dare say never had a young collector been given such an opportunity to revel in a very orgy of collecting." Her first object was the Interior Department, said to have a treasure trove of documents in a subcellar. "Thus I sallied forth that bright May morning" with "two enormous vans, each manned with a crew of husky negroes" and a supply of government mail sacks. (A young white woman with a crew of black men would have been a startling image of the New Woman on the streets of Washington, an essentially southern city, in 1895.) Arriving at the building, they arranged the sacks on the sidewalk in groups labeled with the subdivisions of the department and began their hunt.

> We went down a long, dark, damp corridor at the end of which the object of our expedition was concealed in a room which was said not to have been opened for sixteen years. We could not open it now. The door opened inwards and it was impossible to squeeze in and so much as wink at the treasure. One of the negroes finally forced his way in and, by shifting some of the contents he was able to clear enough space, I thought for an entrance for me. But what I saw was a solid wall of books from floor to ceiling and from side to side of the room—nothing but books.[6]

They determined that there was enough space for Hasse to perch between the top of the books and the ceiling. Wearing gloves and a mask to protect against the dust and mold, she climbed to the top with a lantern, examined each volume, and called out its issuing bureau as she tossed it down to the crew, who placed it in the appropriate sack or discarded those ruined by mold. Back at the office, the documents could be distributed efficiently to the bins assigned to agency subdivisions. In six weeks, Hasse gathered and classified about 300,000 volumes, setting aside a copy for the library and storing the rest in the bins.

Hasse had similar adventures at the Capitol. The clerk of the House documents room told her of a "legend" of early documents in a bricked-up room above them. Soon they had a ladder and tools and had made an opening in the ceiling large enough to see that "there was the room and there were the documents!" After much inquiry, she also found a windowless inner room containing "heaps and heaps of the early documents," from which she emerged "happy, smootched with dust, honest sweat, candle grease, and documents."

Not all the documents Hasse found were old. Sometimes she was distressed to find new documents about to be discarded even as more copies issued from the GPO presses. The wastefulness of printing a stock of costly scientific reports for each member of Congress to make free distribution offended Hasse's sense of efficiency, so she and Crandall developed a proposal to give members vouchers for their constituents, who could then obtain what they wanted from the Documents Office. Crandall promoted the idea to the press, and the author of the Printing Act seemed interested, but nothing came of it, other than giving Hasse firsthand knowledge of the difficulty of persuading Congress to adopt efficient policies.[7]

As she hunted for documents throughout the government, Hasse made the acquaintance of longtime government employees, many of them older men charmed by the attractive and enthusiastic young woman. The clerks of the House and Senate documents rooms entertained her with tales of congressmen and documents. As her father's daughter, she enjoyed the conversation of the government scientists who were making Washington a center of research in the Smithsonian and the Interior and Agriculture Departments, where some of the men knew of her father's study of lichens. She had the thrill of meeting men like the Geological Survey's John Wesley Powell, the great explorer of the Grand Canyon and fighter for a rational western land policy, as well as a prolific publisher of handsomely illustrated scientific reports, and Samuel Langley, head of the Smithsonian Institution and inventor of a flying machine. She studied all aspects of GPO's work, asking the printing foreman if she could watch the entire production of the *Congressional Record*, even if it meant staying all night.[8] Observing the federal government in action gave Hasse a new sense of its publications as part of the great world, "quite another feeling about documents than one acquired in the school or catalogue room."

Hasse also eagerly learned from her elderly colleague J. H. Hickox, a "mine of information" who had years of experience in Washington and had compiled a monthly catalog of new documents (published by Lowdermilk) before joining the Documents Office. He shared expertise as they worked on the second edition of the *Checklist of Public Documents,* which Richard Bowker praised for comprising "more working information about government documents than has probably ever been put under one cover."[9] With his experience, Hickox was able to issue the new *Monthly Catalogue of Government Publications* within a few months of starting work. Hasse may have influenced him to arrange it by government departments, which was not how he had organized his earlier catalog, but now coordinated with the way she was arranging the documents library. It was apparently not the preference of Francis Crandall, who made "profuse apologies" for what he considered a makeshift system. Bowker was favorably impressed, however, and found the new catalog superior to the earlier efforts of Poore (chronological) and Ames (a tabular structure alphabetized by keyword in title). Hasse and Hickox worked together for only a short time, however, before he resigned, unable to "subordinate himself to the direction of others."[10]

~ ~ ~

Meanwhile, Crandall was hiring more librarians. Mary Eileen Ahern declined his offer, choosing instead to go to library school for an educational credential, but two Albany-trained catalogers, Edith Clarke and William Burns, joined the office with responsibility for cataloging the documents and developing the "comprehensive index" (*Document Catalogue*) and the "consolidated index" (*Document Index*). Since these were required by the new law, they were given priority and made a separate department from the library, so that, as Edith

Clarke emphasized, "the office of librarian carries with it no authority over nor supervision of the large cataloging staff."[11] This may have been disappointing to Hasse, who had hastily accepted the librarian's position without clarifying her responsibilities; now she found that the key cataloging positions were not under her direction. Instead, the section was headed by Edith Clarke, an ambitious and self-confident woman who had been head of cataloging at Columbia University and Newberry Library. Like Hasse, she was eager to publish and network professionally, and she had already been in the limelight as librarian of the Woman's Building at the 1893 Chicago world's fair. Clarke was somewhat older than Hasse and had both a college degree and professional certification from Dewey's library school. Soon she added two 1895 Albany graduates to the cataloging staff, which may have created a clique of catalogers certain of their authority as experts, while Hasse was the odd woman out, lacking the status of library school education and skeptical about the cataloging mystique.

Crandall and Clarke seem to have formed a mutual admiration society. He praised her "energy, skill, and executive ability" in the preface to the *Document Catalogue,* which was largely her creation.[12] She consulted him extensively on "various knotty portions" of the project. Clarke later wrote of him as "a man so progressive, of such broad outlook, such high and exacting standards and devotion to the public interests."[13] Hasse seems not to have shared that enthusiasm, though she never publicly expressed an opinion of her coworkers, and her later published recollection, written at a time when she was accused of being difficult, was that at no time did she have "any friction with fellow workers" at GPO. At a meeting of the ALA Catalog Section, she praised the "very excellent catalogs issued by the superintendent of documents . . . [which] cannot be improved upon." The only record of dissatisfaction with Crandall and the catalogers appeared in 1898 in what Richard Bowker referred to as Hasse's private "animadversions against 'a few cataloguers and a journalist,'" but this may have been due more to an unpleasant experience with Crandall after she left than to disputes during her work in the Documents Office.[14]

Some have suggested that Hasse and Clarke argued over the classification of the library, with Clarke favoring use of Dewey's subject-based Decimal Classification, while Hasse preferred to use the agency-based system she had developed in Los Angeles.[15] If there was such a disagreement, it was part of debates about documents that librarians would continue far into the future. The conflict is inferred from the typescript of Hasse's classification, which seems to attempt a compromise between the two systems by showing Dewey classification on the left side and her "classification in use in this library" on the right side of each page of the listings for the executive agencies.

Clarke or Crandall may have suggested such a combination; Clarke, in a book published twenty years later, provided a long list of government agencies linked to the most closely related Dewey classes, which suggests that she may have had such an idea at GPO. In the same book, however, she stated that the usefulness of the Documents Office classification "originated" by Hasse was "indisputable" for its special situation: a library consisting solely of federal government documents and used only by a staff with expert knowledge. This does not support the suggestion that she opposed Hasse's system when they worked together at GPO. For other libraries, however, she argued that its disadvantages outweighed its convenience; the message of her book was that librarians should give government documents "the same footing and treatment as any other works."[16]

Clarke's responsibility at the time was for cataloging, not classification, and her published comments showed her to be fully aware of the importance of issuing agencies as corporate authors of government publications. In answer to those who argued that such author entries would be too confusing, she pointed to the often confusing nature of the titles of government publications, which were not a practical alternative to agency authors as main entries. She insisted on the "golden principle" of Cutter's rule that "bodies of men are to be considered as authors of works published in their name or by their authority." Without this principle, she said, the staff of the Documents Office library "could not shelve, catalog, nor refer with any accuracy to the government publications in their charge."[17] Thus she had used agency authors in cataloging, and with an appendix "table of 'Governmental authors' . . . as a pilgrim staff, catalogers will find the labyrinth of public documents a plain and easy road to travel."

Clarke made no mention of an aspect of her corporate authors that soon would be debated among librarians, the use of an inverted form of the agency name that provided a kind of keyword order and avoided a long list of entries starting with the words "department" or "bureau": "Education Bureau" instead of "Bureau of Education." Hasse agreed with Clarke on the inversion issue and may have been involved in what would prove to be a controversial decision. Some would object that inversion created a new problem by placing the author entries in the midst of subjects starting with the same word, and some couldn't tolerate what seemed a violation of cataloging principle. When the issue came before the ALA cataloging section in 1903, Hasse and Clarke joined forces with a motion in support of inverted entries, but ultimately the Library of Congress decided not to accept them for its printed cards.

Clarke and Crandall rejected the idea, suggested by Bowker, that the *Document Catalogue* be arranged according to government structure, explaining in the preface that "no effort to originate some new and unfamiliar form of catalogue will here be found to add to the confusion in which public documents are already enveloped."[18] Clarke recognized the problems presented by agency names in a dictionary arrangement, using the inverted form and providing the appendix guide to agencies to make it easier to use, but she seems not to have grasped the desirability of a guide to government structure that would show all the subdivisions within a department. Since her appendix table of government authors was only an alphabetical list, Bowker complained of "the difficulty of finding out comprehensively the publications of any one department, and perhaps this want could wisely be supplied by a second appendix giving a bird's-eye view of the departments with their several subdivisions logically arranged underneath, and in each subdivision the regular lines of publications."[19] Such an outline of agencies and all their subdivisions later would be issued by GPO as the 1909 edition of the *Checklist* and the serial *List of Classes*.

All that can be said with certainty is that Hasse and Clarke were struggling with issues that had no perfect, easy solution. Both were under great pressure, Hasse to organize the large number of documents and Clarke to produce the *Document Catalogue*, and decisions had to be made quickly. Presumably the small staff of librarians discussed the issues, and Crandall was used as a sounding board, but there was little time for debate. Although Hasse's historical reputation derives largely from creation of what became the Superintendent of Documents Classification, there is little more evidence of how it developed at GPO than in Los Angeles. Responsible for organizing and maintaining the library, Hasse naturally would have been inclined to adopt the system she had already found practical for the LAPL collection and the Agriculture Department checklist, the work that had led to her being hired by Crandall. Her system was efficient for organizing documents as she gathered them from agencies and for responding to the many requests from those agencies, few of which had complete collections of their own publications. The later criticisms of the system did not apply at the time. Since the library consisted solely of documents, there were no books in a different classification. The issue of classification changing as agencies were reorganized was not addressed by Hasse in her Agriculture list and might not have seemed a problem for the Documents Office library, where staff would be familiar with reorganization as a fact of life in government that necessarily would be reflected in the classification.

Hasse's contemporary statements do not show any zeal to impose her system on other libraries. In her preface to the checklist, she attributed the classification to "practical experience" and offered it "merely as a suggestion to librarians who keep their files of Government publications apart from their general collection of books." In 1896, she advised the Connecticut Library Association that documents should be kept in a collection "by themselves" because most were published in numbered series, but in a library that was not attempting a "complete collection," it would be reasonable to break up sets and classify individual documents by subject. In both Los Angeles and Washington, Hasse's staff was limited in size and experience; being able to assign documents to a classification by agency and series seemed more efficient than trying to determine the subject of each document. As her understanding of government information deepened over time, Hasse became ever more convinced that work with documents required an understanding of the structure and functions of government as an organization, but she always said that classification was a practical choice for each library. For her in 1895, faced with a huge workload and a small, inexperienced staff, the classification was "adequate and simple."[20]

Though not advocating it for all libraries, Hasse certainly took pride in her system. She later recalled that when John Shaw Billings visited the library, he examined her classification "quite carefully." She worked on it with the intention "of providing a notation for any collection of United States documents which was to be kept together as a unit."[21] When she left GPO, she kept her original typescript (leaving behind a working copy that was much annotated as the staff developed the system) and later donated it to GPO as a historic document. Crandall and Clarke may have had reservations, but Hasse was not alone in her ideas about classification; her concept had the approval of two knowledgeable men, Richard Bowker and William Leander Post.

During Hasse's GPO years, support for agency-based classification came from Richard Bowker, an authority on the bibliographic control of government documents from his work on the *American Catalogue* and as chair of the ALA Public Documents Committee. In the 1884 *American Catalogue* appendix on U.S. documents, he had listed them by issuing agency, considering it only a makeshift arrangement at the time. A decade later, he was inclined to think it the best way to arrange documents in a printed catalog. He made this point as early as September 1895 in an editorial comment on the new *Monthly Catalogue*'s agency arrangement as "the most practical way of Government cataloging," one that also should be adopted for the annual documents catalog being developed: "We suggest that, after all, the best method may be to make the annual catalog on the lines of departments and bureaus—which is practically a subject classification and a classification by publishers—supplementing this with an index by author, title, and specifically by subject." If another system were used, the catalog then should include an appendix of the agency plan for the *Monthly Catalogue,* "which is the natural classification for government documents." [22]

A few months later, he reiterated this to Hasse: "I have always thought that in the case of Government publications arrangement by departments and subclassification by bureaus was perhaps preferable to an alphabet by bureaus, as the department arrangement gives a rough classing which is in itself valuable, while the strict alphabetical arrangement . . . brings a great mass of entries under the absolutely nominal term Bureau." [23] Bowker seemed to be thinking of the problems of agencies as author entries in catalogs and bibliographies. American librarians would be grappling with the rules of corporate entry for government agencies for another decade, and the difficulties inherent in government agency entries would bedevil libraries (and Adelaide Hasse) long after that. Bowker's only comment specifically on Hasse's classification, in his review of the Agriculture Department checklist, found it "partly but not wholly satisfactory; evidently it will be some time before we can have a comprehensive method of notation for government documents, desirable as it is." [24]

The full development of the Superintendent of Documents Classification came when William Leander Post held the office from 1906 to 1909. Post, who had worked in the Documents Office library since Hasse's time, had no doubt that agency-based classification was the correct concept, explaining that as "it was seen to be impossible to arrange such a large and uncertain collection of special publications by either the 'decimal' or 'expansive' system . . . , governmental author arrangement was adopted, corresponding in the main" to Hasse's system for the Agriculture Department. Over time, this was found to be "not capable of meeting the needs of a great Library of government literature, and a new classification became a necessity." After much experimentation and consideration of various systems, Post adopted a classification that proved "satisfactory in every way." Post did not go into detail about his decisions for what he referred to as "my scheme," but Hasse described it as an "expanded form" of her classification. [25] More complex than her original concept, it went further into the levels of agency structure, reflecting a decade of experience with the collection.

Post and Hasse were on friendly terms and probably discussed the system's evolution.

~ ~ ~

When Crandall issued his first official report in October 1895, he explained that the development of the library had been slowed by various factors. The shelving for ten thousand volumes soon proved to be insufficient, requiring a delay to obtain more fireproof shelves. The need to concentrate on producing the catalogs required by law, particularly the annual *Document Catalogue*, meant that "the force which had been assigned to the work of making the library and its card catalogue had to be pressed into the printed catalogue service," which implies that Hasse's staff was reassigned within a few months of her arrival. He concluded his lengthy comments with praise for the efforts of his "trained experts," Hasse, Hickox, Clarke, and Burns.[26]

Whether Hasse helped with the *Document Catalogue* is unknown, but she did work with Hickox on the new edition of the *Checklist of U.S. Public Documents* as they extensively revised and expanded copy prepared by Ames. Showing her interest in bibliography, she contributed three appendixes: a list of government reports of explorations and surveys; a bibliography of government catalogs; and an index to important executive department reports within the congressional serial set. Bowker praised them in his review, a month before he also praised her Agriculture Department checklist.[27] At a time when development of the library was not going well, she was encouraged to see bibliography as the path to appreciation and success.

By mid-1896, Crandall reported to ALA that the library struggled under "discouraging circumstances" in which "the work has been enormous, the number of assistants at the disposal of the librarian has been small, and they have been mostly without experience or training." Moreover, some branches of the office had "been stripped almost bare in order to give the catalogers all possible help." Without mentioning Hasse's name, he summed up her achievement:

> That so much has been accomplished under such conditions is to me a constant surprise. A reference library containing 12,000 documents has been established, and a quarter of a million duplicates have been assorted and made ready for immediate exchange or sale. These books, belonging to the government, which before were as unavailable and as useless as if they lay at the bottom of the Potomac, have been restored to use and are as accessible and as available as the day they were printed. It does not seem to me an extravagant estimate to say that this government property thus reclaimed is worth a half-million dollars.[28]

In his official report of the office's first full year, there was no mention of the shortage of staff and no praise for Hasse or anyone else as Crandall pointed with pride to the library of fifteen thousand documents "created, accessioned, shelf-listed, etc., so that it is immediately available for reference, not only in our own work, but for the convenience of all who choose to use it." Everything Crandall reported implied a heavy workload: creation of the library; production of four major publications; more depository libraries; increasing sales of current documents; an "almost overwhelming" volume of inquiries from people who expected the office to function as an "information bureau for documents."[29]

Probably it was the frustration of inadequate support for her work that caused Hasse to seek new employment less than a year after arriving in Washington. In March 1896, she wrote to John Shaw Billings at the newly formed New York Public Library, seeking to be put in charge of the cataloging of documents. Kelso, who had joined Hasse the previous summer, had already been to see Billings about a job, but neither was successful. Hasse was told that there were no openings, but her inquiry would be kept on file pending organizational changes. When she promptly wrote back to expand on her ideas for documents, Billings promised to visit GPO when next in Washington, but no job offer was forthcoming.[30]

~ ~ ~

Interest in a new job was only one thing on Hasse's mind as she enjoyed the stimulating atmosphere of Washington and the professional contacts in the East. Hearing from Alice Kroeger of the Drexel library school that Dewey would be visiting Philadelphia, she wrote to urge him to come on to Washington. Richard Bowker visited and left with Hasse's proposal for a handbook on government publications for the ALA publishing section, though he worried that she planned "a pretty large book."[31] That project was deferred, but she did produce a brief appendix, "Public Documents," for John Cotton Dana's *Library Primer* in 1896. Added to her appendixes in the *Checklist of Public Documents* and the publication of her agriculture checklist as *Agriculture Department Library Bulletin 9,* she was moving quickly to establish a reputation as a bibliographer and an expert in government publications. Her *Library Primer* contribution appeared first in *Public Libraries,* the new periodical Dana and Mary Eileen Ahern had created for small public libraries, and then in the revised version published as a book in 1899. In what would be a continuing theme, Hasse warned librarians not to try to collect more documents than were actually needed. As to how to organize documents, Hasse said she didn't have space to discuss fully what must be decided by each library "chiefly upon the extent to which the library can afford duplication," meaning that the serial set should be kept as a separate entity, while individual copies of some agency reports might be integrated into the classified book collection.[32]

Professional organizations provided more networking opportunities. In May 1896, Hasse and Kelso traveled to New Haven to address the Connecticut Library Association. Hasse reported on the Documents Office library and discussed what would be a perennial topic among librarians, the separation or integration of government publications within library collections. She gave what would be her standard advice, that large holdings of documents should be kept together as a separate collection, primarily because most were in numbered series, but libraries not collecting complete series certainly could choose to integrate individual government reports into the subject classification. Kelso spoke of the librarian's duty to make the library vital in the life of the community, "a place where class distinctions are forgotten and where workmen and employers can meet on the common ground of common interest."[33] Such hopeful idealism was a common element of librarians' meetings; it also reflected the national mood of 1896, with the economy reviving and the voters' turn to the Republican presidential candidate, the unfailingly bland William McKinley, as a refuge from years of turmoil.

The two women also attended the 1896 ALA conference in Cleveland. Kelso was, as always, a lively participant in the discussions. When *The Red Badge of Courage* was condemned, she lightened the priggish tone by remarking that its offensive language (some hells and damns) did make an effective antiwar statement. Hasse was not reported as joining the public discussions, but as a member of the Committee on Library Schools, she submitted a report on the Pratt Institute school, one of the few uncontroversial statements she would ever make to ALA. The committee's report was rather bold in making some criticisms of the schools, however, and it also was unusual in attempting comparative study of the programs, though ultimately finding too little consistency to make comparisons. Hasse did not continue on that committee, but she was appointed to a special committee to consider a proposed "American Libraries Clearinghouse" for the centralized distribution of privately published books and pamphlets.[34]

The Cleveland ALA conference was notable for a speech that made a lasting impression on Hasse. In his presidential address, John Cotton Dana of the Denver Public Library urged librarians to "Hear the Other Side," to take action to improve the mausoleum-like atmosphere of their libraries, their own poor reputation, and the quality of their users, perceived to be children, novel-reading women, and "loafers." Already known as a rebellious Westerner (though originally from New England), Dana was criticized by *Library Journal* for negativity. To Hasse and Kelso, however, he was trying to stir librarians to action about issues they had addressed in Los Angeles; as Kelso had just told the Connecticut librarians, "western libraries are much more important in the life of cities than eastern ones." Dana would be both a friend and an influence on Hasse's professional values, as his sardonic skepticism reinforced Kelso's iconoclastic attitudes.

Back in Washington, Hasse was so active in the Washington Library Club that she was elected vice president in December 1896. The group had seventy-one members, librarians and bibliographers from the agencies, the Smithsonian, and the Library of Congress, who were eager to discuss the possibilities of a union list of periodicals, interlibrary loans, centralized printing of catalog cards, and, of course, the future of the Library of Congress in the magnificent building rising on Capitol Hill. For professional contacts, Washington was infinitely better than remote Los Angeles with its handful of small, struggling libraries. Hasse was meeting librarians and bibliographers who specialized in the sciences and law, most of them men serving a clientele of men engaged in important work. They especially appreciated her efforts to develop the much-needed comprehensive library of public documents.

There were also antiquarian specialists like Lowdermilk and William Boyden of the Scottish Rite Masonic Library, where for several months Hasse spent her evenings cataloging its collection, enjoying the "fine bindings, rare editions and . . . books on unusual subjects" while being well paid and then awarded a bronze medal that had never before been given to a woman.[35]

Hasse and Boyden also worked together to obtain a patent for a catalog card sorting device that would "save labor and time." This too was part of the atmosphere of Washington librarians. Forty years later, Hasse reminded the local library association that its early members had been advocates of technology as well as bibliography, citing the influence of Walter Swingle in promoting the photostat for copying in libraries and John Shaw Billings' contribution to the Hollerith punch card computing machine, which became the basis of the development of computers in the United States.[36]

~ ~ ~

After almost a year of unemployment, Kelso found what she wanted, a job in New York City. She worked with the publisher Charles Scribner's model library and then moved to the book wholesaler Baker and Taylor, where she would spend the rest of her career in a business that served libraries. Hasse was increasingly dissatisfied with GPO, where there were signs of political interference, and eager to join Kelso in New York. Still hopeful of persuading John Shaw Billings to hire her, she wrote to him again in March 1897. He was not encouraging at first, but she persisted so persuasively that by May she could submit her resignation and depart triumphantly for the New York Public Library.

In his annual report, Francis Crandall commented, "The resignation . . . of the librarian of the office, whose reputation, gained chiefly by her work here, secured her a flattering engagement in New York, checked for a time the work in the document library."[37] Actually, the new job had been won by her persistence with Billings and by the energy and ability demonstrated over seven years of library work. Crandall felt inconvenienced by Hasse's departure, and he probably also envied her move to what he regarded as a "much better situation," while he was left to deal with the new Public Printer and continuing problems with Congress. At the time, he told California's senators, who had inquired about filling Hasse's place with a patronage appointment, that "the wisdom of her appointment has been demonstrated by the success of her work here,"[38] but his annual report gave her no public praise, and he made at least two attacks on her after she left, accusing her of improperly taking a government record with her and then writing a highly critical review of one of her first published bibliographies.

Crandall's allegation that Hasse had taken a government record was sent to Billings in the fall of 1897, just as she was settling into her new job. In the style of Kelso, she responded with an indignant and vigorous counterattack. Since Crandall had embarrassed her by contacting her boss, she did the same with his, Public Printer F. W. Palmer, to ask that Crandall "be directed to either substantiate his charges or to retract his statements to Dr. Billings." She sent a copy to California Senator White, who had only recently received Crandall's praise for her work and knew of her good reputation in Los Angeles, to request that he contact Palmer in support of her request, telling him that Crandall "virtually accuses me of theft," a charge "so grave in its possible consequences that I cannot do less than bring the matter to the notice of the Public Printer." White promptly wrote to express his concern that "a great wrong had been done" by Crandall's letter to Hasse's employer "for the purpose of injuring her." He asked Palmer to investigate and "take such action as seems to you compatible with fair dealing."[39] The new head of GPO would not have been pleased with a subordinate who caused such an inquiry from a senator, and probably it was not coincidental that, a month later, Crandall was replaced as Superintendent of Documents by Louis Ferrell, secretary to a member of the Senate Appropriations Committee. In perfect irony, Crandall was demoted to Hasse's former position as librarian, where he remained for many years.

The removal of Crandall dismayed Richard Bowker and many librarians, who feared that political hacks would undo the progress of the past two years. As chairman of the ALA Public Documents Committee, Bowker led the protests and calls for Crandall's reinstatement, which Hasse declined to join. Now a member of the documents committee, she even objected to praise for Crandall in its report, distressing Bowker with "the touch of personal bias which has crept into your animadversions against 'a few catalogers and a journalist.'"[40] Though she kept his telegrams offering her a job for the rest of her life, Hasse showed no fondness for the man who hired her. While always warm in praising the inspiration and encouragement she received from Kelso and Billings, she never had anything to say about Francis Crandall.

It remained for Crandall's successor, Superintendent of Documents Louis Ferrell, to pay official tribute to Hasse as "one of the foremost librarians of the country," responsible for creating the library that "will remain a monument to her zeal and industry." Many years later, soon after she presented the typescript of her classification to GPO, the Superintendent of Documents wrote that the catalogers and library staff who knew Hasse regarded her as "an indefatigable worker, very competent, enthusiastic, intelligent, and of high personal integrity and character."[41] Almost a century after her arrival in Washington, GPO honored her memory by naming a meeting room Hasse Hall, with a plaque explaining that it was "Named for the First GPO Librarian Adelaide R. Hasse."

Notes

1. Adelaide Hasse, *The Compensations of Librarianship* (privately printed, 1919), 4-5; "Miss Adelaide R. Hasse," *New York Times Illustrated Magazine* (27 June 1897):15; Lowdermilk to AH, April 25 [1895], AH-NY.
2. Crandall to AH, 24, 26, 27 April 1895, AH-LC.
3. "Report of the Superintendent of Documents" in GPO 1898 Annual Report, 17-18.
4. LJ 20 (June 1895): 197.
5. "Report of the Superintendent of Documents," in GPO 1895 Annual Report, 15.
6. Hasse, *Compensations*, 5-9, is her account of her work at GPO.
7. Hasse, *Compensations*, 8; *New York Times*, 22 Dec. 1895.
8. James Cameron, "GPO's Living History: Adelaide R. Hasse," *Administrative Notes* 5 (May 1984): 26.
9. Richard Bowker, review of *Checklist of Public Documents*, LJ 21 (Feb. 1896): 74.
10. LJ 20 (Sept. 1895): 293; LJ 22 (Feb. 1897): 113.
11. Edith Clarke, *Guide to the Use of United States Government Publications* (Boston: Boston Book Co., 1918), 35.
12. Francis Crandall, preface to *Catalogue of the Public Documents of the 53d Congress and of All Departments of the Government of the U.S. for the Period from March 4,1893, to June 30,1895* (Washington: GPO, 1896), 5.
13. Francis Crandall, "Public Documents and the Proposed New Public Document Bill," LJ 21 (1896 conference proceedings): 22; Clarke, *Guide*, 35.
14. Hasse, *Compensations*, 9; Adelaide Hasse, "The Cataloging of Government Documents, United States and Foreign," LJ 28 (1903 conference proceedings): 177; Bowker to AH, Feb. 2, 1898, AH-NY.
15. Gail K. Nelson and John V. Richardson Jr., "Adelaide Hasse and the Early History of the U.S. Superintendent of Documents Classification Scheme," *Government Publications Review* 13 (Jan.-Feb. 1986): 92.
16. Clarke, *Guide*, 8-9, 154-87, 237.
17. Edith Clarke, "Corporate Entry," LJ 22 (Sept. 1897): 435.
18. Crandall, preface, 4.
19. Richard Bowker, review of *Catalogue of the Public Documents*, LJ 22 (Jan. 1897): 43.
20. Adelaide Hasse, preface to *List of Publications of the U.S. Department of Agriculture, from 1841 to June 30, 1895, inclusive* (Washington: GPO, 1896), 5; "State Library Associations," LJ 21 (June 1896): 284; Adelaide Hasse, "Classification for United States Public Documents," typescript in possession of GPO.
21. Hasse, *Compensations*, 9.
22. LJ 20 (Sept. 1895): 293.
23. Bowker to AH, 13 Feb. 1896, AH-NY.
24. Richard Bowker, review of *List of Publications of the U.S. Department of Agriculture*, LJ 21 (March 1896): 111.
25.William Leander Post, preface to *List of Publications of the Agriculture Department, 1862-1902, with Analytical Index* (Washington: GPO, 1904), 8-9; William Leander Post, "Outline for a Working Collection of Public Documents and Aids to Its Use," LJ 34 (Dec. 1909): 545; Hasse, *Compensations*, 9.

26. "Report of the Superintendent of Documents," in GPO 1895 Annual Report, 16-17, 29.

27. Bowker, review of *Checklist*, LJ 21 (Feb. 1896): 74; Bowker, review of *List*, LJ 21 (June 1896): 111.

28. Crandall, "Public Documents," LJ 21 (1896 conference proceedings): 23.

29. "Report of the Superintendent of Documents" in GPO 1896 Annual Report, 15-16.

30. Kelso to Bowker, 4 Dec. 1895, Bowker papers, NYPL; Billings to AH, 14, 25 March 1896, AH-NY.

31. AH to Dewey, 5 Dec. 1895, Dewey papers, Rare Book and Manuscript Library, Columbia University; Bowker to AH, 26 Dec. 1895, AH-NY.

32. Adelaide Hasse, "A.L.A. Library Primer . . . Appendix F Public Documents," PL 1 (Nov. 1896): 263-64; "Public Documents" in *Library Primer* (Chicago: Library Bureau, 1899), 110-12.

33. LJ 21 (June 1896): 284.

34. LJ 21 (1896 conference proceedings); Sarah Vann, *Training for Librarianship before 1923* (Chicago: ALA, 1961), 82.

35. LJ 22 (Jan. 1897): 40; John Y. Cole, *Capital Libraries and Librarians: A Brief History of the District of Columbia Library Association* (Washington: Library of Congress, 1994); Hasse, *Compensations*, 9.

36. PL 2 (June 1897): 268; Adelaide Hasse, "A Backward Glance," *D.C. Libraries* 6 (Nov. 1934): 5.

37. "Report of the Superintendent of Documents," in GPO 1897 Annual Report, 15.

38. Crandall to George C. Perkins, 7 May 1897, AH federal employment file, National Archives and Records Administration, Civilian Personnel Records, St. Louis.

39. AH to Stephen M. White, 4 Oct. 1897; White to F. W. Palmer, 12 Oct. 1897, AH federal employment file.

40. LJ 22 (Dec. 1897): 747; Bowker to AH, 2 Feb. 1898, AH-NY.

41. GPO 1898 Annual Report, 18; Alton Tisdel to Public Printer, 4 Nov. 1933, AH federal employment file.

PART II

NEW YORK

Chapter 4

Astor Library, 1897-1904

Hasse's move to New York took her to the nation's largest and most dynamic city just as the consolidation of Manhattan and the Bronx with Brooklyn, Queens, and Staten Island created a colossus second only to London. New York was the financial and intellectual capital that drew the ambitious and the idealistic and those, like Hasse, who were both.

The New York Public Library (NYPL), whose consolidation coincided with the city's, had been formed in 1895 from collections and endowments established by three rich men: the Astor Library, the Lenox Library, and the Tilden Foundation. The new institution was intended to be a great research collection that would be open to the public. Not a public library in the usual sense of being established and funded by the city, it was primarily supported by an endowment and contributions, governed by a self-perpetuating board of trustees drawn from the WASP establishment, with heavy representation of associates of J. P. Morgan, the Wall Street titan who dominated much of the nation's economy. In 1901, an assortment of independent libraries would become the circulating branches of NYPL, making two distinct parts, the research library formed from the Astor and Lenox collections, known as the Reference Department because none of its materials circulated, and the Circulation Department, consisting of the original branches and the many additional branch buildings funded by Andrew Carnegie. The operation of the Circulation Department was supported by the city, as was construction of a new central building that would house the administration, the Reference Department, and some services of the Circulation Department. The two departments often functioned as two distinct library systems, and, in an additional complication, the public libraries of Brooklyn and Queens remained separate despite the city consolidation.[1]

The relations with city government of the semiprivate public library became increasingly complex and problematic over time, but the initial response to the consolidation agreement was nationwide praise for the prospect of a public library in New York that would be the equal of the great libraries of Europe. The appointment of the distinguished Dr. John Shaw Billings, creator of the world-renowned library of the Surgeon General's office (later the National Library of Medicine), its *Index Catalog,* and the *Index Medicus*, added to the sense of a great undertaking that would match the scholarly resources of European libraries while establishing an American model of practicality and accessibility. Even when Hasse was still in Los Angeles, the local press had reported the exciting prospects of the new library in New York, and *Library Journal* had been near euphoric in enthusiasm for the new library and the choice of Billings to head it.[2]

~ ~ ~

Hasse's later account of her hiring gave the impression that Billings happened to see her work at GPO and immediately called her to New York: "I had fairly well developed the classification for the documents when, one day, Dr. Billings . . . paid us a visit. Dr. Billings examined the library, but especially the classification, which he went over quite carefully. . . . A very short time after . . . I received an offer from him to come to the NYPL, there to build what Dr. Billings wished to be a great documents collection."[3]

What really happened is more complex and ambiguous. Both Hasse and Kelso had contacted Billings soon after his appointment in December 1895. Hasse wrote in March seeking to be put in charge of cataloging public documents. Billings replied that he had as many catalogers as currently allowed but would keep her letter pending probable reorganization. He was somewhat encouraging, assuring her that he was "fully aware of the importance of a complete index to government documents, which index may include much more than an ordinary catalogue," but his priority was clearing a cataloging backlog of fifty thousand books and pamphlets.[4]

Hasse promptly wrote back, urging him to visit and see what she had done at GPO. Billings assured her he would try to do so when next in Washington, adding that the Astor and Lenox libraries had fair but far from complete collections of documents, for which he would eventually list desiderata.[5] His interest seemed to be getting her help in arranging for NYPL to receive the congressional series both as the individual documents were issued and in the bound volumes sent to depository libraries after each Congress. Showing his grasp of a basic problem of documents in libraries, he wrote that "a great library like this" required two sets of the documents, both the individual documents to be classed by subject and the compilations in the serial set (which then included many executive branch publications as well as congressional documents) to be maintained as a distinct collection. As he sketched rough plans for the new building that year, Billings included a public documents room on the main floor, along with rooms for periodicals, newspapers, children's books, and patents, the materials he expected to be most in demand by the public.

Billings' visit did not produce a job offer, but a year later Hasse wrote again, telling of her dissatisfaction with the situation at GPO and her eagerness to establish a government documents department at NYPL and develop as a bibliographer. Billings was not encouraging, warning, "Probably the only position in this country that would give full scope for the work in accordance with your tastes and wishes would be in charge of Government Documents in the Library of Congress. Probably no other library . . . would feel justified in using any considerable portion of its income in this direction, and the setting apart of government documents in a library as a specialty under the direction of one person does not fit in with the usual system of organization, class, and management."

Having dismissed her ambitious proposal, Billings offered her work as a cataloger of materials "which would include Government Documents but not be confined to them" at $75 per month, with no guarantee of promotion. He conceded that the salary was below "what you should receive," and a few days later he wrote again to explain more fully why he could not make "the arrangement you propose" or offer a better salary. There was an "unlimited" supply of people eager for cataloging work at $50, and he had fourteen applications from experienced catalogers willing to start at $60, while his chief cataloger, "a thoroughly competent and highly educated man," received $125, and the chiefs of the cataloging divisions, who included "a thoroughly educated Dane . . . and two . . . Harvard graduates who are doing excellent work," were paid $75.[6] The reference to these men's educational attainments was a reminder of Hasse's lack of higher education, but she never acknowledged that limitation, and indeed many of the men who worked in the Astor and Lenox libraries were self-educated in their specialties. Billings himself, though graduate of college and medical school, had no special training for various fields in which he had excelled; his talent was for organizing and managing large undertakings that, in the title of his most recent biography, brought order out of chaos in the burgeoning age of information.[7] Undeterred by his reservations, Hasse persisted, and Billings reconsidered. Early in May, she was hired at $100 as assistant cataloger for documents.

A few days later, Hasse received a stunning telegram from Los Angeles asking if she would accept the position of librarian at LAPL for $150.[8] The membership of the library board had changed, and Clara Fowler was leaving. Hasse could have gracefully withdrawn from her agreement with Billings; she had not yet started work, and the Los Angeles offer was a directorship at better pay, as well as a triumphal return to the city where she had been insulted two years earlier. She savored the irony enough to keep the telegram for the rest of her life but unhesitatingly wired back, "TOO LATE. HAVE JUST CLOSED WITH ASTOR LIBRARY." A great research library in New York offered better opportunities. She would be able to work intensely with documents, learn from the distinguished Dr. Billings, network with leading librarians, and enjoy the vitality of the city with Kelso. Aa Hasse approached the milestone of her thirtieth birthday, New York offered exciting personal and career prospects, while Los Angeles meant a return to an isolated provincial city and the pressures of her family, not an appealing prospect to an ambitious young woman as the promise of a new century beckoned. Her hopes were summed up by *Library Journal* in reporting a meeting of the New York Library Club, where Billings spoke about development of an index of the scientific literature, and another speaker predicted the development of a catalog of all books published in the world: "It would seem that the coming century is to be the bibliographers' millennium."[9]

Hasse was determined to be part of those bibliographic achievements, and New York would give her a base on which to build the career she envisioned.

Hasse's sense of importance was encouraged by the press attention that greeted her arrival at NYPL. The *New York Times* sent a man to report on her first day on the job in "Miss Hasse's Unique Task." He suggested that she knew more about documents than any other woman, while the *New York World,* in a report picked up by the *Los Angeles Times,* credited her with knowing more "about this unusually uninteresting literature than any other woman, and, for that matter, any man." At the end of June, the *New York Times* ran another story, a short profile in its new Sunday magazine, recounting her career as a series of achievements leading to recognition and opportunities for more achievement. Hasse was portrayed as bright, energetic, and attractive, an "outdoor girl" who also was an expert dedicated to making government publications accessible to the public, the very model of the American New Woman and the antithesis of the librarian as fusty hoarder of dusty tomes.[10]

Over the years, Hasse would court the press and be the subject of admiring features in New York's many newspapers, as well as frequent favorable mention in *Library Journal* and *Public Libraries.* She was encouraged by Kelso, who kept a hand in journalism with freelance writing and a column in the *New York Post,* then the nation's leading progressive paper. Kelso was the only woman on its staff, and her weekly column reported on the activities of the city's multitudinous women's organizations, most of them eager to reform education, public health, and factory conditions, as well as campaigning for the vote and "equal pay for equal work." Hasse also was eager to publish her own work; as Billings had told her, "You want to become known as a skilled bibliographer and for this purpose you must write." Within a year of moving to New York, she had written "The Nation's Records" and "Presidents' Messages" for leading periodicals and was preparing several bibliographies for publication.[11]

The *Times* articles said that she had come to NYPL as assistant cataloger responsible for government documents, but by the time the *San Francisco Call* reported on her appointment in July, it was "to take charge of the public document department." Writing about her work in 1906, Hasse firmly stated, "In June 1897, the New York Public Library established its department of public documents," an assertion repeated in later NYPL publications.[12] The department may have existed in Hasse's mind on the day she began work, but Billings seems to have hired her to catalog documents and related materials in international affairs and the social sciences, with no reference to such a department in his annual report for the year. The report for the year ending in June 1899 referred for the first time to the Oriental, Slavonic, and Public Documents Departments, and two years later he called for expanding the collection of periodical public documents, noting that a fifth of the volumes requested in 1899-1900 were documents. Hasse's determination to develop a department devoted to documents had not been dampened by Billings' initial doubts, and once she was established, he seems to have let her go fullsteam ahead with a department where she could specialize as a cataloger, collector, and bibliographer of government publications. The unpleasantness about Crandall's allegation did not affect her standing with Billings, who had long experience with such attacks, and after a year on the job, her salary was raised to $125. Observing Hasse's determination and drive, Billings may have been reminded of his younger self, single-handedly creating the world's largest and best medical library in the office of the Surgeon General.

~ ~ ~

Billings was a pragmatist who approved the development of special collections without reference to a theory of library organization. Some were based on subject, some on language, some on form. Hasse's enthusiasm for documents seems to have influenced his planning; when he presented his plans for the new central building to ALA, he had decided that the public documents reading room should be located on the second floor, in an area planned for special collections that would serve advanced research, away from casual visitors who might wander into the first floor. He was warned to keep the special collections close to the main reading room on the third floor, but perhaps not fully recognizing the potential problems of communication and coordination, Billings expressed confidence that what mattered was ready access to the central stack area for all reading rooms. Late that year, he announced NYPL's intention to collect pamphlets, reports, and documents "on a very broad scale."[13] He referred mainly to publications of civic, business, and professional organizations, with state and municipal documents also mentioned. Hasse would become a dedicated collector of such material, later criticized for overcollecting ephemera, but the record is clear that Billings intended to go beyond books and periodicals in collecting in the large and growing area of materials related to business, public administration, and the budding scholarly disciplines of the social sciences.

Billings had an immense task requiring innumerable decisions, and with his military experience, he seems to have regarded the catalogers he hired in the 1890s as junior officers who could be promoted to greater responsibilities as they proved themselves. Since the trustees had authorized him to hire catalogers, he was able to get promising librarians at low salaries and then give new or expanded assignments to those who measured up. J. W. Freidus, a Pratt library school graduate hired as a cataloger at the same time as Hasse, went on to build the Judaica collection as Hasse developed the documents collection. Though his relations with Billings and other librarians were sometimes tense, Freidus' ability as a specialist was encouraged as Hasse's was. Harry Lydenberg, one of the Harvard graduates Billings had mentioned to Hasse, soon was promoted from cataloger to the director's assistant. A shy, self-effacing man with a notable attention to detail, Lydenberg was well suited to assist a director with Billings' wide responsibilities and strong personality.

Billings was the kind of leader Hasse craved. His achievements as a librarian, researcher, and medical scientist, combined with an air of military authority and his general force of character, inspired respect in some of the most prominent men of the day, particularly NYPL trustees Andrew Carnegie, the self-made steel magnate who was devoting his later years to philanthropy, and John Cadwalader, the eminent Wall Street lawyer. Cadwalader and his brother-in-law, the influential neurologist S. Weir Mitchell (known for his "rest cures" for nervous breakdowns), were personally close to Billings in what Hasse saw as bonds of "rare friendship." She especially appreciated the "extremely gracious democracy" of these men; when he escorted prominent visitors around the library, Billings would introduce them to the staff "quite informally," while Cadwalader sometimes stopped to chat with her about documents. She was touched that Cadwalader remembered her interest in Alexander Vattemare, an early library promoter, and presented her with an envelope containing a lock of Vattemare's hair that he had come upon while browsing in a secondhand book stall.[14]

To the library staff, Billings was a revered father figure whose austere manner overlay both a fierce temper and a gentle sympathy. They could never match his achievements, nor could anyone else in library work, with the possible exception of Melvil Dewey. Harry Lydenberg pointed to the contrast between Billings and Ainsworth Spofford as Librarian of Congress: "The one was static, the other dynamic. Spofford was content with a passive development of the Library of Congress; Billings not only made the Surgeon-General's Library one of the great collections of medical books, but by his creation of an index to its contents he made it an active instrument for the increase of medical learning." Lydenberg's memoir of Billings reflected the staff's awe of their godlike leader:

> He had done so many things and all so well, . . . that life in his later years offered little that was new to him. He took things in quickly and made few obvious comments. Under ordinary circumstances he was taciturn, not to say reserved. Austere he was. . . . But lovable he was too, charming in his manner, kind, thoughtful, considerate. The army officer was apparent in countless ways, in what he expected as well as what he did. The medical man and the scientist appeared with equal frequency, in his attitude to life, in the way he faced the great problems of nature, in his scrupulously careful weighing of evidence, in his methods of attacking new problems, in his survey of a situation, in his balancing the facts apparent with proper weighing and valuation of all phases of the question. . . . He was a born leader and had unshaken confidence in his own judgment. . . . I never knew a man who could say "No" so frequently, who could brush aside so summarily one's pet schemes and yet send one away marveling how that refusal brought increased respect and affection. . . . One of his most helpful, most delightful characteristics was his uncanny ability to see the essence of a thing, its real meaning, its real consequences, and when considering it to brush aside extraneous qualities. He seized upon essentials and settled them once and for all. . . . Through all . . . stands out, preeminent and persistent, his love of books. . . . His book and his cigar formed his constant companions. He read as he worked, easily . . . grasping the idea quickly and retaining it in a way that made ordinary men admire and despair. . . . He had a strong temper, usually well under control. His frown could be emphatic, but when he smiled the kindly soul behind those eyes shone forth with equal emphasis. As reticent in praise as reproof, the weight of either was unmistakable when he did express it. Loyalty to friends and ideals, wideness of sympathy and of vision, tenacity of purpose, ceaseless industry, consideration of others before himself, gentleness combined with firmness, were

some of the characteristics of this remarkable man, a soldier and a scholar, a bookman and a scientist, above all, a gentleman.[15]

Hasse's published memories of Billings included both his intimidating and sympathetic sides. Once when she launched into an explanation of the difficulties of a task, Billings delivered the "reprimand of a soldier" that was also a compliment: "Miss Hasse, if it had been easy, I would not have asked you to do it." Encountering Hasse one evening in the Lenox Library, he noted the notes for a bibliographic project under her arm and smiled with the understanding of a fellow workaholic, "You are happy, aren't you?" She was indeed happy, working intensively with government documents, planning bibliographies, and learning from men like Billings and the Lenox Library's distinguished bibliographer Wilberforce Eames. Twenty years after her arrival at NYPL, she summed up what Billings had meant to her:

> By travel, by association, by personal achievement, by breadth of vision and great gentle manliness, Dr. Billings was an ideal person to direct the destinies of an educational public service institution. He stood for something. A hard worker himself, he was extremely critical of the capacity for work in others, and his tendency was towards minimum appreciation in this regard. Had you, however, proven yourself to the contrary, then he was most generous, helpful and encouraging.[16]

Hasse emphasized Billings' effectiveness as a leader who, like Kelso, encouraged his staff to develop themselves as well as the library. He had, on a larger scale, the same qualities she had found in Kelso: an innovative spirit, human sympathy, capacity for hard work, decisiveness, and wide acquaintance among the movers and shakers of the day. And he was similar to Hasse's own father, a doctor with a dedication to scientific research and service as an army surgeon in the Civil War. In an era shaped by memory of the Civil War, some of Billings' power over others must have come from awareness that here was a man who had come through unspeakable horrors as a battlefield surgeon at Gettysburg and Chancellorsville.

Hasse always insisted that her aim at NYPL was to implement Billings' plans. Certainly in the early years, when the staff was small, Billings was well acquainted with the librarians and involved in their decisions. Both Hasse and Anne Carroll Moore, NYPL's noted children's librarian, later wrote of Dr. Billings' active interest in their very different specialties. Ambitious women in their early thirties, Hasse and Moore appreciated a director who related to women as "a sincere friend or kindly mentor," not concerned with feminine beauty or charm. Notes from Billings that Hasse kept show his kindly but rather remote interest, urging her not to damage her health with overwork (advice her father also sent) and telling her, "We shall be glad to have you back with us," when she was away on a bibliographic project. From his military career, Billings had mastered the art of conveying sympathetic interest while retaining a commander's distance. To Hasse, he was her great leader in a great enterprise, "to build up what Dr. Billings wished to be a great document collection."[17]

~ ~ ~

Hasse began work in the Astor Library, an imposing Italianate brick building on Lafayette Place, a few blocks east of Washington Square and just around the corner from the equally impressive Cooper Union. When she arrived on June 1, 1897, no arrangements had been made for her to begin work on the documents, and she didn't even have a desk. The *New York Times* reporter found her improvising a table on a window seat.

The library was a bequest of John Jacob Astor, the richest American of his day. Having made a fortune as a merchant and real-estate investor, Astor left $400,000 for a library that would be open to the public for reference. His descendants gave further support, and his friend Joseph Cogswell, former Harvard librarian, developed the building, collection, and catalogs into an outstanding scholarly library. Though open to all over age fourteen, the Astor Library offered no popular circulating material, and its limited hours, due mainly to lack of either gas or electric light, effectively restricted access. The general public probably made more use of the nearby periodical reading room in the Cooper Union. By the time of the NYPL consolidation, it still had a major collection but had not been keeping up with the trends of leading libraries, from lighting to card catalogs to reference service. The Lenox Library, housed separately far uptown, had similar limitations.

Billings had to simultaneously improve the two research libraries, plan and oversee construction of the central building, and organize the circulating branches into one system, greatly expanded by the construction of the Carnegie buildings. It was the sort of challenging atmosphere Hasse had learned to deal with in her previous jobs, and she threw herself into this new phase of her career, determined to develop her reputation as an expert, publish bibliographies, and become a leader in the library profession. She was in her element in New York, approaching the new century amid the dynamism of a city that became the second largest in the world with a spectacular fireworks display as midnight rang in the New Year. Equally exciting was the prospect of the huge new library building, expected to open in a few years (but instead delayed until 1911). At the end of her first six months at NYPL, Hasse must have been thrilled by *Library Journal*'s editorial forecasting a future worthy of her ideals and her ambition:

> With the acceptance of the plans for its new building, the New York Public Library enters upon the final stage of its preparation for the great work that waits it as the centre of library interests in the second greatest city in the world. . . . The difference between the library conditions in New York today and those of five years ago, great as it is, is as nothing to the contrast that can surely be predicted between the conditions as they exist today and as they will be five years hence. Nor can it be doubted that the same wisdom and foresight that have created, within two years, the New York Public Library, will recognize the great opportunities now opening before it and guide it to a future of usefulness the limits of which it is hard to forsee. . . .

The plans as a whole deserve the careful attention of librarians, and the hearty thanks and congratulations of the library profession should be extended to the library authorities, whose careful planning and wise direction have made possible the production of a building not only beautiful in itself but promising to be the most practical and satisfactory library building that has yet been given to the world.[18]

Ironically, the same pages that predicted a glorious future at NYPL had word of GPO that validated Hasse's decision to leave. Perhaps she even felt a bit of *schadenfreude* at the report of Crandall's demotion and a letter dismissing Edith Clarke's paper on corporate entries as illogical. But now her focus was on the future, to develop her ideal government documents department as a model for large libraries. She was proudly aware that she was doing something new, that "no library had . . . specialized in public documents" as she intended.[19]

~ ~ ~

In the Astor Library, Hasse found an assortment of documents she estimated at ten thousand volumes. Their scope was much broader in time and geography than what she had worked with previously. Besides federal and state publications, there were historic documents of the American colonies and the European powers, including "the great British, French, German, Spanish, and Portuguese series of calendars and reprints of state papers," collections of treaties, and a "very fragmentary file of statutes." As she worked on the cataloging records, she also prepared checklists of holdings that gave an overview of the collection and a start on her bibliographic goals. Once she had the records in order, Hasse devoted herself to developing the collection, so that by the time the trustees reported on the library's first ten years, the documents department was reported to number 185,000, a fifth of the total collection and "one of the most important collections in the world" for research in history, political science, economics, and municipal government. At the beginning of the twentieth century, Hasse built what would remain "one of the world's great collections of government publications."[20]

Hasse had to fill many gaps in the files of historic documents while also keeping up with current documents, which meant constantly contacting governments, for "unless appeals were periodically renewed, files would regularly lapse." Once a system was in place to keep track of such renewals of state and federal publications, she tackled municipal documents, contacting all American cities of more than twenty-five thousand population and comparable European cities to request "collected documents, charters, ordinances and financial documents." The second annual report of the Documents Department reported receiving three thousand serials per month.

Both historic and current documents required alertness to myriad sources of information, for as Hasse explained, "There is no medium which regularly announces official publications." Reference to current documents might turn up in newspapers or any number of periodicals, while historic documents necessitated combing through secondhand dealers' catalogs. Billings was an "inveterate reader" of such catalogs, and Hasse felt she was working closely with him to develop the collection, sharing the delight of finding a rare document at a low price and preparing lists of lacunae for him to take on his summer trips abroad: "Always after his return from Europe there would come to the library through the autumn, through the winter, box after box of documents. Gloat is the word that most nearly expresses my feelings. . . . I shall always be grateful for the joy of those days. Documents or pearls, the emotions of the collector are the same."[21]

Gifts were also a prime source of acquisitions, notably a collection of congressional documents related to foreign affairs presented by John Cadwalader, who had learned about the value of documents and their inadequate indexing in his youth while serving in the State Department. Hasse was soon indexing the volumes, which would lead eventually to one of her finest bibliographic achievements and to other projects of interest to Cadwalader. Working on an index to all the information within the reports encouraged her steadily increasing awareness of the need to go beyond collecting and recording documents to provide access to their content.

~ ~ ~

The rapidly growing collection provided Hasse with all the challenges involved in cataloging documents. She summed up their differences from the trade books librarians usually cataloged: "official literature, a literature as a rule authorless, so far as personal names are concerned, a literature having a whimsical relationship in its parts and volumes and series, a literature alienated, so far as convenience of treatment according to accepted forms is concerned, entirely from the ordinary type of market literature."[22] There were no established rules for dealing with government publications as such, so Hasse took an exploratory approach, confident that she would find solutions as she worked with the documents. In the beginning, the library's cataloging was not particularly systematized, and she seems to have been able to develop documents cataloging as she wished, without objections from catalogers protecting their policies and rules. There was no single public catalog of the Astor Library (records were in a card catalog and two book catalogs), no shelflist, and no subject cataloging until Billings decreed that it must be done, which meant that cataloging staff often worked on subject headings at home at night, with results that sometimes were inconsistent or erroneous.

Hasse's recollection was that the "obvious" first step was formation of a "departmental" documents catalog by separating existing documents cards from the catalog and cutting up a set of the two book catalogs to create cards from their documents records. These author-only cards then were arranged in a single alphabet of inverted entries like those at GPO, replacing "the now generally discarded one of graduated entries under departments," apparently meaning "Public Lands Bureau" instead of "Dept. of Interior. Bureau of Public Lands." A few years later, such inversion became an intensely debated topic, but Hasse had the practice of GPO as precedent supporting her decision. She considered the inverted names "simple, sane and natural" in most cases, though "awkward and unsatisfactory for temporary or special bodies in most cases," but with the staff struggling to keep up with accessions, she determined to invert consistently in the interests of workflow and producing "some sort of orderly record."[23]

Soon Hasse was designing special cards for serial records, first for "those dependent on the fiscal year and those dependent on the legislative period," then a system of separate cards for volumes having "bibliographical value." Next came a system of showing serial volumes that also appeared in sets of collected documents, first in the "official catalog" of the documents department, and then a simplified version for the library's public catalog. By the end of Hasse's first year, there were thirty thousand cards in her documents catalog, which would grow to over four hundred thousand cards in its first decade.[24]

Then there was the issue of subject cards: "Contrary to other departmental catalogs in the library, the official catalog of documents contains both subject and author entries," but not for all documents or subjects, only "where public economics was concerned . . . to show primarily the serials which governments issued illustrating their own activity, rather than to show what the library contained on a given subject." Subject entries for the documents catalog "corresponded at first to those of the public catalog," but Hasse soon realized that something more was needed: "My material demanded a record which should disclose . . . the degree of uniformity and of minuteness with which various governments publish their revenue or expenditure accounts, their estimates or appropriations, their assessments, valuations and to what point of development the various systems of maintenance or regulation may have arrived in the several states. I read, I heard learned discussions, I reflected and I experimented with my material."[25] She was developing a system of analyzing government reports in terms of public administration and economic history at a level that library subject headings couldn't match, something that would be of great value to her as a bibliographer. Much to Hasse's later regret, however, there never was time to include full subject cataloging in the departmental catalog.

Another unusual feature of Hasse's catalog was the inclusion of references to documents found in bibliographies and secondhand catalogs but not owned by the library, showing her intention to make it a bibliography of documents as well as a record of holdings. This involved creating and filing more records in order to have information about weak areas of the collection and indications of desiderata. Working intensively with the author, title, and subject problems of a wide range of documents, she became convinced that existing cataloging rules could not be applied routinely to government publications and might even be detrimental to making their content accessible, so she developed modifications that seemed practical and "reconcilable with current cataloging customs." As she found solutions, she began speaking and writing about her ideas.

In 1901, she persuaded the Library Bureau to publish her cataloging handbook. Partly as a convenience to users and partly because the Library Bureau was doubtful about sales, it was planned to be a series of four pamphlets, but only two were published: *Part 1—The Government at Large; the Constitution, Statutes, and Treaties* and *Part 2—The Legislative Body.* The sections on the executive and judicial branches never appeared. Why it was not completed is unclear, but several factors seem to have been involved. Correspondence shows that the Library Bureau told Hasse that sales were unsatisfactory, then reversed itself and wanted to complete the set. Hasse, busy with other projects, probably had tired of dealing with her unenthusiastic publisher and concluded that there was less need for a handbook when GPO began distributing printed cards for documents in 1904. That lasted only two years, but Library of Congress cards also were available to libraries. At the same time, the ALA Cataloging Committee had recognized the need for rules for government corporate entries. Hasse was not a member of the committee, but she consulted with the chairman, J. C. M. Hanson of the Library of Congress, and influenced the rules it developed.[26]

In the handbook, Hasse addressed some of the problems of government author entries with an innovation that was practical and uniform but challenged librarians to think in different terms. This was her standardized form of main entries for treaties, laws, and constitutions (or ordinances and charters, in the case of city governments):

United States. Constitution.
Japan. Treaties.
New York. Laws, statutes.

Her creation of these main entries for the innumerable individual copies and collected sets of laws and treaties brought them together under a standard entry. As Hasse explained, the only "author" of such publications was the government at large; with no agency author, something was needed to bring together these types of publications and provide a uniform entry where they could be found. She saw her method as "expedient, simple and adapted to all countries." It was baffling to some librarians, who wrote to argue that such "author" entries seemed to be subjects. In her preface, Hasse was careful to explain that she had "no intention to establish precedents or to lay down rules," that she hoped only to offer her experience with documents. She had struggled to apply conventional cataloging rules and concluded that they were "often a detriment" to access in libraries. Since much of the problem of cataloging documents came down to the corporate author entry, she had developed her alternative approach. "In cases . . . where divergence is suggested from accepted methods, it is not done in a spirit of reform or overrule," she assured librarians, "but only with the desire that, having proved by actual experience the satisfactory results of the use of a not generally accepted form, its exploitation may help . . . to minimize some of the difficulties of the cataloger."[27]

Hasse's unconventional approach did not worry *Library Journal*'s reviewer, who proclaimed it the "first step towards a consummation devoutly to be wished—the formulation of a practical uniform method" for cataloging documents, concluding that the "modifications and exceptions required to make the cataloging of public documents at once practical and systematic are cogently set forth, both in the text and in the series of excellent facsimile cards."[28] "No one could be better fitted than Miss Hasse, by her thorough and varied experience, to undertake this task . . . [which] has added a much needed tool to the librarian's working equipment," said LJ, in an instance of its recurring praise for Hasse's expertise. The unsigned review also commended her attention to the need to make clear the historical and political relationships between documents and their issuing governmental bodies, something Hasse had stressed in her first sentence on the nature of official authors: "The study of government documents, or government publications, or official literature, is the study of the mechanism of modern government as expressed in its publications."[29] This would be her consistent theme, not advocating that libraries should adhere to any particular model, method, or rule, but rather that the librarians who worked with public documents must understand the history, nature, and functions of the issuing governments and how these related to their publications.

In 1903, Hasse was the lead speaker at the ALA Catalog Section. Although apparently expected to clarify the issue of inversion of author entries for government agencies, she brushed that aside as a matter for each library to decide and spoke mainly of general principles that offered little guidance for the debate over inverted entries that followed.[30] A committee of the Association of Departmental Librarians in Washington had been studying uniformity of entry of U.S. documents on printed catalog cards. The Library of Congress was printing cards for libraries, and GPO was about to start distribution of its cards in depository shipments, but they disagreed on the inversion of agency entries. Unable to reach consensus, the committee referred the issue to the Catalog Section, where it received an exhaustive discussion that illustrated the inherent difficulties of cataloging documents. The committee's report identified five reasons against inversion and five reasons in favor. Then J. C. M. Hanson of LC spoke at length against inversion and in favor of standardized acceptance of the names of agencies as they appeared, with the proviso that libraries could mark the keyword in such entries to file as if inverted. GPO expressed its preference for the inverted form, arguing that most depository libraries preferred it and the public instinctively requested documents "by the significant word." That view was supported by librarians who did reference work, several of whom expressed their unhappiness with entries that seemed to serve the convenience of catalogers more than the interest of the public. Roland Falkner of the LC Documents Division was one of those speaking in favor of inverted entries as "on the whole the most convenient" way to enter federal and state documents, providing a kind of keyword access to agencies whose correct names were rarely known to the public, while another LC librarian, Charles Martel of Cataloging, pointed to various problems lurking in inverted agency names. Martel informally suggested an alternative similar to Hasse's standard main entries, a system of establishing distinctive terms, as in LC's policy for the varying names of commercial firms, "best known surname, followed by the definition firm, name of business and place, e.g. Scribner, firm, publishers, N.Y." His idea deserved consideration, but since it wasn't part of an official report or offered as a motion, it seemed to get lost in the discussion of two problematic alternatives. Finally Hasse proposed a compromise solution, adoption of inverted entries for English-language documents (avoiding the complications of inverting in foreign languages). She was vigorously supported by Edith Clarke, and the two women offered a motion that was approved by those at the meeting. LC ultimately decided it would not invert in its printed cards, however, while GPO discontinued its cards after a few years but continued to use the inverted form in its publications.

~ ~ ~

Hasse's expertise was recognized with appointment to the ALA Committee on Public Documents in 1897. With its third member not very involved, the committee was essentially Hasse and Richard Bowker, a situation that might have intimidated a less confident young woman. Bowker was twenty years her senior and had long been a leader of ALA and the documents committee, doing much of ALA's lobbying in Washington while pursuing his remarkable career as a leader in business, publishing, civic reform, and the library and bibliography movements. Though not a librarian, Bowker ranked with men like Billings and Dewey for the effort he put into libraries as editor and publisher of *Library Journal* and the *American Catalogue*, ALA leader, and trustee of the Brooklyn Public Library. He had been involved with the problems of documents bibliography and distribution far longer than Hasse, but, not inclined to defer to his authority, she firmly asserted her views.

Hasse's inclination to independent thinking had been encouraged by her 1896-97 service on the special committee on a proposed government clearinghouse to distribute the large pamphlet literature of the time to libraries. The idea came to ALA from the editor of a German American newspaper in St. Louis. Two of the three committee members reported favorably on the proposal, suggesting that the Library of Congress might perform the function. Hasse dissented in a minority report, arguing that the government had no duty "to assist the librarian to the knowledge of ephemeral private publications, much less to supply . . . such publications gratuitously." She dismissed the idea as unrealistic with "the Library of Congress already overburdened, the copyright system inadequately provided for, the document problem yet in chaos—all matters of greater moment to librarians than the free distribution of private pamphlets." When someone questioned whether LC really was overburdened, given that its staff would be increased in the new building, Billings came to Hasse's defense, pointing out that LC would be occupied for years in clearing backlogs and dismissing the majority report as "entirely impractical." Minority reports, especially from a young woman, were unusual in ALA, and Billings' support must have contributed to Hasse's sense of a special bond with him.[31]

In their two-person Public Documents Committee, Hasse and Bowker soon were involved in a vigorous but good-humored debate about their conference report and resolutions. Hasse emphatically did not share his wish for Crandall's restoration as Superintendent of Documents, to the point that Bowker reproved her for the tone of her comments. Her objection to any commendation of Crandall was so insistent that Bowker removed it from his draft report, leaving only reference to previous ALA praise that was, he reminded her, "a matter of record, not of opinion."[32]

Hasse also wanted the committee to address the whole depository library program by making specific recommendations for the reorganization of the system, instead of just reacting to Senator Henry Cabot Lodge's bill to transfer the Documents Office to the Library of Congress building while leaving it administratively within the Government Printing Office. Bowker, long a supporter of civil service reforms, was always eager to reduce political appointments related to libraries and favored an amendment to make the office administratively part of LC; while he was at it, he drafted the resolution to include another pet idea, that LC be officially designated the national library. Hasse had other points she wanted to put on the ALA agenda, including reform of the designation of depositories by members of Congress and the need for selective distribution to small depository libraries, which were swamped by quantities of documents not needed in their communities. Bowker had negotiated with Congress for years to achieve the 1895 reforms and saw no point in pursuing a hopeless cause; Congress would not give up the depository designation privilege, he told her, even if it did mean bad choices. Hasse also pressed for ALA to recognize the problems with state documents and direct the committee to survey the state libraries about "existing files" of state publications. Bowker shared her interest, but he was doubtful of making much impression on the state librarians, many of whom "are the most impossible people possible."[33]

Less than a month before the conference, Bowker sent Hasse a draft of the report. She promptly sent back her alternative draft on depository reorganization. Bowker didn't think he could agree but graciously assured her that even if they made separate reports, it would not "be in any sense an act unfriendly to anybody, or that the chairman or anybody else would have a right to complain, outwardly or inwardly." Committees were "for the sake of discussion and not merely for the registry of some one person's opinion," he wrote, and then followed through by revising the report to accommodate her views, while recognizing that she might "desire to make a minority report." On June 10, only a few days before the conference, he sent a draft modified "so that I think it cannot but have your approval." Besides toning down the praise of Crandall and including a report and resolution on state documents, it acknowledged that a member of the committee wanted an ALA committee to be assigned "the task of suggesting modifications of the present bill or framing a substitute," but the majority recommended only supporting the Lodge bill. Though there was no discussion of what Hasse wanted, she at least had influenced the report. Gracefully accepting Bowker's draft, she assured him, "Of course I do not propose to be a bigot about this affair, and in fact I am much subdued by your gentle caution against becoming opinionated."[34]

When Bowker presented the report and resolutions, there was concern among some ALA leaders that the sensitivity of the subject required careful consideration, so the vote was postponed. At a later session, the resolutions endorsing the Lodge bill and calling for inquiry into state documents were readily approved, but Bowker's pet idea to designate LC the national library and incorporate the Documents Office into it was considered too sensitive for action and instead was referred to the ALA Council. There may have been some satisfaction for Hasse in seeing Bowker's preferences challenged, but ALA's cautious reaction also showed that he was right about the difficulty of raising issues related to the depository program. Hasse took no recorded part in the discussion; her only public mention was in the safe area of bibliographic work, when the Foreign Documents Committee, of which she was also a member, reported that she was doing the editorial work for a bibliography of French serial documents to be published by the New York State Library. She was reappointed to both documents committees.[35]

The 1898 conference drew record attendance to a resort on Lake Chatauqua, where five hundred librarians escaped the summer heat for refreshing lake cruises, bicycling, golf, lawn teas, July 4 fireworks, and dancing past midnight. ALA members, "whose motto is 'We never sleep' spun around the floor" until the musicians were exhausted, Caroline Hewins reported.[36] The sociable atmosphere gave Hasse more opportunities for networking, especially with Kelso also in attendance. Since Kelso's new career in marketing required her presence at ALA, both women were able to attend the conferences at Philadelphia and Chatauqua, where Kelso was as irrepressible as ever in joining discussions and again disputing the opinionated Dewey. Amid the whirl of meetings, parties, and sightseeing, Hasse and Kelso could congratulate themselves on how successfully they had reinvented their careers after the fiasco in Los Angeles, with both now established in the nation's greatest city and able to enjoy their trip to ALA without harassment by press or politicians.

The following year, the Public Documents Committee's report consisted largely of the results of Hasse's resolution on a survey of state documents holdings. She was not present at the conference or at the next two, which were not held near New York, and there is little record of her active involvement in the committee, other than a letter to Bowker about another bill proposing to tinker with the publication of documents. She complained that "such constant alteration of minor matter is as confusing in its result as the original condition was"; what was really needed was "a simple and effective solution, viz. an editorial board," to oversee government publishing.[37]

With no major developments at the federal level, Hasse shifted her focus to state documents, where there was greater need and opportunity for improvement, especially with the formation of the National Association of State Libraries (NASL) as a possible coordinating group. In 1900, Hasse addressed the NASL meeting on how government documents might be made more useful to the public, a forceful articulation of the needed improvements in federal and state documents, which she described as "a primeval forest, where the vegetation is rank, and through which scarcely a trail has been cut."[38] The key to improvment, she argued, was not simply catalogers trained in library schools but rather "people who understand the relation of this literature to the government." She was preceded on the program by Herbert Putnam, the new Librarian of Congress, who spoke of his vision of a national library as an information bureau for the entire country. Bowker, who had been instrumental in Putnam's appointment, was delighted at his interest in working with the state librarians to improve the bibliographic control of state publications, but Putnam's attitude towards documents was about to cause a problem for Hasse.

Bowker, whose heavy workload was complicated by deteriorating eyesight that would soon leave him almost blind, withdrew from the Public Documents Committee in 1901. The appointment of a new chair must have been distressing to Hasse; despite her reputation as an expert, her service on the committee, and her ten years of ALA activity, the position went to a newcomer without experience as a librarian. Roland Falkner had been appointed head of the new public documents division at the Library of Congress in 1900, because Herbert Putnam wanted a man with advanced education in statistics and economics, effectively rejecting Hasse's career model for women without such credentials. Falkner was a professor of statistics at the University of Pennsylvania who had no library experience with documents nor any background on the issues in ALA. Soon he was writing to Hasse for help with reference questions, acknowledging, "Your extensive experience in handling public documents gives you a grasp of the subject which I feel that I lack entirely." When Falkner asked the committee members for suggestions for his report, he was surprised by the range of topics Hasse sent; it hadn't occurred to him that state documents were within the committee's scope. Besides, Falkner wrote, as a "wholly untrained librarian," he would be out of his element and probably quite bored at ALA, but he looked forward to "instructive as well as agreeable shop talk" with her.[39] Educating Falkner probably was not so agreeable to Hasse, but she was not inclined to give up on ALA because of a slight. Instead, she increased her visibility, attending conferences, serving on committees, and speaking in programs about documents. When Falkner departed in 1904, Hasse finally was appointed chair of the Public Documents Committee.

~ ~ ~

Meanwhile, Hasse had become involved in controversy on another committee. At the urging of John Cotton Dana, she had returned to the Committee on Library Schools, where she and Dana joined in what would be their continuing goal, trying to stir up substantive discussion in ALA. Since Hasse's service in 1896, when the committee had shown interest in evaluation, it had fallen back to its pattern of simply identifying and commending the schools, but in 1900 Hasse and Dana issued a mildly critical report with recommendations that ALA take on responsibility for evaluating education for librarianship and accrediting programs "with an assurance born of full knowledge," to be acquired by inspecting the schools.[40]

Though Hasse had warned Dana that the committee was "a delicate business," the two of them in combination couldn't resist submitting a somewhat rambling report of their impressions of the four existing schools at Albany, Drexel, Illinois, and Pratt (summer schools and library training classes were not considered) that even sixty years later distressed the writer of a dissertation with its "petulant and captious tone."[41] This seems an excessive reaction to some teasing remarks aimed at puncturing pomposity. The report did try to compare the library schools in a single table of data, but the authors admitted their analysis was "very inadequate" because firsthand inspection had been "almost nil." They nevertheless went ahead with criticism of the education and experience of the faculties, the overemphasis on cataloging and classification in the curricula, and the lack of the specialized training needed for positions in larger libraries.

Dana and Hasse, both having organized training classes in public libraries, expressed their preference for such apprenticeship programs as preparation for most library work, possibly excepting the administrative positions in larger libraries. The weakness that most disturbed them was not so much in the schools as in the many libraries that did nothing to develop staff. "Every library should be a library school," they urged. "Every assistant capable of growth should be encouraged to grow, in knowledge, breadth and zeal." Yet, in a seeming contradiction, they wanted "such scholastic and professional training as will eventually lead to the universal recognition of librarianship as a learned profession." They also "granted that library schools did impart a breadth of vision and general zeal" not often found in apprenticeship trainees, but ALA should not overestimate the schools' quality nor evade the need to improve them.

Their tart comments stirred resentment, particularly when they pointed out the obvious, that a library school, "with its graduates as its friends, with the prestige of its name," had an advantage in placing its students, even though most librarians would rather hire a person who had worked in a similar library for two years than a library school graduate with no experience. There were denials that librarians favored graduates of their alma maters, but Hasse and Dana probably were expressing their awareness of the female networks among library school alumnae; the graduates would have been unusual for their time, when sisterhood and school spirit were powerful ideals, had they not developed abiding bonds of loyalty to the women leaders of their schools and friendship with their fellow students, almost all women. Adding more offense to the clubby world of the schools, Dana and Hasse dismissed the library school graduate as offering "a little more enthusiasm, a little wider acquaintance with the literature of her profession and a certain glibness in the use of the patter of her calling which she sometimes mistakes for breadth, and others not initiated sometimes take for depth."

However annoying the report was to some, it won the support of Dewey and other ALA leaders, most of whom had not attended library school themselves. In the ten years since classes began at Pratt, there had been growing concern about the various new programs, and now Dana and Hasse had prodded ALA to take some responsibility for professional education. The association responded promptly with a by-law that watered down their proposal but did establish a new committee authorized to visit and report on the schools and make such recommendations as it saw fit. Dana was a member, but Hasse avoided what now was regarded as a hot potato, and it would be many years before she again entered the perennial debates about the education of librarians.

~ ~ ~

Her reservations about library schools didn't inhibit Hasse's willingness to address their students, and her location made it convenient to lecture at the schools
at the state library in Albany and nearby Pratt Institute. In 1902 she had a more
extensive teaching job that was ideal for career development, providing publicity
and networking, along with a triumphant return to her native state. In August,
she traveled to Wisconsin to give a three-week course on documents in the summer school of the Wisconsin Free Library Commission. It was publicized in the
library press, of course, and Hasse also managed to get attention in the *New
York Times*, including her usual quote about the value of current and historical
documents.[42] Wisconsin was a leader in the library world, due largely to the indefatigable efforts of two women, Cornelia Marvin, director of the summer
school, and Lutie Stearns, who lectured in the school and also organized a
meeting for midwestern librarians at the end of the session. Among the lecturers
was their friend Mary Eileen Ahern, now editor of *Public Libraries,* who gave
the summer school publicity and published the paper Hasse gave during the Library Week meeting; in an indication of Hasse's reputation, *Library Journal*
also ran it.[43] That summer, the faculty included a newcomer who shared Hasse's
interests, a lecturer on state documents named Charles McCarthy, who had recently been hired for the new legislative reference service that Cornelia Marvin
had guided into existence. McCarthy was an outsider, an unpolished Irish
Catholic warned away from an academic career despite his brilliant dissertation
at the state university. Like Hasse, he would find in government information an
opportunity to invent a new career, developing the Legislative Reference Library
into an activist information service that would be an essential part of the reforms
in which Wisconsin led the Progressive Era.[44]

Hasse's class involved a heavy workload, with forty-nine students from
thirteen states in classes that met daily from nine to five. Although limited to
those with library school training or equivalent experience, the students came
from so many different kinds of libraries that the class had to be "more general"
than Hasse had intended. After three weeks of dealing with her large and diverse
class, Hasse was probably relieved to escape further questions by departing for
New York immediately after her address to the first session of Library Week,
"much to the regret of everyone, as her advice on the vexing question of public
documents is always helpful."

In her paper and her prospectus for the course, Hasse reiterated her themes of
the period: the need for library staff with thorough knowledge of documents and
the governments that issue them; the value of local collections of state and city
documents; and the desirability of more efficient systems of distribution, especially a method of selectivity for federal depositories. She was particularly concerned that so many small depositories were swamped with federal depository
documents that were of little use to their communities and were not well cared
for, while they overlooked the importance of collecting local documents, which
were likely to be needed by their communities and unlikely to be preserved elsewhere for the historical record.

~ ~ ~

Hasse had told Billings of her ambition to become a distinguished bibliographer; now she pursued this goal with her usual energy and focus. Her first task was to finish two bibliographies of U.S. documents published in 1899, one on the interoceanic canal and the other on reports of explorations, an interest she shared with her father.[45] Hasse had been working on the latter at least since 1895, when it was an appendix to the *Checklist of Public Documents*, and had consulted outside experts, one of whom sent six pages of comment.[46] The bibliography was subjected to a highly critical review in *Library Journal*, however, by none other than her former boss, Francis Crandall, who pointed to examples of "numerous discrepancies . . . more confusion in the treatment of series, editions, imprint data, etc., than is consistent with careful bibliographical work . . . somewhat numerous omissions which will be noted by those familiar with the material under treatment." His comments had the tone of a fatherly reproof:

> Probably many readers will be surprised to see 90 pages filled with the mere titles of these reports, but not even Miss Hasse's industry and intimate acquaintance with the tangled maze of the public documents have sufficed to make a complete collection of such titles. While recognizing fully the great amount of intelligent labor bestowed upon this "contribution towards a bibliography," a service will perhaps be done to the author and to her public by pointing out . . . a few of the more important omissions and a few respects in which the work has not been so carefully done as its value seems to demand. . . . Miss Hasse has not done herself justice in her present work. It is to be hoped . . . she may build upon it with more care, tracing all the varied forms in which each publication has appeared, giving increased care to revision and proof-reading, and thus producing a comprehensive and accurate bibliography. Certainly no one is more competent thus to extract the kernel from the dry document husk, and as a pioneer in a most perplexing and difficult bibliographic field her work demands appreciation, even though its details in the present instance must call forth criticism.[47]

To have one of her first publications so criticized was a useful lesson for Hasse, but it must have greatly increased the tension under which she worked on the endless details of what Crandall had conceded was a perplexing and difficult field, while also keeping up with her job in a library with a demanding director and a workweek of six nine-hour days. And her history with Crandall and the aggression behind his pious tone was another lesson in how men might attack an ambitious and independent woman.

Meanwhile, Hasse was engrossed in "transcribing, compiling, revising and editing" the list of French government serials that would finally be published in the New York State Library's bibliography series. Though begun by Clement Andrews, it required Hasse's "long continued assistance" to prepare its 164 pages for publication. The introduction by the chair of the ALA Foreign Documents Committee reflected what must have been Hasse's anxiety in asking "for indulgence from a portion, at least, of its critics." The compilers acknowledged that "there are discrepancies . . . [and] a defect particularly hard to eliminate from a cooperative list . . . want of complete uniformity in the entries." It was hoped "that the connection between related entries has been made clear by means of notes and references." Though Hasse began work in 1898, the bibliography was not published until 1902.[48]

At the same time, Hasse began issuing bibliographies with a convenient publisher, NYPL's own monthly *Bulletin,* which Billings established in 1897 to issue bibliographies and other scholarship derived from the library's collections. Hasse could combine aspects of her work, publishing the checklists she prepared in analyzing the library's holdings of documents. By 1902, *Library Journal* was singing her praises:

> For the past three years the New York Public Library has been printing in its monthly *Bulletin* lists of parts of its collection of public documents. . . . This is a notable contribution to the bibliography of public documents, especially in its illustration of practical methods of arrangement and form of entry for material that is full of perplexities and variations, . . . the work of Miss Adelaide R. Hasse, chief of the Document Department. . . . Careful annotations give record of the establishment or historical development of each office or bureau and register changes or special characteristics of the various issues. . . . The methods of entry adopted for the list will repay study on the part of catalogers. The variations of form found in document material are indeed legion . . . but Miss Hasse has managed to give varying data in the most compact way. . . . The methods worked out are clear and effective, and the list sets an excellent model for like work elsewhere.[49]

The following year, LJ added more plaudits for "the valuable work [NYPL] has been doing for public document bibliography." Hasse's bibliography of publications of the General Assembly of New York in the colonial period was "a model of careful and authoritative work." Her annotations were again praised, and she was credited with including far more documents than earlier bibliographies, including twenty-four that had not previously been recorded.[50] Hasse's early bibliographies in the *Bulletin* were primarily historical and based on NYPL's holdings:

The Northeastern Boundary (1900)
New York State Boundaries (1900)
Check List of Foreign Government Documents on Finance (1901)
Check List of American Federal Documents Relating to Finance (1902)
Check List of . . . State Documents . . . Relating to Finance (1902)
Check List of . . . Municipal . . . Documents Relating to Finance (1902)
Some Materials for a Bibliography of the Official Publications of the
    General Assembly of the Colony of New York, 1693-1775 (1903)
List . . . Relating to Political Rights,Constitutions, and Constitutional
    Law (1904)

Hasse was not shy about calling attention to her bibliographic work. She sent copies to the chairman of the Public Archives Commission of the American Historical Association, offering to help the commission's work. He warned that he could not pay her, but Hasse eventually volunteered to prepare a bibliography of colonial documents for the commission anyway. She also sent copies to scholars like John Bassett Moore at Columbia and bibliographers like Thorvald Solberg, head of the Copyright Office at the Library of Congress, who complimented her on "solid careful intelligent work" that would advance her reputation. When Hasse received such letters, she marked the words of praise for Billings' attention, which usually brought a quick note of his approval.[51]

As Hasse worked intensively with historical bibliography, she was able to identify previously unlisted New York colonial documents, "putting on record some 900 where before less than 100 had been known." Her pursuit took her to other American libraries with historical holdings, and she became obsessed with finding an early document that was believed to have been printed but had been lost in the succeeding three centuries. After much research, she "finally had a suppositional structure, as complete as that back of any mystery best seller." Accordingly, she set sail in October 1902 for a "holiday" that only a bibliographer could appreciate, a visit to London spent mostly at the Public Record Office, on the trail of the lost Bayard's (the author) or Bradford's (the printer) journal, *A Narrative of an Attempt Made by the French of Canada Upon the Mohaque's Country.* Printed in 1693, it was considered the first book published in New York; it might also be described as the first government document, since it was printed at the direction of the colony's governor as a report of his defense against a French invasion. A quarter century later, Hasse still vividly remembered the thrill of the hunt:

> My fortnight in London was drawing to a close. I had not found the treasure and the world was drab. Return passage had been booked and there were two more days of tenseness. . . . Thursday through busy Holborn, down Chancery Lane to the Record Office. Too early. At last. Scurrying down dark and chilly corridors to a small, dim, chilly room. Then another wait for the containing volume to be brought from some internal, infernal region. Oh, why this excruciating indifference! . . . Perfunctorily an apparently damaged quarto of bound up broadsides and pamphlets was laid before me with the stern injunction that I could use it this day only as the Editor was at work on it and could dispense with it no longer. Leaf by leaf, each one scanned with magnified scrutiny. The room was chilly. I was burning. Had anyone spoken to me, I would have shouted. . . . And then quite simply there was my quarry, a 15-page quarto. The moment of realized discovery was truly quite overwhelming. I was dazed. Then a feverish taking of notes, counting lines and folios, measuring margins, description of each page, the corroborative original signature and all the other bibliographical items for the proper recording. . . . That day I had to be turned out of the premises. . . . Back the next day with a personal plea to the Editor for a postponement of the return of the volume . . . and for one more day I could leaf and examine, describe and count. My notes must be submitted to Mr. Eames, the dean of Americana bibliography, and his test would be thorough.

She need not have worried. When she presented her notes, "I saw in Mr. Eames' face the frank pleasure which a true craftsman takes in the work of a colleague, and heard his simple remark: 'Well, you've got it.'"[52]

Hasse also located the only copy of the first published proceedings of an American legislature, the 1695 *Journal of the House of Representatives for His Majestie's Province of New York in America.* The year after her discovery, Dodd Mead published facsimile editions of both with introductions by Hasse. Her account of Bradford's journal was an amusing tale of early political image-making in which Governor Fletcher got the printer William Bradford out of jail in Philadelphia, where he had run afoul of the Quakers, so as to have a printer for his account of his defense of the colony against the invasion from Canada. His successor claimed that Fletcher had concocted the story, but Hasse reported that French sources confirmed the incident.

The year 1903 was triumphant for Hasse, with publication of the two lost books and her extensive bibliography of the colonial New York General Assembly. Having demonstrated mastery of historical bibliography, she now wanted to do something big in the neglected area of state documents, and soon she was preparing a proposal for an index to the documents of the states. She also was involved in the guide to colonial records and the index of the foreign relations documents donated by John Cadwalader, which she hoped to publish. Increasingly, she was dissatisfied with the traditional bibliography that focused on physical aspects, "the bibliography of the missing frontispiece, the usually missing 27th plate, the millimeter marginal variations, the one of five known perfect extant copies." The real need was for access to the content, not description of the physical "container." In reviewing an index to the congressional documents series, Hasse complained that it was "constructed from the headings only of the documents, and no attempt has been made to analyze their contents." A proper index would be "infinitely more complex," she argued, citing the example of a document with one entry, "Mexico, diplomatic affairs," while in the index to foreign affairs documents in preparation at NYPL "between 500 and 600 cards have been made for this document."[53]

She expanded on this theme in a paper at the 1904 ALA conference, "On a Bibliography of Public Documents." Since the meeting was in St. Louis, site of the world's fair, all programs were asked to take an international perspective. ALA president Herbert Putnam had invited Hasse to speak at the session on international bibliographic projects. She sent him an outline of a proposal for an international documents bibliography and suggested that representatives of other nations be invited to start discussion of such a project. Putnam was doubtful that many would attend but urged her to make a proposal "as explicit, as positive, and as vigorous as you can make it." When he received her paper a month before the meeting, Putnam asked her to be more specific about a plan, but Hasse declined "to indulge in the, as yet, premature consideration of ways and means." She chose instead to discuss the broader implications of a bibliography of documents, which to Hasse meant an index to their contents, not merely a list of titles with perhaps some subject entries derived from titles. She wanted an index that would locate the statistics, laws, treaties, and other information "stored away in public documents." Hasse reviewed the limitations of existing catalogs and indexes, described the international conventions that established central bureaus of information, and ended with a brief suggestion for an "international index . . . published by a central bureau."[54]

Since the other papers on the program all dealt with existing projects or organizations, Putnam's concern with Hasse's lack of specificity was not misplaced, but it would have been awkward for her to propose a definite plan for an international organization. At a time when few governments provided adequate bibliographies of their own publications, Hasse was describing an ideal, trying to point the library world towards her vision of an index to the contents of all government publications. The ideal of international cooperation and central information bureaus would be Hasse's lifelong dream, a reflection of the hopes for bibliography at the beginning of the twentieth century. The year after her ALA paper, Helen Haines of *Library Journal* passed along a new pamphlet by Paul Otlet, leader of the European bibliography movement, in which he envisioned an international system of economic information centers with a central office, all coordinated by an international office of "universal" information and documentation. But, as LJ had warned two years earlier, with the "growing desire for organized bibliographical work," there was a tendency to overlook practical considerations in the theories of "a great organization or chain of organizations, with international and local branches all working together to record and classify the literature of the world."[55]

With such a system of international bibliography only a hope and U.S. federal documents being cataloged in Washington, the full force of Hasse's bibliographic ambition turned to state documents, where she saw the greatest needs and opportunities for creativity. She helped Bowker with the second part of his *State Publications: A Provisional List* and then wrote a highly technical review that showed how much she was thinking about the problems of state documents. At the 1903 conference of the National Association of State Libraries, she "read what was perhaps the most pertinent and timely paper of the session, 'The Function of the NASL,' in which she suggested a very important and useful line of work," that the state libraries produce a documents bibliography. Appointed chair of a committee to develop the idea, Hasse reported back the following year with a concept of a central depository for one copy of all documents of all the states as the basis for bibliographic work. No specifics were offered for where it would be located and how it would be funded. Her report also urged a system of "uniform publications of records of state official literature," by which she envisioned a standard bibliographic structure and terminology based on government functions. Herbert Putnam, who entered after Hasse spoke and perhaps did not realize that she again had sketched broad concepts, urged support for the development of documents bibliography as a "special responsibility" of the state libraries. The committee was enlarged and continued with Hasse as chair.[56]

Back in New York, Hasse learned that her interest in state documents was known outside the library world. She received a letter from Henry Gardner, professor of economics at Brown and member of the Carnegie Institution's Economics and Sociology Department, asking if she had "any thought of preparing" an index of state documents. The department intended to produce a major scholarly economic history of the United States, and Gardner, as chair of its committee on bibliography, was acutely aware of what a morass state documents were for the researcher. Hasse immediately replied that she would be glad to meet with him on a subject "of the highest interest to me." She also informed Billings, who had great influence within the Carnegie Institution. In what proved to be a sign of trouble to come, the initial meeting was disappointing, as Gardner was "staggered" by her estimate of the cost, finding it completely beyond what might be funded by his department. Once the possibility had arisen, however, Hasse would not rest until she had found a way to undertake the project.[57]

~ ~ ~

As she worked on collecting, cataloging, and bibliography, Hasse's interest in getting at the content of publications was stimulated by referrals from the library's reference desk, due to the "impossibility of supplying by catalogue the information sought after and . . . the great need for a method other than cataloging to discover the contents of public documents." Lawyers and teachers were the most frequent inquirers, but Hasse also dealt with some notable researchers in economics. A young economist, John R. Commons, worked in one of the alcoves, trying to develop the first index of price changes. Soon he moved to the University of Wisconsin as a specialist in labor history; there he worked closely with Charles McCarthy of the Legislative Reference Library to provide the information needed by Governor "Fighting Bob" LaFollette and his successors as they made Wisconsin an engine of the Progressive movement. What McCarthy called the "Wisconsin Idea" intensely utilized the organized information of his library and the expertise of the state university's faculty in support of reform. With Teddy Roosevelt in the White House, the momentum for reform produced not only legislation but also regulations, commissions, and boards that contributed to the rapid growth of administrative law, a new area of government publications that drew Hasse's attention. She began to develop proposals for reference works that would use government information, but publishers were not encouraging; in 1904, Macmillan told her there was little public interest in a book on American fiscal policy.[58]

Another of Hasse's early clients involved her in history-making research that showed what could be done with public documents and also provided a model of what a woman could achieve in New York. Ida Tarbell of *McClure's Magazine* called on Hasse's help with the research for her vastly influential *History of the Standard Oil Company*, published in *McClure's* in 1902 and as a book in 1904. Tarbell's carefully documented account of the unscrupulous methods of John D. Rockefeller and his company was a powerful blow to the laissez-faire business philosophy and led eventually to the government's breakup of Standard Oil. Marshaling the damning facts that had accumulated in the public record as Rockefeller implacably consolidated the oil industry, Tarbell's indictment could not be dismissed as the ranting of a radical or a crank. As Tarbell pursued her research, however, she was repeatedly frustrated by difficulties in obtaining public documents. Then, as she recalled in her memoirs, she would call on Adelaide Hasse:

> For instance, there was the important Hepburn investigation of the relations of the railroads and private industries. . . . I could not find a copy in the Oil Region where I was working. The Standard had destroyed them all, I was told. At that time, there was in the Public Library of New York City one of the ablest of American bibliographers —Adelaide Hasse. She had helped me more than once to find a scarce document.
> "How about this Hepburn investigation?" I wrote Miss Hasse.
> "Here in the library for your use whenever you will come around."
> But she added: "Only one hundred copies were ever published. It is a scarce piece. . . . It was understood at the time . . . railroad presidents whose testimony was given before the committee bought up and destroyed as many sets as they could obtain."[59]

~ ~ ~

Ida Tarbell was only one of the achieving women Hasse met in New York. Through Kelso, she became acquainted with Lucy Salmon, head of the history department at Vassar, a prominent feminist and reformer whose many interests included the library movement, both for its educational value and as a career for women. Salmon was among the high-minded educators who invested in Melvil Dewey's Lake Placid Club, but she became convinced that he had cheated her, a sign of Dewey's increasingly stormy relations with others. To Hasse, she wrote warmly, "A summer in London with Miss Kelso has made you an old and intimate friend!"

Hasse made a point to notify Tarbell and Salmon of her publications, just as she informed prominent men, and both would pay tribute to her work many years later, Tarbell in her autobiography and Salmon in a letter to the *New York Times*. Commenting on a debate over who was the greatest American historian, Salmon suggested that too much credit was being given to those who published the most volumes. She argued that many diverse contributors to the literature of history deserved recognition, among them A. R. Hasse for developing classifications that "clarified previously unintelligible relationships . . . to bring order out of chaos for the often bewildered historian."[60]

Another intellectual woman friend was Mariana Griswold Van Rennselaer, author of a noted biography of the architect H. H. Richardson and other books on architecture and New York colonial history, as well as a contributor to leading periodicals. Van Rennselaer entertained Hasse in her house on West Tenth Street, a few blocks from Hasse's home at 114 Waverly Place.[61]

The Washington Square area was identified with the "Bachelor Girl," a variation on the theme of the New Woman that worried the press. There was worried comment about female bachelors who actually preferred the single life, and President Roosevelt stirred general alarm about the danger of "race suicide" caused by women unwilling to marry and have children.[62] Hasse's location, just off the square, was an easy walk to work, past the elegant brick houses facing Stanford White's triumphal arch, along Astor Place to Lafayette, where the imposing Astor Library on the east side of the street faced a handsome block of commercial buildings. On the way, Hasse passed within sight of the Triangle Shirtwaist factory and other garment sweatshops, where young Jewish and Italian immigrant women labored for a few dollars a week. Lower Manhattan teemed with struggling immigrants, the Italians south of Washington Square, Eastern European Jews on the lower east side, the Germans of Kleine Deutschland. The cacophony of cultures and languages crammed into a small area was part of the city's energy. There was also a bohemian element—artists, writers, reformers, New Women—increasingly drawn to the neighborhood around Washington Square, along with middleclass professionals and a few of the rich who had not moved uptown. Though Kelso was involved in good-government groups, there is no record of Hasse participating in the reform movements that flourished in the cafes and settlement houses of lower Manhattan. Her work brought her in contact with some of the leading reformers of the time, but her little free time apparently went to her social life and cultural interests in the arts and collecting for a personal library that included forty first editions of the poetry of Algernon Charles Swinburne, the passionate voice of youthful rebellion against convention.[63]

Much of Hasse's socializing made use of the National Arts Club, founded in 1898 to promote awareness of the arts but mainly to serve artists and elite art lovers as a social club and hotel, first in a building on 34th Street and later in the Tilden Mansion on Gramercy Park. The club was unusual in being open to both men and women, giving Hasse a respectable place to socialize with prominent men and entertain in a way that would have been difficult for a woman living alone in an apartment. Her companions for dinners and teas included John J. Murphy, secretary of the influential Citizens' League; Walter Logan, prominent attorney, writer, and speaker; Gutzon Borglum, the volatile sculptor whose ambitions to make big American artworks would culminate in Mt. Rushmore; and Adolph Bandelier, the pioneering ethnologist of the Southwest.

Bandelier was a close friend of the writer Charles Lummis, whom Hasse had known in Los Angeles, and came from a familiar background, a Swiss immigrant family in the St. Louis area. Like so many men Hasse knew, he had invented a unique career, a combination historian, novelist, anthropologist, and archaeologist, doing research in both historical documents and the sites of the native cultures of the Americas. His work was assisted by his multilingual wife, Fanny, daughter of Swiss immigrants to Peru. When Bandelier moved to New York to work for the American Museum of Natural History, he and Fanny used the Astor Library, and Hasse was quick to befriend them, attending his lectures and inviting them to the National Arts Club. Bandelier found the club crowded and noisy, and after dining with Hasse, Borglum, a young man, and three women, he complained to his journal that Hasse "is very kind, but she invites too many people," though dinner for eight hardly seems excessive. During dinner, Walter Logan asked them to lunch with some Mexican friends the next day. Bandelier noted a "pleasant time," with Logan, Hasse, the two Mexicans, a

Scotch couple named Turner, and three women, one of whom "acted like a comedian." Fanny and "Don Adolpho" continued to see Hasse over the next few years, sometimes joined by Borglum, who sculpted a bust of Bandelier.[64]

Hasse corresponded affectionately with her parents but saw little of her family. Her sisters Hilda and Jessie spent time with her in New York but returned to California, while Elsa married and settled in Wisconsin. Their brother Carl, an engineer in Arizona and California, was regarded as uncommunicative by the family, perhaps a reaction to being the only male among four lively sisters.[65]

Hasse had achieved the dream of New York's New Women, freedom from the domestic roles of wife, mother, or daughter. She was self-supporting in intellectually stimulating work, lived alone, and created her own circle of friends and colleagues. One of her few family obligations must have reinforced her satisfaction in being a modern career woman with wide acquaintance in New York. When her German cousin, Hermann Hasse, visited on a postdoctoral trip around the world, she was able to arrange a tour of an Edison electric power plant for him through Richard Bowker, former president of the company.[66]

Probably influenced by his cousin Adelaide, Hermann would become involved in the bibliographic movement in Germany. He was a director of the International Institute of Social Bibliography, which began issuing its bibliography of the social sciences in 1905. When the government granted subsidies to the institute and bibliography in 1908, Hermann's Social Democratic politics were unacceptable, and he moved on to various businesses and causes that reflected his idealistic interest in social problems. As a liberal, modern-minded young man, he was in conflict with his father, Ernst Hasse (1846-1908), leader of the Pan-German League, which sometimes embarrassed even the Kaiser's government with its virulent racialist views and demands that Germany acquire more territory.[67]

Adelaide Hasse's father and Ernst Hasse were half first cousins, descended from different wives of the same grandfather. Ernst had begun his career in the family tradition, as a respected professor and civil servant in Leipzig, head of Saxony's statistics bureau for many years. Obsessed with Germany's need for colonies abroad and more land in Europe, he became a zealot for the extreme nationalist position of the Pan-German League. A tireless organizer, Ernst Hasse worked to develop the league as its president and a member of the Reichstag. Despite his efforts, the Pan-German League was not very influential in his lifetime, and he was widely derided as a simple-minded fanatic, but his views grew increasingly popular, and later events would make the league seem a precursor of the horrors that grew from radical German nationalism. In time, the obsession of Ernst Hasse would cast a shadow over the lives of his son and their American cousin, but when Hermann and Adelaide met in New York at the beginning of the new century, their futures seemed to hold only promise of political, intellectual, and technological progress in an era of peace and prosperity.

Notes

1. Background information is drawn especially from Phyllis Dain, *The New York Public Library: A History of Its Founding and Early Years* (New York: NYPL, 1972).

2. *Los Angeles Herald*, 28 April 1895.

3. Adelaide Hasse, *The Compensations of Librarianship* (privately printed, 1919), 9.

4. Billings to AH, 14 March 1896, AH-NY.

5. Billings to AH, 25 March 1896, AH-NY.

6. Billings to AH, 27, 31 March 1897, AH-NY.

7. Carleton Chapman, *Order out of Chaos: John Shaw Billings and America's Coming of Age* (Boston: Boston Medical Library, 1994).

8. G. A. Robinson [presumably Dobinson] to AH, 13 May 1897, AH-LC. Her reply is noted on the telegram.

9. LJ 22 (April 1897): 209-10.

10. *New York Times*, 2 June 1897; *Los Angeles Times*, 4 June 1897; "Miss Adelaide R. Hasse," *New York Times Illustrated Magazine* (27 June 1897): 15.

11. Billings to AH, 27 March 1897, AH-NY; Adelaide Hasse, "The Nation's Records," *Forum* 25 (July 1898): 598-602; Adelaide Hasse, "Presidents' Messages," *Nation* 67 (24 Nov. 1898): 389.

12. *San Francisco Call*, 9 July 1897; Adelaide Hasse, "Building Up a Document Department," PL 12 (Jan. 1907): 48.

13. LJ 22 (Aug. 1897): 411.

14. Hasse, *Compensations*, 12-13.

15. Harry Miller Lydenberg, *John Shaw Billings* (Chicago: ALA, 1924), 79-82.

16. Hasse, *Compensations*, 10-12.

17. Dain, *NYPL*, 106; Fielding Garrison, *John Shaw Billings: A Memoir* (New York: G. P. Putnam's Sons, 1915), 387; Billings to AH, 21 Nov. 1902, AH-LC; Hasse, *Compensations*, 9.

18. LJ 22 (Dec. 1897): 736-37.

19. Hasse, "Building Up," 48.

20. Hasse reported on her collecting in NYPL's annual reports and in "Building Up a Document Department." There is little about her early collecting in her papers. The trustees' report on the first decade is in NYPL's 1906 Annual Report. The later reference to the collection is in Sam P. Williams, *Guide to the Research Collections of the New York Public Library* (Chicago: ALA, 1975), 170. Another account is in Karl Brown, *A Guide to the Reference Collections of the New York Public Library* (New York: New York Public Library, 1941), 241-48.

21. Hasse, *Compensations*, 10.

22. Adelaide Hasse, *United States Government Publications: A Handbook for the Cataloger* (Boston: Library Bureau, 1902), 3.

23. Hasse, "Building Up," 48-49.

24. Ibid., 49.

25. Ibid., 49-50.

26. Library Bureau to AH, April 1902-July 1907, AH-NY; AH exchange with T. Franklin Currier and J. C. M. Hanson of ALA Cataloging Committee, Nov. 1905-March 1906, AH-NY.

27. Hasse, *Handbook*, 3-4.

28. LJ 27 (June 1902): 340-41.

29. Hasse, *Handbook*, 7.

30. LJ 28 (1903 conference proceedings): 176-89.

31. LJ 21 (1896 conference proceedings): 67; LJ 22 (1897 conference proceedings): 99-101.

32. Bowker to AH, 4 Jan., 2 Feb. 1898, AH-NY.

33. Bowker to AH, 5 Oct. 1898, AH-NY.

34. Bowker to AH, 2 Feb. 1898, 10, 13, 23, 29 June 1898, AH-NY; AH to Bowker, 30 June 1898, Bowker papers, NYPL.

35. LJ 23 (1898 conference proceedings): 117-121, 127-28.

36. Ibid., 185-86.

37. AH to Bowker, 3 Jan. 1900, Bowker papers, NYPL.

38. Adelaide Hasse, "How May Government Documents Be Made More Useful to the Public?" PL 6 (Jan. 1901): 28-34.

39. Falkner to AH, 18 March 1901, 20 March 1902, AH-NY.

40. LJ 25 (1900 conference proceedings): 83-86, 112-13.

41. AH to Dana, 22 Dec. 1899, Dana papers, Springfield (Mass.) Public Library; Sarah Vann, *Education for Librarianship before 1923* (Chicago: ALA, 1962), 96.

42. Wisconsin Free Library Commission, *Special Announcement: Course of Instruction in Public Documents, August 6-27, 1902*, AH-LC; LJ 27 (March 1902): 149; PL 6 (Dec. 1901): 625; *New York Times Book Review* (23 Aug. 1902): 12.

43. PL 7 (Oct. 1902): 372, 387; Adelaide Hasse, "Public Documents," PL 7 (Oct. 1902): 355-59, also "The Vexed Question of Public Documents," LJ 27 (Sept. 1902): 815-18.

44. John R. Commons, *Myself* (New York: Macmillan, 1934), 108-9; Marion Casey, *Charles McCarthy: Librarianship and Reform* (Chicago: ALA, 1981).

45. Adelaide Hasse, *Bibliography of United States Public Documents Relating to Interoceanic Communications, Nicaragua, Isthmus of Panama, Isthmus of Tehuantepic, etc.* (Washington: GPO, 1899); Adelaide Hasse, *Reports of Explorations Printed in the Documents of the United States Government* (Washington: GPO, 1899).

46. T. S. Palmer, USDA Biological Survey, to AH, 31 Aug. 1897, AH-NY.

47. LJ 24 (Sept. 1899): 536-37.

48. ALA Committee on Foreign Documents, *Partial List of French Government Serials in American Libraries*, New York State Library Bulletin 70 (January 1902), Bibliography 33.

49. LJ 27 (Sept. 1902): 835-36.

50. LJ 28 (March 1903): 140.

51. William MacDonald to AH, 30 June, 8 Dec. 1900, 7 Jan. 1901; Moore to AH, 1 Jan. 1901; Solberg to AH, 27 Feb. 1903, all AH-NY.

52. Adelaide Hasse, "Bibliography: Today and Tomorrow," SL 21 (March 1930): 75-76; Hasse, *Compensations*, 11.

53. Hasse, "Bibliography," 75; Adelaide Hasse, review of *Tables and Annotated Index to the Congressional Series of United States Public Documents*, LJ 27 (May 1902): 282.

54. Adelaide Hasse, "On a Bibliography of Public Documents," LJ 29 (1904 conference proceedings): 116-20; Putnam to AH, 18 May, 24 Sept. 1904, AH-NY.

55. Haines to AH, 21 Nov. 1905, AH-NY; LJ 30 (Nov. 1905): 886-87; LJ 27 (Aug. 1902): 753.

56. Adelaide Hasse, review of *State Publications: A Provisional List . . . Part 2*, LJ 28 (Feb. 1903): 78-80; LJ 28 (Aug. 1903): 609; PL 10 (Jan. 1905): 28-30.

57. Gardner to AH, 19 Nov. 1904, AH-NY; AH to Billings, 23 Nov. 1904, AH-NY.

58. NYPL 1904 Annual Report; Commons, *Myself*, 65, 108-8; Macmillan to AH, 22 Aug. 1904, AH-NY.

59. Ida Tarbell, *All in a Day's Work* (New York: Macmillan, 1939), 209.

60. Salmon to AH, 15 Jan. 1906, 15 Nov. 1908, AH-NY; *New York Times*, 7 March 1926.

61. Van Rennselaer to AH [n.d.], AH-NY. Waverly Place was one of four known addresses, gleaned from her papers and city directories, during AH's Astor Library years.

62. Dee Garrison, *Mary Heaton Vorse: The Life of an American Insurgent* (Philadelphia: Temple University Press, 1989), 23, 28; Elizabeth Israel, *Bachelor Girl* (New York: William Morrow, 2002), 108-10, 116.

63. Her Swinburne collection was donated to NYPL: Receipt, 29 June 1910, AH-LC; NYPL *Bulletin* 14 (1910): 413, 454-55.

64. Adolph Bandelier, Journal, 19, 20, 21 Feb., 20, 21, 22 April 1904, New Mexico State Museum, Santa Fe; Charles Lange, *Bandelier: The Life and Adventures of Adolph Bandelier* (Salt Lake City: University of Utah Press, 1996), 186-87, 190.

65. AH-NY and AH-LC contain a few letters from her parents and sisters about family matters.

66. AH to Richard Bowker, 19, 22 Oct. 1903, Bowker papers, NYPL.

67. Peter Burger, e-mail on his research on Hermann Hasse for his dissertation on the Berlin bibliographic movement. Burger lost the trail of Hermann, who had a Jewish wife, during the Nazi regime. On Ernst Hasse, see Mildred Wertheimer, *The Pan-German League, 1890-1914* (New York: Octagon Books, repr. 1971) and Roger Chickering, *We Men Who Feel Most German: A Cultural Study of the Pan-German League, 1886-1914* (Boston: Allen & Unwin, 1984).

Chapter 5

Astor Library, 1905-1910

One day in 1905, Hasse might have seen Henry James studying the houses on Waverly Place, recalling his childhood in a New York that had been swept away in the city's perpetual tumult of change.[1] The brick row houses off Washington Square were one of the few reminders of the novelist's past in a city where skyscrapers now rose more than twenty stories, the palaces of the rich lined upper Fifth Avenue, and tenements were crammed with immigrants. Hasse would find pleasant spots to live amid the crowds and noise, but neither nostalgia for old New York nor skepticism about change were part of her values. She was a New Woman, determined to be part of the striving, driving energy that was the essence of New York.

By now, Hasse was well established in the career she had invented as an expert in government publications. Starting with an obscure position in an isolated provincial city, with no higher education, she had astutely taken advantage of opportunities to attain professional status in a new field at a time when the most women could hope for was "the lower ranks of professional hierarchies" as teachers, nurses, or secretaries.[2] As a super performer who worked harder to produce more, she had developed a national reputation as an expert in government information at a time when American women were not allowed to vote in most states. Word of her achievements had even reached her ancestral homeland; a speaker at the 1906 meeting of German librarians mentioned New York Public Library as an example of advances made in the organization of government documents in the United States that ought to be emulated in Europe.[3] Hasse had job offers, but she preferred to remain at NYPL, where Billings and Cadwalader appreciated her work, and there were such great expectations for the long-delayed new building.

For all her success, Hasse had reason for uneasiness as she saw how often men, especially those with advanced degrees, were hired to work with government publications. Roland Falkner had left the Library of Congress, but his successors in the documents division were men. Charles McCarthy was having

great success with the Wisconsin Legislative Reference Library, and Robert
Whitten, another Ph.D., was doing similar work at the New York State Library.
Their appointments were a warning that she could be shunted aside in favor of
men. For women seeking professional status, even when they held prestigious
academic degrees, there was a constant struggle against marginalization, and in
large libraries, despite their overwhelmingly female workforce, women were denied the highest positions.[4]

All around her were signs of women's precarious economic position. Everyone was reading *The House of Mirth,* Edith Wharton's novel of a New York society beauty who failed to land a rich husband and was destroyed by her inability to support herself. The Triangle Shirtwaist factory that Hasse passed near on
her way to work became a symbol of the plight of the immigrant women who
labored for pitifully low wages, first when its workers set off the great strike of
garment workers in 1909 and then in the infamous fire that killed 146 women in
1911. Hasse had escaped such fates and established herself as a professional with
expert status that women seldom attained, but she could not feel much more secure than the girls she saw heading for the garment factory.

As the suffrage campaign gained new energy, there was growing awareness
that economic independence was crucial to women's emancipation. New York
was a center of efforts to improve women's pay and working conditions, linking
the struggles of working-class women with those of the middle and upper
classes seeking the vote. The Women's Trade Union League was established in
1903, and four years later Harriot Stanton Blatch, the feisty daughter of Elizabeth Cady Stanton, founded the Self-supporting Women's League for Equality,
in recognition that economic opportunity, suffrage, and civil rights for women
were intertwined. The efforts to bring together women across classes and conditions were not without tensions, but contact with the unions contributed to the
more aggressive tactics of a revived suffrage movement less concerned with ladylike behavior. In 1905, Blatch led women's groups in endorsing the third-
party candidate for mayor, William Randolph Hearst, the newspaper publisher
loathed as a rabble-rouser by respectable men.

Hasse would become involved in the issues of working women in the
course of helping researchers in the library, but she had little time for reform organizations as her career moved into a phase of intense work, so consuming that
friends and family worried about her health. Under pressure, she was sometimes
irritable and sharp-tongued, apparently indifferent to the hazard of being labeled
a difficult woman. For Hasse, with her great energy and ambition, the times
called for large undertakings and a hectic life. The dynamism of the era was
epitomized by the man in the White House, President Teddy Roosevelt, of
whom Henry Adams wrote, "His restless and combative energy was more than
abnormal. . . . He was pure act."[5] Roosevelt was not merely a colorful personality; his high-spirited combination of energy, idealism, and shrewdness transformed the federal government and focused Americans on reforming their institutions to adapt to the conditions of the new century. As the Progressive Era
moved into high gear, change at all levels of government in all parts of the
country made current government publications more vital than ever to reformers

and more in demand for research. Economics, sociology, and public administration were rising disciplines, overlapping with history and law, all using government documents as research became integral to reform movements.

Innovation in research and information service was what Hasse admired in librarians. With all his responsibilities at NYPL, Billings still found time to be a key figure in the new Carnegie Institution in Washington, founded by Andrew Carnegie to encourage American research. Charles McCarthy's legislative reference library took an activist approach that included bill drafting service; what interested him most about public documents, McCarthy wrote to Hasse in 1905, was making them "live for the purpose of modifying and clarifying legislation."[6] If able to overcome "many discouraging circumstances to my work here," he hoped to prepare analytic guides to all the legislation that came before the Wisconsin Legislature, make them available to libraries, and ultimately "make our legislation better and more intelligent." Across the Hudson, John Cotton Dana had moved to the Newark Public Library, where he was advertising the library, even on billboards, and developing a special branch to serve business. And back in Los Angeles, another old acquaintance, the writer Charles Lummis, was appointed to head the public library and soon was busily making changes, some of which had been suggested by Kelso fifteen years earlier.

Lummis' efforts were in line with her own views, and Hasse appreciated him as a bright and charming Renaissance man who, like so many men she knew, had invented a unique career, but the circumstances of his appointment were another warning of the precariousness of a woman librarian's position. Lummis got the job because the trustees decided a man was needed; they proceeded to fire the incumbent woman, Mary Jones, who was capable, experienced, and professionally trained, but had been frequently criticized by the all-male board. Lummis was a friend of the board's chairman and happened to be in need of a job. Even more assertive than Kelso, Mary Jones fought her dismissal as a case of sex discrimination, making it a *cause célèbre* among librarians and women's organizations. When Susan B. Anthony addressed a thousand indignant Los Angeles women about Jones' firing, she linked it to their lack of political power, in words similar to what Hasse had said in 1895: "Of course, the man will win, because there are only men to settle it."[7]

Hasse might have created a place for herself as an "honorary man," an expert in government information, but she could not feel entirely secure or accepted. Now in her prime and determined to do major bibliographic work, she would encounter new complexities and tensions as a woman professional. Showing her awareness of the courage needed to risk mistakes and endure criticism, Hasse began 1905 with the publication in *Library Journal* of a brief piece titled "Analyticals," consisting simply of four aphorisms that expressed her determination to act.

AN OCCASIONAL REFLECTION.—In the world of activity there are two classes of persons—the one, to which belong those who do many things, not faultlessly, and are criticised; and the other, to which belong those who do nothing, faultlessly, and criticise.

EST CE QUE C'EST UN BIBLIOTHECAIRE?—"D'un beau papier il porte un diademe, et sur son front it est ecrit systeme." (*Voltaire*)
A POSSIBILITY?—Ought one to respect the motives of those who are not willing to purchase the success of a good cause by a seeming inconsistency—persons who are eternally metaphysically right and practically wrong? (*Extr. Congressional Record*)
AFTER TENNYSON.—'Tis better to commit yourself and stand corrected than never to have committed yourself at all.[8]

~ ~ ~

By 1905, Hasse had built the public documents collection from 3 percent to 20 percent of the Reference Department. Henceforth, she would maintain it at that level, collecting less intensively but keeping up with ever-changing developments and always alert to special opportunities for acquisitions that came to her attention through contacts with librarians and dealers. The collection was not strong in Latin American documents, so late in 1905 Hasse pounced on the possibility of getting some of the Bancroft Library's holdings when they were acquired by the University of California. She advised Billings that she had inquired "guardedly" about the documents, which "will always be isolated, as Berkeley is never likely to collect these things. . . . I should so like to have them here. Is there not someone who could be interested?" She followed with a more pointed letter to John Rowell, the Berkeley librarian, asking about the Central American ministries of war, finance, and foreign affairs and pointing out that if he did not continue the files, they would be "an isolated block of material which will always remain a fragment." Since there was no condition on the sale to prevent "alienation of a portion of the collection," could they arrange exchange or purchase? Rowell avoided a definite answer with the graceful suggestion that Hasse move to Berkeley instead: "There is an isolated 'block of material' in the N.Y. public library—to wit Hasse, which I should like to 'alienate' from said library. I suppose it is out of the question."[9]

After years of cataloging documents and thinking about the problems they presented, Hasse became dissatisfied with her dictionary arrangement of agency entries in the documents catalog:

> The simple alphabetical arrangement of the author catalog proved itself to be unsuited to my purpose. As representing my subject, it was incoherent, vacant and meaningless. It began nowhere and led to nothing. What I needed was an arrangement which would assemble and co-ordinate . . . divisions of government. I proceeded to construct such an arrangement.[10]

She turned again to her belief in relying on the structure of government in working with documents, developing a kind of classed catalog that would have been a shelflist if she had been using her classification developed in Los Angeles and Washington. In New York, there was a unique classification designed by Billings and Harry Lydenberg for the NYPL collection; it was subject classification but had "star" categories that could be used to bring together materials for the special collections, such as government documents or Judaica. *S was the identification for the documents that were kept together as a group, primarily those dealing with aspects of public administration that did not lend themselves to subject classification, while many others were integrated into the subject classes.[11] Without her preferred documents classification, Hasse used her catalog to create a system based on political and administrative organization. Not only did the structure work better than a dictionary catalog for much research, it also had the advantage of reducing the importance of the form of main entry and the amount of time spent establishing the correct names of agencies. She also avoided the problems of documents' titles by filing them chronologically rather than alphabetically, in recognition that researchers usually were interested in a specific period; the chronological arrangement could be used either to locate a particular document or to see if an agency had issued titles of interest in a particular period.

Perhaps without fully realizing it, Hasse was creating a dual system of cataloging for the library's public catalog and the "official catalog of documents." The documents catalog seems to have been both a working record in the absence of a shelflist and a reference tool for the planned documents room in the new building, which would serve sophisticated researchers. The documents catalog was what really interested Hasse, both as a tool for her job and as a base for bibliographic work. To her it was a kind of work of art that she was continually refining as she learned more about documents, but she was also developing something that would increasingly seem problematic to other NYPL librarians, whose discomfort with the complexities of government documents would be projected onto Hasse and her cataloging.

Having made the major decision to refile the documents catalog in 1906, Hasse had little time for further tinkering in the next few years, as her staff was "reduced to three catalogers" in addition to herself, while she took on the direction of a dozen indexers for a major bibliographic project. As the move to the new central building approached, however, she turned again to looking at how to provide more information in both catalogs and initiated what became an increasing emphasis, analytics of the large sets in which so many documents were issued. A later account summed up her achievement: "During the first decade and a half of the [twentieth] century, nearly all of the government documents were catalogued and 'back indexed' with an enthusiastic thoroughness which will be met with in few libraries."[12]

~ ~ ~

Hasse's reputation as an expert on documents brought inquiries from all over the country, so that she was effectively operating a kind of national information center. Letters came from librarians seeking guidance on acquiring, cataloging and using documents; Cornelia Marvin, now with the Oregon Library Commission, Ida Kidder, and Margaret Mann were among the prominent women requesting information and advice. So too did bewildered librarians in isolated small towns, like the librarian in Traverse City, Michigan, who needed help

with the entry for the Fur Seal Arbitration papers, and Mary Grant, librarian of
the State Normal School in Winona, Minnesota, who wrote gratefully, "I knew
no one else to help me out but you."[13] Joanne Passett has described the plight
of women librarians trying to manage impoverished libraries in the West:
"Many encountered disheveled piles of government documents that proliferated
with astounding regularity, and few librarians knew how to organize them. They
often stored documents in closets, basements or any other available space until a
request . . . necessitated that they be retrieved."[14] These women so much wanted
to do the correct thing professionally, and who better to advise them than Miss
Hasse in New York, who was so confident and knew so much about documents.

Then there were the questions about finding information within the documents. From Los Angeles Public Library came the pleas of Grace Pinney, who
apologized for "bothering you so much," but needed to know whether the four
maps spoken of in Emory's report on the Mexican Boundary Survey were ever
published, as they were needed in determining the boundaries of the new Imperial County. With her usual rather overwhelming thoroughness, Hasse replied
that the maps didn't seem to be in any congressional documents but were available in NYPL and LC, as described in the 1901 LC list of maps of America,
which identified five maps, although only four were cited by Emory: "Item 6 on
p. 411 of the List is a map made under Weller who was U.S. commissioner in
1849 preceding Fremont, who never served, and Emory whose commission was
an ad interim one until Bartlett came in to complete the work. Emory in his report has apparently intended to include only those maps made under his direction. You will no doubt have noted the account of the Emory methods in the report of the later survey under the treaty of 1882, published in vol. 23, Sen. docs
55 Congress, 2nd sess."[15] There were also queries from academic researchers, including professors at Harvard, Yale, Columbia, Cornell, and the universities of
Chicago, Pennsylvania, Illinois, and Oklahoma. From the Census Bureau came
thanks for Hasse's notes on marriage and divorce statistics and for one of her
published bibliographies, "the greatest possible labor saver."

Librarians and researchers came from afar to use her resources and learn
about working with documents. Miss Cross of the Census Bureau "enjoyed
working with you extremely and was most grateful for the aid you gave." Rosa
Hubbard of the Kansas State Library asked to study Hasse's methods, as she felt
"very ignorant regarding public documents and will confess they frighten me
somewhat." An eager young reference librarian at Ohio State, Charles Reeder,
wrote and visited. Thanking Hasse for her attention, he assured her that he
agreed with her lesson "that the government publications of any country cannot
be taught or understood without a knowledge of the organization of that government and the functions of the various departments."[16]

Her location in New York continued to bring Hasse into contact with
prominent Progressive Era researchers, most notably in working on the historic
"Brandeis Brief." Her involvement began late in 1907 with a note from Florence
Kelley of the National Consumers League, perhaps the greatest reformer of that
age of reform, requesting "help in getting the official foreign information concerning the regulation of hours of labor of women and children." It was needed

by the leading Progressive attorney Louis Brandeis for his brief to the Supreme Court in *Muller v. Oregon,* in which the Court would judge the constitutionality of the Oregon law limiting women laundry and factory workers to workdays not exceeding ten hours. Given the Court's record of striking down interference with "liberty of contract," there was fear that the case would make such protective labor laws unconstitutional, leaving women laundry workers (the nation's third-largest women's occupation) at the mercy of their employers. As Kelley wrote to Hasse, "I feel sure that you, personally, share the anxiety we are all feeling lest the court decide wrongly this most important case."[17]

Brandeis' strategy, which is invariably described as having "changed the course of legal history," was to minimize legal argument, which might only stir the justices to another defense of liberty of contract, and instead overwhelm the Court with evidence that protective labor laws were long established as a normal government response to public health problems. He took the case pro bono on condition that the Consumers League provide him with such evidence within two weeks. League members, led by Josephine and Pauline Goldmark, Brandeis' sisters-in-law, turned to the Astor Library, and most of the information was found in government publications, particularly those of Great Britain, where the government had been reporting on working conditions for seventy-five years. The result was a brief consisting of two pages of legal argument and more than a hundred pages of a topically arranged, annotated bibliography of laws, legislative hearings and reports, labor bureau studies, factory inspections, and other reports from Britain, major European countries, and twenty states. Each citation was accompanied by key quotations that provided an extensive base of facts about the public health problems in long hours of labor, particularly relative to the health of mothers and children. Though Brandeis gave Josephine Goldmark public credit for the research, Hasse's contribution is evident to anyone familiar with her work, and her papers contain thanks from Florence Kelley.[18]

Brandeis argued the case in January 1908, and in February the Court upheld the Oregon law, mentioning how impressive were the extensive citations. The brief was published and widely distributed to support the enactment of such laws in other states. Brandeis and the Consumers League continued their work on the issue, gathering information for use in similar cases. By 1916, Oregon had expanded the ten-hour limitation to male workers, and Brandeis and Goldmark were again preparing for battle, now unable to rely on the maternal health materials from the first brief. When Brandeis was himself appointed to the Supreme Court, the case was taken by the equally shrewd and determined Felix Frankfurter, who successfully argued *Bunting v. Oregon*. Florence Kelley again expressed appreciation for the help of NYPL, "particularly of Miss Hasse . . . and thanks her for her unfailing assistance in the preparation of the brief defending the Oregon ten-hour law."[19] At that point, such gratitude probably did Hasse more harm than good with men who did not sympathize with Kelley and her causes. But for Hasse, the Brandeis Brief was a powerful experience of how organized access to government information could move the levers of history, reinforcing her shift away from traditional bibliography with its emphasis on the physical characteristics of the "container." Her goal for the rest of her long career would be to make the content of government publications accessible, to make them "live" as Charles McCarthy said, when decisions were made.

~ ~ ~

Finally, Hasse achieved her goal of publishing major scholarly bibliographies. One was for the Public Archives Commission of the American Historical Association, which she had approached originally in 1900, only to be told it could not pay her. She later volunteered to prepare a bibliography that was issued as part of the AHA's 1906 annual report (not published until 1908), *Materials for a Bibliography of the Public Archives of the Thirteen Original States.* Somewhat misleadingly titled, it was essentially a checklist of the published records of the original states from their earliest colonial days to 1789, most of which were in London, not in American state archives. Though making "no claim to completeness," it was a notable achievement, over three hundred pages of fine print listing the known public documents of a period when colonial government publishing was haphazard. In it, Hasse again turned to the structure of government as her organizing principle, an approach that would be understandable to the historians and archivists using the bibliography.

At the same time, her correspondence with Henry Gardner of the Carnegie Institution about a subject index to state documents continued as Hasse sought funds and a publisher. Her search would make it a period of highs and lows, unexpected complications and strange twists of fate, the beginning of years of stress that were bibliographically productive but took their toll on Hasse.[20]

When Gardner had reacted with dismay to the amount of money and time in Hasse's initial proposal, she suggested two possibilities for funding: the ALA Publishing Board, which had a $100,000 endowment from Andrew Carnegie (arranged by Billings), might make a grant to the Public Documents Committee to work with Gardner's committee on such a project, or the state libraries might support the printing of indexes for their respective states. The latter was encouraged by the Virginia state librarian, who wrote, "Your plan is not too full, nor should it be cut down. It should be a bibliography, and a volume thoroughly indexed should by all means be made." He was ready to cooperate in compiling a bibliography according to the form Hasse suggested, to be printed as a state document or any other way that could be arranged. Gardner, who had been experimenting with Rhode Island documents "as a test of what might be accomplished at a reasonable cost" and found it took much more time than he expected, was eager for ALA support. Hasse asked if his committee could bear half an annual cost of $7,500 for two years, with ALA taking the other half, with perhaps some states' support for printing. This would enable them to proceed with her original plan; she was wary of Gardner's inclination to go ahead with some quick work, telling him she would "rather go slow, planning to do the work on a final scale, than to begin at once" in a way that would result "only in a fragment." But if it was done properly, "I am prepared to begin . . . tomorrow." As Hasse worked on proposals for both ALA and the state librarians, she raised the question of pay with Gardner, who agreed that she ought to be paid at her suggested "reasonable" rate. He continued to feel uneasy, however, about whether her proposal could be done on time and within budget.

Hasse meanwhile had received an encouraging reaction to her feeler to the ALA Publishing Board. Melvil Dewey had responded enthusiastically and gave Hasse the impression he would make a "liberal contribution" to the project, which Gardner thought would enable them to raise the remainder of the money. Hasse wrote to Dewey in April, suggesting that they prepare a report on the project for the 1905 ALA conference, scheduled for Portland, Oregon, in July. Dewey urged her to come to Albany early in May, so that he could "talk it out with you for an hour or two and get into the spirit of it fully from your standpoint." With his usual confidence, he assured her, "I can carry it through for you." Dewey's invitation included a sociable long weekend, from Friday, May 5, through a music festival on May 8-9, to include rides in the country with Dewey, who had "horses and an auto and will give you a lot better air than you breathe in great and wicked Gotham." Dewey's eagerness to take women on drives in the country had already disturbed some of the library school students, but Hasse could hardly avoid meeting with him once she had suggested collaboration on the proposal. She was not going to Portland, and the Publishing Board's chairman was reputed to oppose publication proposals from women, so it seemed vital that Dewey serve as her advocate.[21]

Hasse accepted the invitation, but her visit was brief and disappointing. All that is known is that she and Dewey went for a long drive, and she then departed hastily, "ran away so suddenly" in Dewey's words. Henry Gardner was sorry to learn that arrangements with Dewey "did not proceed as smoothly as you had hoped." Whatever happened, Hasse had joined the ranks of those who had disturbing experiences with Dewey at a time of "a kind of building frenzy, in his life and his relationships with others."[22] His tendency to go beyond the bounds of propriety in kissing and hugging women librarians had become particularly problematic and would lead to a scandal in ALA the following year. A letter about the ALA turmoil indicates that Hasse was one of the women offended by Dewey, presumably on her visit to Albany. Emotionally dependent on women, Dewey had been surrounded by devoted female disciples, some of whom lived with him and his wife, Annie. At the time, Annie was away for long periods and thought to be terminally ill, while Salome Cutler Fairchild, who ran the Albany library school, was on the verge of a breakdown, due in part to conflict with Dewey over the nature of library education. Dewey was tangled in more conflict and crisis than usual, under attack by his superior, the New York Commissioner of Education, as a poor manager, by New York's Jewish community for the anti-Semitic policy of his Lake Placid Club, and even by the library school students for excessive emphasis on mechanical detail. Dewey was prone to suspect conspiracies, and the stress of a situation in which he felt surrounded by enemies probably intensified his craving for female admiration and affection.

Showing no recognition of Hasse's disappointment, Dewey dashed off a warm note asking if she was home safely "after your flying visit," of which "I'm inclined to think it a dream but a very pleasant one. Only a day!" He went on flirtatiously, "But I am very glad that I know you better. Sometimes I think of you as Cordelia for your voice is hers. Sometimes as Brunhild fair blue eyed Saxon." Urging her to send him a word to help in his "hardest week in the year," he asked, "Aren't you missionary enough to want to do this?" There is no record that Hasse replied to his effusion. In June, with the ALA conference near, Dewey sent a businesslike, typed letter, asking for her statement on the proposed index to use in "lobbying as you suggested." He assured her that she could "command my good offices in helping on this important work. You have done so much already for public documents that you deserve support in any further work." Whatever Dewey may have done, it was not effective; his influence in the association had been in decline for years, and he had angered the other Publishing Board members in a recent dispute over the *A.L.A. Catalog*. The board declined to publish the index, unwilling to bear the costs of compilation as well as printing and finding Hasse's plan insufficiently specific.

Hasse also attempted to stir interest among the state librarians through a report of her Committee on Systematic Bibliography of State Literature. Her index project was the only subject of the report. Without mentioning the Carnegie Institution, she said $4,000 had been made available to produce a card index of state documents "having an economic bearing," with funds available only to provide copies to "the promoters of the work," and no means at hand to print the index for libraries. She suggested that her committee be discharged and replaced with a committee to explore "the ways and means to provide libraries with copies of this work." With Hasse not present to answer questions, the state librarians reacted with uncertainty but showed strong interest in having the index in their libraries in some form. Making no mention of the Publishing Board, Dewey expressed confidence that the Librarian of Congress could be persuaded to print the cards with support by the state libraries.[23]

Meanwhile, Hasse had continued to negotiate with Gardner, informing him that she "would prepare an index of economic material in state documents . . . to be completed in not over two years at an expense . . . not to exceed $3600." This was less than half the amount she had suggested earlier, and Gardner must have felt qualms as he wrote, "You feel confident that you could complete the work within the time and at the cost stated." Both wanted the project to go forward, so he suppressed his doubts, while she underestimated the time and cost. At some point, she gave up hope of being paid, when it was agreed that she could direct the indexers as part of her work at NYPL. After a meeting to work out differences on the scope of the project, Gardner was concerned that the index must cover economic material in "reports not primarily economic, such as education and agriculture," which Hasse had planned to omit to reduce costs. At the end of June, he had approval from Carroll Wright, head of the Economics and Sociology Department, to use $1,000 for six months of work on a card index, with further contributions dependent on the success of the initial work.

Billings approved this with his usual brevity, "Seems OK." Gardner then sent a statement of his understanding of their discussions: The "general method of procedure" would be agreed upon by Hasse, Gardner, and the other committee member with the work "under the direct charge of Miss Hasse," to produce card sets for the Carnegie Institution, each division of the Economics and Sociology Department, and NYPL, and Billings to have "general supervision of the work so long as Miss Hasse remains at the NYPL and to render monthly account to us of the expenditure incurred." Billings immediately disclaimed responsibility: "I do not expect to exercise any general supervision, as I shall leave the whole matter to Miss Hasse."

Gardner and Hasse thus embarked on a relationship that would often seem like a bad marriage, as they negotiated at a distance about the scope, cost, and time of their project, as well as numerous details, from cross references to title pages. Gardner continually pressed Hasse to finish quickly and fussed that her accounts were not accurate (though the errors were minor), while Hasse soon became irritated with the confusion that arose among those involved, particularly as she came to feel that the men failed to respect her as a colleague and appreciate the sacrifices she made for a project that took many hours beyond her library schedule and would continue years longer than originally estimated.

Problems began only two weeks after the index was authorized, when Gardner wrote about "some difference of opinion among the various collaborators in regard to the necessity of including the pages of the references." Since some regarded it as important, "I suppose we had better do it," he concluded, without any acknowledgment of how much additional work would be involved in page citations. A month later, he wrote that he had received her statement of expenses but wanted vouchers prepared in duplicate. He was worried that there seemed to be no schedule of subheadings for such key topics as money, banking, manufactures, or the labor question, while Hasse objected to his insistence on arrangement by broad topics that corresponded to the subdivisions of the Economics and Sociology Department, which forced her to develop large numbers of cross references from narrower subjects and to design subdivisions of the broad headings. Though he had agreed to the omission of the publications of labor bureaus, which were being indexed by the Bureau of Labor Statistics, he wanted to be sure to include boards of arbitration, factory inspectors, and tenement house commissions. On the other hand, he hadn't understood that Hasse intended to go into the area of legislation, which would "more than double the work and I fear make the whole scheme impracticable." A week later, he sent her a detailed list of suggestions with the comment, "The detail in which you have worked out the reference, much greater than I anticipated, have led me to make my suggestions in detail also." The next week, he advised her confusingly that she should continue to make the cross references she considered necessary, even though few would be needed by the experts using the index, who "will have in mind practically all possible cross references," but if it were to be published, "cross references would of course be essential." A month later, he suggested that she somehow give more information about the content of regular reports than had Bowker's *State Publications,* but without analyzing each one. At the same time, he was worried about the scope and time involved, suggesting that at "the rate at which the work is going . . . we shall have to cut down as much as is compatible with accomplishing the main result." By December, they would need to "show such progress as to clearly justify going ahead . . . on the assumption that we can get the results we are after without too great expense." He assured Hasse that there was no question of the "very great value of what you are accomplishing," but he feared that the project would seem so large that the Carnegie Institution "will be afraid to go on with it."

Gardner's letters were exasperating, but Hasse had fresh hope for the ALA Publishing Board, where new members, Henry Legler and Electra Doren, had been appointed to give representation to the interests of the Midwest. Legler, the dynamic head of the Wisconsin Free Library Commission, soon took an interest in Hasse's index and visited NYPL in the fall to examine her work. Here was a man on Hasse's wavelength. Born to a German-Swiss father and Italian mother who immigrated to Wisconsin when he was twelve, Legler had begun humbly as a typesetter and gone on to create a brilliant career as a journalist, historian, politician, and public administrator, serving as secretary of the Milwaukee Board of Education for fourteen years. His appointment as secretary of the library commission brought the library world a leader whose energy and intelligence were matched by charm and good looks. Legler immediately became a force on the Publishing Board, and once he took up Hasse's cause, it was only a matter of time until the board reversed itself and agreed to publish the index. He also arranged for a Milwaukee newspaper to publish a feature on Hasse as a native daughter who was a distinguished expert on government documents.

Perhaps it was Legler's encouragement that made Hasse more assertive with Gardner. When she informed him of the ALA interest, she also registered her concern about the quality of the project and her sense that Gardner was displeased with what she was doing. Gardner assured her that he favored the work as she had planned and was impressed with its quantity and quality, but he feared (rightly, as it turned out) that her output for the first state, Maine, "has been so great as to make it appear that it will take considerably more than two years to cover the whole country." Soon he sent suggestions for simplifying and reducing detail for discussion on his upcoming visit, though he warned that he wouldn't have much time. Gardner's frequent references to his lack of time must have been an added irritant to Hasse, who was working on the bibliography on top of the other demands of her job. Hasse then shocked him with proposals for more indexers and publication as books, rather than on cards. Gardner wrote that he was "rather loath to give up cards" (which he expected to receive on an ongoing basis, without having to wait until each state index was complete) and asked about printing costs. Hasse had been receiving optimistic letters from Legler throughout November, and, at this point, she either decided she had had enough of Gardner or felt that ALA funding gave her the clout to get tough. She explained that the issue with cards was not printing costs but rather the sorting and filing of the card sets and, in an apparent dig at Gardner's chronic uncertainty, the possibility of having to revise cards already printed if changes were made. She then told him that after January "it would be wise for you to employ a head worker as secretary, a person who could give his or her whole time to the work and one who could be in more direct communication with you." She had cleared this with Billings, asking if it would be "dishonorable" to withdraw from the project after the initial six months, since "what they want is secretarial and not bibliographic work." Billings advised, "Not at all dishonorable or objectionable if you give them timely warning."

Even as Hasse was telling Gardner she wanted out, Legler was writing to the other members of the Publishing Board to urge support. Electra Doren had already approved, and two other members promptly sent favorable comments on the sample pages and the concept of publishing as a series of fascicles, which could spread the cost over a long period. Dewey, who was in the midst of the trauma of the end of his career at the New York State Library, took three weeks to send rambling comments about the desirability of doing it on cards, arguing that separate volumes for each state would lack uniformity, but he was basically favorable to "Miss Hasse's great state document index." "She is easily the best woman in the country in this field and we should give her all possible support," he wrote, but then confusingly added that it "must be published either by our board, the state librarians, Library of Congress, or some other agency," as if other publishers were readily available. Legler replied to Dewey's "general tenor," "I am glad you are so heartily in favor of going on with this work."

His interest in Hasse revived, Dewey sent her a carbon of his letter and another invitation to visit. "I want to help you all I can in this whole matter which should be a lasting monument to your own work," he assured her, suggesting that she address the library school and get the support of "Anderson and Wyer, our new men," an odd reference to the fact that he was being replaced by Edwin Anderson. Dewey offered to pay her expenses and promised another ride in the country, although "the snow may prevent our having as long an auto trip as before, but I have a pair of nice horses and will give you a little fresh air that will do your Manhattan brain good." Hasse had no interest in another visit with Dewey and was annoyed with his pushing the idea of cards ("Not for this sort of work," she noted on his letter). She left his letter unanswered through the holidays, until just before she departed for Maine to work on the index.

Meanwhile, Gardner had written to urge that she "go on with the work and see what can be accomplished under the new conditions" of ALA support for publication and Carnegie funding for two additional indexers. Hasse warned again that "it would be wiser for you to employ a secretary" to do the work full-time, but Gardner assured her that he was "perfectly satisfied" with her work and confident they could achieve "substantially what we are after within a reasonable time and at a cost not beyond our means." He told her to be frank about her reasons for wanting to withdraw from the project, "but I certainly don't want you to give it up under the impression that we feel any dissatisfaction. . . . We know of no one in whom we would have as much confidence as in you." Hasse sent this to Billings with a request for a consultation.

At this point, Gardner and Hasse could see the problems in their partnership. Gardner had grasped that what Hasse wanted would take far more time and money than estimated. Hasse found Gardner an annoying colleague who pressed her to work quickly and cheaply without understanding the implications of his suggestions. She also resented the demands on her time for unpaid work. Hasse's withdrawal would have saved them from years of conflict, but neither was willing to make the break. After conferring with Billings, Hasse agreed to continue, with an increase in the number and hours of the indexers, and soon she was off to Maine in search of documents.

The new year soon proved to be a repetition of the tensions of 1905. By February, Gardner again worried that the quantity of Hasse's Maine output meant delay in finishing and again complained about errors in her accounts. In March, there was confused correspondence about public finance headings, with Gardner reversing his earlier opinion, while assuring Hasse that she should feel free to raise objections and regard his comments "purely as suggestions and not as final determination." And with the support of the ALA Publishing Board seemingly assured after a meeting with Hasse, Gardner changed his position and suggested that the Carnegie Institution might provide more money after all. In the spring, there was continuing uncertainty about Carnegie funding; Gardner finally reported that Carroll Wright had authorized Hasse to proceed with a plan to complete the work by July 1, 1908, but there was some doubt about the Carnegie Executive Committee.

Hasse had now committed herself to complete a major bibliography of the notoriously difficult documents of the states in only two years. June was a hectic month as she faced the overwhelming state documents project while preparing for the ALA conference (June 29 - July 7) where she would present two reports and obtain the Publishing Board's official approval. She also had the worry that her name would be involved in a public scandal about Dewey. The strain was visible to Billings. As he departed for his annual trip to Europe, the doctor wrote soothingly, "The most important thing in the whole business is, that you shall keep your health and strength and not over do things in the summer heat. My final word is, take care of yourself."

At least there were no last minute problems with the Publishing Board's formal agreement to publish the index, which was said to have been "done with great care and in great detail, and includes a large amount of useful material." The board expected to publish it "one state at a time, and finally issue the indexes for all the states in a combined volume, or volumes, with some general index which will give a clue to the contents." Its report was not entirely clear on the status of the work, stating that it "has been compiled, state by state, by Miss Hasse," as though it were almost complete.[24] Although Hasse had thought originally that NYPL's collection and the state libraries would provide most of the documents, her trip to Maine had shown how much more she would find as she delved into additional libraries in each state.

As Hasse finished the first volume, she proposed a title page that Gardner accepted, though it would later be another source of tension:

Economic Material
in
American State Documents
A Topical Analysis and Checklist
Maine

Prepared for the
Department of Economics and Sociology of the Carnegie Institution

by
Adelaide R. Hasse
Librarian Department of Public Documents
New York Public Library

Then in September the question of the publisher was thrown back into un-certainty when the Carnegie Institution showed interest in publishing the index itself, despite all the effort that had gone into arranging ALA publication. Hasse was meanwhile having difficulty with turnover in her workforce of a dozen in-dexers; it was not easy to find, train, and keep staff for such detailed work under Hasse's strict supervision. "It must be extremely trying to have to constantly break in new people," Gardner wrote in a long letter about the problems he found in her accounts. For all his criticism of Hasse's financial records, Gardner was never sure just what information Wright wanted her to provide.

In October, the Carnegie Institution Executive Committee, of which Bill-ings was a member, recommended a substantial sum, $17,500, for the indexing and expressed a preference for publishing itself, asking Hasse to estimate the printing costs. While she was preparing that, Gardner was sending frequent let-ters about subject headings, the necessity to include health-related reports, and his wish to review pages before printing. Early in December, he wrote about a new mix-up about the printing: Carroll Wright had somehow misunderstood Hasse's written estimate of $40,000-$50,000 to be only $10,000. Gardner was exasperated by Wright's error and fumed to Hasse that it was "extremely unfor-tunate" that the board "could not have left things alone after everything had been arranged" with ALA. Soon after, the Carnegie Board of Trustees finally ap-proved both the $17,500 appropriation and $20,000 to begin printing; after two years of Hasse's efforts to find a publisher for work the Carnegie Institution was supposedly unwilling to fund fully, there suddenly was ample support, and Car-negie would be the publisher after all. Gardner felt embarrassed by the change after he had joined Hasse in soliciting ALA publication. He assumed that Bill-ings had persuaded the board, which makes it even stranger that the matter wasn't settled earlier. Billings knew how much effort, over more than a year, had gone into persuading the ALA Publishing Board, apparently without any suggestion from him that the Carnegie board might solve the problem.

With the Carnegie Institution now supporting the whole project, Carroll Wright proved to be a continuing source of confusion. In February 1907, he wrote to Gardner that he and Billings objected to the lack of cross references. Gardner explained that some cross references would be included, but more would add to the costs, which opened confused discussion of what was meant by cross references. Wright then offended Hasse by insisting that the title page by changed from "prepared for" to "prepared under the direction of" his depart-ment. Gardner added a petty indignity by suggesting "further testing of the ac-curacy of the work" by hiring someone to work full-time checking whether all publications had been included in the index. Having urged Hasse to work faster and restrain the quantity of output, he now worried that there would be criticism of possible omissions. Hasse responded indignantly, asking where he got the impression "that the work is not subject to the most rigid scrutiny by me personally" and warning that he was "laboring under a grave misapprehension."

Gardner again assured her of his "confidence" and "admiration," suggesting only that errors would creep in, so why not have someone check each page "whether every item of economic bearing had been included." How this person would see what wasn't there was unclear, unless Gardner expected reexamining every document indexed, an expensive idea from one who had constantly nagged Hasse about controlling costs. He added a postscript on how to "get on without misunderstandings." His ground rules were that the committee had "perfect confidence" in her work but was free to offer suggestions, just as she was free to make suggestions or criticize their ideas without offense to anyone. Frankness did not offend him, but he objected to her feeling that any suggestion implied lack of confidence.

With the first volume coming off the presses, Hasse seemed to have reached the end of her rope; she replied with a denunciation of Gardner's failings as a collaborator. His confidence and her responsibility "were settled when you hired me." The problem was Gardner's inefficient attitude: "You have, quite unconsciously, I believe, observed what amounts to an obstructive policy." She pointed to the delay in setting a format ("You finally settled on one which, because it is cumbersome and out-of-date, will . . . be criticized by librarians.") and the problems caused by his haphazard suggestions, sometimes changing previous suggestions and requiring "that hours would be consumed in making your required changes in references, etc., etc." Certainly the freedom to offer suggestions was understood, but she must "most respectfully urge you to make them at the proper time and stick to them." Both cards and sheets were sent for his suggestions while the work would be least disturbed by changes, but he had had the copy for the first three states for nine months, and the preface was still unsettled, though he had had it for months. "We absolutely can not go on this way," Hasse told him. "You must . . . rely somewhat on my judgment as to detail, and you must make your suggestions in season, and proof must come back to me when asked for." His delays were adding to the printing costs, she complained, and his instructions directly to the printer had confused the printing and proofreading. As for his worries about errors, there would be faults, but she knew the work was being done "as well as it could be under the circumstances." If the Carnegie board wished "to hire an inspector, it is of course at liberty to do so without consulting me." She ended with a plea that he consider her requests from a "fellow worker" and again threatened to drop out if he did not respond promptly in the future. And in another indication of the stress she was feeling, Hasse wrote self-pityingly of the project's impact on her life: "I re-arranged my personal life and dismissed my friends in order that I might give you an undivided 14 hour day. . . . I am not only not being paid but I am money out of pocket owing to my increased expenditure for care, 'maintenance,' etc. for when a machine is being driven as I am, it requires extra looking after. You have practically demanded and have accepted these sacrifices."

Hasse had no sooner fired off this blast than she was further infuriated by receipt of a title page from the printer that differed from the revision she had been directed to make by Gardner and Wright. She dashed off a protest that "any one who has any feeling for books appreciates the importance of the title page." Now she told Gardner to remove her name, though "I am afraid you will think my attitude is one of stubbornness and wanting to have my own way." He didn't understand that she had hoped to do the work "in the best way, regardless of one's private taste, but with every deference to the knowledge of all concerned." (In the end, the title page appeared as she originally had proposed.)

Gardner replied immediately with a thirteen-page apology, promises to improve, and assurances of appreciation for "the tremendous amount of work you are doing and the sacrifice of time and strength you are making with no pecuniary inducement and no motive other than to do a good piece of work." As for the title page, he had no idea where it came from. "This whole business has been a kind of nightmare," he wrote, "but with a little patience we will get things running smoothly again." Two days later, he reported that the title page change came from the Carnegie Executive Committee, of which Billings was "the dominant member . . . in regard to all matters of publication." He gently expressed his own frustration with Billings' actions, from the publishing change, which put them in a "very disagreeable position" with ALA, to the title page change made with no consultation. Putting the ball back in Hasse's court, he noted Billings' intimidating style: "I have noticed a disinclination, on the part of those who know him, to try to influence him. . . . Any attempt on my part to argue the question with him would be apt to do much more harm than good. If you think you can do so without danger of giving rise to more serious complications, I am perfectly willing for you to do so." The embarrassing revelation that Billings hadn't communicated with her may have deflected Hasse's anger, and meanwhile she was off to the ALA conference, to show proof sheets to much praise. Then at last, the first volume, Maine, came off the presses.

Immediate congratulations on the "splendid work" came from Charles McCarthy, and there was praise from *Public Libraries*, noting that Hasse's role "guarantees that the work is done in a scholarly manner."[25] But, as Hasse had feared, the organization of the Maine index was criticized. In an otherwise highly favorable review, Richard Bowker found it difficult to describe "the method adopted for the main headings and their sub-arrangement. . . . [C]onsiderable study is needed to learn the system by which under the several headings, sub-headings and sub-sub-headings a special subject is organized, although the abundance of cross-references makes individual reference easier than would at first sight appear." Noting idiosyncratic headings and apparent inconsistencies, he suggested that "key to what may seem . . . an anachronism and not in line with Miss Hasse's well-known preference for pure dictionary method" lay in the organization of the Carnegie Economics and Sociology Department into subdivisions that corresponded to the subject categories used in the index. Hasse wrote to assure him that it was "entirely beyond my control."[26] She had tried to persuade her collaborators that the dictionary arrangement was best for an index, but they had insisted that it match the divisions of their department and use some headings that seemed odd to Bowker.

Bowker knew from experience with his own *State Publications* how much work and little reward there were for guides to state documents, and he would always be supportive in praising the index. That summer, he boosted Hasse's morale with an editorial urging support for "the great work which Miss Hasse is editing, largely for the benefit of libraries." He reminded librarians, "Her work in the interests of students and of libraries is everywhere acknowledged to be of the very highest value, and if such work is not appreciated, what encouragement is there to do work of this sort, which always costs far beyond its price?" His concern proved justified, for after the first seven volumes, Hasse informed him that publication had been cut from a thousand copies to five hundred.[27]

Bowker and Hasse exchanged warm letters as she followed in his path as a bibliographer of state documents and chair of the documents committee. *Library Journal* praised each volume as it appeared, usually in reviews by Bowker or his assistant William Seaver, a young Harvard graduate whose work on *State Publications* made him familiar with the "perplexing irregularity" faced by Hasse. Seaver was unstinting in praise of a "great work . . . so thoroughly and masterfully done." "The achievement . . . has been marvelous," he concluded, adding that the index "may without adulation be called the product of genius, for it is conspicuously the result of taking pains—that gift which, combined with experience and rare ability, has distinguished Miss Hasse as pre-eminently the person to undertake this work and carry it through."[28]

They also exchanged inscribed copies of their bibliographies, with Hasse telling Bowker, "Such appreciation makes it easier for me to go on." A few months later, he wrote about "how cordially and with what admiration of your energy Mr. Tillinghast [Massachusetts state librarian] spoke . . . of you, that he expressed some depredation in venturing to approach you when under full headway, lest he should be run down by the momentum of the work!" Like many who knew Hasse, Bowker felt some unease about her phenomenal hard work, hoping that her energy would not wear out, "but that you will survive to complete the magnum opus." Hasse confidently replied, "As for the 'magnum opus,' one thing is certain—one of us is going to be finished & if I have my way it will be the m. o. I don't think I'm going to give out—for I play just as hard as I can work—but I do not try to do both at the same time."[29]

The Maine volume was followed promptly by those for Vermont, New York, and New Hampshire in the fall of 1907 and Massachusetts, Rhode Island, and California in 1908. In the Carnegie Institution's 1907 *Yearbook*, Carroll Wright proudly reported "many commendatory references" to the index, adding, "Probably no better person could have been selected for this very important work" than Hasse. He was confident that the compilation would be "practically completed by July 1, 1908, according to her agreement" at below the estimated cost. His 1908 report said that the "main work of compilation has been completed," with Hasse "filling the gaps," as fast as the volumes could be printed.[30] By the end of the year, Gardner was again pressing her about completion. He assured her that he was not complaining, that she "certainly must not overwork," but urged focus on the volumes that could be quickly published, reminding her that she had led him to believe she could "furnish the material as fast as the Carnegie Institution could print it." In 1909, only the Illinois volume appeared, and Gardner continued to urge more production, telling Hasse that the Carnegie Institution would provide "whatever funds may be necessary to complete the index" and suggesting that she hire someone to hunt for documents in the states. Instead, Hasse herself went to Ohio in the autumn, locating many previously unknown early documents in six libraries from Cleveland to Cincinnati. When she thought the Ohio index was well under way, she found variant editions that required revision. Rather desperately, Gardner asked for a meeting on the completion date and "any suggestion you may have for expediting it."

Hasse again reacted with indignation and an offer to drop the project. If Gardner felt the work "could be pushed along by someone else," she was ready to turn it over: "If I am to be crowded into doing bad work, as I was in the beginning through the New York volume, which was very bad, there is nothing in the whole scheme for me. I am out of pocket and out of time. Since you are now getting good work for practically nothing, & if you and the Carnegie Institution do not feel that you are getting your money's worth, then of course you must consider your own interests." Her resentment of her unpaid status and the pressure to finish was hardly fair to Gardner. Hasse had embarked on the project knowing she would not be paid and had repeatedly agreed to finish quickly. As she got into the work, her ideas changed, just as Gardner's did, and after the first volumes, she added time- and space-consuming improvements, such as the names of localities as subjects. She seemed to be both determined to make more improvements, such as the addition of references to the names of prominent men connected with particular Ohio documents, and unhappy with so much unpaid work, and she would lash out at the anxious Gardner when he prodded her to honor her original agreement. Gardner was not alone in emphasizing the importance of finishing, as some of the scholars working on the economic history of the United States had planned on the availability of the index to do their research. L. C. Marshall of the University of Chicago sent Hasse a copy of a paper in which he said there was no more important single economic bibliography than her index "when it shall have been completed." In his enthusiastic review, William Seaver had praised the prompt issuance of the early volumes, unlike so many bibliographies "that drag along anywhere from a decade to a quarter century" due to inadequate support. Hasse's index did not lack support; in November 1909, Gardner reported that another $10,000 had been authorized by the Carnegie Institution, which would continue to support the index for years.

The delays and Hasse's unhappiness with the lack of pay were not unusual in the Carnegie Economics and Sociology Department, which generally found its projects hard to forecast and subject to delays when scholars abandoned their unpaid work for more lucrative opportunities. Hasse may have been desperate to prod Gardner to be better organized, without recognizing how harsh her written words would seem, or she may have aimed for the intimidating style that worked for Billings, but her apparent unwillingness to acknowledge her own failings while snapping at Gardner showed a puzzling indifference to the hazard of being labeled an angry, unreasonable woman. Since Gardner remained polite and the Carnegie Institution continued to support her work, Hasse was encouraged to adopt an aggressive style with male colleagues that would be damaging as she grew older and no longer had Billings as a protector.

Gardner seems to have given up on the collaboration after another letter from Hasse blaming him for delays in reviewing her manuscript and galley proofs: "I am appalled. . . . At this rate—no matter how hard we work to get copy ready—the thing will be years in coming out. I do not want personally to be tied up with it beyond a certain time—as I have already made plans which are far more satisfactory to me than this work." Gardner's last letter in Hasse's files was a routine matter in May 1910. According to the Carnegie Institution *Yearbook*, illness in his family limited his work for the next few years. Since Carroll Wright had died in 1909, Hasse henceforth dealt with Henry Farnam of Yale, the new head of the Economics and Sociology Department. Farnam had not been involved in the original planning and was comfortable reporting that it was "impossible at the beginning to anticipate the mass of material that would be involved." His report for 1909 pointed proudly to the index "carried forward energetically" by Hasse as the only work of the department to be published by the Carnegie Institution. He noted that the index "virtually constitutes a thirteenth division," which must have pleased Hasse, after years of chafing under the direction of Gardner and Wright. The next year, he again was hopeful that "substantial progress has been made . . . and every effort will be made to bring the work to a conclusion at as early a date as possible." But only two more volumes, Kentucky and Delaware, were published in 1910 and none in 1911, which Hasse blamed on the pressures of moving to the new building.[31]

Work on the index may also have been slowed by Hasse's taking on another large, multiyear project, the indexing of the papers of Hamilton Fish, secretary of state in the Grant administration and mentor of John Cadwalader. Hasse was always eager to please Cadwalader, and she hoped her indexing would lead to the papers being donated to NYPL. John Bassett Moore of Columbia, who hoped to write a biography of Fish, worked with her and controlled the funding, but his location in the city made it easier for them to consult.[32]

~ ~ ~

Gardner would have been even more uneasy if he had known the extent to which the entrepreneurial Hasse was pursuing other publishing possibilities, particularly those that might pay her. At the same time that she was complaining to Gardner of the strain of fourteen-hour days, she was making ambitious proposals to various publishers. Late in 1906, Hasse corresponded with a midwestern publisher about an information service or reference works using the data in government publications, "official sources" but not "inside information." Hasse abruptly ended their negotiations for reasons that are not clear. Then in May 1907, she offered a proposal for reference works in administrative law to several New York publishers, suggesting two types of publications: (1) current or retrospective indexes, digests, topical analytic guides, of materials ranging from royal instructions to colonial governors up to state attorney generals' opinions; (2) a sixteen-page monthly, "topically arranged, analytically treated" review of current federal, state, and city administrative reports. She estimated that 595 li-

braries, corporations, and government agencies would pay $25 for annual sub-
scriptions, producing revenue double the cost of publishing. The guide would
be produced by the NYPL Documents Department from the publications it received. Hasse said that she believed she was "safe in saying such an arrangement
could be made with the authorities," which would seem to indicate she had discussed it with Billings, but there is no record of approval of what was a sensitive proposal to use NYPL staff and resources for the profit of a commercial
publisher. When no publisher was receptive, she approached a printing company
with a proposal for a trade paper on federal, state, and city documents; that also
was rejected. The closest she got to any such publication was contributing to
two annual editions of *Review of Legislation*, which Robert Whitten edited for
the New York State Library. Each chapter was an overview of the year's legislation on a topic, written by a leading expert; Hasse's was "Public Printing and
Records." After contributing once, Hasse asked to be paid, but Whitten told her
that his administration already thought the *Review* cost too much and would not
allow payment to authors. Hasse contributed a second time but then declined to
continue, saying she was too busy with other work. Her only paid involvement
in a commercially published reference book was for contributing material on cities and countries to the *Perpetual Looseleaf Encyclopedia*, an opportunity to
show her expertise but not creating the kind of reference works she envisioned.
The editor asked for her assistance in revising articles on cities in 1910, as
Hasse was becoming intensely involved with municipal documents; she was
paid $10 per thousand words or $5 for revisions.[33]

The only other publisher to pay for her work was H. W. Wilson, who sent
her $5 in 1908 for time spent evaluating the manuscript of a guide to documents
by Elfrida Everhart, an Atlanta reference librarian. Wilson had asked for her
judgment of likely sales and was surprised to get a nine-page report on the numerous flaws she found. Both Hasse and Superintendent of Documents Post
were scornful of Everhart's effort, with Hasse describing sections as variously
"inadequate . . . erroneous . . . incorrect." Everhart responded that Hasse's
"super abundance of technical detail is confusing and bewildering . . . and unnecessary" for what was meant to be a practical guide for the nonspecialist, but
Post found her criticisms "useful and to the point and [I] trust they will bear
fruit in preventing the publication of Everhart's book." Instead, 1909 correspondence suggests that Hasse relented and tried to help find a publisher for the
book, which finally was issued by Wilson in 1910, with thanks to Hasse in the
preface. James Wyer, himself the author of a guide to documents, reviewed it
negatively for "lack of definiteness and the absence of detailed information."[34]

Hasse continued to be visible in the library press, publishing reviews and
her papers from meetings and the Public Documents Committee, and offering
proposals to *Library Journal*, where the editors, Helen Haines and Isabel Lord,
were encouraging, though Haines did urge her to keep contributions brief. Both
were among those who worried about Hasse's frenetic pace. "Don't work too
hard, dear," Haines wrote, telling Hasse that she was inclined "to come over on
a Sunday and take you to church with me." When Hasse was working day and
night to get the state documents index to the printer, she still managed to offer a

paper on the *City Record* to Lord, who wrote, "It was good to see your handwriting—but I would rather see your face." In 1908, she reviewed the Superintendent of Documents latest annual report, reiterating her disapproval of the government's "unbusinesslike" method of disposing of documents simultaneously by sale and free distribution. Hasse also offered a column on documents to *Public Libraries*, which Mary Eileen Ahern was "delighted" to accept, but "Public Document Queries" appeared in only a few issues. Hasse introduced each column with an amusing quotation from *Middlemarch*: "To collect documents is one mode of serving your country, and to remember the contents of a document is another."[35]

After that, with the index taking so much time, she appeared rarely in either journal. In 1909-10, Hasse's only contribution to the library press was a sharp reply to a paper in *Public Libraries* that dared to criticize NYPL. In "The Social Opportunity of the Public Library," Emma Louise Adams had urged the Connecticut Library Association to join with social workers and civic organizations in the "great social awakening" of the times, stock up on current material about public issues, and employ researchers to analyze their communities. Rather alarmingly, she added that these researchers should also investigate "the large number of breakdowns among library workers," a problem much discussed among librarians at the time. Adams particularly advocated "a department of social bibliography equipped with the best facilities and competently manned." Unfortunately, she chose NYPL as an example of a library that failed to encourage access to "the literature which would aid in the solution of social problems." The NYPL *Bulletin* had "given scant attention to such subjects," instead publishing on such arcane topics as Islamic law. Adams claimed that a Mr. Brunère, secretary of several commissions on public welfare issues, had found that the material he needed was unavailable at NYPL. Hasse's indignation at the suggestion that NYPL lacked material on current social issues was understandable, given the library's policies and her own constant efforts to acquire and catalog such information. She pointed to "misrepresentation" as inviting her response:

> Mr Brunère is reputed to be a public official, and . . . said to have been in search of material on the milk supply system and the welfare of school children. From the lady's description of Mr Brunère I should say that he belongs to that type of person which thinks straight as a die in its own office, but which, in a library, is hopelessly at sea. Mr Brunère is reported as not having been able to find any material contributing to his knowledge of sanitary milk supply systems. Possibly. It is, however, but fair to record that on June 29, 1909, the catalog . . . contained a total of 387 entries on Milk, 52 of which related exclusively to public milk supplies and 47 to milk tests. These comprised books, government reports and recent magazine articles in English, French and German.
>
> The lady's reference to the bulletin of the library is thoughtless and inept. Her selection of the list on Mohammedan law . . . is but an illustration of the pernicious habitual misrepresentation of the agitator. She refrained from making mention of the library's recent list of its material on banking . . . . While this . . . is hardly social from the agitator's point of view, it does have a very direct bearing on the welfare of the present day. . . .

More within the lines of the lady's denunciation is an index to just such material as she quotes Mr. Brunère as having been in search of. Eight volumes of the index have been completed and its compilation is made possible only by the liberality of the library she uncomprehendingly misrepresents.

After almost two pages of sarcasm about Adams' "nonsense," Hasse assured her readers that "neither has undue sensitivity to criticism nor yet a spirit of harshness occasioned these remarks." She was motivated only by "apprehension . . . lest we stray too far away from that which is our work to do, when a New England audience of librarians will seriously accept a proposal to turn public libraries into a combination clipping bureau, newspaper morgue and Rogues' gallery."[36]

Some aspects of this suggest that Hasse was reacting with hasty defensiveness, perhaps from the stress of her workload, the general turmoil of the times, or sheer irritation with Adams' carelessness. Given the genteel values of the library world, however, she would have been wiser to limit herself to a factual refutation of Adams' statements or leave it to the administration to send a correction. She also could have investigated the matter of "Mr. Brunère," probably Henry Bruère, an influential reformer and founder of the Municipal Research Bureau. If Adams got his name wrong, she may also have been misinformed about what he said (no source was given), and Hasse would have had more grounds to refute the criticism. If Adams' story was true, it offered an opportunity to contact Bruère and educate him about NYPL. Hasse wrote as though she had no idea who he was and had made no effort to find out, but she must have been aware of Bruère, if only because he had been quoted in the press demanding that more city departments publish timely reports of their work.[37] Oddest of all was Hasse's hostility to ideas similar to what she and Kelso had long advocated and that she soon would be promoting with a vigor that far outdid Adams. Within a few years, Hasse would be building a large clippings collection, publicly criticizing libraries, including NYPL, for insufficient involvement in their communities, complaining about oppressive conditions in library work, and calling for "socialized bibliography" similar to Adams' social bibliography. And she, who had scorned Adams for "the pernicious habitual misrepresentation of the agitator," would be subject to the same accusation, with disastrous results.

~ ~ ~

Hasse's involvement in the American Library Association was particularly intense and complex in this period. Chairing the Public Documents Committee was a major responsibility, but there were also personal and professional difficulties that seemed to complicate each annual conference.

For the 1905 conference in Portland, Oregon, Hasse had to prepare both what proved to be an unsuccessful proposal to the Publishing Board, which involved her with Dewey, and her first report of the Public Documents Committee. The latter was a thorough factual review of the year's developments affecting documents: legislation, developments in cataloging, library school courses, important documents and bibliographies. She noted a "tendency towards reaction against miscellaneous public printing" in congressional action, including authorization of a joint commission of inquiry into public printing, but did not discuss the implications for libraries, nor did her report offer any resolutions or say anything about the work of the committee. Now that she was chair, Hasse was faced with the problem of dealing with widely scattered members, who had to be consulted by mail. She sent the committee circular letters about her ideas for its work, with copies to Helen Haines at *Library Journal*. Over time, Hasse would become frustrated with the difficulty of operating by mail, but initially there was the pleasure of a long letter from Charles McCarthy with his frank judgments (current library school courses in documents "seem to me to be absolutely useless") and his hopes to prepare comparative analytic guides to all Wisconsin bills, "if I do not get burnt out every few months."[38]

Besides her committee responsibility, this was the period of negotiations with the ALA Publishing Board. In March 1906, Hasse met with the board in Atlantic City at the meeting of the New York and Pennsylvania library associations. She also gave her paper on building the documents collection, which both *Library Journal* and *Public Libraries* published, and met with J. C. M. Hanson to discuss catalog cards for documents.

Meanwhile, there was a movement afoot to censure Dewey at the 1906 ALA conference for behavior that had disturbed a number of women at the 1905 meeting and the post-conference cruise to Alaska. In June, with everyone looking forward to meeting amid the sunshine and sea breezes of the Rhode Island resort Narragansett Bay, Hasse was alarmed to learn that her name had been mentioned to those seeking ALA action against Dewey. The leaders were Bowker, Isabel Lord of the Pratt Institute library, who also helped edit LJ, and Edwin Anderson, Dewey's successor at the New York State Library and brother-in-law of Mary Wright Plummer of the Pratt library school. Lord, Plummer, and Anderson were proud alumni of the Albany library school and admirers of its leader, Salome Cutler Fairchild; they were already furious with Dewey at his unilateral efforts to relocate the school and his dismissal of Fairchild's emphasis on reading and culture in library education. Anderson had just made a clean sweep of the Dewey regime in Albany, rejecting Dewey's plans to continue to work with the library school and with his longtime associate May Seymour on the Decimal Classification. Anderson fired Seymour in February and sent Dewey into exile in Lake Placid, but he, Lord, and Plummer also were deeply offended by Dewey's behavior towards women and wanted him banished altogether from the library world. Bowker apparently heard about it from Lord and wanted the matter handled by ALA's leading men, whether to protect women from sordid discussions or to protect ALA from overwrought women is unclear.[39]

When Hasse learned that she had been mentioned as one who had problems with Dewey, she immediately wrote to Bowker, Lord, and Anderson to object to any public censure of "obnoxious" private behavior. By the later standards of what would be known as sexual harassment, Dewey's alleged behavior in ALA activities was a legitimate concern of the association, but no professional organization would want to censure one of its founders and best-known members, especially for something that would be a huge scandal in the sensation-loving newspapers. The previous year's furor over Dewey's anti-Semitic policy at his Lake Placid Club had been bad enough; most ALA members would not want any more commotion about the nation's most prominent librarian. Hasse described the problem as a private matter that a woman could handle, a view held by many women who had known Dewey for years, including Mary Eileen Ahern, who wrote an angry editorial about the "malignant presumption" of those who would try to use ALA "to avenge personal animosities." Hasse tactfully thanked Bowker, Lord, and Anderson for their "chivalrous impulse," but she firmly directed that "under no circumstances is my name to be used," and she urged them not to involve ALA.

> I learn today that a matter which I had regarded as private has been communicated to you through a misunderstanding. I am furthermore advised that action is contemplated which will involve the A.L.A. . . . Leaving quite aside my own part in the matter, you will permit me to say that I should regard it as exceedingly unwise to take any action such as . . . is contemplated.
>
> In every case the grievance is a private one. The A.L.A. is a public body, and it would be, in my opinion, not only very undignified, but distinctly wrong to assume on its part the power to pass judgment on any member's private affairs. We are a professional body, the members of which, encountering obnoxious personal traits in fellow members, must content ourselves to employ those defenses which reason, training, and character dictate.[40]

Though she addressed the issue as a matter of dignity and principle for a professional organization, Hasse must also have feared that any connection with scandal would damage her career, and she may have worried that a brouhaha in the press would damage the career prospects of women librarians generally. Even if women were seen only as victims of the lecherous Dewey, the subtext would be the dangers of women working with men, attending conferences with men, or otherwise straying outside a safely separate sphere.

The Dewey scandal added to Hasse's worries as she approached the meeting where she would be presenting both the Public Documents Committee's report and a paper to the "Major Problems" session of the Catalog Section, as well as getting the Publishing Board's official agreement to issue her index.[41] The conference seethed with the conflict between Dewey's supporters and detractors, but ultimately no action was taken. Embittered by what he considered unfair accusations, Dewey largely withdrew from the library movement that had been so much his creation. The controversy subsided, but Edwin Anderson and Mary Wright Plummer continued hostile to Dewey. Plummer wrote later that she would never agree to meet with him, and Anderson protested to Bowker that any honors to Dewey "would be a serious blow to decency." Almost twenty years later, the issue would be raised again by Tessa Kelso, but her position in 1906 cannot be determined from the scant record of what apparently was the main topic of conversation that week at Narragansett Bay. Hasse was among those asked for their impressions of the conference for *Public Libraries*; while most responded with the usual platitudes about stimulating programs and interesting discussions, she remarked coolly, "It had an atmosphere of its own."[42]

Hasse, who was accompanied by her sister Jessie, had a busy week both personally and professionally. She socialized with her old friend from Los Angeles, Charles Lummis, who was happily playing the role of rambunctious westerner among proper eastern librarians. Since becoming head of LAPL, Lummis was eager to renew contact with Kelso and Hasse; that fall, he published a history of the library in his magazine, *Out West*, in which he praised Kelso's administration and described Hasse as the most famous woman librarian of the day. George Sargent, columnist on bibliography for the *Boston Transcript*, was charmed by the Hasse sisters and soon wrote of his hopes for talk of "bibliographical matters" when he visited New York. (Like Hasse, Sargent had no college education but became a noted bibliographer and bookman.) The acting Superintendent of Documents, William Leander Post, was another old acquaintance eager to confer with Hasse; they shared an outspoken style and similar views on documents and depository libraries.[43]

Hasse's Public Documents Committee report again included a great deal of factual material about legislation, agencies, and indexes, as well as praise for Bowker's *State Publications,* Wyer's documents manual, and Whitten's *Legislative Review.* As she presented her report in person, however, she also used it to advocate change in how ALA addressed "the document problem." She pointed out that requiring the committee to report for the previous calendar year prevented it from addressing current legislation, which usually was introduced in the winter and ought to be the subject of the committee's report at the summer conference. This was especially true that year as Congress was about to pass legislation that finally responded to some depository complaints. It also kept the committee from commenting on recent changes in the *Monthly Catalogue*, which Edith Clarke, now at the University of Vermont, had attacked in *Library Journal.* Hasse suggested that the rule be modified for the documents committee and that its members have a longer term than one year (though they usually were repeatedly reappointed). In discussing the new Commission to Investigate Public Printing, she criticized the depository program for overloading many libraries with more documents than they could handle and for basing designation on congressional districts, which had no connection with libraries' levels of development. She was supported by Post, who told the meeting that in a recent conversation with congressional staff, "I was forced to admit that the librarians of the country . . . were abusing the privilege of receiving government publications."[44]

After reading her formal report, Hasse added a suggestion that had occurred to her in discussions at the conference: what was really needed was not a committee report but rather "a permanent place for the discussion of public documents." This idea was greeted with applause and the encouragement of Post. After consulting with the available members, Hasse made a formal recommendation that the committee be replaced with a public documents section. The ALA Council referred it to the Executive Board with the suggestion that "a round table meeting on public documents would perhaps be more effective and satisfactory." The board agreed and advised Hasse that the Program Committee was ready to approve a request for such a round table, but the constitution provided only for the named standing committees, which were appointed annually. At the same time, however, the board advised a group interested in a law librarians' section of "the course to be pursued in application for establishment of a section."[45] It would be more than sixty years before a section on documents, the Government Documents Round Table, was established within ALA.

For daring to raise issues, Hasse was seen as a bold innovator by those familiar with the dynamics of ALA and depository libraries. Committee member John P. Kennedy wrote that he was glad that ALA "is gradually awakening and doing some good work along our line . . . [and] surprised that the Program Committee is ready to sanction a 'round table' discussion of public documents." He hoped for emphasis on instructing librarians "how to handle" documents, for, "there is not one librarian in one hundred that knows anything about it." The most distant member, Mary Sutcliff, wrote from California that the committee needed more permanency, so that members could learn to be of help to the chair. As for the depositories,

I am afraid you will have a hard time to persuade the depository libraries that they do not need all the stuff that comes to them. The simple life idea has not yet penetrated the library mind. It still holds that the chief aim of man is to "take all you can get and keep all you can." Most depository libraries . . . resent any curtailment of their supposed privileges. Nevertheless, here's power to your elbow in bringing about reform.

The highest praise came from Richard Bowker, who wrote of his "cordial appreciation of the comprehensive and admirable work you have done in your Public Documents report this year. . . . I did an excellent thing, I must admit, in resigning the chairmanship . . . so that it has fallen to so much more effective hands." Hasse replied that whatever worthwhile work was being done by the committee was due to "the pace set" by Bowker, just as her state documents index would be "almost impossible" without his *State Publications*.[46]

With ALA out of the way, Hasse was still busy with speaking engagements, while also dealing with the difficulties of the index project and the demands of her job. She was hired as a lecturer for a New York University class and spoke to a meeting of the Massachusetts Library Club on documents in small libraries.[47] She also was in touch with Superintendent of Documents Post, who appreciated her congratulations on his appointment "much more than the mere sentimental expressions one gets from friends, for you fully comprehend the needs of the office and the necessary qualifications to fill it." Soon he wanted her reaction to his effort to stir depositories "to some recognition of their responsibilities," a goal they would pursue at ALA the next year.[48]

For the 1907 ALA conference in Asheville, Hasse was given a round table as one of the five general sessions. Encouraging open discussion, she announced her plan and asked for suggestions in the March *Library Journal*: "The . . . program has been arranged solely that librarians, and especially those of depository libraries, may have the opportunity of meeting the authorities in charge of the printing and distribution of public documents. This is the first time this opportunity will have been provided." Her announcement brought more letters of commendation and favorable editorial comment in LJ, which hoped that the meeting would clarify preferred policy on depository selectivity for communication to Congress.[49]

Mysteriously, the same issue included a paper that seemed to be an attack on Hasse, though without mentioning her name. Helen Haines had told Hasse of her intention to publish a "general, obvious, and rather trite" paper about documents "to keep people's minds a little on that subject" just before the conference.[50] Haines gave no indication that she recognized its criticism of Hasse, so it is unclear whether she or Bowker meant to send a message. She would soon leave LJ due to nervous strain and lung trouble, and she may have been too exhausted to grasp the article's implications. Led to expect a routine call for more interest in documents, Hasse must have been startled to encounter complaints that discussion of the "vexed question" of documents (the title of her 1902 paper in LJ) had been overly negative and given too much attention to the "mechanical side," as though the questions of organizing and recording documents were not of real complexity. The author, Charles Smith of the University of Washington, claimed that the "main question seems to have been how best to get rid of these refractory publications," either by integrating them into the book collection or establishing a separate collection, but, of course, that question was a debate about how libraries could make documents accessible, not "get rid of them." Smith complained of "a general note of dissatisfaction," of which Hasse's 1906 committee report was an example, for its comment about the cost of documents to libraries relative to their low use. He insisted that to anyone with "knowledge of their contents," documents were of obvious practical usefulness in the public library, and, though he conceded "real and inherent difficulties attending their use," he argued that "any library assistant with a good general education should be able . . . to become readily familiar with the handling of public documents." Documents were of value as a counterweight to the "feminized" state of libraries, mostly providing books to appeal to women and children instead of serving "the men who do the world's work" with collections "strong along technical and commercial lines." Smith finished with an admonition aimed at Hasse's criticism of unselective depository distribution, warning that "the librarian who does not appreciate the generosity of the federal government . . . should at least be cautious of his criticism," since "the unguarded utterances and unappreciative attitude of a few librarians might work a serious and permanent injury to the libraries of the whole country."[51]

Smith had no impact on Hasse's report at Asheville, where she repeated her criticism of depository libraries even more vigorously. She abandoned the conventional report of the previous year's developments for an introduction to the session that was certainly thought-provoking in describing documents in depository libraries as a "white elephant" and blaming the "present crisis" on the "indiscriminate distribution of a public grant and the failure of the grantee to convert the asset into a negotiable factor." She reviewed the history of depository legislation, criticizing the designation by congressional districts as irrelevant to the actual use of documents mainly "by specialists in . . . the natural, technical or historical sciences." Distributing increasing numbers of documents to five hundred depositories created "chronic document indigestion," while libraries had done nothing to develop reference works or sophisticated cataloging that would make the content of documents accessible:

> There is a good deal of cant and more or less enthusiasm about the great amount of valuable information locked away in these documents. How do we know it? Or is it guessing? If we know it, who has convinced us? Not a librarian. For in all the 50 years in which these books have been freely dispensed to librarians, not one has prepared a tool which would unlock this storehouse of information. . . . This fact is significant to me as showing the unpreparedness of the average library to make use of this asset.[52]

She also complained that the government and the depositories had "never taken a single step to bring about a mutual hearing" (which was disputed by Bowker, who pointed out that GPO officials had shown their willingness to communicate by regular attendance at ALA). The volume of federal documents, Hasse said, had discouraged libraries from what should be their priority, collecting local documents. Her solution was the reduction of the federal depository program to "carefully selected" regional libraries, "with withdrawal of all other documents from free distribution and their sale at a minimum cost price." Hasse acknowledged that not all librarians would agree with this suggestion, but if there were to be change, "some one had to make the opening move." She offered a vision of how libraries might improve access to government publications as an alternative to the wasteful mediocrity of the existing system, apparently with the intention of stimulating discussion at a time when there was a federal government commission to investigate public printing. With her blunt comments on the depository program, it must have seemed an unusual opening from the documents committee chair in what was supposed to be a practical discussion between librarians and GPO officials. This was in the same period as Hasse's blow-ups at Gardner, when the stress of bringing the first index volumes to publication may have been a factor in her sharp criticism. No one was disputing the truth of what she said; a few years later, her successor as committee chair would regretfully report that there was justification of the criticism of the depository program by the commission on printing, due to the "laxness and indifference of certain libraries" in responding to its inquiries, but his solution to the problem of depositories not taking "adequate care" of documents was a combination of selectivity in what they received and inspections by the Documents Office.[53]

Hasse was followed by Superintendent of Documents Post, introduced by the session chair, Edwin Anderson, with the sardonic remark that he would "tell us some of our shortcomings." That he did, pointing to the problems for his office when libraries returned quantities of documents and failed to reply to his surveys while deluging him with questions about points of law. He explained his problems in hiring staff and following a law "as illogical as it could possibly be," but he also was eager to report his plans to improve the depository and sales programs with advertising, a checklist of all U.S. documents ever published with their classification, lists of the publications of various departments, surveys of libraries, and establishment of a clearinghouse to provide numbers needed to fill gaps in sets. He praised Hasse's report and joined in her criticism of both congressional district designation and libraries that consigned documents to dusty attics or dingy cellars, but his main emphasis was the need for cooperation with his office to bring about changes.[54]

The discussion period was dominated by Bowker and prominent directors. There were comments on the need for selectivity and a more rational system of designation, but many questions dealt with one issue, whether the law prohibited the circulation of depository documents. Since the Astor Library did not circulate its collection, the question did not directly affect Hasse, but it was of great concern to others. The most perceptive comments came from Bowker, who had a firmer grasp than most of those present of the whole range of documents issues affected by government actions. He spoke of the desired provisions of a more flexible system and pointed to the need for coordination between LC in producing catalog cards and GPO in distributing depository documents. He was the only participant to ask Post about the new checklist, which would show, for the first time, all known documents with their Documents Office classification. In the post-conference *Library Journal*, Bowker's editorial praised Post's "lucid and encouraging statement" and the usefulness of the round table meeting. He commended the only ALA program to have scheduled time for discussion but made no mention of Hasse's address, which he probably considered unrealistic, if not completely inappropriate. *Library Journal*'s report said only, "Miss Hasse's report as chairman . . . was the introduction to a most interesting and useful discussion, opened by William L. Post . . . in an excellent statement." LJ also praised another meeting involving Hasse, that of the state libraries, for its "useful discussion" of state documents and presentation of the proof sheets of Hasse's "most important" index.[55]

While Hasse was trying to encourage open discussion, the 1907 ALA meeting was notable for behind-the-scenes conflict and intrigue that outdid the Dewey controversy of the previous year. The surface reason was the long and bitter dispute over where to locate headquarters, but several power struggles underlay this. There was the long-standing tension between East and West (i.e., Northeast and Midwest), which came to a head over whether headquarters should move from Boston to Chicago. There was intrigue and turmoil over the association's first executive officer, E. C. Hovey, when some members of the Executive Board pressured him to resign. Hovey survived the incident but soon was forced out, after only two years in the job. He had stirred controversy by accepting nomination for the elected office of treasurer, which was questionable for an employee of the association. Vice-president Edwin Anderson was so offended that he refused to run for president in the usual pattern of succession, and Hovey believed that Anderson was the "prime mover," along with his associate James Wyer, among the men of the Executive Board to oust him. Anderson's refusal of the presidency created an awkward hunt for a nominee and opened an opportunity for a group of rebels led by John Cotton Dana to offer a reform slate, the first time ALA voters had a choice. The reformers' candidate for president, Arthur Bostwick of the NYPL Circulation Department, was elected, but the rest of their slate lost, leaving Bostwick a reformer without support in the elected leadership, while Wyer remained secretary. Instead of ALA reform, the result was a split between Dana and Bostwick, who thought the circumstances called for a conciliatory approach; when Dana urged him to take advantage of his office with strong action, Bostwick concluded, "Dana was one of those persons who love an argument and prefer to take an unpopular, or even an impossible side."[56] *Library Journal* expressed dismay that the unity of ALA was marred by electioneering, especially involving the organization's first executive. Hovey then wrote indignantly to Bowker about the "stab in the back . . . from those who never opened their mouth, as was their duty, in criticism of their own paid and appointed official," those members of the board who had communicated "no word of criticism" before suddenly pressing him to resign. He believed that the reform ticket would have won if the issue of the board's "arbitrary action" had been presented openly; as it was, there was outrage from many prominent men, and "many ladies came forward to support the independent ticket."[57]

The indignant ladies were not identified, but Hasse's friendship with Dana and her increasing impatience with ALA make it likely that she was among them. The atmosphere of intrigue may have contributed to Hasse's reaction to another action of the Executive Board, the creation of a special Committee on Relations of Libraries to Federal and State Governments to handle questions of library postage, copyright (then a major ALA controversy), and other government issues affecting libraries that were not within the province of existing committees. Its five members included Bowker and Robert Whitten but not Hasse, who apparently saw it as a check on her Public Documents Committee. Her perception was that the new committee would deal with policy issues, leaving her committee with nothing to do unless it took on a bibliographic project. There is no evidence on the record that this was the ulterior motive for the new committee; it was proposed by the chair of a committee on library postal matters, who saw a need for a broader charge, and there was no mention of government publications or depository libraries, which had long been within the scope of the Public Documents Committee. Hasse would at least have to coordinate with the new committee, however, as well as communicating with her own committee's far-flung members. With her contacts, Hasse may have heard rumors about hidden reasons for the new committee, at a time when ALA was full of speculation about Hovey's problems with members of the Executive Board. A key figure in the covert attacks on Hovey in 1907 and Dewey in 1906 was Edwin Anderson, who also had presided over the session where Hasse criticized depository libraries. If Hasse suspected Anderson and Wyer of setting the new committee against her as chair of the Public Documents Committee, it would help explain the future tensions between them. From the perspective of the Executive Board, however, there was reason to fear that her views would be heard as representative of ALA in Washington, particularly by the new Commission to Investigate Public Printing. Anderson, a man of intense discretion, would not have been pleased by outspoken comments from the chair of any ALA committee, and Hasse's public criticism of a government program for five hundred libraries was cause for alarm. The new committee may have seemed an indirect way to control Hasse, but she reacted to it as an attack.

By the new year, Hasse had decided not to continue as chair of the Public Documents Committee, a sensible choice when she was under tremendous pressure to publish the state documents index and had just been through the intensive work on the Brandeis Brief. ALA secretary Wyer expressed regret and asked if she had any suggestion of a replacement who would continue her "thorough, useful, and efficient" work. Hasse made no recommendation, but she did ask Wyer to continue to schedule a documents discussion, urging that it "be carried out informally in the nature of a round table with the Superintendent of Documents present. . . . More real help could be given in this way . . . than in any other I can see at present." Hasse also used her LJ review of the Superintendent of Documents' annual report to note its "appreciative reference" to the discussion at Asheville and express her hope that such discussion would be a "regular feature . . . for the good of the librarians and the ease of the Documents Office." Wyer replied that the general sessions were full but a documents round table would be placed somewhere in the program (where it turned out to be in conflict with the meeting of the law librarians).[58]

As ALA seethed and droned, the high-spirited Charles Lummis sought relief from its "pompous asses." In meetings, he observed those whose expressions showed amusement or cynicism and assembled them in 1907 to form the Bibliosmiles, "a rally of librarians who are Nevertheless Human," devoted to comic songs and speeches that mocked the solemnity of ALA. "The more I see of libraries and librarians," Lummis wrote, "the more evident it becomes to me that we are starting in the nick of time. The thing is something like Poe's 'Pit and the Pendulum,' and the walls are closing in on us all the time." The first members were men, but Lummis was careful to acknowledge that, though women "have never been admitted to those serious and subterranean councils in which the real fate of the A.L.A. is determined, . . . there are women fully worthy to share our efforts to retain humanity in libraries." His old friends Kelso and Hasse were elected in 1908. Hasse was given the title Big Stick (perhaps a reference to her soft voice, as in President Roosevelt's famous "Speak softly and carry a big stick"), while Kelso was Minnehaha.[59]

Hasse was not present to enjoy the songs and speeches, such as Samuel Green on "Why Do People Bother Us for Books?" and Lummis on "Dusting Our Top Shelves." She had decided to skip ALA for a trip to Kentucky to work on her index, much to the annoyance of James Wyer when she wrote, only a month before the conference, to ask him to chair the documents session. "I am sorry to have to do this, as you ought to be present yourself," he complained, with some justification. *Library Journal* had just published Wyer's scathing review of the Superintendent of Documents' *Author Headings for U. S. Public Documents,* to which Post replied cuttingly in the June issue, so presiding over a meeting that featured Post would have been an uncomfortable prospect, but the two men managed a gracious exchange of compliments, and Wyer had only to make introductions for the extensive program Hasse had arranged. The lead speaker was none other than Elfrida Everhart on popularizing documents, followed by a discussion of instruction in documents by two library school instructors, and concluding with Post's speech and audience discussion. Wyer expressed regret at Hasse's absence, for "Miss Hasse is perhaps the best informed person on public documents in the United States and could lead this meeting in a way that no one else can." Post added that she "has done more than any other person to present to the world the public documents in their proper light."[60]

Despite such compliments, Hasse seemed to feel only frustration with ALA. In May, she recommended abolition of the Public Documents Committee in a letter to its members, suggesting that the work could be done by other committees. The reactions to this drastic last-minute proposal were mixed. Theodore Koch agreed with her, as did Bernard Steiner, who wanted aspects of documents divided among four other committees. Johnson Brigham wrote that Hasse was "the best judge," but he feared that the "real needs of the average library as to documents and their availability may wholly 'lose out'" without the committee, as nothing "of a practical nature" would come from the others. Robert Whitten, also a member of the new committee, thought the committee on documents still was needed: "I have no doubt that you are tired of carrying on the work but think it very important that it should be continued." Hasse submitted only a brief, perfunctory report, explaining that she had been "too much engaged with documents to draft a report on documents." She mentioned that "the question has arisen" of eliminating the committee but found "no unanimity" among the members. Hasse would continue as a member of the committee off and on for years, occasionally suggesting projects but not putting much energy into it.[61]

Hasse may have been unhappy with the association, and some insiders may have been unhappy with her, but her contributions were valued enough to earn her nomination to the ALA Council. The conference she chose not to attend elected her in a tie for the second-highest number of votes. She never served, however, for the next year's conference adopted a new constitution that enlarged the council but deprived it of power. In what one member described as "the most autocratic constitution I have ever heard of outside of Russia," decision making was concentrated in the Executive Board.[62] Hasse was not elected to the new council, and she did not attend an ALA annual conference again until 1914. She also chose not to participate in the elite American Library Institute, which was intended to consider the major issues facing the profession, after her election in 1907.[63] She provided a "valuable paper" for the 1910 Brussels Congress of Archivists and Librarians, held in conjunction with the Congress of Bibliography and Documentation, but since she did not go to Europe to present it, there was no discussion at the meeting.[64]

As Hasse reduced her organizational participation, she continued some involvement with the National Association of State Libraries, which made her an honorary member in 1910, in recognition of "her invaluable work on the bibliography of state publications." Henceforth, she would be an occasional committee member or program participant in various organizations, but her sustained involvement in ALA was over. For Hasse, the most important organizational development was the 1909 establishment of the Special Libraries Association (SLA), formed on the initiative of John Cotton Dana as a venue for the legislative, business, and technical librarians who were more active in serving business and government than the typical public library. The founders were not entirely clear on their definition of "special library," and "dissatisfaction with ALA was perhaps the one common bond" among them.[65] Dana's criticism of the status quo had long been resented, and now his establishment of a rival organization, albeit one that met in conjunction with ALA, roused more hostility in the ALA establishment. For Hasse, however, SLA soon would become an inspiration and a refuge. The special librarians were oriented to what librarians could do, in the sense of active information service, which would become Hasse's obsession in the new library building.

~ ~ ~

The stress of Hasse's workload continued to worry her family and friends. She had a period of ill health late in 1908 that alarmed her father, who warned again about her work: "You are wearing yourself out by such incessant application." He worried also about her being alone, since her sister Hilda had returned to California, and suggested that she "take a rest and come home." The next month, he wrote about her neuralgia, advising "dry heat and rest . . . something I fear you cannot get."[66] Hasse's letters to Gardner showed her awareness that she was overworking, and she was sometimes "sighing for the West," as she told Charles Lummis.[67] With her sisters gone, Hasse needed to cultivate connections, but her long hours made that difficult. Kelso was still in New York, however, and the two developed a friendship with Yvette Guilbert, the French singer whose unique dramatic talent made her an international star, as popular on the American stage as she was in French and British music halls. Hasse continued to see the Bandeliers and remained involved in the National Arts Club, which had moved into the Tilden mansion on Gramercy Park, an area popular with writers and artists and near where Hasse now lived on East 15th Street, between Third Avenue and Stuyvesant Square. The neighborhood had the elegance of the handsome old Friends Meeting House and the Romanesque St. George Episcopal Church facing the square, while the elevated trains on Third Avenue offered access to much of the city. Kelso lived and worked nearby, and several blocks north was a popular beer garden, part of the Kleine Deutschland neighborhood where German restaurants and delicatessens were reminders of her roots.

Besides the Bibliosmiles, Hasse became a member of another satirical group, the Association of Easy Marks, whose motto was "Another of the same kind, born every minute" (presumably an allusion to P. T. Barnum's "There's a sucker born every minute."). Its president was Ellis Parker Butler, a Wisconsin-born humor writer, and the members were mostly writers and editors, along with an assortment of librarians, curators, politicians, and artists. Hasse kept her letter from Butler and the membership list for the rest of her life, suggesting that she particularly valued either its style of humor or the sense that other prominent New Yorkers shared a feeling of being an "easy mark."[68]

Hasse's election to the Bibliosmiles was a sign of Charles Lummis' visibility in her life during his five years at LAPL. Lummis hoped to recruit her, and he always relished the company of bright and attractive women, so his charm was sometimes turned on Hasse around 1907-08, at ALA, in letters (urging her to join him and his young daughter in Washington because he wanted his daughter "to see a Real Woman"), and on a visit to New York in the summer of 1908.[69] Descending on the Astor Library, he swept her off to Newark for lunch with Dana in the handsome building that Lummis considered "the best organized public library in the country." They returned to New York for dinner before Lummis dashed off to visit the writer Ernest Seton Thompson in Connecticut. Returning the next day, he arrived at Hasse's apartment bearing their dinner from a delicatessen, and then he was off to catch the midnight train to Washington, where he knew President Roosevelt, his Harvard classmate, and everyone else who mattered. Hasse must have felt like Cinderella after the ball as she returned to the routines of the library and the problems of the state documents index. The values of men like Lummis and Dana encouraged iconoclastic tendencies that were deeply rooted in Hasse's life, going back to her Forty-Eighter grandfather and her formative library experience with Kelso. She apparently did not realize that this could be hazardous for a woman now in her forties, particularly as circumstances changed in the library.

~ ~ ~

There was a major change in the administration of the library with the arrival in 1908 of Edwin Anderson as the associate director, in waiting to succeed Billings. Anderson had been encouraging in offering the state library's cooperation on the documents index, but his involvement in secretive maneuvers in ALA may have made an unfavorable impression on Hasse. She probably also had heard that May Seymour, one of Dewey's longtime associates, believed that Anderson had fired her because he wanted to hire a man in her place at the state library.[70]

Anderson had been at NYPL only a month when Lummis visited and noted "nice little pow-wow with Andrews [sic] who is the coming man to supply old Dr. Billings." To Anderson, Hasse's association with free-spirited critics like Lummis and Dana probably added to doubts about her going back to the Dewey matter in 1906 and the 1907 documents committee report. Anderson had a strict sense of propriety, a strongly judgmental streak, and a proclivity to secrecy. Lummis' unconventional style—he wore a battered Spanish-style corduroy suit, red Navajo sash, and no tie, and usually had a flask of apricot brandy in his pocket—his mockery of ALA, and his reputation as a Casanova, one who even had recently recognized an illegitimate daughter, were bad enough, but he also had taken the job of a properly trained librarian who, like Anderson, had attended the New York State Library School. Anderson was always concerned to bring more men into library work, but not men like Lummis, who had rejected his New England heritage for a life of "getting out from under the shadow of the Mayflower." The proper and reserved Anderson was not the sort to share Lummis' flask or sing comic songs with the Bibliosmiles. He preferred lecturing to librarians and women's clubs on "Children and the Public Library," in which he showed slides of children's rooms and exhibited the dime novels boys would read unless "they came under the influence of children's librarians," such books as *Bowery Bill's Secret* and *Diamond Dick's Hobo Train, or the Man with the Long Blue Scar*. Kelso had dutifully reported in her newspaper column that his presentation "aroused much discussion," but she and Hasse probably snickered at such priggishness by the state librarian of New York.[71] Kelso had herself portrayed libraries as an alternative to unwholesome children's reading when she was under fire for *Le Cadet*, but within ALA, she consistently criticized sentimental emphasis on children's service and urged librarians to develop and publicize other services, especially to businessmen.

A midwestern doctor's son, Anderson had tried various careers in law, teaching, journalism, and mining, a pattern Dee Garrison described as typical of the period's "somewhat downwardly mobile" library leaders, most of whom "did not become librarians until they had tried one or more other occupations."[72] At twenty-nine, he entered Dewey's library school. Many years later, when they both had reason to regret ever encountering Edwin Anderson, Dewey told Hasse that Anderson had always been a "disappointment to those of us who care most for the hyer thins of life and unselfish devotion to the library cauz."[73] Whatever Dewey's doubts, they did not slow Anderson's advancement. He left school early to take a cataloging job in Chicago and then made a propitious move to become librarian of one of Andrew Carnegie's first libraries, in Braddock, Pennsylvania, site of a Carnegie steelworks. From there, he became head of the Carnegie Library of Pittsburgh, where he had access to Carnegie's deep pockets in developing the staff, catalog, and collection for an impressive new building. His success soon persuaded Carnegie to pay for an additional wing. The library was regarded as a model, with extensive cataloging, reference services, including a technology department, and children's services in the central building and all branches. After a decade, Anderson left Pittsburgh to try lead and zinc mining in Missouri, but soon he had the satisfaction of returning to Albany to take over the state library and its library school from Dewey. Two years later, he was recruited to NYPL, where Carnegie was a trustee, with the understanding that he would succeed Billings.

Dignified and rather handsome, Anderson appealed to the trustees as discreet, deferential, and businesslike. He was given a great deal of credit for having business experience, despite not having been notably successful in it. To librarians, he represented the new wave of directors with library school education. Bowker was quick to praise his appointment and James Wyer's promotion to succeed him in Albany: "The rapid promotion of Mr. Anderson, Mr. Wyer and others of the younger men in the library field emphasizes afresh the demand for men and women of large executive ability and trained skill in the library profession."[74] To Hasse, whose experience with Anderson had not inspired confidence, the newcomer stirred some uneasiness. His designation as Billings' successor was a reminder that the leader she revered was now seventy and in declining health, and library school training was not something she regarded as an essential qualification to lead the New York Public Library.

Hasse would not have been reassured by the changes that soon followed Anderson's arrival: the departure of Arthur Bostwick and the promotion of Harry Lydenberg. Bostwick had seemed well qualified to succeed Billings as director of the library which he had served as head of the Circulation Department in a difficult period of transition. Holder of a Ph.D. in physics from Yale, he had worked in publishing for ten years as an editor of reference books and periodicals, before entering library administration as head of the New York Free Circulating Library and then the Brooklyn Public Library. Returning to the consolidated NYPL in 1901 as head of the Circulation Department, he had dealt with the challenges of putting together a system from an assortment of independent libraries and the new Carnegie branch buildings. An energetic and personable extrovert, remembered by Keyes Metcalf as the best extemporaneous speaker he ever heard, Bostwick was tolerant of personality differences and skilled at dealing with conflict within his large staff. He and Billings had clashed, however, and bringing in an associate director was a message that Bostwick was not the heir apparent. To Anderson, Bostwick was both a possible rival and the man who had just been elected ALA president on the rebel ticket after he refused the office; one of his first acts was to write a confidential report critical of Bostwick for laxity in hiring and promotions. Anderson was insistent that hiring the right people was an administrator's most important responsibility, and he did not doubt his own ability to identify the best. Bostwick soon left for a long and successful career as director of the St. Louis Public Library.

In another change that would particularly affect Hasse, Harry Lydenberg was appointed Chief Reference Librarian, a new position whose responsibilities were not entirely clear, as Billings retained control of most aspects of the Reference Department, and Anderson also involved himself in its operations. Lydenberg, who was not inclined to question the wishes of Billings or Anderson, had neither authority nor much interest in administration. The division chiefs were told that they reported to all three men. Hasse and Lydenberg shared affection and admiration for Billings, the man who had hired them, and both were dedicated to building the collection, but their temperaments were profoundly different. He would not provide the leadership Hasse wanted for the library, and she probably resented his advancement, while he certainly came to resent her vigorously expressive style.

Hasse later wrote cryptically of her fear that Billings' successor represented "the same evil shadow which once so shamefully fell on the A.L.A."[5] But whatever her unease about the future, Billings was still in charge, and Hasse's hopes centered on the magnificent building rising on Fifth Avenue. There Billings had designated a room for her public documents division. There, in her professional prime, she would be able to implement her ideas in service to the public.

Notes

1. Leon Edel, *Henry James: A Life* (New York: Harper & Row, 1985), 612.

2. Christine Stansell, *American Moderns: Bohemian New York and the Creation of a New Century* (New York: Metropolitan Books, Henry Holt, 2000), 245. Stansell is particularly good on the New Woman's feelings about work, 241-48.

3. LJ 31 (Sept. 1906): 673.

4. On the struggles of professional women, see Ellen Fitzpatrick, *Endless Crusade: Women Social Scientists and Progressive Reform* (New York: Oxford University Press, 1990) and Penina Glazer and Miriam Slater, *Unequal Colleagues: The Entrance of Women into the Professions, 1890-1940* (New Brunswick, NJ: Rutgers University Press, 1987).

5. *Education of Henry Adams* (Modern Library edition), 417.

6. Charles McCarthy to AH, 14 March 1905, AH-NY.

7. Mark Thompson, *American Character: the Curious Life of Charles Fletcher Lummis and the Rediscovery of the Southwest* (New York: Arcade, 2001), 271-73; Margaret F. Maxwell, "The Lion and the Lady: The Firing of Miss Mary Jones," *American Libraries* 9 (May 1978): 270.

8. Adelaide Hasse, "Analyticals," LJ 30 (Jan. 1905): 20.

9. AH to Billings, 23 Dec. 1905; AH-J. E. Rowell exchange, 8, 12 Feb. 1906, AH-NY.

10. Adelaide Hasse, "Building Up a Document Department," PL 12 (Jan. 1907): 50.

11. For a description of the collection in the *S class, see Karl Brown, *A Guide to the Reference Collections of the New York Public Library* (New York: New York Public Library, 1941), 241-48. Brown emphasizes that documents are in "nearly every part of the classification" (p. 241).

12. Brown, *Guide*, 242.

13. These and other inquiries, AH-NY.

14. Joanne Passett, *Cultural Crusaders: Women Librarians in the American West, 1900-1917* (Albuquerque: University of New Mexico Press, 1994), 68-69.

15. Grace Pinney to AH, 27 March 1908; AH to Pinney, undated draft, AH-NY.

16. These and other letters of inquiry and thanks, AH-NY.

17. Florence Kelley to AH, 21 Nov. , 30 Dec. 1907, AH-NY.

18. Josephine Goldmark, *Impatient Crusader: Florence Kelley's Life Story* (Urbana: University of Illinois Press, 1953), 150-59; Philippa Strum, *Louis D. Brandeis: Justice for the People* (Cambridge: Harvard University Press, 1984), 114-23; *Felix Frankfurter Reminisces* (New York: Reynal, 1960), 94-103.

19. Extract from minutes of Executive Committee, National Consumers League, 1 Feb. 1916, AH-CB.

20. All letters on the state documents index in this section are in AH-NY. Most of the correspondence with Gardner is together in box 2, but a few letters are in box 3, as are related letters from Dewey, Legler, and some state librarians.

21. Dennis Thomison, *A History of the American Library Association* (Chicago: ALA, 1978), 51.

22. Dee Garrison, *Apostles of Culture: The Public Librarian and American Society, 1876-1920* (New York: Free Press, 1979), 138.

23. LJ 30 (1905 conference proceedings): 238-40.

24. LJ 31 (1906 conference proceedings): 157.

25. McCarthy to AH, 6 Aug. 1907, AH-NY; PL 12 (Oct. 1907): 329-30.

26. Richard Bowker, review of *Index of Economic Material in Documents of the States: Maine, 1820-1904*, LJ 32 (Aug. 1907): 377-79; AH to Bowker, 24 July 1907, Bowker papers, NYPL.

27. LJ 32 (Aug. 1907): 350; AH to Bowker, 18 Aug. 1909, Bowker papers, NYPL.

28. William Seaver, review of *Index of Economic Material in Documents of the States of the United States: New York, 1789-1904* and *Massachusetts, 1789-1904*, LJ 33 (Nov. 1908): 466-67.

29. AH to Bowker, 2 April 1909; Bowker to AH, 17 Aug. 1909; AH reply, 18 Aug. 19 09, all Bowker papers, NYPL.

30. Carnegie Institution of Washington, *Yearbook*, 6 (1907), 75; 7 (1908), 85.

31. Carnegie Institution of Washington, *Yearbook*, 8 (1909), 80; 9 (1910), 73; 10 (1911), 77.

32. There are few references to this index in Hasse's papers. Allen Nevins' biography of Fish says the papers were indexed under the direction of John Bassett Moore, with no mention of AH, but her "Biographical Record" [typescript, ca. 1939], AH-LC, says they "collaborated." A note from Moore to AH, 21 Sept. 1911, in possession of Ariel Fielding, shows him making payments for expenses, but details about the project and its funding are lacking. AH toCadwalader at the end of her work, 29 Dec. 1913, AH-NY, expressed hope of the papers being donated to NYPL.

33. Correspondence about these projects, AH-NY.

34. H. W. Wilson to AH, 24 March, 15 May, 18 May 1908, AH-NY; Post to AH, 1 April, 14 April 1908, AH-NY; J. I. Wyer, review of *Handbook of United States Public Documents*, by Elfrida Everhart, LJ 35 (May 1910): 221.

35. Haines to AH, 21 Nov. 1905, AH-NY; Adelaide Hasse, "The New York City Record," LJ 32 (May 1907): 207-8; Lord to AH, 12 March 1907, AH-NY; Adelaide Hasse, review of the *13th Annual Report of the Superintendent of Documents*, LJ 33 (March 1908): 98-99; Ahern to AH, 12 Oct. 1907, AH-NY; "Public Documents Queries" PL 13 (Jan. 1908): 29-30, (March 1908): 107-8, (May 1908): 179-80.

36. Emma Louise Adams, "The Social Opportunity of the Public Library," PL 14 (June 1909): 247-49; Adelaide Hasse, "The Social Opportunity of the Public Library: A Reply," PL 14 (Nov. 1909): 344-45.

37. *New York Times*, 26, 28 Jan. 1906. Hasse may have been in Maine, working on the state documents index, but it is unlikely that she did not hear about Bruère's call for improved New York City government publications.

38. LJ 30 (1905 conference proceedings): 92-97; Haines to AH, 21 Nov. 1905, AH-NY; McCarthy to AH, 14 March 1905, AH-NY.

39. Garrison, *Apostles,* 153-56; Wayne Wiegand, *Irrepressible Reformer: A Biography of Melvil Dewey* (Chicago: ALA, 1996), 301-9.

40. PL 11 (Oct. 1906): 441; AH to Lord, Bowker, and Anderson, 12 June 1906, Bowker papers, NYPL.

41. Adelaide Hasse, "Subject Headings for State Documents," LJ 31 (1906 conference proceedings): 123-26.

42. PL 11 (Oct. 1906): 456.

43. Lummis, Sargent, and Post letters to AH, all AH-NY.

44. LJ 31 (1906 conference proceedings): 140-45, 219-20.

45. Ibid., 279.

46. John P. Kennedy to AH, 31 July 1906; Mary Sutcliff to AH, 22 June 1906; Bowker to AH, 13 Aug. 1906; AH to Bowker, 15 Aug. 1906, all AH-NY.

47. Adelaide Hasse, "Documents for Small Libraries," PL 11 (Nov. 1906): 511-13.

48. Post to AH, 1 Sept. 1906, 16 Oct. 1906, AH-NY.

49. LJ 32 (March 1907): 120; LJ 32 (May 1907): 194.

50. Haines to AH, 11 March 1907, AH-NY.

51. Charles Smith, "Public Documents as a Library Resource," LJ 32 (May 1907): 195-98.

52. *ALA Bulletin* 2 (1908 conference proceedings): 132-35.

53. *ALA Bulletin* 4 (1910 conference proceedings): 759-60.

54. *ALA Bulletin* 2 (1908 conference proceedings): 135-39.

55. Ibid., 139-45; LJ 32 (June 1907): 245-46, 269.

56. Thomison, *ALA*, 56-57.

57. LJ 32 (June 1907): 246-47; Hovey to Bowker, 14 June 1907, Bowker papers, NYPL.

58. Wyer to AH, 31 Jan. 1908, AH reply, n.d., Wyer to AH, 21 April 1908, all AH-NY.

59. Dudley Gordon, "Charles F. Lummis, Litt.D., Librarian Extraordinary, and Founder of the Bibliosmiles," *California Librarian* 22 (Jan. 1961): 17-22; Turbese Lummis Fiske, *Charles F. Lummis: The Man and His West* (Norman: University of Oklahoma Press, 1975), 128-29.

60. Wyer to AH, 3 June 1908, AH-NY; *ALA Bulletin* 2 (1908 conference proceedings): 382-406.

61. Committee correspondence, AH-NY; *ALA Bulletin* 2 (1908 conference proceedings): 178.

62. LJ 33 (July 1908): 283; Thomison, *ALA*, 58-59.

63. LJ 33 (Nov. 1908): 447-48.

64. LJ 35 (July 1910): 319, (Oct. 1910): 451.

65. Thomison, *ALA*, 60.

66. Hermann Hasse to AH, 28 Dec. 1908, AH-LC, and Jan. 1909, AH-NY.

67. Lummis journal, 12 July 1908, Lummis papers, Braun Library, Southwest Museum, Los Angeles.

68. Butler to AH, 25 Feb. 1910, AH-LC.

69. Lummis to AH, 31 Oct. 1909, AH-NY; Lummis journal, 12, 24 July 1908, Lummis papers, Braun Library, Southwest Museum, Los Angeles.

70. Garrison, *Apostles*, 279.

71. *New York Evening Post*, 12 Jan. 1907. Another account of his lecture is LJ 32 (Feb. 1907): 85-86.

72. Dee Garrison, "Rejoinder," *Journal of Library History* 10 (April 1975): 111.

73. Dewey to AH, 13 Feb. 1923, Dewey papers, Rare Book and Manuscript Library, Columbia University. Dewey was using simplified spelling, of which he was the nation's leading advocate.

74. LJ 33 (June 1908): 211.

75. Adelaide Hasse, *The Compensations of Librarianship* (privately printed, 1919), 13.

Chapter 6

Documents Division, 1911-1914

At long last, the New York Public Library's new central library opened in the monumental Beaux Arts building that *Library Journal* compared to both a palace and a cathedral.[1] In the heart of Manhattan, facing Fifth Avenue, pillars and stairs gave the entrance an air of grandeur, reinforced inside by the marbled entry hall with staircases sweeping up on either side. The location of the card catalog and the vast main reading room on the third floor provided quiet and natural light, as Billings intended, and also sent a message that the library's resources were for serious research.

Moving the collections from the Astor and Lenox libraries had been an overwhelming task, organized by Harry Lydenberg with his usual attention to detail. Planning the shelving of the government documents had been particularly difficult, as fifty thousand were stored in boxes, making it hard to estimate how much shelf space they required, given the variations in the size of documents. Hasse fondly remembered Billings' brusque "reprimand of a soldier" as she began explaining the problem: "Miss Hasse, if it had been easy I would not have asked you to do it." After months of measuring and planning, the Lenox Library moved first, followed by the Astor Library from April 13 to May 18, 1911, in five hundred loads of eighty three-foot-long boxes, each labeled with its exact location down to the specific shelf. Despite the painstaking preparation, many books ended up misshelved or piled on the floor in the stacks.[2]

On the evening before the opening ceremony, everyone was in place at seven for the final inspection and test of the equipment, which included public elevators, ninety telephone extensions, pneumatic tubes for call slips, and an elaborate system of lifts and conveyors to transport materials within the vast building with its huge central stacks and numerous reading rooms. At nine, the staff assembled to hear Billings' thanks and receive commemorative medals. The director also presented boutonnieres to the men and bouquets to the women, and then refreshments were served.[3]

The next afternoon, the senior staff gathered on the north stairway, over-looking the entrance hall filled with five hundred invited guests. As the orchestra in the gallery struck up the "Star-Spangled Banner," Billings and Anderson led in the trustees and the most important guests, including Governor Dix and President Taft. Afterward, there were complaints that none of the speakers had been inspirational about the value of literature, but for Hasse, their addresses were in tune with her professional values in emphasizing information as a form of energy, powering the nation's culture of commerce and individual opportunity.

After the opening prayer, a trustee reviewed the history of the library from its roots in the arrival of a German immigrant, John Jacob Astor, who became the richest American of his day and bequeathed the original endowment. Seated on the platform was the richest American of the current day, Andrew Carnegie, who had devoted part of his vast fortune to building public libraries. The other key figure in the library's history, Samuel Tilden, the New Yorker remembered mainly for having been cheated out of the presidency in the notorious election of 1876, was recalled for his bold motto: "I will lead where any dare to follow. I will follow where any dare to lead." Tilden was also on the mind of the chairman of the Board of Trustees, John Bigelow, who remembered his doubts about endowing a library for New York after learning that Boston Public Library's circulation was 90 percent fiction; once again, the message was that libraries must be more than recreational reading for women and children. For Hasse, here was the lesson that some of the most dynamic and powerful men in America had recognized the potential of libraries, just as they had understood how to lead great economic and political enterprises.

Governor Dix followed to proclaim that the library would be "called upon to meet the needs of keener and more complex activities than are manifest in any other city in the world." It was more than a collection of books, it was "the generator of moral and intellectual energy" that no longer waited for people to come to it, for "the new library goes to them." He might have been describing what Hasse would see as her mission in the coming years, to take the initiative in publicizing her department's resources and reaching out to those who might use them.

Finally, President Taft, speaking from long experience in the complex conflicts of public life, commended the "master minds" whose "genius and statesmanship" had managed to pull together all the public and private interests involved in creating the New York Public Library and its central building. The president spoke of the "national importance" of the library, "a model and example for other cities." The building they were opening showed the final perfection of the concept that went back to the founding of the Astor Library in 1849.

After the speeches, the guests were free to inspect the building, and then fifteen thousand additional ticket holders were admitted. The next day the building opened to the public, and fifty thousand New Yorkers came through the doors. Many were merely curiosity seekers, but the numbers were a sign of the mass use of the new building that would seem overwhelming to a staff accustomed to a less hectic atmosphere in the Astor and Lenox libraries.

~ ~ ~

The Documents Division and the other specialized reading rooms intentionally had been located at a distance from both the entrance and the main reading room to protect them from casual or unsophisticated inquiries. Users were expected to obtain cards of admission from the director giving them access for "extensive research," while the "casual reader" needing a few volumes from one of the special collections could call for them in the Main Reading Room. As William Gamble explained in *Library Journal*, his Technology Department was a research library for experts, such as engineers, inventors, and manufacturers, not "the boy who desires to make a wireless outfit for $3, or the fireman who would 'bone up' for a civil service examination." Billings kept up the emphasis on "serious, scholarly" research, not mere fact checking, making it the subject of a staff meeting in 1912 for which Hasse was one of those asked to give a five-minute talk on "research of this type carried on in your division and the people engaged in it." Billings thus became one of many librarians who would try to design levels of service that would efficiently meet the varying needs of library users. His plan was a reasonable attempt to address a fundamental problem of service to a large and diverse public, but with previous experience in a medical library, he may not have fully realized the difficulties inherent in coordinating so many reading rooms with so many and varied researchers, especially as use of the library proved heavier than anyone had anticipated.[4]

The Documents Division, Room 229 at the northwest corner of the second floor, had shelving for eighty thousand documents and seats for thirty readers. The room had an entry directly into the stack area that filled much of the west side of the building, providing "ample overflow" space for documents, and another door directly into the Economics and Sociology Division (usually referred to as the Economics Division, though it was meant to cover the social sciences generally) in Room 228, which had space for twenty readers and twenty thousand volumes. There was a carrier link with the Science Division at the northeast corner, which in turn had a book lift connection with the Technology Division below it on the first floor, all evidence of Billings' effort to design efficient links among the reading rooms. Within a year, however, the head of the Economics Division was complaining about the problems of locating volumes that might be wanted in his room when they were somewhere in the process of going to or from the main reading room.[5]

The Documents Division had a staff of about a dozen to deal with cataloging documents for the divisional catalog and the public catalog located on the third floor, maintaining the reading room, including 1,424 current periodicals, bindery preparation for many more government periodicals held in the Current Periodicals Division, and providing reference service for on-site inquirers as well as many telephone and mail queries. Hasse also continued to supervise the indexers on the state documents project. She and her staff had no separate office space, doing their cataloging and bibliographic work in the same room with readers or in the stacks.

Hasse had helped many researchers in the past, but now she was acutely conscious of having new responsibility for full-time reference service as well as her department's established collecting and cataloging work. The average number of inquiries was not large at first, and Hasse was concerned to increase it to justify the division's existence, since reference work was measured in terms of numbers of users (which would seem to conflict with the emphasis on substantive scholarly research by a presumably small number of experts). Though she made a point of reporting that there was no publicity for the division, Hasse soon was promoting reference service by contacting prominent researchers about the resources her department offered. She and her staff were quick to prepare bibliographies for influential researchers from city government. When a city official asked for a list of sources on waste disposal, Hasse and an assistant worked until ten that night and were able to get the list to him by noon the next day; soon after that, a bibliography on signs and billboards went to Commissioner Raymond Fosdick. By September 1912, the division could report a 60 percent increase from the previous year, but Hasse was "not quite satisfied . . . and says we must have 400 and more every month." By 1914, the division had over eleven thousand users, but Hasse was sure that the possibilities of reference work "are at present barely realized." Her annual report didn't even mention cataloging as Hasse focused on service to researchers, "chiefly men connected with commercial, industrial or civic organizations" who might spend days or even weeks in the division. She quoted the reaction of a lawyer who observed one of the staff being consulted about information on taxation of stock exchanges and exclaimed, "Is it possible it is expected of you to give such information as that? Why there are trained men downtown earning their living by preparing briefs on special questions of that kind."[6]

Despite her eagerness to develop a clientele, Hasse told her staff to take on only questions that could be answered with their own resources, sending readers to other rooms when appropriate. Sorting out how to handle inquiries among the various divisions and the central Information Desk soon proved to be difficult, however, as tensions developed over who should be sent where for what. Hasse also realized that both reference and cataloging might suffer if librarians could not concentrate fully on one or the other, so she and her assistants Margarite Lawlor and William Seaver each took entire days of reference duty, with a backup person for busy times, rather than giving "haphazard" attention to reference as an interruption of cataloging. Lawlor also was assigned to scan the *City Record* and *Congressional Record* daily to spot matters of interest to the division and its users. In 1912, the division also took on the work of a newspaper clippings file that could provide background information about documents and government actions. Soon it was Hasse's pride and joy, growing rapidly, "mounted on manilla backs, kept in vertical files, arranged by simple classification."

Always eager to describe the skilled work done by librarians, Hasse initiated a monthly journal of her department's first full year in the new building. Written by her energetic first assistant, Margarite Lawlor, it was mostly a sprightly account of the Documents Division's work, ranging from humorous anecdotes to copies of the written policies and procedures Hasse developed, "on the lookout for all that will increase the efficiency of the department." The journal aimed to report the division's efforts in a way that would both encourage esprit de corps in its staff and inform the administration of what was being accomplished, but it also made frank reference to problems with other staff and praised the division chief in a way that probably seemed inappropriate to some. When Hasse suggested that the other divisions prepare such chronicles, Lydenberg replied that, interesting as the report was, "we have only one Miss Hasse and Miss Lawlor" with the energy to prepare it. To other division heads, it was evidence of Hasse's egotism, what Charles Williamson of the Economics Division described as her "policy of carefully recording and enlarging upon every case in which she had succeeded in doing only what was expected of her."

Hasse had always been a self-promoter, originally encouraged by Kelso, and publicity for her work also was publicity for her staff, for NYPL, and for libraries generally. But as she publicized herself and her division, there was growing resentment, later expressed by Williamson: "A librarian who is not willing to do her work without getting instant recognition and publicity is unfitted for the business." Billings and Anderson both saw a need to promote NYPL in a suitable manner, but ambivalence about publicity was ingrained in the genteel culture of libraries, particularly if it was personal promotion, as Hasse's often was, or seemed commercial, as with Dana's billboard advertising. This uneasiness was expressed by *Library Journal* in an editorial on the attention to publicity at the 1912 ALA conference, where there was much discussion of the ignorance of libraries' potential among influential classes of the community, particularly businessmen, who still saw the library only as "a building resorted to by women and children." Citing a talk by Kelso in which she reiterated her view that the "responsible librarian should spend more than half the time" outside the library, LJ worried that such ideas "savor too much of commercialism" but conceded that "libraries have much to learn in this direction." The editorial didn't even mention another of Kelso's points, that libraries must promote more than children's service: "Sentimentality has played too large a part in the library, and women librarians should interest themselves in the work men are doing."[7]

As libraries groped for suitable publicity, Hasse would follow Kelso's ideas about being visible in the community by attending meetings, contacting researchers, and offering information to the press. The publicity in the New York newspapers sometimes had a personal component, as in her 1912 piece about library careers for women, which was accompanied by a large photo of Hasse. Coworkers might be resentful, but she was promoting the resources of a library that had been the subject of constant press attention for years and was considered important enough for the president of the United States to attend its opening and describe it as a national model. The new building was extensively discussed in newspapers and magazines, and *Library Journal* was practically euphoric in its lengthy reports and editorials in the May and June issues. At year's end, Bowker published an editorial on the vastly improved collection and bibliography of public documents, which "have now reached remarkable efficiency in this country, primarily at the Library of Congress and in the New York Public

Library." Only one librarian was mentioned in regard to this achievement: "The public document department of the New York Public Library, with Miss Adelaide R. Hasse at the head, is a library in itself, so completely equipped and so well organized as to form a model of its kind, comparable fully with Library of Congress methods and probably superior to methods in other countries." Hasse responded with suitable modesty: "Didn't you rather pile it on in the LJ editorial? It embarrassed me."[8]

Such praise seemed a sign that Hasse was indeed in her prime in the magnificent building on Fifth Avenue. The move had taken her time away from the state documents index, but now the Ohio volume was nearing completion, finally appearing in 1912 as two volumes totaling 1,336 pages. Its increased level of detail met her standards, with the addition of personal names of those prominently identified with reports and the identification of many previously unrecorded early documents and variant editions making it much longer than previous volumes. Instead of concentrating on finishing the index, however, she was immersing herself in municipal documents, publishing a bibliography in the NYPL *Bulletin* that she intended to be the first of a monthly series. Before it even appeared, she had an inquiry from John Fairlie, a rising expert in public administration at the University of Illinois, who heard of it from a fellow political scientist who had spoken with Hasse in the library.[9]

~ ~ ~

As she was dealing with the move to the new library, Hasse made a major change in her personal life by adopting a three-year-old boy, Leslie Maynard. Hasse had a middle-class income, but the care of a child would be a major increase in her expenses, as well as demanding of her time, energy, and attention. She may have seen it as a way to compensate for neglect of her personal life after years of fourteen-hour days. A few years later, she told a reporter that her son gave balance to her life, that she "purposely picked a red-headed lively youngster who would discipline me and be a big responsibility," though it is hard to see why she needed more responsibility at that point.[10]

Adoption was a trend for single women with adequate incomes. It was more common among social workers than librarians, but several prominent women librarians adopted around the same time. Hasse's family thought she was influenced by her sister Elsa's adoption of a son, but Elsa was married and financially comfortable. Single motherhood by adoption was seen as a New Woman's choice, and Hasse was said to enjoy startling people by introducing herself as "Miss Hasse" and son. Sometimes adoptions were a way of regularizing secret out-of-wedlock births, and there may have been some such suspicions about Hasse. Her whereabouts can be established around the date of Leslie's birth, however, the week she was socializing with the visiting Charles Lummis.[11]

~ ~ ~

After the triumphant atmosphere of the opening came the adjustment to the new environment. Conditions were far from easy for the staff of the Reference Department. Though the size of the staff doubled with the move, mass use of the new building seemed overwhelming, and the stress was intensified by long hours at the reference desks, further compounded by the addition of evening and Sunday hours in 1912. It would be many years before the administration realized that the reference schedules were too stressful.[12] The pressure at the catalog and the main reading room did lead to establishment of the Information Division to operate the central reference desk at the public catalog, while the Readers Division remained responsible for the stacks and main reading room.

Then there were the problems of the catalog that Keyes Metcalf described as a hodgepodge of inconsistent subject headings. Metcalf felt that, for all the catalog's limitations, one could always find at least one or two things on a subject, but for Hasse, with her experience in scholarly bibliography and her hope of serving advanced researchers, such a casual attitude was unacceptable. For technical services staff, there was the volume of material to be processed and the absence of a shelflist as well as the inconsistencies of the subject entries. Once the library acquired a photostat machine, creation of a shelflist from copies of the catalog cards became a priority, to be followed by an inventory.[13]

For all staff, salaries were less than in other large libraries, and there were no pensions, because the trustees would not surrender their independence from the often corrupt city government in order to join its pension system. In defense of their prerogatives, some of the richest men in America denied pensions to the underpaid library staff, with the result that some aging employees could not afford to retire. Billings, their strong leader for fifteen years, was now over seventy and nearing the end of his career. In this atmosphere, Hasse was determined in pressing for action on problems that affected service to readers, increasingly vocal about the need to improve working conditions, and energetic in promoting her division to the public, none of which endeared her to the administration or the other division heads. A pattern began to develop in which she was labeled a difficult woman within the library while receiving frequent praise from outside.

The first sign of conflict involved the adjacent Economics Division. The plan of the two reading rooms, adjoining and linked by a door between, indicated Billings' expectation that there would be communication about their related materials, but Hasse was insistent that her division be recognized as "separate and independent." Charles Williamson, the newly hired chief of the Economics Division, later said that Billings had "especially requested" him to report any difficulty with Hasse, who had wanted his job and would be jealous and difficult, but he "seldom made complaint about her."[14] This may be Williamson's way of justifying the lack of documentation for his later claim of constant problems; the only evidence of conflict was put on the record by Hasse herself in regard to one incident. Hasse did want to lead a division that would include documents and related materials in the social sciences, law, and public administration, which had long been her responsibility in cataloging and bibliography. In a report on the first twelve years of her department, she emphasized that she had not collected documents as such but rather had specialized in three areas: international arbitration, public administration, and economics and sociology. The latter was the largest subject component of the documents she collected and cataloged, Hasse explained, calling attention to her expertise in the area.[15] The establishment of a separate division headed by a newcomer may well have seemed an injustice after she had compiled such a record of achievement, and it may have contributed to her suspicion of Edwin Anderson, who had come from a library with a social science department headed by a male Ph.D. and had recruited Williamson for the position established only six months before the building opened. Hasse had other reasons for feeling resentful towards Williamson, who had a Ph.D. and solid knowledge of the bibliography of economics but had never worked in a library when he was appointed to head a division at NYPL. He had decided to change from teaching to library work after some difficulties with the woman president of Bryn Mawr College, M. Carey Thomas, who had doubts about his teaching ability, particularly whether he had the requisite energy.

By determination and force of personality, Thomas had established Bryn Mawr as the peer of the best men's colleges, and she was insistent on maintaining high standards. She and Williamson initially disagreed over her preference for teaching economic theory rather than the practical aspects that he wanted to emphasize; Thomas opposed any tendency to steer Bryn Mawr women to low-status feminized occupations instead of preparing them for advanced study and professional work. In his first year on the faculty, Williamson was stricken with typhoid fever and was slow to recover, which caused Thomas to require more time to evaluate his teaching. In his third year, he was informed that his contract would not be renewed. The record in Williamson's biography does not show Thomas to have been anything other than fair, reasonable, and courteous; she gave Williamson a favorable letter of reference that said he was not renewed because she could not promise the advancement he had "a right to expect." She did damage his hopes for a position at Bowdoin College, however, by telling its president of some feeling that Williamson was "not a very inspiring teacher," due partly to his illness. Williamson felt bitter, complaining that Thomas was difficult with male faculty and "has been known to knock a good man out of a good position for no other reason than a slight personal grudge." His experience with a woman president must have been a particular shock to one who had risen from humble circumstances by attaching himself to prominent men, working as secretary to the president of Western Reserve and the economist Richard Ely at the University of Wisconsin to pay for his education. Uneasy about his future in academia, he decided to investigate library work, which had long interested him, and almost immediately was hired by NYPL at a salary better than he could have hoped for in teaching. Edwin Anderson had made inquiries at Columbia, where Williamson's Ph.D. adviser recommended him. Once on the job, Williamson consulted often with Anderson.[16]

With her contacts, Hasse probably heard what happened at Bryn Mawr and naturally resented the appointment of a man whose qualifications seemed to be his Ph.D. and his gender, not any record of achievement in libraries. She had devoted years of labor to establishing her reputation as a librarian and bibliographer; now a younger man who had been neither and had failed as a teacher effortlessly obtained the status she had after a quarter century of library work and bibliographic publication. As the only woman division head in the Reference Department, Hasse had reason to fear that she might be marginalized or even made subordinate to Williamson, whose graduate training gave him an assumption of superiority. Personally, they had different temperaments, likely to grate on each other; Williamson was easily annoyed by self-promoting extroverts like Hasse, while she was scornful of those who lacked her energy. And if Hasse objected to his advantages as a man, Williamson's anger with M. Carey Thomas showed his resentment of strong women.

Hasse's negative predisposition towards Williamson was reinforced soon after his arrival when the division chiefs were asked by Billings to present brief statements on the work of their departments at a meeting. Hasse recalled:

Unfortunately Dr. Billings called first on a newcomer, a former teacher, possessed of a remarkable flow of words. Simple courtesy would have dictated less than ordinary brevity, but having once begun, it was apparently difficult for the speaker to stop. Dr. Billings began to watch the clock, then he grew stern, and finally, I believe, the physician's curiosity was aroused, for he kept his cold blue eye steadily on the talker. When at last the flow of words abated, Dr. Billings arose and in icy tones said to us: "Ladies and gentlemen, the hour is late. We will adjourn."[17]

Later, at a time when it was in his interest to demonize Hasse, Williamson said that he found her impossible from the beginning and soon heard that the other division chiefs felt the same. As an example, he cited Hasse's decision to treat publications of the nongovernmental Bureau of Municipal Research as documents, moving them from his division to hers. Williamson said he "protested courteously but vigorously, but he might as well have talked to the moon." He offered no contemporary documentation of what seems to be one of many mysteries of NYPL management. Disputes over the location of materials are common in libraries, especially those with special collections and reading rooms, but Williamson gave no indication that there was any process for resolving the issue, just as he reported Billings' warning about Hasse without any suggestion that the director had done anything to prevent problems. Instead, he portrayed himself as the long-suffering victim of an unreasonable, intransigent woman. A later memo from Lydenberg seems to say that Hasse argued that the publications were not being properly cataloged and won approval to transfer them to her expert care. This was not without precedent, as the Documents Division's journal mentions that several types of material that were not strictly government publications (foreign chamber of commerce reports, state university publications) were assigned to the division in its first year. Hasse's male colleagues would increasingly join in labeling her an impossible female, while she increasingly felt that the tact expected of a woman would only encourage them to take advantage of her. Where there are records of their conflicts, they show that Hasse had justification for her positions, often was in the right, and felt that she had to be assertive to get anywhere with unreasonable, intransigent men.

Another source of tension between Hasse and Williamson was William

Seaver, who had been Bowker's assistant in compiling *State Publications* and decided to enter library work without first going to library school. After a long job search, during which he gave Hasse as a reference, he joined the Documents Division in September 1910. Hasse soon "felt a lack of confidence in him and his work," finding him "particularly inept" at the reference work required in the new building (not surprising in one who had not worked in a library or attended library school). In 1912, she removed him from reference duty and put him in charge of documents cataloging, and soon after, Seaver transferred to the Economics Division. His place in the Documents Division was filled by a woman who was paid $30 per month, which was "ludicrous," Hasse complained to Lydenberg, when she immediately could do the same work as Seaver "wrapped in the cotton wool of $100." She even protested to Williamson about Seaver coming into 229 to get a document for a reader in 228.

> I think we might as well come to an understanding now that the Documents Division is a separate and independent division and not an adjunct to the Economics and Sociology division. Courtesy as well as business, since the work of the reference divisions is measured by the numbers of readers, would seem then to dictate that we be very fair about the use of our respective rooms. If, as in the case . . . of the inquirer yesterday (and which is not the first of its kind) you had no material to answer the question, and all the material had to be taken from this room, it would have been only fair to have sent the reader here. This was particularly annoying both because all the material was from temporary records and is open to the danger of not getting back properly, and because your messenger had to be helped to get the material. I should much prefer not to have Mr. Seaver sent here to do reference work. If I had found him efficient in document reference work, he would not have been transferred.

Williamson's explanation was that he had already referred the reader for a specific document and only sent Seaver when the documents staff knew nothing about it. Clearly, Hasse was worried about the independence of her division, her status as chief, and even the possibility that Williamson would take credit for service that used documents. In further evidence of her strong feelings, the letter was included in the division's journal with the comment: "Dr. Williamson did not draw a clear line between his division and this one, so Miss Hasse drew one for him."[18]

According to Williamson, Seaver was a victim of Hasse's jealousy of his superior knowledge of documents, an improbable claim.[19] Hasse's hostile tone does suggest some deeper problem, perhaps suspicion that Seaver was subverting her to form alliances with Williamson and Frank Waite, another newcomer recruited by Anderson, who helped with the initial organization of the Economics Division and was a sympathetic listener to young men. As a Harvard graduate and associate of the influential Bowker, Seaver may have irritated Hasse with expectations of status and advancement (perhaps wanting the rank of "first assistant" that went to Margarite Lawlor), and when lack of experience made him seem "inept" at reference work, she may have given offense by switching him to full-time cataloging (where he somehow felt obliged to spend two hours a day of his own time at home cataloging the state university publications the division had taken on). Presumably Seaver wanted to make contacts and develop his career, not be pigeonholed as a documents cataloger with an impossible workload. Tensions with Hasse would have been particularly distressing at a time when he was dealing with his mother's illness and death. With Willamson and Waite organizing the economics and sociology materials next door, he had a chance to cultivate congenial men and move into a better situation with a boss who also was new to library work.

In an instance of the ever-shifting narratives at NYPL, Hasse publicly praised Seaver a few years later at ALA, describing him as "a very careful, conscientious worker" who had done an exceptional job of cataloging the publications of the state university at home on his own time. "And then he resigned," she said, as though it had been a great loss, with no suggestion that she had wanted him transferred. This may have been aimed at conciliating Bowker, who was present at the meeting. Hasse's troubles with Seaver probably chilled her relations with Bowker; there is no more record of friendly exchanges between them after Seaver left the Documents Division, but *Library Journal* continued to publish her writings, and it was gracious in mentioning her along with the compliment to Seaver: "In referring modestly to her own remarkable bibliographies of state publications, she illustrated the difficulties by instancing Seaver's 'painstaking and excellent work in bringing order out of chaos as to the publications of the University of the State of New York . . .—and then he resigned!'"[20]

Seaver remained under Williamson's wing for the next five years. They seem to have bonded as young men in an unfamiliar environment with a shared resentment of powerful women. When Williamson left NYPL in 1918, Seaver was not promoted to his position, and his new boss found fault with him. He decided to join the library war service program and did not return to NYPL, pursuing a library career successfully in his native Massachusetts instead.[21]

~ ~ ~

As Hasse and Williamson sparred over turf issues, they did agree in their initial opposition to calls for the establishment of a municipal reference library, which would have overlapped with their collections and services. Other cities had established such special libraries to serve city government, and the idea had been discussed in New York at least since 1908. Late in 1911, Commissioner of Accounts Raymond Fosdick proposed that NYPL create a municipal reference library. Anderson was politely receptive, suggesting that Fosdick meet with the librarians who already did a good deal of work with city officials. The trustees approved the concept soon after but without committing to establish such a library. In the meantime, another proposal came from William H. Allen of the influential Municipal Research Bureau.[22]

Much of the reform energy of the period focused on conditions in the nation's large cities, which had grown quickly to enormous size without the traditions of public administration that existed in Europe's much older cities. In

New York, establishment of the private Municipal Research Bureau in 1907 provided a new approach to urban problems, adding to the city's anticorruption reform tradition an emphasis on scientific management and research, by which the careful gathering and analysis of information would lead to the adoption of efficient operations. The bureau's founders were three bright young reformers, William H. Allen, Henry Bruère, and Frederick Cleveland, who set out to identify the methods of sound public administration. In 1911, they added a training school, which attracted hundreds of applicants to its program of preparation for government work. One of the students had prepared a case study on the need for a special library for the city's government, which Allen used as the basis of his proposal for a municipal reference library.

Hasse drafted a response with which Williamson and William Gamble concurred. She explained that all the information needs cited in the study already were being met every day in the Reference Department's special reading rooms. Now that the library had space for its collections, the staff was concentrating on "making accessible the results of years of collecting." She warned that it was a "delusion" to think that a collection could be readily duplicated for a municipal reference library; the cost of periodicals alone would be staggering. It would make more sense to employ an indexer in the central building to prepare a card index that would provide references for officials downtown at city hall instead of trying to develop a separate, overlapping library for them.

Anderson passed this on to Allen, who only persisted in urging that the library accept the services of his student to begin collecting the materials needed by city officials. Hasse, again with Williamson concurring, warned Anderson that the proposal was "unwise," as aldermen had expressed hostility to the idea at a recent meeting. She thought the city would get a municipal reference library when officials really wanted one; in the meantime, NYPL shouldn't get involved in "pulling Mr. Allen's chestnuts out of the fire." Anderson advised Allen that it was not the time to pursue something opposed by aldermen, and, in any event, amateur collecting efforts were not needed when NYPL already had "people who have had years of experience in collecting such material and know how to trace it and where to beg or buy it." This put off the issue for awhile, but a year later the city opened a municipal reference library, and a year after that NYPL took over its operation.

Hasse's reservations about a municipal reference library did not indicate any lack of enthusiasm for municipal documents, which became her priority in the new building. She had collected them from the beginning, but now she was aiming to develop bibliographies and reference service that would meet the growing demand for information about cities. This put her in conflict with Willamson over the Bureau of Municipal Research publications and with Allen over a municipal reference library, and it even seems to have led to some tensions with Billings, who was admittedly more stubborn and crotchety in old age and declining health. In March 1912, he directed that her list of municipal documents be discontinued, not made a monthly feature of the NYPL *Bulletin* as Hasse had planned; the division's journal commented that "a great deal of interest had been shown in the list and its decease was mourned."[23] Undeterred by the setback, Hasse promptly offered it to the new *National Municipal Review,* where it began appearing in the July issue, with Hasse named an associate editor, joining John Fairlie, John Lapp of the Indiana Legislative Reference Library, and Charles Beard of Columbia, who was about to shake the study of American history and government with his *Economic Interpretation of the Constitution of the United States* (1913). Hasse was the only woman editor and member of the large editorial board.[24] A month later, Billings also rebuffed her request to establish a special collection of New York City documents, with duplicates remaining in the subject classes. Hasse's note to Billings was returned with a comment from Lydenberg: "Director acknowledges it through me and requests that you and I have a talk about the scheme some time."[25]

~ ~ ~

Hasse's desire to establish a special collection of New York City documents was an indicator of her growing realization that it was problematic to have a division specializing in government documents without a comprehensive separate collection of documents. Although thousands of documents were in 229 or the adjacent stacks, many others were scattered throughout the stacks or in the other special collections. The classification Billings had designed was essentially subject-based but included special "star categories" that allowed the grouping of some types of material, such as public documents and Judaica; this system made it possible to locate many documents in or near 229, while others were simply classed by subject and located in the stacks or other reading rooms. Hasse complained that the division's work was "peculiarly difficult" because it received such a wide range of questions without having either a complete collection of documents at hand or a subject catalog.[26] Her preference for organizing documents in a separate collection went back to the beginning of her career, originally because of the greater efficiency in processing, but reference work had reinforced her belief in specialized work with government publications. With her knowledge of the use of government information, she was sometimes frustrated by flaws in NYPL's classification and would occasionally suggest pulling together a special collection of some type of heavily used documents. Other librarians seem to have opposed her ideas. Hasse's concerns about the quality of classification and subject cataloging would become a source of conflict with Lydenberg and others.

Hasse and Williamson also agreed that the library's policy of not collecting law (on the assumption that it was available in law libraries) was not realistic when many users of their divisions needed law materials at hand. Williamson argued vigorously in his annual report that, regardless of whether NYPL ever established a law division, it must acquire sets of state laws, which were essential to researchers in his division. Hasse was authorized to build the collection of statutory law and soon could report the "most noteworthy feature" of 1913 for her division: "the library now has a good law collection." She regretted that the foreign law collection remained weak but noted that few Americans could read laws in foreign languages anyway.

Hasse seems to have felt no hesitancy in suggesting changes in locations, classifications, subject headings, procedures or any other aspect of the library's operations and services, which, perhaps inevitably, irritated other division chiefs. Such suggestions were not unreasonable or unusual, however; many organizational and personnel adjustments were made during the first decade in the new building. Sometimes Hasse's suggestions were accepted, as when the mild-mannered head of cataloging, Axel Moth, agreed to her request for a change in the search procedures for documents, but, as often happens in organizations, other department heads reacted negatively to suggestions that they change procedures, relocate materials, or correct errors. William Taylor of Accessions tangled with Hasse in 1912, when she wanted to change the classification procedure that was delaying documents after they had been cataloged by her division and were being requested by readers. Documents staff would have to walk the equivalent of four city blocks to search for items that couldn't always be found in Accessions, making the division appear inefficient to users. Taylor "took a personal attitude and seemed to feel I was infringing on his domain," Hasse told Lydenberg in explaining why, as a "last resort," she decided to ignore Accessions' procedure for classification and just directly shelve some pamphlet series in 229. This may have also reflected her underlying desire to retain the documents as a special collection rather than lose them to another division by subject classification. Taking a self-righteous tone that spelled trouble ahead, Hasse told Lydenberg she had to take action in the interest of providing service to readers: "I feel it is my duty to make documents which I have collected accessible, and any little internal system which interferes with that duty I shall disregard. My present action was not taken without first consulting the proper department, and was only taken for the good of the service. It seemed the only way to effectively raise the question."

Taylor denied all fault and accused Hasse of making unnecessary problems for his department, but he finally suggested sending one of his staff to Documents to do the classifying there. Lydenberg, in what would be his continuing response to conflict, urged that "with a bit of forbearance and charity for mistakes on all parts we can work out some satisfactory arrangement." He did tell Hasse of his concern that ignoring the established system of classification deprived other divisions of material, but there was no stern warning that she must not act unilaterally.[27]

Lydenberg was a hands-off manager whose response to conflict among his bickering librarians was to urge patience, civility, and awareness that there were no perfect solutions. Reserved and absorbed in the details of collection building, he spent much of his time perusing book dealers' catalogs or indexing periodicals (for the references NYPL included in its catalog), which he would continue when staff came to his office to consult him. Even Keyes Metcalf, who greatly admired Lydenberg, admitted that he had no interest in administration and didn't spend enough time on it. He was not encouraged by the awkward lack of clarity about his responsibilities as Chief Reference Librarian in relation to Billings and Anderson, both of whom were involved in the operations of the Reference Department. Metcalf later observed that Lydenberg often disagreed with

Anderson but "never would argue with his superior and would leave the office quietly." [28]

Adjusting to new responsibilities with a detached superior could not have been easy for Hasse, but she usually was polite to Lydenberg and careful to keep him informed. Beneath the surface, however, mutual irritation was growing. In dealing with male peers, Hasse did not go out of her way to avoid conflict, and she could be indiscreet in putting her exasperation in writing, apparently not realizing that Edwin Anderson would accumulate a file of Hasse's memos as evidence that she was a classic difficult woman, selfish, bad-tempered, and unreasonable.

With the departure of Madeleine Day of the Periodical Room, who married Lydenberg in 1912, Hasse was the only woman division chief in the Reference Department. Women librarians did head departments and branches in the Circulation Department, but this was perceived as lower status work with lower status people, dealing with women, children, and immigrants. At a time when determined women were aggressively campaigning for the vote, the turmoil in the outside world probably was a factor in the increasing tension between Hasse and her male coworkers. With new leadership, the suffrage movement adopted new tactics for increased visibility, using modern advertising and publicity techniques in the mass mobilization for state referenda that were fought year after year. Women won the vote in Washington state in 1910, California in 1911, three states in 1912 (while losing three others), and Illinois in 1913. In New York the struggle went on for years, with women orating and parading in the streets and campaigning around the state in trains and automobiles. To Hasse, it was an exciting time of women demonstrating their ability to organize and publicize their cause. To some men, it was disturbing, even frightening.

Even had there been no women's movement and had Hasse been a less zealous personality, the times did not encourage calm and patience. The year 1912 was the crest of the great wave of change known as the Progressive Era, the point when mainstream, middle-class America decided that reform was essential. Change did not come without conflict, and Hasse's disputes with Williamson and Taylor were nothing compared to the political storms visible in each day's headlines or at the very doors of the library, in the case of twenty thousand suffrage supporters who marched up Fifth Avenue in May. For most of the year, the nation was transfixed by the spectacle of President Taft and his predecessor, Teddy Roosevelt, engaged in a furious battle for the Republican presidential nomination. As the spring primaries went for Roosevelt, Taft denounced his former friend and mentor, who replied so forcefully that some questioned his sanity. Roosevelt's arrival in Chicago for the convention was greeted by huge crowds chanting, "We want Teddy." In an atmosphere of high drama, he delivered the oration that ended with his stunning call to action, "We stand at Armageddon and we battle for the Lord." When the convention, chaired by the iron-willed Elihu Root, nominated Taft, Roosevelt and his supporters bolted to form a new party dedicated "to social and industrial justice." The Progressive Party's convention in August was noted for the presence of women delegates and the appearance of a woman as a platform speaker, when Jane Addams seconded

Roosevelt's nomination. The turmoil was felt in the Documents Division, where a list of Roosevelt's messages was compiled in response to "persistent demands from his friends and his enemies, who all told us the reasons why they were one or the other."[29]

The Democrats nominated their own reform candidate, Woodrow Wilson, whose career demonstrated the way in which scholarship had become a force for change. A political scientist who had written a classic study of Congress, Wilson had become prominent as the reforming president of Princeton University and governor of New Jersey. In the election, with the Republican vote split, he swept to an overwhelming electoral college victory. He and Roosevelt represented a clear vote for reform, winning forty-six states and ten million votes between them (plus a remarkable one million votes for the Socialist Eugene Debs) to Taft's two states and three million votes.

For Hasse, closely following developments in government and always tuned into the zeitgeist, it was a time to press ahead for change, ignoring any small-minded bureaucrats who stood in her way. As she wrote in the *Times* that year, if a woman librarian had real ambition and a "fixed purpose . . . there is nothing that can stop one working towards and ultimately arriving at one's goal." She might encounter difficulties with coworkers, but there was always the satisfaction of helping users and appreciation from outside for her bibliographic work and reference service. Hasse had a special thrill that fall in the appearance in her department of Vilhjalmur Stefansson, the explorer just back from more than four years in the Arctic; he wanted a particular report in the British Parliamentary papers, but the title could not be found in the indexes. After he left, Hasse identified the probable report, compared it with a paper in a geography journal mentioned by Stefansson, and notified him that they were identical except for one map. Stefansson sent a note of thanks that Hasse kept for the rest of her life, a sign of her fascination, inherited from her father, with the courage and endurance of explorers like Stefansson and later Amelia Earhart.[30]

The year ended with good news. Trustee John Cadwalader and his brother-in-law Weir Mitchell sometimes stopped to visit Hasse when in the library; Cadwalader had long been interested in her indexing of U.S. diplomatic papers, and as they chatted in December, Mitchell remarked that the Carnegie Institution ought to publish it. Cadwalader promptly asked for a description of the index to take to Washington to pursue the idea. Hasse gave him a statement prepared years earlier and sent a copy to Billings with a note mentioning that she was "startled by the singular coincidence in the dates," as the original had been prepared for him on December 8, 1903 and was now copied for Cadwalader on December 8, 1912.[31] She thus informed the quick-tempered Billings that she had merely given a plan originally prepared for him to Cadwalader, who had requested it and was responsible for any communication with the Carnegie Institution. The Carnegie board soon agreed to publish her index to diplomatic papers for the period when there was no single collection of diplomatic correspondence, from the end of *American State Papers* in 1828 to the beginning of the State Department's annual compilation in 1861. The three-volume *Index to United States Documents Relating to Foreign Affairs, 1828-1861* would be one

of Hasse's finest achievements, praised by a historian as a "justly celebrated . . .
monument of bibliographical labor and intelligent and lucid organization."[32]
With no end in sight to the state documents project, Hasse now had a second
major index to prepare for publication, in addition to another year of work to
finish indexing the Hamilton Fish papers and her monthly obligation to the *National Municipal Review*, plus the bibliographies her division prepared for the
NYPL *Bulletin*, which in 1912-13 included a list of city charters, ordinances,
and collected documents sets that took almost four hundred pages in six issues,
plus a bibliography, prepared for the influential City Club, of material related to
New York's City Plan, so thorough it went back to 1643 in its references.

~ ~ ~

A few months later, Billings told Hasse, "Don't work too hard. Take care of
yourself. There's something I want you to do." These words would haunt Hasse.
Her leader had another mission for her, but she would never know what it was,
for Billings died suddenly following surgery on March 11, 1913. Though his
retirement had been expected, losing Billings suddenly and completely to death
created a vacuum within the staff he had directed with a fatherly combination of
sternness and kindness. The grieving Hasse felt privileged to be among the staff
chosen to follow his coffin from the funeral in Georgetown to burial at Arlington National Cemetery. "As we slowly followed the flag-draped caisson over
that long road to beautiful Arlington, I was aware that I had lost a friend," she
remembered, but there also was a feeling of apprehension, a sense that "the same
evil shadow which once so shamefully fell on the A.L.A. would have to be contended with." Hasse did not explain this ominous allusion; it could have been a
general reference to the secretive and autocratic atmosphere of ALA, but written
in the context of her later bitterness towards Edwin Anderson, it may refer directly to Anderson's intrigues, always devious and behind-the-scenes. She later
said that a coworker warned, "Never get mixed up in an argument with him.
You can't find a smoother person in making you appear to be in the wrong
without committing himself." The change in administration would have been
difficult for longtime staff in any circumstances, but Hasse seems to have been
especially uneasy. A year after Billings' death, *Library Journal* urged that the
national medical library be transferred to the Library of Congress to provide
continuity with Billings' original organization, which was threatened by
"haphazard conditions" in the Surgeon General's office; Hasse soon would suspect that Billings' intentions for NYPL were also threatened, that his heritage
was being undone by lesser men.[33]

　　Wanting to keep her connection with John Cadwalader, she wrote him an
emotional note of thanks for including her in the funeral party as one of the
seven NYPL staff representatives. He assured her that she was an obvious choice
for the delegation of those Billings would have wanted to be present.[34] A year
later, Cadwalader too was dead. Elihu Root, his successor as the board's dominant figure as chairman of the Executive Committee, was as cool and remote as
Edwin Anderson. Billings and Cadwalader had taken a paternal interest in Hasse

and encouraged her work. No longer young, Hasse was now without those powerful male mentors and dealing with very different men.

Elihu Root was one of the most eminent Americans of his time, former secretary of state and secretary of war, winner of the Nobel Peace Prize, senator from New York, leader of every conceivable civic endeavor, counselor to Roosevelt, Carnegie (longtime chair of the boards of both the Carnegie Corporation and the Carnegie Institution), and many others of the rich and powerful. He also was the man who had led the fight against women's suffrage in New York for twenty years. In a city where New Women were so visible and vibrant with the thrill of new roles, Root held to the view that women must be protected from life: "In politics there is struggle, strife, contention, bitterness, heart-burning, excitement, agitation, everything which is adverse to the true character of woman. . . . Woman in strife becomes hard, harsh, unlovable, repulsive; as far removed from that gentle creature to whom we all owe allegiance and to whom we confess submission, as the heaven is removed from the earth." The purpose of government is protection, and "the duty and right of protection rests with the male . . . and I, for one, will never consent to part with the divine right of protecting my wife, my daughter, the women whom I love and the women whom I respect, exercising the birthright of man, and place that high duty in the weak and nerveless hands of those designed by God to be protected rather than to engage in the stern warfare of government."[35] Root might feel protective of women he loved and respected, but Hasse would learn how punitive he could be towards a woman who was not a "gentle creature."

Root's opposition to women's suffrage was not due only to Victorian delusions about the angelic female. As a top Wall Street lawyer, he was closely identified with the financial interests that fought suffrage from fear that women voters would support reforms they opposed. Root had once been close to Teddy Roosevelt, who had the highest opinion of him until 1912, when Root ruthlessly chaired the Republican convention that rejected Roosevelt and reform. In the Senate, he was a leading opponent of Wilson's New Freedom legislation. He would lose that fight, and finally he would lose the battle against women voting. In 1912, the shrewd suffrage organizer Carrie Chapman Catt decided that New York, the most populous state, must be won and began to organize the massive campaign that would involve "all sorts of novel techniques and . . . grassroots canvassing never before seen on such a scale." It would take five years to prevail, and for Root, those years would be a nightmare of assertive, noisy women parading, orating, *demanding* the right to vote.[36]

Edwin Anderson expressed no public opinion on women's suffrage or anything else. He did not write for publication and seldom spoke in public, aside from his talks on the dangers of dime novels and his presidential address to ALA, which surprised the members with a complaint about the tariff on imported books instead of the usual effort to inspire with a vision of the profession. In 1912, however, he participated in a panel discussion where he called for ALA attention to the importance of recruiting college-educated men to library work. To the suggestion that the "housewifely" routines taught by library schools were unappealing to men, he asserted that the methods learned in library school had been useful to him. The schools could not be expected to impart wisdom or administrative talent, he said, for that was "the gift of the gods." Since such ability was inborn, Anderson's priority was hiring staff who had the special talent. Not surprisingly, he found that aptitude for management in people much like himself: mostly old-stock midwestern men with college and library school degrees. The men he hired were happy to repeat Anderson's constantly reiterated view that employing good people was his most important task, establishing the conventional wisdom that Anderson's greatest contribution was his ability to identify and hire outstanding talent. His protégés formed an old boy network that would advance into administrative positions in other large libraries, always repeating the narrative of Anderson's special talent for spotting librarians with executive ability.

In the hope of attracting men to library school with the lure of New York City and work experience in NYPL, Anderson persuaded Andrew Carnegie to fund a training school at NYPL. It was headed by his sister-in-law, Mary Wright Plummer, who left her longtime position at Pratt to start the new program. Billings had not required the library school credential, hiring people with a mix of education, languages, and experience, and he apparently had little respect for the "profession," commenting on the smug atmosphere at an ALA conference: "There are about four hundred librarians here and probably there were never so many people together so thoroughly satisfied with their own knowledge."[37] In Billings' last years, several men without library school degrees were hired for the new building, including Williamson, Seaver, Frank Waite, and Rob Henderson. But now *Library Journal* greeted Anderson's accession with special praise for his "full training of the professional school" and the hope, which would have annoyed Billings, that his record would "prove worthy of comparison with the great man who has gone, and who came to his work without those advantages of professional training which later librarians enjoy."[38] Once established as director, Anderson was determined to improve the staff by employing young men with library school training. Keyes Metcalf and Charles McCombs were hired in 1913, followed by Paul North Rice and Rollin Sawyer in 1914, and Carl Cannon in 1917. If Metcalf's views are typical, they were scornful of the older librarians and eager to establish themselves as executives who would make the library efficient. All would become enemies of Hasse, as would a prominent female library school graduate, Minnie Sears, hired in 1914 to improve subject cataloging and generally shape up the Cataloging Division as assistant to its diffident head, Axel Moth, a Dane who knew many languages and had a European university education but lacked a library school certificate.

Metcalf and McCombs were both Ohioans (as were Lydenberg, Taylor, and Williamson), and they soon became friends and allies, but their relations with others were not so congenial as they encountered problems indicative of Lydenberg's often mystifying management. Metcalf had been promised a job without even applying, as Anderson was eager to hire a man from the NYPL school's first class. Metcalf felt well qualified, since he had experience as assistant to his brother-in-law, Azariah Root, librarian of Oberlin College, and had worked almost full-time in the various reading rooms at NYPL as a student. When he went to the administrative office for his formal offer, Anderson was busy, but Lydenberg told him he could supervise the main book stack for $75 a month; despite Metcalf's experience in the reading rooms, Lydenberg said he wasn't ready to work with the public. Instead he was given a major responsibility for which he wasn't particularly prepared, dealing with the problems of the huge central stacks and its staff of young men. When Metcalf started work in July, he was infuriated to learn that McCombs, hired by Anderson to supervise the main reading room, was paid $125. McCombs' qualifications didn't seem markedly superior to his—he had worked in the library throughout his undergraduate years at Ohio State and briefly in the Library of Congress after graduating from the Albany library school—and Metcalf felt that Lydenberg had taken advantage of him. Since there was no schedule of salaries, such resentment was common as staff members discovered that others were better paid. Metcalf seethed in silence for months before complaining that he had chosen the wrong profession; Lydenberg made no reply, but his salary was raised to $100 in January 1914. There was some consolation for Metcalf to learn that his $75 salary was more than any of the women in his class were earning.[39]

McCombs may have been making more money, but his problems were worse. Both he and Metcalf were supervised by C. H. A. Bjerregaard, the elderly chief of the Readers Division, but Bjerregaard seldom descended into the stacks to see Metcalf. McCombs, however, was intensely disliked by Bjerregaard and the man who had been his chief assistant before McCombs' appointment. Their constant criticism was so distressing that Metcalf thought the administration should intervene to stop the harassment, but when he spoke to Lydenberg about it, the reply was only, "If McCombs is the man we want there, he will pull through." Eventually the resentful assistant was transferred, and McCombs survived what Metcalf decided was a kind of test of whether he was "tough enough." Gradually, Metcalf concluded that aspects of Lydenberg's behavior that seemed puzzling or disturbing often were such indirect tests. Though they had many disagreements over the years, Metcalf ultimately put Lydenberg "at the top of my list of great librarians," but in the early years of their acquaintance, he seemed "one of the most conservative men I had ever known, politically and in other ways." Lydenberg's attitude towards the young library school graduates was summed up by his gruff response to one of Metcalf's complaints: "When are you going to grow up?"[40]

One man Metcalf could discuss his troubles with was Frank Waite, another midwesterner, who had come from St. Louis to help with the move and then became head of the new Information Division. Waite was as conservative as Lydenberg, a man "who objected vigorously to shifting from the position he was in to another," and in his later years he became withdrawn from inability to tolerate new people, but for most of his long career, he showed "a genius for becoming well acquainted with the younger men," often inviting them home to meet his wife and three daughters, all of whom married NYPL librarians.[41]

With Anderson and Waite both mentoring the younger men, Hasse soon saw signs of cliques and favoritism. From the beginning of her career, she had been a star, encouraged to tackle big projects and new challenges that had

brought her praise and prominence. Now, in middle age, she found herself dealing with administrators who wanted her to do her job dutifully and quietly,
without bothering them. Uneasy about the new administration, Hasse probably
wondered if she should follow those who left for other employment. Bostwick
departed in 1909, and Everett Perry, who was close to Billings and on good
terms with Hasse, left in 1911 to head Los Angeles Public Library. When such
men saw no opportunity for advancement at NYPL, directorships in other cities
were readily available, but, as a woman and with no higher education, Hasse's
opportunities were limited. In her prime, she found herself bumping against
what would later be known as the glass ceiling; despite being a leader in an occupation that was mostly women, she had little opportunity for advancement.
Directorships of large libraries rarely went to women, usually only when they
had long service as assistant to a departing man. Preference for men to head library schools was increasing, as Hasse could observe at Pratt, where a man succeeded Mary Wright Plummer, creating decades of tension with the passed-over
assistant director, the "tart-tongued and assertive" Josephine Rathbone.[42] At the
Library of Congress, Herbert Putnam preferred men as department heads. Hasse
probably assumed she could always get another job if necessary, but leaving
would be difficult when she had invested so much in the Documents Division
as a kind of work of art and in NYPL as the ideal of a great urban public library.
NYPL was the base that enabled her to do her bibliographic work; it had given
her prestige and opportunities not readily available elsewhere, at a time when
there were few American research libraries. And she had complicated her life by
adopting a child, making it even harder to relocate or accept a lower salary.

Feeling stressed after Billings' death, Hasse complained about the street
noise when her division's windows were open that summer, but she pressed on
with all her projects, readying the first volume of the foreign affairs index for
printing, finishing the New Jersey and Pennsylvania volumes of the state documents index, and completing her index of the Hamilton Fish papers. She was
"specializing in city documents," producing bibliographies on municipal topics
for the NYPL *Bulletin*, and along with her bibliography in the *National Municipal Review,* she now offered its readers reference service for individual questions, which brought inquiries by phone and letter from around the country.[43]
Asked by a graduate student at Berkeley if she had a bibliography on municipal
efficiency, she offered to prepare one. After corresponding about definitions and
coverage, Hasse produced an initial "couple of hundred cards" within a month,
but the project ended with arrival of a new book covering the subject.[44]

~ ~ ~

As Hasse intensified her work with municipal documents, she returned to addressing library meetings in an effort to stir interest in how public libraries
could support change in their communities. In September 1913, she appeared at
the conference of the New York Library Association to urge the "heresy" of
"Socialized Bibliography."[45] Always ready to attack complacency, Hasse sharply
criticized public libraries for maintaining costly buildings and catalogs while

doing little to meet the information needs of their communities:

> It employs countless tireless women to erect that curious structure, the catalog. It is wasting its substance in the endless revision of blundering experiments. The average public library is pathetically deficient in . . . meeting the spirit of the time. It is being called on for bread and it gives a stone. The establishment of special libraries, of municipal reference libraries, is only an expression of the failure of the average public library to grasp the golden opportunity. . . . I know very well that there are individual, or groups of individual, progressives who are breaking away from convention and orthodoxy, but collectively I doubt we are meeting our obligations.

Pointing to the campaigns of the public health movement, she urged librarians to be equally active in analyzing and meeting the information needs of their communities. Her vision was of "expertly trained" librarians who would "work largely outside the library" to learn the needs of civic organizations, government officials, and business, "to discover every instance where the library's resources could be made to be of service." Back in the library, other librarians would maintain "a definitive index of information, especially that contained in periodicals, society proceedings and public documents," updated daily.

> Socialized bibliography will reduce orthodox cataloging to a minimum by centralization and will then equip each library with a card directory of every man, woman and institution, club and organization in the city and its environs interested in a special subject or subjects. Library workers will be expertly trained to serve these specialists intelligently. It will be required of them to be reasonably familiar with local and national questions not only of the day but of the day before and the day after. . . . There will be close cooperation between the outside and the inside force, and can you not see the real, practical civic service that socialized bibliography may be made to render? It will make the library a city-wide, or even a nation-wide concrete reality, not as now often is the case, an abstraction you hear about casually, if you hear about it at all. As I visualize the plan it lends itself to a variety of adaptation, but always with the result that it gets over to the people. This the average public library has not yet learned to do.

An unsigned editorial mildly reproved Hasse for the awkwardness of the term "socialized bibliography," but praised her "saving heresy," noting that "no one can read Miss Hasse's earnest pleas without realizing the possibilities that are open to public libraries for new life and enlarged service, in the method she outlines." The writer summarized Hasse's vision as three key ideas, "none of which has received due emphasis thus far in the common management of the library." [46]

Dana also appreciated her intentions, but with some skepticism: "Socialized bibliography: I don't see how you can do it." His staff's effort to keep up with the news was time-consuming enough, and how they "ever could get the money . . . for assistants who could and would gather this information, then gather information about those who need it, and then put the former in the hands of the latter, I can't see." Still he urged Hasse to join him for lunch and "prove to us that you are right—as I presume you are." Chronically unhappy with the library establishment, Dana included some typically frank comments: "I have reached the point where I feel like fighting whenever I come near a group of librarians, especially the Council, the Institute, or the ALA. I don't think they have done themselves credit or have added anything to the standing of our profession."[47] He had no idea, of course, that his letters would end up in Anderson's evidence against Hasse, as guilt by association with a man resented for his critical outlook and founding of the Special Libraries Association. When Dana wrote of his exasperation with ALA, Edwin Anderson was serving as its president.

In November 1913, the reform spirit swept New York with the election of Mayor John Purroy Mitchel, who was closely associated with the Municipal Research Bureau. This probably contributed to Hasse's messianic spirit when she addressed the state librarians a few months later. James Wyer had asked her to speak on "recent state and city bibliographic enterprises," but Hasse decided her audience already was informed on that topic and should hear instead her vision of a "city bibliography which I hope may be an enterprise of tomorrow."[48] Pointing to the "awakened civic consciousness of the American people" as a movement sweeping the country, she urged librarians to take responsibility for a systematic, uniform, national civic information service based on an established standard nomenclature and reporting current developments and trends not to be found in conventional bibliography.

> Don't wait for books and magazine articles. Watch the newspapers, and by all means watch the conventions of men who are promoting live issues. The proceedings of a snow removal conference in Philadelphia, a traffic discussion in New York City, a cooperative farmers' meeting in Iowa, an agricultural credit conference in Wisconsin, don't get into books or magazines and consequently not into conventional bibliography. Yet the material can all be had and if you are running the right kind of a municipal or any other reference library, it is what your readers want.

Hasse ended with the suggestion that the National Municipal League and the federal Bureau of Education be enlisted in an effort led by libraries: "It is most eminently the place of the public library, the most splendidly democratic of our institutions, to promote such a bibliography." Her concept was taken up by the Municipal League the next year, when Hasse became the chair of its new Committee on Civic Bibliography.

~ ~ ~

In the meantime, Hasse had still another project, one that would involve her in a stunning turn in the course of history. ALA had decided to provide an exhibit for the Leipzig Exposition of the Book and Graphic Arts, a celebration of printing and books in Germany's publishing center, in the summer of 1914. Although European countries were providing impressive exhibits, Congress declined to appropriate funds for United States participation, despite the urging of President Wilson and the *New York Times,* so ALA would be the main representative of American print culture. German-speaking librarians were needed to staff the exhibit, and Hasse took responsibility for August and September. She had never been to her ancestral homeland, and now she, the American New Woman personified, would officially represent American libraries in the region where her father and grandparents had once lived. Her father wrote of relatives who might still be there and reminisced about his student days in Leipzig, of dueling societies and suppers of "diche milch . . . und schwarzbrodt."[49]

As Hasse prepared to sail on July 20, there were reports of rising tensions among the European powers stemming from the assassination of the Austrian Archduke Franz Ferdinand, but few expected that the incident in the Balkans would have serious impact. In a fatal miscalculation, Austria issued a provocative ultimatum to Serbia on July 24, and France and Germany mobilized. Hasse arrived in a Europe that seemed suddenly caught in an inexorable surge towards war. On August 4, Germany invaded neutral Belgium in a sweep towards Paris and the channel ports. The next day, Britain declared war, and Europe fell into the abyss that would destroy so many bright hopes for the new century.

Americans, including many librarians touring Europe en route to Leipzig, now fled in panic to Paris and London, desperate to get home, but Hasse remained at her post. The exposition was still open, and she was in no danger in the early days of a war that was expected to be over in months. Attendance was not heavy, so she had ample time to learn about Germany. Adjoining her area were the exhibits of the Berlin State Library and the Leipzig University Library, putting her in daily contact with German librarians, and she also learned about the library school, Germany's first, that opened that fall in Leipzig. All around her was the drama of a nation mobilizing for war with German efficiency and a tribal fervor that swept even the Reichstag's large group of Social Democrats into abandoning their antiwar principles to support the fight against encircling enemies, Russia, France, and Britain. In a proclamation "To the Civilized World," ninety-three distinguished German scientists, scholars, and artists insisted that Germany bore no blame for the war and committed no atrocities. Hasse's first month in Leipzig coincided with the crucial period of the German advance through Belgium from August 4 to 23, when the British and French were able to stop the German army but not defeat it, setting the stalemate that would last for four years of slaughter on the Western Front. She remained through October, not able to get home until November 11.[50]

Hasse's presence in Germany in 1914 would do her great damage when the United States eventually entered the war, and little trace of a fascinating experience that became a painful subject remains in her papers. There is practically nothing about what she saw and whom she met. It would be interesting to know if she discussed cataloging with the German librarians; since the German cataloging code, commonly known as the "Prussian Instructions," did not recognize corporate entry, Hasse could have received reinforcement for her skepticism about the value of government agency entries, which would be a source of conflict back at NYPL. Soon after her return, she reviewed a new Austrian library periodical and made passing mention of Austrians' "unit and team efficiency," but said nothing of personal observations. She brought material from the Leipzig library school to Mary Wright Plummer and wrote a short piece about it for *Public Libraries,* noting that several men had applied to attend a "technical women's school in Germany, where opinion as to the progress of women is supposed to be so conservative."[51] Several months later, she mentioned having observed German shepherd dogs, "whose intelligence seemed almost human," being trained for work on the battlefield.[52] Some harmless actions would be held against her, such as appearing at a library reception in "German peasant dress," presumably a dirndl acquired on her trip, and presenting the German viewpoint at a staff program where Richard Gottheil, who had been in France in 1914, gave the French perspective. More than a half century later, Keyes Metcalf remembered it as a "rather heated" exchange at a time when most Americans wished to remain neutral.[53] As *Library Journal* editorialized, "Our sympathy is with each and all of the contestants, our only hope an early return of peace."[54] At year's end, with opposing armies entrenched in Flanders, President Wilson declared it a "war with which we have nothing to do."

~ ~ ~

Once back at work, Hasse would not have had Germany foremost in her mind, for she returned to find changes of great importance to her career. Williamson and Seaver were gone, having transferred to the Municipal Reference Library, and Hasse was asked to take over the Economics Division, which would merge with the Documents Division. Her salary was raised to $3,000, making her one of the best-paid women librarians in a field where women rarely earned more than $2,000. Her new salary was $360 more than she would have received in 1915 as documents chief alone, a substantial increase but less impressive relative to taking on what had been two full-time jobs.[55] She would receive no further raises during a period when the cost of living soared in New York, and she may have heard that Williamson was making more.

Although her new position seemed to be a promotion, it soon would be clear that Anderson regarded Hasse as a problem, not a team player in the Reference Department. This raises the question of why he didn't move her to the Municipal Reference Library instead of Williamson. She had expressed skepticism about the need for such a library, but so had Williamson, and Hasse had a national reputation for her work with municipal documents and had helped with a course on municipal reference in the NYPL library school. A few months after Williamson's move, she addressed the Connecticut Library Association on the very subject of municipal reference.[56] It was her usual thoroughly researched account of the history and function of this new kind of library, operated as a branch of the public library within city hall. Unlike the municipal research bureau concept promoted by William Allen and the legislative reference library movement, which "owes its recognition wholly to the hammer and tongs method of its originator, Charles McCarthy," municipal reference libraries had not been "pushed in the same energetic manner," Hasse said, probably reflecting a desire to be that promoter and her doubts that Williamson had the energy of men like Allen and McCarthy. In effect, however, Hasse was operating a municipal reference library for cities all over the country, so she could enjoy the prospects for an expanded division, relieved to be free of the tensions with Williamson and Seaver.

Anderson, who was always ready to promote young men to advantageous positions, said at the time that he and city officials thought a man should head the Municipal Reference Library.[57] Williamson was the kind of man he preferred in a job that reported directly to him and represented NYPL at city hall. Williamson later claimed that the move was not of his choosing but was pressed by Anderson. Since early in 1914, however, Williamson had been discussing the library with Henry Bruère, who had moved from the Municipal Research Bureau to a powerful position as the new mayor's chamberlain.[58] There is no indication that Bruère knew of Hasse's earlier dismissive comments about "Mr. Brunère," but, with his research orientation, he would have been impressed by Williamson's doctorate and experience in the Economics Division. With Bruère's influence in the mayor's office, there was much emphasis on research and scientific methods of public administration, making the Municipal Reference Library an attractive career move for Williamson.

When Hasse later accused Anderson of personal animosity, he could point to having promoted her and raised her salary as evidence of his good intentions. He may have hoped that combining the two divisions would eliminate a source of conflict, while satisfying Hasse's ambition and giving Williamson a promising new situation. It would also reduce costs, a major concern as he found the Reference Department's endowment inadequate to cover its operations, with prices rising and the value of the endowment declining in an atmosphere of economic uncertainty. A more cynical interpretation would be that he eliminated the "separate and independent" Documents Division that was Hasse's bastion, established by Billings and praised by *Library Journal*, and then undercut her in ways that seemed intended to pressure her to leave. What appeared to be an honor and an opportunity was instead the beginning of the end of her career at NYPL.

But Hasse, always looking forward to new challenges, was more enthusiastic and dedicated than ever as 1914 ended. As usual, she was encouraged by the appreciation of those she helped in the library that December. A young woman about to start work at Virginia's legislative reference bureau sent thanks for an evening of "helpful advice and generous interest." A college professor was effusive in his gratitude for her help on a Saturday afternoon in finding data on European police systems and then following up with a list of the titles of heads of police departments of Zurich, Bern, Budapest, and Copenhagen. He acknowledged her "enormous sacrifice of time" and wished he could make some return "for your unfailing kindness on this as on all previous occasions."[59]

Notes

1. LJ 36 (May 1911): 217.
2. Harry Lydenberg, "Moving the New York Public Library," LJ 36 (June 1911): 296-97; Adelaide Hasse, *The Compensations of Librarianship* (privately published, 1919),12; Keyes Metcalf, *Random Recollections of an Anachronism* (New York: Readex Books, 1980), 144.
3. "Dedication of the New York Public Library," LJ 36 (June 1911): 293-95.
4. "The New Building of the New York Public Library," LJ 36 (May 1911): 224; William Gamble, "Technology and Patent Divisions of the New York Public Library," LJ 36 (Dec. 1911): 634-35; Billings to AH, 21 May 1912, AH-LC.
5. "New Building," LJ 36: 225; NYPL 1912 Annual Report.
6. Information about the Documents Division is from NYPL 1911-14 Annual Reports and the 1912 journal, consisting of monthly accounts of the division's work by Margarite Lawlor, AH-CB.
7. LJ 37 (Aug. 1912): 417, 439.
8. Adelaide Hasse, "What a Girl Should Know Who Wants to Be a Librarian," *New York Times*, 1 Dec. 1912; LJ 36 (Dec. 1911); 610; AH to Bowker, 23 Dec. 1911, Bowker papers, NYPL.
9. Fairlie to AH, 5 Dec. 1911, AH reply, n.d., AH-NY. Her bibliography first appeared in the NYPL *Bulletin*, Jan. 1912.
10. *New York Evening Mail*, 17 Sept. 1915.
11. Adelaide Fielding Kerr to David Laughlin, 3 Oct. 1990, in possession of the author. Kerr was AH's niece, recalling what she heard from family and friends. Leslie Maynard's military records, AH-LC, give his birth date as 23 July 1908, in Hartford, Connecticut. The 1910 census lists him in Hartford in some sort of orphanage or foster care in which sixteen children of various ages and last names are listed as "boarders," their parents "unknown."
12. Metcalf, *Random*, 294.
13. Ibid., 126, 130-31, 135-36.
14. "Comments of Dr Williamson," n.d., AH-CB.
15. NYPL 1909 Annual Report.
16. Paul Winkler, *The Greatest of Greatness: The Life and Work of Charles C. Williamson* (Metuchen, NJ: Scarecrow Press, 1992), 51-77.
17. Hasse, *Compensations*, 12.
18. Documents Division journal, Sept. 1912, includes both comments about the incident and copies of the letters, AH to Lydenberg, 11 Sept. 1912, and AH to Williamson, 7 Sept. 1912. The latter is also quoted in "Comments of Dr. Williamson," AH-CB, and Winkler's biography of Williamson.
19. "Comments of Dr. Williamson," AH-CB.
20. *ALA Bulletin* 10 (1916 conference proceedings): 446; LJ 41 (Aug. 1916): 602.
21. Barry Seaver, *The Career of Rebecca Browning Rankin, the Municipal Reference Librarian of the City of New York, 1920-1952* (Diss., University of North Carolina, Chapel Hill, 1997), 21, 40.
22. Fosdick and Allen correspondence and AH comments to Anderson, 13 Feb., 20 March 1912, all RG 6, Director's Office, Municipal Reference Branch file, NYPL archives.

23. AH to John Fairlie, 11 April 1912, AH-NY; Documents Division journal, April 1912, AH-CB.

24. Adelaide Hasse, "Recent Municipal Documents," *National Municipal Review* (July 1912-Dec. 1916).

25. AH to Billings, 12 April 1912, Lydenberg to AH, same date, both AH-CB.

26. NYPL Annual Report, 1912, 1913.

27. AH to Lydenberg, Taylor to Lydenberg, Lydenberg to AH, all 13 June 1912, AH-CB; Documents Division journal, June and Sept. 1912, AH-CB.

28. Metcalf, *Random*, 131, 134-35, 121.

29. Documents Division journal, Oct. 1912, AH-CB.

30. Hasse, "What a Girl Should Know"; AH to Stefansson, 7, 25 Oct. 1912, Stefansson to AH, 5 Nov. 1912, AH-LC.

31. AH to Billings, 9 Dec. 1912, AH-CB.

32. Samuel Flagg Bemis, *Guide to the Diplomatic History of the U.S., 1775-1921* (Washington: GPO, 1935), 314.

33. Hasse, *Compensations*, 13, 21; LJ 39 (June 1914): 417.

34. Cadwalader to AH, 17 March 1913, AH-LC.

35. Quoted in Philip Jessup, *Elihu Root* (New York: Dodd, Mead, 1938), 178.

36. Eleanor Flexner, *Century of Struggle: The Woman's Rights Movement in the U.S.* (Cambridge: Harvard University Press, 1959), 301-4; William O'Neill, *Everyone Was Brave: A History of Feminism in America* (New York: Quadrangle Books, 1971), 124.

37. Quoted in Dennis Thomison, *A History of the Americann Library Association* (Chicago: ALA, 1978), 49.

38. LJ 38 (June 1913): 314.

39. Metcalf, *Random*, 128-30.

40. Ibid., 126-30.

41. Ibid., 144, 147-49.

42. Barbara Brand, "Pratt Institute Library School: The Perils of Professionalization," in Suzanne Hildenbrand, ed., *Reclaiming the American Library Past: Writing the Women In* (Norwood, NJ: Ablex, 1996), 255.

43. *National Municipal Review* 2 (April 1913): 353. The editor announces that "questions requiring documentary research" will be answered "through the cordial cooperation of Miss Hasse, who has expressed her willingness to make the bibliography department a library service department for the *National Municipal Review*."

44. AH to Charles Haines, 21 Aug. 1913, AH-NY; AH exchange with J. R. Douglas, Oct.- Dec. 1913, AH-NY.

45. Adelaide Hasse, "Socialized Bibliography," *New York Libraries* 4 (Nov. 1913): 11-12.

46. *New York Libraries* 4 (Nov. 1913): 5.

47. Dana to AH, 15 Jan. 1914, AH-CB.

48. Adelaide Hasse, "A Bibliographic Enterprise," *ALA Bulletin* 8 (1914 conference proceedings): 306-9.

49. Hermann Hasse to AH, 5 June 1914, AH-LC.

50. LJ 39 (Sept. 1914): 657, (Oct. 1914): 768-69, (Dec. 1914): 881, 920.

51. Adelaide Hasse, review of *Beitrage zur Bibliotheksverwaltung*, LJ 40 (April 1915): 279; Plummer to AH, 17 Nov. 1914, AH-CB; Adelaide Hasse, "A New Library School in Germany," PL 19 (Dec. 1914): 470.

52. AH to Jesse D. Burks, 19 March 1915, AH-NY.

53. U.S. Federal Bureau of Investigation (1922) File 62-329; Metcalf, *Random*, 181.

54. LJ 39 (Sept. 1914): 657.

55. Extract from minutes of Executive Committee meeting, 4 Dec. 1914, AH-CB.

56. Adelaide Hasse, "Municipal Reference Libraries," LJ 40 (Oct. 1915): 699-703.

57. Seaver, *Rankin,* 46.

58. Winkler, *Greatest*, 83-85.

59. Mabel Haines to AH, 1 Jan. 1915, AH-NY; Jacob Hartmann to AH, 15 Dec. 1914, AH-NY.

Chapter 7

Economics Division, 1915-1916

Leading the new Documents and Economics Division was Hasse's opportunity to expand and promote information services to government, business, and reformers. With her confidence that the division was performing vital work in the great world, she continued to encourage esprit de corps in her staff, despite salaries that were poor and growing worse. The years 1915 through 1918 would be intensely productive as Hasse threw herself into speaking, teaching, publishing, and reference work that she pursued with her unfailing energy.

Hasse seems initially to have referred to the new department as the Documents Division, as though her unit had absorbed the Economics Division. Others referred to it as the Economics and Public Documents Division, but gradually it became known as the Economics Division. Hasse pressed ahead with her development and promotion of the division, having a leaflet about its resources printed and contacting individuals and companies with offers of assistance. With two rooms now available, she allowed typewriters in one, a very popular innovation. Her version of the division's transformation was described by an admiring journalist several years later:

> [W]hen she took charge of the Division of Economics, a few students, some elderly habitués of the library, and an occasional woman would drift in, glance over a book or two, and drift out again. No real use was being made of the department; the books remained untouched on the shelves; the seats were empty. . . . [T]oday you almost have to reserve a seat in advance if you want to use this department. The rooms are crowded with readers, young and old, and the clack of four or five typewriters can be heard. One glance will show that here are gathered serious workers, men and women who have come for valuable information. And Miss Hasse has accomplished this miracle merely by applying business methods to her department. "I had something to sell" she said, "and I sold it. . . . I realized . . . library service must be sold just as any other goods are marketed. So I adopted a few business methods and the results came, slowly but surely." . . . So to individual and business corporations she sent cards saying: "Why build up enormous,

expensive libraries which can never be as good as ours when you have our library right at hand? . . . Send your men here with your typewriters. I'll give them a special room. . . . Tell me what subjects you want information on, and I will see that all the available material is placed at your disposal. Our office is for you and it is free of charge. Please consult us."[1]

This was the vision that Hasse promoted to many admirers in a narrative that Charles Williamson would have indignantly disputed. He took pride in having tripled the division's collection, prepared bibliographies on current topics, and developed "ever-widening use," but he was no match for Hasse's energetic publicity. She cultivated an intensely busy atmosphere with an eager young staff, and use increased greatly over the next few years, in part because of research on war-related issues.

The zeitgeist continued to encourage Hasse's zealous temperament. President Wilson had declared reform accomplished at the end of 1914, but there was still plenty of reforming energy in New York, particularly among women fighting for emancipation. The suffrage campaign was defeated at the polls in 1915 but pressed on to another referendum in 1917, providing constant examples of women grasping every means to advocate their cause. Hasse particularly admired Inez Milholland, the glamorous young Vassar graduate who was the Joan of Arc of the New York suffrage movement until her untimely death in 1916. One of those influenced by the militant tactics of British suffrage campaigners, Milholland had told the press that men "never won much freedom . . . without fighting for it. They have used the boycott, the gun, the sword, violence of all kinds. If we borrow men's methods . . . it is because the men refuse to do us justice."[2]

Librarians were not visible among the suffragists—many prominent women librarians opposed the suffrage amendment—but one of the most passionate campaigners was an NYPL clerical worker named Maud Malone, who organized the first open-air suffrage rally (considered a radical innovation) and was notorious for adopting the British tactic of aggressively disrupting political speakers, even Theodore Roosevelt and Woodrow Wilson, with demands for women's suffrage. Malone frequently created uproars that led to her forcible removal and even a jail sentence, the first American to be imprisoned for suffrage protest. A judge denounced her as "one of those scatter-brained, loose-tongued, ill-mannered viragoes," but it all supported Malone's goal of publicizing the cause and making it clear that women would not stop demanding civil rights, even if it meant jail.[3]

Malone was not the only crusading woman to face imprisonment in New York; in 1914, Margaret Sanger was indicted and fled the country to avoid jail for sending birth control information through the mails in her magazine, the alarmingly titled *Woman Rebel,* with its equally alarming motto, "No Gods, No Masters." She returned in 1916 to open the first American birth control clinic and soon was arrested and sentenced to thirty days in jail. Sanger later recalled the bold spirit of the time: "I defined a woman's duty, 'To look the world in the face with a go-to-hell look in the eyes; to have an idea; to speak and act in defiance of convention.' It was a marvelous time to say what we wished. All America was a Hyde Park corner as far as criticism and challenging thought were concerned."[4]

Hasse described herself as "keenly interested in the woman movement and in suffrage incidentally," indicating that she saw the vote as only a part of emancipation.[5] She was most visible in regard to economic status, especially in publicizing careers for women in libraries by speaking, writing, and giving press interviews. From her first day at NYPL, her career had drawn the attention of the many local newspapers, and her new position attracted fresh interest. A feature in the *Evening Mail* used Hasse's single motherhood as an attention-getting lead, but mostly it was about her work, describing her as "probably the most learned woman in New York and certainly the highest authority in the world on public documents and technical reports." Hasse provided colorful tales of the varied users of the Economics Division and their needs, all of which were met with the expert aid of Hasse and her "able assistant," Joanna Strange. Her work was "as full of variety as a vaudeville show" as she assisted "men and women whose names are famous for doing big things in the world."[6]

One of the division's users, Eva vom Baur, a young Barnard graduate who edited the women's page of the *Evening Sun* and directed a program on vocations for women at New York University, asked Hasse to speak in her lecture series on women's work. Hasse sought suggestions from Dana, teasingly consulting "an exponent of conservatism" to balance her "radical and unorthodox" ideas about women librarians. Dana replied with sardonic comments about "library mediocrities" that Hasse kept permanently in her personal papers. His analysis influenced her thinking and encouraged her increasingly frank comments about library working conditions, including the inadequacies of library administrators and the discrimination against women. To Dana, women librarians were "as good as conditions permit," which wasn't very good when both teaching and business offered more rewards to educated women. Like Kelso, he disdained the sentimentality of children's librarians, "women of extreme motherly temperament who are ready to feel they are doing the world good merely because they feel good while doing it." As a "pioneer land" without strong traditions of education, the library profession would have to rely on the "half-prepared," and women certainly had brought "a fine lot of ideas (and many not so fine!) and a boundless zeal" that was doing some good. The "hardships of women in library work" he attributed "largely to the dreadful fact that all women are of a servile class, and partly to the fact that they are just now beginning to get out of their condition of servility." The biggest problem was that "women in libraries are not sufficiently stimulated to learn, most of them do nothing . . . but float along." The need was for "library women of brains [to] set forth on a campaign to promote the continuous and all pervading education of women in libraries."[7]

Hasse's lecture was the basis for an article for the *Hunter College Bulletin* that emphasized the demands of library work, asking, "Have you a reasonable amount of intelligence, common sense, scholarship, general knowledge, accuracy, stick-to-it-iveness, tact, health, enthusiasm, open-mindedness, executive ability, sympathy, presence, reasonableness, patience, imagination, interest in all kinds of people, and in everything in the world, inside and outside of books?" She advised that the main reason for getting a library school degree was to qualify for better pay, although one could learn much from on-the-job training. Women should not anticipate good pay, however: "Being women, you need never expect anything wonderful in the way of the salaries. It's the men in the library profession who command the big salaries. But you can command a living wage, and perhaps help to persuade the world that equal pay for equal work is absolutely essential in this profession as in any other." Instead, the rewards would be "a great deal of joy" from "constantly learning" and dealing with all sorts of people in work where "you will never be bored." Such public mention of pay equity in libraries was unusual and probably stirred alarm among library directors, particularly at NYPL, with its secrecy about salaries in a city where women teachers had recently won their battle for equal pay.[8]

Women were campaigning for more than their civil and economic rights. They were active in all areas of reform, including those that threatened male indulgences by closing brothels and banning the sale of liquor. And with the European war bogged down in slaughter on an unparalleled scale, American women were campaigning for peace, trying both to stop the war and keep the United States neutral. There were also fears that war, with its emphasis on men as warriors, would undercut the effort to establish women's equality. Hasse's sister Elsa was deeply involved in both the peace and suffrage movements.

Tensions over the neutrality policy grew as the war dragged on. Emotions were stirred by British propaganda about atrocities by the "Huns," much of which later was found to be false, but German actions often seemed designed to prove the British claims. American suspicions of Germany were aroused by the sinking of the *Lusitania* in May 1915, followed in August by the dramatic seizure of a briefcase containing German government plans to influence American opinion and prevent Britain from buying supplies. The papers were turned over to the *New York World*, which reported them as sensational evidence of German plots, though Germany and its sympathizers argued that its actions were legal and similar to what Britain was doing. In the summer of 1916, New York was shaken by a huge explosion of ammunition stored on an island in the harbor; German sabotage was suspected, and the island city grew anxious about its vulnerability.

The eastern establishment, men like the NYPL trustees, inclined to sympathy for Britain, due in part to belief in the superiority of their own British ancestry. There was also the financial interest of the mighty House of Morgan, which was Britain's American fiscal agent and loaned millions to finance purchases in the U.S. The old-stock supporters of the Allies were a small minority of New York's population, though dominating its cultural and financial institutions, and the city's other ethnic groups saw things differently. German Americans naturally favored neutrality, not wanting their country to join in war against the ancestral land to which they had cultural attachments. Irish Americans had no interest in helping Britain maintain her power, and Jewish Americans wanted no part of an alliance with France, of the Dreyfus Affair, and viciously anti-Semitic Russia, which many of them had fled, against Germany and Austria, which had given Jews civil rights. In the rest of the country, there was ambivalence, mixing sympathy for Britain with suspicions of a Wall Street plot to maneuver the nation into the war. Progressives tended to be anti-war and respectful towards Germany as the most advanced nation in Europe, marred by its Prussian militarist strain and the folly of Kaiser Wilhelm, but otherwise superior to imperialist Britain and despotic Russia. This was Hasse's attitude, and she didn't hesitate to express it, declining to help with a bazaar to raise funds for the Allies because, "I am on the other side of the fence."[9] She apparently shared the widespread view that the war was essentially an economic conflict among European powers, and her position enabled her to contribute expertise in economic data to help the supporters of neutrality, but it was no more than what she did for other researchers in the library.

In what should have been a warning to Hasse, the hazard to women who ventured into the controversy was shown by the experience of the revered Jane Addams, who had moved beyond her work for domestic reform to become a leader of the women's peace movement. Just back from a tour of Europe in July 1915, she spoke at Carnegie Hall in an effort to bring some reality to the intensifying emotions about the war, explaining the damage being done to European civil life and the fears of all the warring nations that willingness to negotiate signified weakness. She ended with comments on the tragedy of young soldiers sent by old men to kill and be killed. As evidence that young men had no natural inclination to violence, she claimed that it was common knowledge that before bayonet charges, so glamorized in the press, soldiers had to be emotionally numbed with rum or absinthe. This brought a storm of anger and ridicule down on Addams for insulting heroic soldiers and the honored dead. The press that had built her up into a national heroine for her work with poor immigrants now turned on her, and Addams felt the pain of "being an easy mark for the cheapest comment." As she pressed on with her work for peace, old friends and supporters broke with her, and she was isolated as a foolish and disloyal woman. A British observer noted that in 1912 she could not mention Jane Addams to an American audience without being interrupted by applause, but ten years later her name brought only chill silence.[10]

~ ~ ~

Hasse's father died in 1915, another reminder that she was well into middle age and losing the paternal figures who had influenced her. Dr. Hasse's children soon would think it a blessing that he did not live to see a hysterical hatred of all things German sweep his country. With no relatives nearby, Hasse tried to develop a full life with her son, moving to a house in suburban Tuckahoe, an easy commute via the magnificent new Grand Central Station a few blocks from the library. With her hectic schedule, she needed a housekeeper and cook, plus a governess for Leslie, and, with no raises after 1915, her income was strained by both expenses and inflation. Still she enjoyed entertaining, gardening, and hiking in Westchester County, often joined by young colleagues, including members of the NYPL Young Men's Association, which used a shed on the property as a base for outings.[11]

In 1915, the household was joined temporarily by another boy, about whom nothing is known. A note from Caroline Hewins hoped that "the new boy is quite at home with you and Leslie," and a 1918 letter from Frank Hill refers to Hasse's "children," but there is no mention by Hasse of the second child. Both the 1915 article about her adoptive motherhood and a 1916 note from Hasse about a vacation trip with Leslie refer to only one boy. Most mysteriously, an informant told the Secret Service that Hasse had adopted an English boy but returned him when he proclaimed that Germany would lose the war. The informant had no direct knowledge, having heard it from someone else. Since the story was not repeated by those who would go to great lengths to demonize Hasse as a German sympathizer, it probably was an instance of the sensational, usually untrue tales that spread as anti-German feeling intensified.[12]

There is little record of Hasse's experience as a mother. She enjoyed chatting about "small boys' antics" with other women and telling the reporter for the *Evening Mail* that being an adoptive mother was her main interest in life, that her child kept her from becoming "all warped and lop-sided mentally," but her only anecdotes portrayed Leslie as prone to "frank criticisms" of his mother. "We have plenty of problems and plenty of fun," Hasse told the reporter, but nothing in the interview or Hasse's papers gives examples of family fun. In 1916, when they were delayed in returning from an upstate vacation because the "pestiferous" housekeeper was late in joining them, Hasse's note to Lydenberg was mostly a complaint about a holiday that was "tiresome and a terrible bore" because a polio epidemic restricted children to the grounds of their resort, preventing her from having the long walks she craved. She expressed neither anxiety about the polio danger nor enjoyment of her time with Leslie, to whom she referred only as "the boy." The scant evidence suggests that Hasse adopted Leslie in the hope of enriching her emotional life through motherhood, which was always said to bring fulfillment to women, not realizing that her situation was not well suited to the needs of a child. Several boys in her extended family remembered Hasse as a kindly figure, but a friend who knew mother and son felt that either she had adopted Leslie too late to bond properly or had not had enough time for him.[13]

Though Hasse insisted to the *Mail* that "all business women who have been too busy hitting the bulls eye of success to marry and have sonnies of their own would be one hundred per cent happier if they adopted one or two as soon as their incomes permitted," in reality she seems to have experienced more maternal satisfaction with her young staff in the library. Hasse was a demanding boss but also ready to praise those who met her standards, and most of her staff over the years seem to have regarded her with admiration and affection. She was described as "the best employer I ever had," by one, who wrote of her "broad-minded and intelligent treatment of all people working under her." She made an effort to bring women into a department that might be seen as more suited to men, telling Alice Holden of Vassar that she wanted an "energetic woman" for an opening as her first assistant, and she mentored a series of hard-working, ambitious young women in that position. From what can be learned about the women who worked in the division, they were mostly experienced library

school graduates with social consciousness and ambition to develop as profes-
sionals. Joanna Strange was a graduate of Iowa State and the New York State
Library School with extensive experience in the public libraries of Detroit and
Pittsburgh; she came to the division from a job as secretary of the Anti-Capital
Punishment Society. Alice Ramsburg had nine years' experience in the District
of Columbia library and had gone to England for special study of indexing.
Rose Eichenbaum, a graduate of the Western Reserve library school, left the
Cleveland public library to do social work temporarily in New York and then
joined NYPL.[14]

Though Hasse clashed with two male assistants, William Seaver and Rollin
Sawyer, she also had valued men on her staff, such as J. H. Friedel, Morris
Kolchin, and Sidney Zimand, immigrant Jews who shared her interest in developing library services. Hasse's rapport with ambitious women librarians and
male staff with names like Friedel, Zimand, Kolchin, and Halper, in contrast to
her tensions with the old-stock men favored by Anderson, suggests gender and
ethnic tensions in the Reference Department. As she felt more an outsider as a
middle-aged woman and a German American, Hasse appreciated multilingual
young Jews with backgrounds in European culture. Like Hasse, they would have
to be "pushy," in the common WASP sneer, to get ahead, while Anderson's
young men seemed to advance through a sort of entitlement from the male network that favored those of similar background.

Records show that Hasse gave sympathetic support to several former NYPL
employees who probably were Jews. Sarah Shoninger, who felt unjustly treated
by Axel Moth, gave Hasse as a reference and wrote to report her exciting new
work in words that must have warmed Hasse's heart. Just as she was about to
accept an offer from the Cleveland Reserve Bank, she got a job with the Signal
Corps, where "the pressure is intense and I am working overtime nearly every
day but as long as I am interested, it doesn't matter. It's so alive." In the case of
Eugene Weiss, an indexer whose claim of having worked as a librarian was disputed by someone at NYPL, Hasse wrote that "classification of employees in
any library is a purely arbitrary one," and she wished the library profession "had
more minds of the calibre of that of Mr. Weiss." The letters ended up in Anderson's file on Hasse, along with those from J. H. Friedel.[15]

Friedel's correspondence shows a young man of considerable enthusiasm
and ambition, eager to keep in touch with Hasse from his post-NYPL jobs, especially when he joined the National Industrial Conference Board, the newly established economic research organization headed by Magnus Alexander, long the
chief design engineer for General Electric. Friedel's effusive compliments reflected his gratitude for what he had learned from Hasse: "We who have been
trained under the Hasse system do not recognize such a thing as failure." He
complained of "lazy" public libraries that didn't have any understanding of the
needs of businessmen. In contrast, Hasse's expertise had impressed the men at
the Conference Board: "Mr. Haines is continually talking of you and when Mr.
Alexander wants the last word on a library matter, it is 'Why don't we ask Miss
Hasse?'" Friedel looked forward to seeing her in New York, "for I know how
much I gain from the minutes I am able to spend with you," and he and his wife

hoped the Conference Board would move there from Boston so they could "be near our Miss Hasse who is so much in our affections and in our thoughts."

Hasse defended Friedel to Dana, who complained that a letter from him showed "very considerable ability but overpowering conceit." Hasse assured him that he would feel differently when he met Friedel, "an enthusiastic hard worker with a fine idea of the potential possibilities of public libraries. . . . He is Austrian by birth, a Hebrew, a Cornell Man, well read, and personally likable." Friedel "certainly has ability," Dana conceded, and perhaps his conceit was "largely the exuberance of youth." Dana was well known for publicizing his library, and he enjoyed promoting himself and his views by public speaking and writing for leading periodicals, but his New England temperament was uncomfortable with the eager energy of Friedel, who might have been advised to heed the warning of Adolph Ochs of the *New York Times* to his fellow Jews: "Don't be too smart. Don't know too much." But if Jews and women didn't call attention to their abilities, they would be ignored in what often seemed a no-win situation. While Anderson and his protégés sneered at the self-promotion of outsiders like Hasse and Friedel, their own advancement was assured in an occupation where the gender structure benefited the small number of men of similar backgrounds.[16]

Hostility towards open ambition and confidence was easily adopted to the stereotypes applied to outsiders, "pushy" Jews and "unnatural" New Women. Both were said to have more energy than intelligence and personalities that did not fit among the well bred. This attitude was particularly treacherous in the case of women librarians, who were perpetually told that they were naturally devoted to self-sacrificing service. A woman who enjoyed praise and sought publicity was not natural and could no longer claim moral superiority. As Mary Eileen Ahern had warned in the 1890s, "no woman can hope to reach any standing . . . in the library profession . . . who does not bring to it that love which suffereth long and is kind, is not puffed up, does not behave itself unseemly, vaunteth not itself, thinketh no evil." Twenty years later, at the time when Hasse was being labeled a problem by the men of NYPL, the same values were expressed at the memorial meeting for Mary Wright Plummer, where leading male librarians expressed reverence for their ideal of the modest, quiet, serene True Woman.[17] In what was effectively a warning to women like Hasse, Herbert Putnam spoke of one "whose strength lay not in aggression of opinion or of expression but rather in quiet steadiness." Plummer was modest, diffident, and embarrassed by public attention, Putnam continued: "Her judgment and personality . . . were especially important to us during a period when the enthusiasm of new discoveries and new impulses tempted to hysteria." Though Plummer had lived as an independent career woman, head of two library schools, traveling extensively in Europe, and often writing for publication, her image of gentle femininity moved Richard Bowker to thoughts of her "lovely poem 'My Own,' in which she voiced the tender yearning to touch and mother little children, which is a part of true womanhood." William Warner Bishop added that her career gave the lie to "those gloomy prophets who foretell that men and women cannot work together on the basis of mutual respect and admiration." But Plummer's work with men was not that of the typical woman librarian; as head of a library school, she directed women faculty and the women students who were being prepared to be the poorly paid workforce in organizations headed by men. Her status as a leader in library education and ALA was dependent on not making waves that would disturb the equilibrium of male library directors like Putnam and Bishop. In working with men in ALA (she was its second woman president), Plummer benefited from her personal relationship with Edwin Anderson; as his sister-in-law, she had the connection with a prominent man that elevated a woman's status and made her an auxiliary member of the men's club of ALA insiders. To Anderson, Plummer and another library school leader, Salome Cutler Fairchild, were ideal women librarians, but Hasse regarded such devotees of fine literature as a genteel cult that kept women librarians from entering the real world. Fairchild had publicly doubted that women had the strength for executive positions, but Hasse would point to the suffrage campaign as evidence of organizational ability that women could put to use in libraries.

Friedel's compliment about training under the "Hasse system" was a sign of the special spirit that Hasse cultivated in her staff, sharing her sense that they all were a vital part of the real world. Such emotional rewards were partial compensation for the notoriously bad pay at NYPL, a cause of increasing dissatisfaction and turnover in an inflationary period. Many staff found that experience with Hasse could lead to better opportunities in business, government, or civic organizations. Friedel had gone to a financial firm and then to the Conference Board, where he made $2,500 "with promises of early promotion," while at NYPL, Hasse complained, he had been "night man in my Division at $55 per month, and the library felt they were overpaying him then."[18] Morris Kolchin and Sidney Zimand were recent immigrants, for whom NYPL was a good opportunity regardless of the pay, but their ambition, hard work, and knowledge of languages, economics, and bibliography represented a threat to Anderson and his fellow midwesterners in a city that had absorbed a great wave of European Jews, many with knowledge and interests suited to the Reference Department. The library employed many Jews, of course, and there were branches serving immigrants, along with the Jewish and Slavonic Divisions as suitable niches for scholars. But when such immigrants teamed with Hasse in the Economics Division's promotion of expert service on business and public affairs, they effectively raised a question of what library school graduates offered a research library. Hasse publicly said that they usually offered little, that their training could even be detrimental. She sought bright, energetic young people for every position and encouraged all her staff, including the part-time pages, to develop their skills. She was as proud of the typing ability of Cornelius, "a $22.50 boy who had never touched a typewriter when he came into the Division at $20.00," as she was of Morris Kolchin's bibliographies in the *Bulletin*. She became increasingly vocal about the need for better pay and opportunities, and when Joanna Strange had a job offer in 1915, Hasse asked Anderson to persuade her to stay, prodding him to address the problem of staff turnover.[19]

~ ~ ~

The staff of the Economics Division had no offices, nor even a workroom. They worked in 228, 229, and the adjacent stacks on reference inquiries, bibliographies, collection building and maintenance, and cataloging documents. Hasse had always been a zealous collector, and now her focus widened to the whole developing field of the social sciences and the range of current issues arising from activist government and the war in Europe. A flood of letters went out requesting pamphlets and other material from scholars, corporations, civic and professional organizations, banks, chambers of commerce, and governments. Developing the vertical files of pamphlets, clippings, business catalogs, and pictures was a priority, and with her usual high standards, Hasse required that clippings be mounted on manila cardboard. When her ideas on vertical files were published, Dana wrote that he enjoyed reading it and sensed her pleasure in writing, but "I wonder if it is worth while, even for NYPL, to mount its clippings?"[20] Lydenberg was even more doubtful about the resources going into the files and some of Hasse's other projects when the division was having trouble keeping up with documents cataloging; material about Hasse's vertical file ended up in Anderson's collection of evidence against her.

Reference inquiries continued to come in by letter and telephone, as well as in person. Hasse had long made a point of reporting examples of reference questions to show the challenging nature of library work, and in her first year in the new division, she sent Lydenberg a four-page, single-spaced list of recent queries on topics such as lead poisoning of lapidaries, Venezuelan banking laws, women in industry, auto registration by state, and naturalization law before 1857. Some questions came from far away, encouraged by Hasse's offer of help in the *National Municipal Review* and other publicity. Hasse pointed with pride to these signs of the division's reputation, telling Lydenberg, "[W]hen you phoned about the wire from Cleveland . . . calling for a banking list, we were at work on a wire call from upstate for: 'which of the third class cities in New York State (there are 54) elect and . . . appoint their water commissioners.' We got it out by the skin of our teeth on time. It was for the city of Auburn. The Governor had called on the mayor for a brief which was to be submitted the next morning and the information was wanted for the brief."[21] It apparently did not occur to Hasse that the administration might wonder why NYPL should do work for someone in Cleveland, which had a good public library, or for an upstate mayor's brief to the governor, who had the resources of the state library. Hasse could have pointed to all the publicity about NYPL as the flagship of the great public libraries, a national model in showing what libraries could do. For any library, defining limits on reference service was (and still is) difficult; as services developed, librarians had often debated in their meetings and periodicals how much to do for the public, with opinions ranging from strict limits to no limits. Within NYPL, there was resentment of Hasse for not playing by the unwritten rules. As she continued her practice of passing along letters of praise for the director's information, Anderson replied politely, while privately sneering at such egotism.

Throughout 1915, Hasse made persistent outreach efforts to promote the division's services. She attended meetings of businessmen to get ideas of what they needed, and in the fall she surveyed engineers, manufacturers, and economists for suggestions on how libraries could prepare for the expected intensification of research "with the cessation of European hostilities." In November, she wrote to the chairman of the new Federal Trade Commission to urge that its study of foreign trade include an appendix volume of the statistics needed by "the great reference libraries" that were being "overwhelmed" with requests for commercial statistics and information about economic factors in the war; she was brushed off with the familiar excuse that such statistics were more the responsibility of other agencies. At the same time, she was contacting the business press, sending the editors of *Coal Age* a list of references on the social welfare of miners that received an immediate expression of interest. A few months later, she wrote to *Economic World,* noting its recent editorial on profit sharing and offering a list of material on the subject at NYPL. This brought an enthusiastic response; her bibliography was published, and a list of sources on the "development of insurance in various countries" was requested. Hasse immediately set to work on it, assuring the editor that he need not be concerned that she was being put to a good deal of trouble: "We are in business for just this kind of trouble. We welcome the opportunity of cooperating in work as important as yours." When the work was done, he expressed himself "astonished" and "overjoyed," but when it wasn't published, Hasse asked for its return in order to give it to another publication.[22]

Many of the letters that went out under Hasse's signature were actually written by her closest associate, Joanna Strange. Hasse made sure the reporter for the *Mail* mentioned her assistant, and soon the two women were working on a book about libraries' unfulfilled potential with the tentative title "An Idle Business." As Kelso had once taken her to ALA, Hasse took Strange to the 1916 ALA conference in Asbury Park, where they both presented papers, and introduced her to prominent attendees.[23]

Hasse's paper was one of her ever more vigorous calls for sophisticated reference service, "Library Preparedness in the Fields of Economics and Sociology." Her theme picked up on the debate about national "preparedness," which had become the subject of intense controversy as the European war raged on; President Wilson had tried to defuse the issue of military readiness by advocating preparedness, not for war, but for the postwar world that would be vastly changed. In the Wilsonian spirit, Hasse issued an impassioned call for librarians to join "manufacturers, engineers, scientists" in their "sense of an impending revolution in the existing order," particularly for "intensified research" and the vast readjustments that would come after the war. Hasse offered few specific recommendations, saying that "it would be out of place to consider here the best method of preparation," suggesting only development and distribution of a map showing every state's "library resources and probable consumers" and a "program" for reference workers which "will enable us to co-operate on a common basis, which will relate us closely as a body to those men and women in the world of affairs" who needed the materials that libraries "religiously subscribed to, bound, and shelved, and considered our duty ended there." Hasse was sharp in her criticism of the status quo, starting with the admonition, "Whatever

I have said about the failure of librarians to get to the crux of the document question, I see now is only part of the general failure of librarians to value the essentials of their whole business." "Don't think I am knocking," she added, for library work was "the finest business in the world," but library neglect of reference service had produced " a vast storage place, a warehouse," with an "effective padlock on the contents" due to the failure to develop means of "a practical display of contents." She described herself as "heartsick" at the "shortsightedness of our business," which if it "were one of material profit and loss we would all have been in the receivers' hands years ago." In a remark that would not please the many directors present, Hasse said that most libraries "are overloaded at the business end and undermanned at the reference end," even though it was the reference service that "brings the solid business to the library." Administrators and trustees must be informed of the "impairment of plant which an inadequate reference service is." Calling for improved reference work, Hasse again dismissed the faith in cataloging and library school training, scorning the "orthodox catalog" as "wholly inadequate" and the "overlong training in routine matters." It was unfair to young librarians that reference service was not being developed, and, in an indication of Hasse's feeling that Billings' heritage was being lost,

> It is not fair or loyal to the great men, Winsor, Poole, Dewey or Billings, who believed so mightily in the American library, to allow this most dynamic phase to lapse into insipidity. . . . The nation needs what we can give it. Then why not rouse ourselves out of our professional complacency and do what another group of men, no more fit than we are, surely will do. By our own inertia we are condemning ourselves to a deserved inconsequence.[24]

Hasse's call for change was sandwiched between two forward-looking but narrowly focused talks, "Possible Results of the European War on the European Book Market" and "The Utilization of Photographic Methods in Library Research Work with Especial Reference to Natural Science," both of which seemed to be of greater interest to the library directors who joined in what was described as a "spirited discussion." One wished that Hasse had given "some definite pointers" on the cooperation she wanted. Did she mean cooperative cataloging, lists of special collections, or his particular interest, union lists of periodicals? Another brushed aside talk of "what we are going to do after the war," arguing that libraries needed "munitions" in the form of purchase of research materials, use of interlibrary loan, and a revolutionary development, the photostat (which NYPL was one of the first libraries to acquire). The only woman to speak was Tessa Kelso, who tried to call attention to the needs of small communities that did not have access to "that great central arsenal, the New York Public Library Document Division" and needed information service that would provide more than bibliographies. Hasse and Kelso seemed to point towards some kind of national coordination of libraries' information services that would provide equality of access, much as the recently established Federal Reserve system was improving access to capital, but, perhaps because Hasse didn't offer specific proposals, no one seemed to know how to respond to her call for a unified effort to improve reference service. As Dana wrote when her talk appeared in *Library Journal*, "Your eloquence . . . is quite moving," but he wondered, "What are you going to do about it?"[25]

Other than setting an example and inspiring with speeches, there wasn't much Hasse could do. From her perspective, she was trying to rouse librarians with the kind of sweeping language that President Wilson used that summer in establishing the Council of National Defense, which some thought should be called the "Council of Executive Information," and its Advisory Commission, "a new and direct channel of communication and cooperation between business and scientific men and all departments of the Government." The aim was somehow to coordinate the chaotic American economy in the interest of efficiency, fairness, and progress, although no one seemed to know just how to go about it, and most businessmen were skeptical. Coordination and cooperation joined efficiency as articles of Progressive faith, in the hope that government could provide new systems of organization based on research and facts. To anyone looking at American libraries, the desirability of coordination and efficiency was evident, but no mechanism existed to bring it about. Even on an issue directly involving the federal government, Hasse had made no lasting impression (and probably had stirred enmity) with her calls for more efficient distribution of documents. The diffuse nature and governance of American libraries, operated by thousands of local governments and diverse colleges and universities, made it difficult to suggest specific changes. All Hasse could do was try to speak forcefully enough to influence opinion among librarians and, increasingly, among decision makers outside libraries who understood the value of information.

~ ~ ~

Within NYPL, Hasse was making suggestions for change on matters large and small, particularly involving her ideas for reorganizing her division and her concerns about the quality of cataloging and classification. Her lack of success in redefining her division's mission and obtaining more space did not deter her from continuing to seek changes, but the frustration probably contributed to her sharp tone in complaining about problems, particularly with cataloging, where she saw resources wasted on the details of catalog rules while nothing was done to overhaul classification and subject cataloging. The often negative reaction of her colleagues, and perhaps her sense that they were secretly criticizing her, reinforced her feeling of being a lone voice calling for change. Lydenberg's usual reaction to conflict was to urge forbearance, but beneath the surface he increasingly identified Hasse as the problem.

One of the first signs of trouble ahead concerned Hasse's suggestion for a new name for her department: the Public Affairs Division. She explained that the term was used in universities and would be a more accurate description of the division's work than the original "Economics and Sociology" and "Public Documents," since most of the research in the division dealt with legislation, administrative law, government operations, and statistics. Startlingly for one who had based her career on building a documents department, she suggested,

"The abolition of the Public Documents Division is desirable," essentially because it caused too much confusion and waste to direct the public to a department for expert help with that "special kind of material but that material is then located in other Divisions where the attendants are unfamiliar with its use." Apparently she had had enough of trying to be a reference center for government documents located elsewhere, but she made no mention of who would catalog documents, which turned out to be of greater interest to Anderson and Lydenberg. Her proposal also involved considerable shifting, moving economics books out of 228 and replacing them with legal sets (statutes, reports, and periodicals) from various locations. In addition, "all material of an international character" should be located in one place near this law collection, she said, apparently meaning the publications related to international arbitration and other aspects of the developing field of international law. There would also be shifting in the stacks, and some remodeling, widening the door between 228 and 229 into an archway with a large desk near it as a reference center.[26]

Hasse had discussed changes with Anderson and Lydenberg early on and then sent her proposal to Anderson six months after taking over the combined division. He passed it on to Frank Waite, Charles McCombs, and Keyes Metcalf with a request for their comments. They replied in a single memo that acknowledged merit in Hasse's proposals to centralize law research, shift economics books, often called for in the Main Reading Room, to the stacks from 228, and move other material to stack six from lower levels. But, while agreeing that economics books would be better located in the stacks, they confusingly questioned giving up a "good economics collection" for a "second rate law collection" (which Hasse had rated "good"). And the advantages of the relocations had to be weighed against shifting an estimated 240,000 volumes, a costly, difficult change only four years after the move to the central building, and particularly annoying when it involved materials that Hasse originally had wanted in stack six near her division. Reflecting a chronic tension between Hasse and Metcalf, who objected to Hasse's staff treating stack six as an extension of their division from which they could take books to the reading rooms, the memo insisted that anything shifted closer to 229 must be regarded as "a part of the main stack collection that cannot be taken from the stack for any purpose without leaving an adequate record." In this regard, they asked for a policy "prohibiting the taking over of any material by a special division . . . without the definite permission" of the administration, since this had caused many errors in records; this may have referred to Williamson's complaint about Hasse taking Municipal Research Bureau publications, but no examples were given, and the wording suggests it was a practice of the older, special collection librarians from the Astor and Lenox libraries.[27]

They also objected to consolidation of "all material of an international character," since "we have a subject classification" that should be maintained consistently but was being undermined. As an example of the proper working of the subject classification, they pointed to publications of the Hague peace conferences classified with other materials on the subject of peace. When Hasse later saw their comments, she wrote a long, exasperated memo on why "I adhere to my contention that it is desirable to classify all material of an international char-acter together" and questioning the "competency of my contestants to discuss this question." She ridiculed the ignorance of their comment about classifying materials on peace together, pointing out that "peace conference" was only a popular name for the Hague conferences that produced conventions on various aspects of international arbitration and the codification of international law. (Though the conferences were promoted by peace activists, the participating governments regarded disarmament and other plans to ensure peace as hopelessly impractical.) She provided a six-page list of international arbitration documents scattered in various classifications (e.g. documents of the 1899 Hague conference in ten different classes) and generally a "hopeless muddle." International arbitra-tion was a major interest of influential Americans, including NYPL trustees An-drew Carnegie and Elihu Root, who had won the 1912 Nobel Peace Prize for his work to establish it. To Hasse, simplistic comments from librarians who lacked her in-depth knowledge was a symptom of the decline from Billings' standards of expert service.[28]

After hearing from the three men, Anderson sat on the matter for six months, leaving Hasse dangling. She would persist in raising the issue over the next few years without ever obtaining his approval for a reorganization, though she was able to arrange various piecemeal shifts. It might be assumed that An-derson did not see the need to spend money on such changes soon after the building opened—except that much of what Hasse suggested actually was adopted within a few years, but only after she had left the Economics Division. Soon after her departure, there was major expansion of the division's space, giv-ing it the Science Division's rooms along the east side of the floor, and in 1920 Metcalf willingly undertook a major shift of documents and economics books. The division later was renamed the Economics and Public Affairs Division.

While Hasse tried to get consideration for policy changes, Lydenberg pur-sued his obsessive attention to obscure detail, devoting an inordinate amount of effort to an investigation of thirty cents paid for a lost document. In October 1915, Lydenberg received the thirty cents from Franklin Hopper of the Order Department, who had received it from an assistant, Charles Coombs (described by Metcalf as "a rather feeble old man"), who couldn't remember where he got it. Lydenberg's memo to Anna Burns of Central Circulation produced the expla-nation that the document was borrowed first from the duplicate collection by the Documents Division, then lent through Central Circulation, then lost and paid for by the borrower, with the money sent to Documents. When Coombs told Hasse to see Lydenberg about the thirty cents, she tried twice to reach him by phone and see him in his office before writing that she vaguely remembered re-ceiving thirty cents from a page and sending it on to the Order Department. Lydenberg then sent another memo to Burns asking for more detail as to who the borrower was, when the payment was made, and who set the price at thirty cents. When Burns replied, he sent a memo to Hasse asking if the pamphlet was still in print at thirty cents. Hasse replied that it was and the library had two copies on the shelves and probably more in the duplicate room. Lydenberg fi-nally returned the thirty cents to Burns with a memo explaining what it was.

Hasse's impatience and exasperation become more understandable as one follows this record of confusion and time wasted on nitpicking by the man who was supposed to be leading the Reference Department in a time of tumultuous change. Oddly, the correspondence ended up in Anderson's file on Hasse, though it seems more damaging about the others involved. The record does not explain why Circulation sent the thirty cents to Hasse, why Hopper and Coombs referred such a minor matter to Lydenberg, or why he investigated so assiduously, unless Hasse was suspected of some impropriety, the nature of which is not revealed in the many memos.[29]

Around the same time, Hasse suggested to Lydenberg that readers be required to check their coats, as was the practice in European libraries, both to save space in the reading rooms and to discourage theft, which she was finding a constant problem. Lydenberg replied in his usual fatalistic tone, "In this enlightened country we cannot 'compel' readers to do anything. We urge them to check their wraps. . . . The question has been up time and again, informally and formally, and the Trustees have always felt that our present attitude is as far as we can go." Hasse said no more about it, but as she continued to feel the loss of Billings, she probably wondered why the director wasn't more persuasive with the trustees. Even Metcalf, who owed his advancement to Anderson and Lydenberg, regarded them as "too subservient" to the trustees, in contrast to Billings' attitude of equality and assertiveness in dealing with the board.[30]

Hasse also encountered resistance to her suggestions from Metcalf, who was responsible for the central stacks and binding. His desk was located in the midst of the documents stored in stack six, close to the Documents Division's "noisy book conveyor which frequently went out of order," and the annoyance associated with this equipment may have contributed to Metcalf's resentment of Hasse, who, even before Metcalf was hired, had been complaining about the "carelessness of the stack boys in reporting books unavailable that are on the shelves, in place." Metcalf was under pressure from the condition of the stacks, increasing staff turnover, and Lydenberg's assignment to conduct an inventory, and he found complaints from Hasse particularly irritating. The account he gave long after suggests his discomfort with a forceful woman manager: "She was ambitious, as I suppose many of us are. She had a sharp tongue and she did not 'suffer fools gladly.'" She also was "of German origin," a misleading description of someone born and raised in America. Metcalf, who seemed to be particularly aware of height, remembered Hasse as a "tall, stately figure," while Lydenberg was short and Anderson of average height. Hasse was a great bibliographer and "an extremely capable administrator and organizer," Metcalf admitted, but she was disturbing to her male coworkers, and she gradually "became more and more unpopular with the senior members of the library staff . . . and this naturally did not improve her attitude toward them."[31] Since he describes a great deal of conflict within NYPL, it is not clear whether Hasse's behavior was exceptionally bad or gender anxieties and growing anti-German feelings caused an overreaction to her strong personality and sharp words. Perhaps Metcalf's key phrase is "ambitious, as I suppose many of us are." Hasse's ambition and self-promotion threatened Metcalf and his male allies, both within NYPL, where she might seek a top position, and because of the larger force she represented: the possibility that women librarians, the vast majority of the profession (75 percent in the 1920 census), would demand equal pay and opportunity, as women were so visibly in the streets of New York.

Metcalf's memoir provides little specific information about conflicts involving Hasse. She "thoroughly intimidated" WilliamTaylor of Accessions (though his memos about differences with Hasse show him to be aggressive, not apparently intimidated) by "from time to time" objecting "angrily" to labeling errors by his staff and "made it as difficult as she could" for him. (In fact, Metcalf himself later arranged the transfer of Taylor, partly because he had angered Lydenberg by not getting approval for a four-letter classification in the system where all others were two or three letters.) As for Metcalf's responsibility for the stacks, when Hasse approached him "once or twice a year" with complaints, he decided "that the easiest way to deal with her was to refuse to argue but simply to say, 'I think this is something to refer to the man to whom we both report.'" They would go to Lydenberg's office, where invariably "Mr. Lydenberg supported me and Miss Hasse left practically boiling with rage." Instead of directing Metcalf to negotiate with Hasse before involving him, Lydenberg would only say, "I wish you could find a way to avoid this situation," which Metcalf seemed to take as evidence of what a problem Hasse was, rather than a reflection on his own behavior.[32] Oddly, Metcalf's memoir made no reference to conflicts documented in Anderson's file: his indignant complaints about the Economics Division staff taking volumes from the stacks without leaving records and his claim to have a list of documents entered in the documents catalog but not the public catalog. These issues could have been used to cast Hasse in a bad light, but they involved complexities that didn't fit Metcalf's preferred narrative of men suffering the abuse of a shrewish woman. His memoir is rife with factual errors and convenient omissions, which may only reflect the passage of time, but there does seem to be a considerable element of selective memory editing Metcalf's story to the advantage of its author and the detriment of Adelaide Hasse.

Hasse's difficulties with Metcalf were interrupted when he took a leave to serve as acting librarian at Oberlin in 1916-17, but his replacement, Paul North Rice, was no more congenial. By then, Hasse had learned that she was in serious trouble with Anderson and Lydenberg, barely a year after they had made her chief of the combined division. The roots of the problem may have gone far back and partly originated in differing temperaments, but the immediate cause was Hasse's complaints about errors in other departments at the same time that Lydenberg and Waite were telling Anderson that Hasse's attitude and her documents cataloging were the real problems. In the fall of 1915, Hasse may have been irritated with the lack of response to her reorganization proposal, and she tended to dash off exasperated notes about problems that arose in trying to serve readers. From Anderson's record, it appears that these notes were infrequent and probably fired off in annoyance at failures affecting users. She had become convinced that a forceful manner was the way to get results, but she did not realize or did not care that Lydenberg and other men retaliated with memos about the

Hasse problem.

In September 1915, she and Axel Moth had an exchange that revealed Hasse's irritation and the diffident Moth's distress with her harsh words. Moth wrote that he had made the corrections requested in the heading "Military taxation," but he reminded her that "very radical changes cannot be made in a hurry partly because we have not sufficient help and partly because some changes will involve many others." He had shown his willingness to cooperate with her, he added, "and it really is not necessary to be so severe." Hasse snapped back that the subject "was but an indication of the pitifully inadequate way in which most of the subjects have been handled." There was nothing personal in it, she said, for "my personal regard for the ladies and gentlemen who have heroically wasted their time and the Library's money under a mistaken idea that they were making a subject catalogue is as great as ever." Needing a subject catalog "which is not a delusion and a snare," the Economics Division had put its own catalog "into some form approaching consistency," which involved reviewing four thousand cards for "Taxation" and six thousand for "Population" with no extra help. She offered to show him what she meant by bringing card trays to his office. The problems were "no news to me," Moth assured her, for the catalogers knew "better than anyone . . . the faults of the old system under which we were forced to work for many years." In the hope that discussion might improve the situation, he suggested a meeting of Hasse and Minnie Sears, who was now in charge of subject cataloging and planning changes to deal with the problems. (Apparently this did not have the desired effect; the two women had fundamental differences, and Sears and her companion Isadore Mudge, reference librarian at Columbia, would join the chorus of Hasse's critics.) Meanwhile, Moth was "very glad you called my attention to the ridiculous headings assigned to the medical pamphlet," and her suggestion to refer a "Canterbury Court" entry to the Library of Congress "is a good one and will be done."[33]

The latter esoteric point attracted the interest of Lydenberg, who was also busy investigating the thirty-cent payment. He decided he knew best about the entry, which brought a heated memo from Hasse. After expounding on the nature and history of the ecclesiastical province of Canterbury, she told him she was "not pleading for a reversal" but wanted him to know that "I felt reasonably informed before I challenged the card." Unfortunately for Hasse, Lydenberg's focus on such fine points meant that he would accumulate a list of about a dozen of what he considered erroneous or inconsistent government entries, most of them for obscure foreign documents, that he would cite as evidence of her failings as a cataloger, though he admitted that she was not personally responsible for all of them. (They also were a tiny percentage of the thousands of documents cataloged by the division, which Lydenberg didn't mention.) While Hasse focused on the problems of subject entries that were essential to guide users to content, Lydenberg pointed to errors in government main entries that Hasse considered of less importance, since few people would know the correct entry in the first place. A few weeks later, Hasse sent another complaint to Lydenberg about muddles with records that had resulted in inquirers being misinformed. Not content to just inform him of the problems, she vented her exasperation: "It is difficult not to question a policy which does not know that such things are, or knowing, will allow them to remain so." This was gratuitously offensive to Lydenberg, who thought the administration was trying to address the problems of the catalog, and added to his uneasiness about Hasse's attitude.[34]

In January 1916, Anderson finally replied to Hasse's reorganization proposal, probably because she had inquired about it, by passing on the comments of Waite, Metcalf, and McCombs with a request for her reply and the vague suggestion that later they would try to have a conference of all concerned. Presumably this led to Hasse's comment about their ignorance of the Hague conferences. The record does not show further consideration.

Two weeks later, Lydenberg sent Anderson a long memo about Hasse that seemed to stem from some intemperate statements she had made, possibly in reaction to the handling of her reorganization proposal or to Lydenberg's suggestion that she do something about the backlog of uncataloged documents accumulating in stack six. When Hasse replied that she had unsuccessfully asked him for more cataloging staff a year earlier, Lydenberg arranged for someone to alphabetize the backlog, but he thought to himself that Hasse should have done that much herself. Probably Hasse had screened out the more important documents and left lower-priority items to wait, but Lydenberg blamed her for not doing anything about the "helterskelter mass." Whatever Hasse had written, Lydenberg did not have a copy at hand and made no reference to the context, but he quoted Hasse as having referred to an "antiquated catalog" and a collection "execrably classified." In seven pages of his tiny writing, Lydenberg vented his accumulated resentment at Hasse's insensitivity:

> Some of us have long felt the cataloging of documents was not satisfactory, that there was not sufficient sympathy for the needs of the assistants in the Information Division, that there was not sufficient sympathy for the attitude of the general public. A spirit of cooperation is lacking. The attitude is "The readers can't understand 'document' entries in the public catalogue. Send them to us." It is not always feasable [sic] to "send" people; many of them object to being "sent." The lack of cooperation, the failure to see the other man's point of view is—in essence—the great difficulty other divisions find in working with the Economics Division.

Lydenberg admitted that "unsatisfactory and inadequate" documents records in the public catalog were partly the result of insufficient staff, but Hasse should have set different priorities, concentrating on cataloging new documents instead of "changing forms of entries, redoing work already done," creating two sets of records in the public catalog under different forms of entry. She shouldn't have started a vertical file, a good thing in itself but questionable when there was a large cataloging backlog, but "Miss Hasse, of course, thinks the clipping collection worth all it has cost."[35]

As for the classification problems, Lydenberg said that Hasse had "frequently" been right but was not infallible in her complaints. Again, it was her attitude that was disturbing, not seeming to recognize that classification was often a matter of opinion between equally appropriate choices and describing the classification (which he had developed with Billings) as "execrably bad," though men like Williamson, Metcalf, Waite, and McCombs found it "sufficiently well done to allow them to work with the material classified by it & keep their tempers." His comparison of Hasse with these four younger men is an odd choice, since her position was more comparable to the other heads of special collections; it is unlikely that she was the only one of them to report problems with subject headings and classifications. Of those mentioned by Lydenberg, only Williamson had been chief of a subject division, and that only for two years, while Hasse had been a specialist cataloger and bibliographer at NYPL for eighteen years. The record shows that all four men did their share of complaining about various problems, if not about classification. In his report for his first full year in the Economics Division, Williamson was already registering complaints more pointedly than Hasse ever did in her annual reports, which suggests that Lydenberg would not have found him so agreeable over a longer term, and Metcalf's memoir admits to complaining so annoyingly than Lydenberg asked when he was going to grow up. Perhaps unconsciously, Lydenberg was adapting to Anderson's preference for such men as the agreeable norm to which Hasse, the Other, could be unfavorably compared. The four men formed a clique that, with the addition of Paul North Rice and Carl Cannon, would advance each other's careers and renew their bonds with an annual hiking trip in the Catskills.

Lydenberg made an effort to be fair, acknowledging Hasse's "great abilities, wonderful knowledge, untiring industry." As for the "admirable work" of her division: "We know the entire staff will go to great lengths to help its readers, whether college professors or members of debating teams. Readers appreciate the interest shown them & the help they've received in room 229, and other members of the staff are glad the force in 229 is so enthusiastic and helpful." But in the end he came back to Hasse's attitude and the need for "cooperation, real cooperation. . . . We got it with Williamson, we don't get it now." Again Lydenberg made the contrast with Williamson's brief service, without mention of the other specialists whose service went back to the Billings era or earlier.

Lydenberg's criticism of the documents cataloging echoed those made in a "confidential statement" to Anderson from Frank Waite, who pointed out that efforts to improve the catalog had not addressed documents cards, which were a large part of the catalog and "in regard to uniformity and . . . how near up-to-date rather the worst part." Waite complained of inconsistent entries, rushed cataloging, and the growing backlog. He saw a lack of appreciation of the documents problems in the public catalog because the different arrangement of the documents catalog made variations in entry irrelevant. He did not blame Hasse personally so much as a general problem of older librarians with habits that didn't fit the new library and the tendency of the special collection departments to take a narrow view. Waite's solution was central processing: "I hope for improvement in other special fields than documents. We believe all this can be accomplished only by an imperative rule that all records shall be attended to only by one clearing house whose special business it is."[36]

Waite's approach had an obvious appeal to Anderson, suggesting that the problem lay in attitudes carried over from the previous administration and could be solved by standardized, centralized organization. Had they been part of the discussion, the librarians of the special collections could have pointed out that they were an essential part of Billings' plan for the new building, not just a hangover from the past, but Billings may not have anticipated the extent to which the special collections would become the "kingdoms of their chiefs."[37] The tensions inherent in the structure may have seemed greater with Hasse, because the social sciences and public documents overlapped to such an extent with other divisions and the central information desk. And, as would eventually become clear, Lydenberg and Waite had not fully grasped the cause of the inconsistent entries for documents nor considered what would be involved in a cure. It was, after all, much easier to blame the annoying Miss Hasse.

In January 1916, Hasse had another complaint to Moth about a subject heading for a book on international arbitration, the topic that already was a sore point, which had caused "derisive comments" from a reader. When Lydenberg heard about it, there was an exchange that showed how exasperated they both were. Lydenberg requested a copy of the book and Hasse's note to Moth, and Hasse again was not content to send those items but also added more cards under the heading and more indignant comments, telling him that the public catalog was "a most impressive production as to bulk, but when it comes to making use of it in scientific or intensive way it, in nearly every case, proves itself a jumble and a hodge podge." That the catalog was a hodgepodge was a common complaint; Metcalf repeatedly used the term to describe it in his memoir. But Hasse went on as though determined to alienate Lydenberg: "When I take it upon myself to make criticisms it is only because I want the N. Y. P. L. to produce the best results. I am just as critical of my own work as of that of others. I admit I might be more diplomatic in my expression of criticism, but it is too trying to see grown people go on doing fool things because they have always been done that way. And your [catalog] is irretrievably bad, and it has cost !!"[38]

After mulling this over for several days, Lydenberg took the opportunity to confront Hasse about her harsh words. In a long letter, he gently but firmly warned that there was plenty of criticism of her cataloging and that her use of "unpleasant epithets" and "irritating adjectives" was only undermining her goals.

> I'm going to take this opportunity of telling you that we all of us know the public catalogue—and maybe one or two other catalogues—has mistakes and inconsistencies. Mr Moth and his people are doing their level best to prevent mistakes and inconsistencies occurring and to correct those that have slipped by us. He welcomes every kindly request for correction. I must admit that when diplomatic—or kindly or friendly, as distinguished from carping—criticism is used it smooths matters largely. Frequently people come to me about inconsistencies in the catalogue record of documents in the public catalogue, say they are inadequate or misleading, etc. I invariably tell them that I'm sure you'll be glad to correct the error if it's brought to your attention. I don't believe you would welcome the suggestion if it came to you with a statement that it was an example of a "fool thing." Some misguided people might conceivably think they could apply

such phrases to what they found in the cataloging of public documents. . . .
I'm going to say plainly that I think your attitude is wrong. . . . We're all
part of the Library staff, and we're all working for the good of the same Library. Your work in 229 is not separate from that in 315.

He assured her that her good work with readers was appreciated, as was her
ability to identify errors, but it would be more effective if she took a milder
tone. After all, she wouldn't like it "if Mr Moth used such language about the
corrections on the copy slips for documents entries," of which there were many.
Pointing to specific inconsistencies in documents entries, he admonished,
"There are plenty more incorrect, misleading, inadequate entries in that
'irretrievably bad' catalogue that belong to documents entries. I really don't
think you are in a position to condemn the rest of us in such unqualified and
unrestrained terms." He ended on a conciliatory note, urging that they "pull together" and entreating, "Take this in the spirit I mean it. We've worked together
too long for you to misunderstand my attitude."[39]

Hasse's reply, unwisely written the same date, when she was tired and hun-
gry after a long day, was a *cri-de-coeur* of the middle-aged workaholic whose
patience with the organization had worn painfully thin. As an expression of a
mood close to despair, it is worth quoting at length.

> I thank you for your note. I know I am disagreeable, but I don't mean to
> be carping. The trouble is when I am friendly or kindly or diplomatic, I am
> ineffectual. I was friendly once, but when I saw myself cheated and taken
> advantage of I grew sour. Now I feel only an interest in the service which
> my Division can give and if people or people's work is going to interfere
> with that service I shall have to be disagreeable.
>
>   As to corrections on our copy slips—no slips have been revised by
> any one here for at least 3 months. I used to take them home and sit up
> nights carefully going over each one. Then I learned that Mr. Moth again
> went over them in library time, so I thought I would let him do all the re-
> vising. That is why he finds so many errors now. He gets the cards straight
> from the typewriter.
>
>   There always will be cards under Brooklyn P.L. and N.Y.C., - Borough
> of Brooklyn. P.L. We do not change obsolete forms of govt. or of bureaus
> to superseded ones. The Willard Hospital of course was wrong. There are
> many, many wrong doc. entries, I know. When we send correct ones com-
> plaint is often made that our entries dont file in with others in catalogue,
> etc. etc. However this is all beside the mark. My criticism . . . is only of the
> subject entries, and those are bad through and through. You see I have
> been watching for a good many years for a betterment, but they wont even
> see that something is wrong. My contention is not that it is faulty in spots,
> but that there are no underlying principles sustaining the structure. They
> argue this way: We have adopted a regional subdivision,—and all subjects
> are divided regionally whether by nature they are so divisible or not. Thus
> you may find such headings as Interest Rates, Africa. Formerly when I
> pointed out the impossibility of such a heading in a friendly, kindly way I
> was always told "Well, that is the rule. That is the way we do it." It is not
> for the faults that are made that I lose my temper, but it is the complacency

with which the reason for the faults is ignored.

Don't you see that something is wrong if month after month and year after year one can go on returning finished work? Of course it can be done over and made right, but—. It isn't knowing things, but a certain faculty of coordination that is involved.

I wish we could all pull together—now everyone is pulling apart. I know they are all ready to knife me, but I doubt anyone really cares more than I do about the N.Y.P.L. And I have such aspirations to make my little end of it the very best of its kind there is! How do you think I feel then when I see people falling over each other in 200 [the Cataloging Division], hunting by the hour for the middle name of some obscure person, and I am told off with hardly enough people to help me keep the books moving.

I wish I could make you realize how much—but what is the use, I'd be choked off again—Anyhow I've had nothing to eat since 8 a.m. and it is now 8 p.m., and everything will go on as usual, I suppose, tomorrow and ever after.[40]

At the same time, Hasse and Lydenberg had another exchange when he asked why she couldn't help Accessions' classification work by noting the class of previous editions, as in Moth's system. She explained that of course they did so when known.

The trouble with documents is the official authors change so often. If a manual comes in today issued by Chief of Staff & it is first of its kind by Chief of Staff it is cataloged as such. We cannot in every case go back & see whether last year or the year before the Adjutant General or Secretary of War etc, etc. issued a similar manual, & whether it is in Reference Department & where it was classified. The trouble we all have with documents is due to the way they are issued.[41]

This was an basic problem of government publications, as Hasse knew well, but whether Lydenberg understood her point is unclear, as there is no record of his replying to either of these memos in which she defended herself against criticism of inconsistent entries. As he had told Anderson, it was a matter of priorities, in which Hasse chose to divert staff time to other work when she should have been putting it into better records for the public catalog.

A month later, they had another exchange, when Lydenberg asked her to read proof on documents cards, as "about a ton & a half of linotype metal" was tied up in the print shop waiting for approval of the recent cataloging. Hasse replied that it could only be done by working overtime. She was aware of the complaints about delays, but as she had long ago pointed out to him, "I can do no more than tell you. We are doing the best we can with the facilities we have."[42]

At this point, the accumulation of memos offered Anderson an overview of a host of problems that would cause conflict in American libraries for generations to come. There was the conflict between the catalogers and the reference librarians and between the central information desk librarians and the subject specialists. There were the young men impatient with the old fogies, and the experienced staff resentful of the young whippersnappers. There was the club of men whose status depended on keeping women in their subordinate place, united in their anxiety about a woman who was "ambitious. . . sharp-tongued and didn't suffer fools gladly." There was the documents librarian who felt swamped by her workload with difficult materials versus those who blamed her for making documents complicated. There were the endless calls for more resources, while the administration expected librarians to make do uncomplainingly with what they were given. There was the infighting among departments, all accusing each other of failure to cooperate. And there was the usual organizational conflict between the need for tact and teamwork versus the value of forceful calls for change. Underlying the organizational and personal conflicts were fundamental questions of priorities in collecting, cataloging, and reference.

Faced with the evidence of complex and difficult issues, Anderson's reaction was that his office was "not going to be turned into a debating society." Instead of seeing conflict as a source of information and analysis, he identified Hasse as the problem, and in April he warned her to behave herself. Hasse had sent him a memo about an incident with a newspaperman who threatened to complain to a trustee about how long it took to locate a volume that turned out to be in the Cataloging Division, without a dummy on the shelf. "In the name of good service," she asked for his help to prevent such errors (which, in this case, was part of Metcalf's responsibility). She probably was particularly embarrassed that it happened only a few days after the *Mail* had published her letter encouraging use of NYPL as an educational resource free to all. Lydenberg's response was that the lack of a dummy was an error, but the location was noted in both catalogs, though Hasse "baffled" him by saying that the note in the documents catalog was on an old set of cards that wasn't used. He added that Metcalf felt that Hasse should recognize the similar problems he had when her division took books from the stacks without leaving a record.

Anderson then replied coldly to Hasse, admitting that there should have been a dummy, and a duplicate copy should have been in Cataloging anyway, but adding that he wished "to impress upon you the fact that you are not in a position in your division to determine the proper place of a book in this large institution," when its thousands of users might want volumes in various rooms. That wasn't really the issue Hasse had raised, but Anderson went on to warn that "what is most convenient for you and your readers may be most inconvenient for the officers and readers in other divisions." He admonished, "I am certain you have thrown acid rather than oil on the administrative machinery here," though he couldn't believe she had done so intentionally. She was "somewhat miffed" because he would not let her dictate to Cataloging, but she should realize that her own cataloging was much criticized. Also, he had heard that she was "one of the chief offenders" in taking books from the stacks without leaving a record. He ended with the usual administrative platitudes: "We must all bear and forbear. . . . Let us all pull together. . . . We have not money enough to employ all the people we need, nor of the grade we should have, nor for the purchase of the books we need. . . . We should all work together with a really good will." For Hasse, who had been alerting the director to a possible complaint (and probably also trying to avoid blame for the problem), this must have come as a shock. To be accused of damaging the library was distressing enough, but it was even more annoying when she was in the midst of a series of six lectures in the library school that meant so much to Anderson and had just had a letter about NYPL's value published in the *Mail*.[43]

Three months later, there was another collision, stemming from a memo from the administration about the employment of two half-time boys for her division; it was confusingly worded in a way that seemed to say that they were paid twice the salary of the full-time boy they replaced, a valued employee Hasse hated to lose. Instead of thinking it over and quietly checking, Hasse fired off a protest that showed, all too clearly, her lack of confidence in Anderson: "I have no right to do so, but cannot help question the expediency of administration of this sort where we are continually told there is no money for salaries." Lydenberg explained to Anderson that Hasse had misunderstood the notice, which referred to full-time salaries but said the boys were paid for half-time work. He added, "I'm not certain whether her indignation . . . is a slap at you or at me. From anyone else I suppose I'd resent it, but from Miss Hasse—?" Anderson shot back that she was "entirely mistaken," that "outbursts like your note today have a tendency to throw acid rather than oil on the administrative machinery. . . . I must ask you to use more of the oil of consideration."[44]

After that blunder, Hasse seems to have watched her words and manner, but her sense of being an isolated target simmered, and she blamed Anderson, who was so different from Billings, never emerging from his office, never giving her "a single constructive direction." That summer, the widowed Fanny Bandelier was back in town, desperate to find work; when she asked if it would be useful to meet with Anderson, Hasse replied that he was "not worth knowing." Another division chief, Victor Paltsits, explained that the library only hired "cheap help, mostly students who will work for next to nothing." Hasse's sense of persecution would have been reinforced if, as is likely, Fanny told her what she wrote to Charles Lummis, that Adolph Bandelier's last years had been blighted by lies spread by a colleague, the anthropologist Franz Boas. Hasse's health was not good, and by the time she and Leslie went on vacation at the end of the summer, she was desperate for long walks, but the polio epidemic prevented that. In her depressed mood, Hasse wrote to Lydenberg, "I know I am not needed at the shop particularly & that doesn't help."[45]

Yet, within a month of her return, Hasse was again making positive proposals, reviving her call for restructuring her division and adding a suggestion for informal meetings of the Reference Department librarians to improve communication and coordination. Her spirits may have been improved by another sign of the recognition she received outside the library, an invitation from the Women's Committee of the National Hughes Alliance to write a statement of her reasons for supporting Charles Evans Hughes, Republican and Progressive candidate for president. Unlike Wilson, Hughes supported the women's suffrage amendment, but the Women's Committee, which included many leading women activists, wanted to emphasize that women made political decisions in the same individual way as men, so Hasse was asked to write from an economist's perspective. She made no mention of women or the suffrage question, instead emphasizing Hughes' expertise as a lawyer and administrator with "a full appreciation of the value of business methods." Hughes was a man who believed in regulation, cooperation, and a federal government budget for "administrative efficiency." He stood for the "just interests of labor" and "reform of judicial procedure" and had that "scientific knowledge of the physiology of politics" essential to achieving reform. Hasse's endorsement of Hughes suggests that U.S. neutrality was not her primary concern, for Hughes wanted a tougher foreign policy, while Wilson ran on the slogan "He kept us out of war" and the implicit promise that he would continue to do so.[46]

At the end of September, Hasse again raised the issues of reorganization and her division's "pressing need for space." She presented her memo as a response to Anderson's January message, pointedly mentioning the dates of her original proposal (June 1915) and his reply (January 1916). She firmly advised that soon after the merger, "it was clearly apparent that changes in the administration of the new division would become necessary," and by now it was evident that she had underestimated the division's potential to provide service related to current events. She now requested even more remodeling: in addition to the enlarged opening between 229 and 228, she wanted a door cut through the east side of 228 to provide access to the room on the northeast corner and a stairway put through the floor of 228 to provide space on the first floor for her division. She also mentioned the possibility of switching the locations of the U.S. history reading room in 310 and the Science Division in 225, which would have made the north side of the second floor a center for research on American history and government. Again there was no sign of interest from Anderson, who was instead planning to remove documents cataloging from Hasse's control.[47]

Hasse meanwhile was pursuing her idea for informal meetings of the reference librarians. She had first suggested it to Lydenberg in the spring, and now he approved her asking the other division chiefs for their reactions. These varied considerably, from Victor Paltsits of American History and Manuscripts, who said he was too short of staff to release anyone for meetings, to Heryk Arctowski of Science, who thought it a "splendid idea" to have "simple conversational meetings" that would contribute to "a spirit of sympathetic cooperation" ("This expresses my idea exactly," Hasse noted). Others had doubts about the desirability of more meetings when the chiefs already met, albeit in a formal atmosphere, and a staff newsletter was available, but most recognized the need for better communication, and only Paltsits was unwilling to give it a trial. The meeting on October 17 was attended by fourteen, most of them division chiefs, and the consensus was that "periodical meetings for informal discussion would be desirable." Hasse was asked to give Anderson a plan for meetings of the reference staff "where a more sympathetic spirit of cooperation might be fostered." She asked for "sanction to go on with simple conversational meetings of this sort." He was not receptive, and Hasse later warned Lydenberg that suspicion and misunderstanding within the staff would persist so long as there was a "policy of keeping the workers from getting together and talking over their problems and interests."[48]

Interest in staff meetings was widespread at the time; *Library Journal* editorialized that there was no need for unions when "administration has become wholesomely democratic, as staff meetings have afforded opportunity for helpful cooperation and for enlightened discussion of library plans, methods and aims." To Hasse, reference staff meetings were an effort to improve service in an organization whose complex structure made communication and coordination difficult, and the success of the October meeting gave her hope that the tensions and conflicts in the library could be alleviated. Here again, she may have seen herself continuing on the path of Billings, who had established monthly staff meetings in June 1897. At the time of her arrival, meetings open to the entire NYPL staff were a regular part of the Billings administration, and Hasse had taken her turn on the program committee. Held in the evening, with voluntary attendance, not considered work time, the meetings combined informational programs with socializing to enable staff from the Astor, Lenox, and branch libraries to become acquainted. According to Lydenberg, they were not to discuss "administrative policies," but "suggestions and criticisms" were welcome if "confined to methods and practices and impersonal features of the work . . . free from the airing of personal grievances." Anderson and Lydenberg do not seem to have regarded meetings as a means of organizational development. Anderson had not initiated such gatherings in Pittsburgh, and when Lydenberg described NYPL's staff meetings for LJ, he concluded ambivalently that there were "as many opinions on their value and interest as persons you spoke to; without exception, however, you would find agreement that the best feature, or—some would say—the only good feature of the evening, is the talk by the director."[49]

~ ~ ~

Feeling beleaguered, Hasse struggled on to improve service in an atmosphere of tension and unrest. By the end of the year, however, she received two new shocks, one of which confirmed her fears about Anderson's intentions.

One blow came from the Carnegie Institution, which had continued to publish her indexes as they slowly appeared. The status of its Economics and Sociology Department had been in doubt for years, however, as the trustees became impatient with the slow pace of producing the economic history of the United States that was its only project. To the leaders of the department, this was a monumental undertaking that required a solid foundation in both Hasse's state documents index and numerous monographs, which were complicated by the difficulty of finding qualified scholars able to devote time to unpaid work. Henry Farnam appealed to the wealthy trustees' anxiety about left-wing economics by contrasting the scientific, objective spirit of his department's work with recent publications in economic history "under the influence of the Marxian doctrine of class conflict." Unmoved, the trustees voted to discontinue the department, leaving the future of Hasse's indexes in doubt. The massive Pennsylvania volume was in press, and the South Carolina volume was well under way but slowed by the "inaccessibility of much of the material." Hasse had thought her appropriation would cover completion of the remaining five of the thirteen original states, but that was now uncertain. She pressed on with the foreign affairs index, but publication would be delayed by wartime shortages. Eventually the foreign affairs index was completed in three volumes, while the state documents index ended with Pennsylvania in two volumes.[50]

At the same time, she experienced a profound shock when the cataloging of government documents, which had been her responsibility for twenty years, was transferred to the Cataloging Division. According to Hasse, it happened suddenly, with no consultation. According to Lydenberg, he told her in November that Anderson was considering the transfer, because he wanted all cataloging done in one department, but he had not made a final decision and would be "glad to hear" her views. His version was that she took it as a personal offense, and "the substance of her reply was that she had no desire to talk to Mr. Anderson about the matter."[51] There is no documentation of this meeting, and it is not likely that Hasse would have refused altogether to talk with the director. Since she believed Anderson was acting from personal animosity with the intention of humiliating her, she may have been unwilling to be put in the position of asking him not to do what had already been decided, or she may have pressed for a clear decision-making process, rather than a perfunctory meeting that Anderson could cite as consultation. Uneasiness about the director's decision making was evident in a three-page memo from Axel Moth that expressed alarm at the prospect of taking on documents cataloging and tried to lay out the issues needing consideration. Moth mentioned that Hasse had said she didn't care who did the work "so long as it is done the way she wants it," which suggests an effort to focus on the issues involved in cataloging documents.[52]

The record of Anderson's approach to the issue does not support his later claims that no slight to Hasse was intended. The separate cataloging of documents was a legitimate matter for administrative inquiry, since Waite and Lydenberg had complained about it, and Hasse admitted to difficulty in keeping up with the workload. Anderson's file on Hasse suggests that it had been on his mind for years, starting with some disputes between Hasse and the printing shop Anderson established to produce NYPL's catalog cards. Anderson proceeded deviously, conferring with Moth and Sears, but not clarifying the issues and goals involved. There is no record that he presented all involved with questions about the costs and issues of documents cataloging, nor that he provided leadership in reaching a consensus in place of the various versions of the problem expressed in memos, nor that he carefully analyzed the statements of Moth and Sears, which effectively supported Hasse's complaint of inadequate support.

In his memo, Moth warned that a real change in the cataloging of documents would require a "considerable increase in the cost," due to the need for more qualified staff devoting more time to the complexities of such work. Moth wrote a standard head cataloger's warning of the "many and great obstacles" to taking over documents cataloging, especially without the "friendly cooperation" of Hasse and her staff. Moth worried that there was not enough space for documents work in Cataloging, and he was certain that the existing staff was inadequate, "not . . . competent to do a high grade of work, and . . . probably not capable of the necessary improvement." Not only was their "linguistic and educational equipment" insufficient, "they are also too few to handle work as it ought to be handled." Recruiting enough qualified staff would be difficult and would mean "considerable increase in cost."

Revealing his almost desperate anxiety about the director's understanding, Moth listed six issues that required clarification. (1) What could be done to prevent disputes with Hasse? "Is there really any hope of making Miss Hasse understand that the decision of the Cataloging Division must be absolute? . . . If the change is made, the work will of course in many cases not be done the way she wants it; otherwise, there would be no reason for any change, and she ought to understand that clearly." (2) "Does the director fully realize that if the work is transferred the Library must be prepared for some confusion in the work for at least a year?" (3) How large a staff would be needed and how might efficient workers be obtained? As a further complication, Moth thought some staff should be left to Hasse to analyze large sets, as her division was more familiar with such work than Cataloging. (4) Could the documents catalog be relocated or a photostat copy made so that Cataloging could conveniently work on it? (5) "Is the Library willing and able to assume the necessary additional expense in cataloging documents?" (6) Does the library fully realize that better cataloging takes more time and cannot be done with the speed at present shown in documents cataloging?

Moth ended with regrets "for personal and professional reasons if this . . . has the appearance of an attack on Miss Hasse and her work. It is not meant to be so. I am perfectly well aware of Miss Hasse's great value to the library, and I regret seriously that the relations of the Divisions are not more cordial." What is striking, however, is the extent to which Moth supported Hasse's view of the problem. Her division did not have enough staff, and what it had was not in a high enough grade. Even with limited staff, her division was working faster and doing more complex work (analytics) than Cataloging. Though Moth wanted Hasse to cooperate in sharing her expertise, he would allow her no authority to make decisions or challenge changes made by his division.

At some point, Minnie Sears added her analysis in an undated fifty-three-page memo that both blamed Hasse and called for more staff. Sears began by saying that she would not go so far as those who thought Hasse's document catalog should be thrown in the river, but the "ideal solution" would be to start over with a special appropriation. That is the ideal solution to many problems, of course, but it was not available in this case. Instead Sears tried to suggest affordable changes, though wanting it understood that no miracle could be achieved by a "few surface changes" when "fundamentals need changing." To her, the underlying problem was Hasse's failure to coordinate with Cataloging and the Information Desk. Sears objected strongly to the different structures of the classed documents catalog without subject cards and the dictionary public catalog, which lacked many documents author cards. The structure of the documents catalog meant that it didn't need perfectly uniform author entries, but lack of uniformity caused filing problems and confusion in the public catalog. To Sears, it was obvious that the catalogs must be uniform, and since the public catalog came first, the documents catalog must be made to conform.[53]

To Hasse, her arrangement had the sacred imprimatur of Billings' approval, and the concept probably had seemed logical to him in relation to his design of the building with both general and specialized reference rooms. Sophisticated researchers who wanted government information could go to the specialized division for expert help with a catalog arranged by government structure and chronological period, minimizing the problems of author and title entries for documents, while subject cards in the public catalog would make documents accessible to users and Information Desk staff seeking material by subject. The extent to which Hasse's system actually reflected Billings' intentions is unclear, however, as she never cited any specific administrative approval nor any policy statement on documents cataloging.

Whether such a dual system was sustainable is another question, but no one seems to have raised the possibility of either closing the documents catalog or limiting the agency entries in the public catalog (or making other changes, such as modifying the cataloging rules or ending the inclusion of periodical articles in the main catalog). Sears said the problem was Hasse's overly elaborate system, which would require a large increase in the staff, currently "wholly inadequate in size." She didn't see any way to do the work without more staff, but the workload could be made more manageable by refiling the documents catalog to alphabetical arrangement (which would require revision of cards), making the fullest use of Library of Congress cards, removing some unspecified materials, and reducing both analytics and the cataloging of unspecified "minor" documents. Sears told the administration just what it wanted to hear: "Accurate work under a simple plan better than hasty work under an elaborate plan that may be good in itself but is not affordable."

Sears conceded that there were some desirable features in Hasse's system, such as separating serials and filing titles chronologically rather than alphabetically, in recognition that documents titles often were unclear and more likely to be findable by date. But though Sears could see the problems with titles, she showed no awareness of the problems with government author entries, even as she described Hasse's catalog as allowing varying forms of agency names to file together. She was obsessive about correct author entries to begin with, but she also realized that the way to please Hasse's critics was to present herself as the anti-Hasse, who could provide consistent entries and a comprehensible documents catalog. Hasse's catalog was not a unit, she said, but "a series of different catalogues, or lists, having no connection with each other" (e.g., treaties, international congresses, countries, states of the U.S., foreign cities, U.S. cities, etc.), often with complicated arrangements. Without subject cards, however, there was no reason why it should have been regarded as a unit, nor was it clear that a dictionary arrangement would somehow unify it; for many users it would be more convenient (and unitary) to have the records for types of government, such as states, cities, or treaties, grouped together rather than scattered through the file alphabetically. As for the complex arrangement, Hasse had been explaining for years that government publications had special characteristics and required an understanding of government by the librarian; if her catalog seemed complex, it reflected the historic complexities of governments.

Sears' lack of understanding of documents soon would lead to unintended consequences, but her confidence must have seemed reassuring, and the sheer length of her memo looked impressive while discouraging careful reading, which Anderson and Lydenberg probably weren't inclined to do anyway. There is no indication that Anderson agreed to any increase in support or addressed the policy and operational issues. He simply decided to transfer the cataloging of documents, apparently on the assumption that it would somehow be more efficient or at least would rid him of a source of complaints. Whether he also intended to punish Hasse, as she believed, is unknowable. He may have supposed that she needed relief from the stress of cataloging, but it does seem odd that he didn't combine the question with her suggested reorganization, which could have enabled him to address the cataloging issue as though it were part of her proposal, giving her some of what she sought while making the change he wanted. The only record of his decision, in his presentation to the Executive Committee of the trustees, was disingenuous, stating that there was an "anomalous situation" in regard to "cataloging in the Economics division," which "for some reason" had always been done separately. There was no mention that he was referring to the cataloging of government documents, which had been done under the expert direction of Adelaide Hasse for twenty years. Because of this anomaly, there was "lack of uniformity . . ., some friction between divisions, and . . . cataloging and filing of material relating to economics and public documents were not as well kept up as they were with material handled by the general Cataloging division." He apparently said nothing about Moth's fear that his division couldn't handle the additional work or Hasse's wish to continue to have decision-making authority. The trustees were told that consolidation would produce "greater efficiency of administration," which probably gave the misleading impression that it would reduce costs. Anderson's habit was to attribute decisions to the Executive Committee, but the committee acted on the information that he provided, and it often didn't even meet in the library, preferring a Wall Street office. The minutes (written by Anderson) record no discussion as the committee approved the change on December 8.[54]

With Anderson providing no guidance, it was left to Lydenberg to implement the transfer with Hasse and Moth. He later said that he "suggested that she arrange the details" with Moth before January, but she failed to do so. Since neither Hasse nor Moth wanted the change, Lydenberg's active involvement was needed, but he justified his indirection as tact. In this situation, his hands-off approach verged on passive aggression, vaguely suggesting that Hasse take care of a distressing matter and then accusing her of failing to cooperate. There is no record that Lydenberg gave clear directions to either Hasse or Moth, nor that he monitored the situation during the three weeks in which Hasse allegedly failed to act. He apparently never met with Hasse and Moth together to guide the change that was difficult for both of them. On January 6, he told Hasse that Moth would arrange the transfer with her. Then, when Moth reported that Hasse said she could not give up the catalogers for several weeks, Lydenberg instructed him to tell Hasse that he would "take over" on January 15. On January 8, there was a tense exchange of memos in which Hasse prodded Lydenberg to give her a clear, written, directive on the transfer of staff. Since Lydenberg and Anderson sought to avoid paper trails, Hasse's insistence on written orders was more evidence that she was a troublemaker. "I think I've been sufficiently plain, blunt, and unequivocal in this written communication," he finally wrote, stating that Moth would take over documents cataloging and urging her to "please play the game and help us help you." Lydenberg met with her at the end of the week to assure her that the move was intended to help by giving her "relief from the details of cataloging," and he and Anderson met with her the following week. Hasse again emphasized the need for written policy statements, telling Lydenberg that she would believe in his helpful intentions when she received "in black and white" an announcement that the staff was transferred but the documents cataloging "remains in Miss Hasse's control."[55]

Lydenberg had another example of Hasse's uncooperative behavior, a story that on a weekend in January, she sent thousands of incomplete cards to the area of Moth's desk, where they were left in "indescribable confusion."[56] Again there is no contemporary documentation of the incident, one of the allegations made later in circumstances where Hasse could not reply. Possibly her request to keep her staff for a few weeks was meant to finish the cards, or perhaps she couldn't get clear directions from Moth, who had warned Anderson he didn't have space for documents cataloging.

There are some memos that show Hasse to have been irritated at having to deal with the ramifications of such a major change made by administrators who didn't understand her division's work. When Lydenberg asked about transferring the man he thought checked documents orders, Hasse told him that she had always done that herself and would never have delegated it, but now "I cannot search from another division's catalog." Feeling unfairly treated, she clashed with Lydenberg over issues related to who should do what work, arguing that it was the Shelf Department's job to go through mutilated volumes of the serial set to list replacement needs and venting her chronic annoyance with classification errors, including her lingering anger at McCombs, Waite, and Metcalf for their statements about the classification of peace conferences. Late in January, they had an exchange of memos in which Hasse was particularly blunt that "before spending thousands on shelflists and inventories," he should have "put the foundation i.e. the class in order." When Lydenberg patiently assured her he would be "glad to have any suggestion" for correcting discrepancies she had cited, such as different editions of the same book in three different classes, Hasse snapped, "If I were in your place I would abolish any bureau responsible for such a state of affairs. As it is, there are only two things to be done, to let it go on, which would be cowardly and wrong, or to institute authority where there is understanding of the subject to clear up the mess."[57]

Anderson and Lydenberg would always insist that they intended only a "helpful move" to give Hasse "relief from the details of cataloging." Moth "was anxious to follow Miss Hasse's practice, to co-operate with her in every way possible," but she showed her usual bad attitude, behaving "like a peevish child." Their claim is not supported by Moth's and Sears' memoranda, which show them determined to establish control and change much of Hasse's practice.

If Anderson and Lydenberg read what Moth and Sears told them, it would not have been possible for them to believe that the change was meant only to relieve Hasse of some details. Hasse may have been undiplomatic to tell Lydenberg that she didn't believe him, but her analysis was accurate.

Nor does the record show that Hasse's behavior was a major problem under the circumstances. Pressing administrators to put their decisions in writing does not constitute bad behavior. The revival of her complaint about classification, with its implied criticism of Lydenberg, may have been perceived as a way of getting even, but her concern had been on record long before the cataloging transfer. Perhaps the real problem was Hasse's unwillingness to take dutiful responsibility for dealing with a decision made against her wishes and without addressing the real issues. Her attitude seems to have been that those who wanted the change should clean up their own mess, but, suspecting that Anderson expected "a demonstration on my part which would warrant dismissal," she was careful to avoid action that could be labeled insubordination. Anderson later said that he wanted to fire her then because of her "childish, ill-natured, and insulting" behavior but was dissuaded by Lydenberg; more likely, he knew he didn't have grounds for action that would raise questions in the city and the profession.[58]

With her expressive temperament, however, Hasse did not hide her disapproval or her belief that it was a personal attack to transfer the cataloging that she had done so long, with such an expert reputation. Three years later, she wrote of her anguish at seeing "the result of sixteen years of work and study subjected to mutilation by inexperienced hands." The documents catalog was her creation, developed over many years as part of her idea of a great research library. As Moth and Sears went full speed ahead to dismantle her design, refile it, and remove records and guide cards, she grieved to see her work undone. It must have been especially galling that she was left the responsibility for filing in the reorganized catalog and that she was expected to adjust to its changing arrangement in using it for reference. To Hasse, it was "[u]nthinking vandalism and administrative sabotage . . . actuated by personal motives of the pettiest sort," with the underlying motive of getting rid of her altogether. Inwardly, she cried, "My poor catalogue! My poor readers! And blind trustees!"[59]

~   ~   ~

The transfer of documents cataloging soon would confirm Hasse's fears. Four years later, the situation was described in a memo from Axel Moth to Paul North Rice, who had taken over Accessions from Taylor and then been put in charge of a new Preparation Division that included Accessions and Cataloging. Moth reported on the problems with documents cataloging, which he now blamed on Sears. He began with praise for his own action in directing that the documents catalog be refiled in alphabetical order, which "seems to work very well and make the catalog more usable to readers," a self-serving and unreliable conclusion from one who did not work with the public. The rest of the report described a bogged-down muddle that "would have been as hopeless as ever" had it not been for the withdrawal of many "minor" documents by Hasse's successor. Moth was not sure when a project to consolidate cards would finish with the foreign entries, and it had not even begun the U.S. cards. Vast amounts of unspecified "dead matter" had been removed, but Moth admitted that removal of guide cards had been "a little too radical," to the point of slowing searching. The catalogers' goal of establishing standard main entries had encountered the inevitable difficulties with government agencies, compounded by the "small and inadequate" staff and Sears' elaborate system of determining entries, which required checking as many as five sources to determine an agency name. Moth warned that such careful work made it impossible to keep up with current documents or tackle the backlog without a large increase in the number of catalogers. Sears added to the problem by revising many of Hasse's entries with "endless" scratching out of agency names for replacement by versions only slightly different. Thus "State Dept." in U.S. states became "State, Sec. of," and "California Health Board" became "California. Health, State Bd. of," just the kind of detail Hasse had tried to simplify and avoid revising. Moth thought it a waste of time, especially since Sears assigned it to the two best documents catalogers, but he offered no explanation as to why he couldn't restrain Sears, who now was presented as the difficult woman causing problems for the men of the Reference Department. It seemed to be forgotten that Sears had been led to believe that her priority was to correct the inconsistent government entries of the Hasse era, which inevitably would involve a great deal of authority work.[60]

The administration was desperate to improve cataloging productivity and now blamed Sears for its decline "by nearly one half because of the work involved in making absolutely correct entries in the authority file and of Miss Sears' insistence on following the rules." Metcalf solved the problem with a committee dominated by Anderson's favored young men, Metcalf, Rice, Cannon, and Williamson. Over Sears' objections, they set limitations on how much time could be spent on authority work and distributed their report directly to the staff. In Metcalf's faulty memory, Moth died soon after, and Rice then became chief of the Preparation Division. Actually, Moth remained a cataloger at NYPL until his death in 1932, but he was as good as dead to Metcalf, as Rice's takeover of Accessions and Cataloging showed that the old timers from the Billings era were making way for the efficient young men with library school training. As for Sears, Metcalf's cheerful recollection was that she "took the first opportunity to leave" for a successful career with the publisher H. W. Wilson. At the time, however, *Library Journal* reported that her resignation was "on account of ill health" that required her "to take a prolonged rest." According to Metcalf, productivity returned to its pre-Sears levels under Rice's direction, but a 1929 report reveals that, twelve years after consolidation, documents were cataloged by a specialized subdivision of the Cataloging Division with a staff of seventeen, double what Hasse had.[61]

In a final irony, the subject of documents cataloging appeared many years later in a report by a committee that included two of Anderson's protégés, Paul North Rice and Andrew Osborn (one of Frank Waite's sons-in-law). In 1940, they joined a library school professor, Carleton Joeckel, on a committee of outsiders appointed by the new Librarian of Congress, Archibald MacLeish, to report on LC's cataloging and classification operations. MacLeish, who was not a librarian, had been shocked to find a cataloging backlog of two million volumes that was growing by thirty thousand a year. The committee's solution was "simplified cataloging," minimizing detailed rules for both descriptive and subject cataloging. Avoiding details itself, the committee's first two recommendations called for a codification of simplified cataloging as the way to cut costs for all libraries. The committee became even vaguer on the subject of government documents and could only recommend further study:

> 3. The situation as regards documents cataloging should be investigated very carefully indeed. Should documents be cataloged in general? Should only selected ones be cataloged? Should steps be taken to see that better government indexes to documents are issued? Should the preparation of a document index similar to the periodical indexes be recommended? The whole question of document cataloging is a troublesome one. Countries may change their names. . . . Whole countries have been swallowed up by others. . . . In other countries extensive reorganizations in governmental structure have taken place. . . . What is to be the future of document cataloging in such circumstances?
>
> 4. Rules for change of names should be carefully studied to see if there are not more economical ways of handling the material than re-cataloging each time a change of name occurs. This is not a difficult matter as regards personal names, but considerable thought should be given to the problem of change of corporate names. If a library is 30,000 changes of name behind in its serial cataloging, of what value is a rule calling for up-to-dateness?[62]

The committee feared, "Something closely approaching a breakdown in administration has occurred . . . in the Catalog, Accessions, and Documents Divisions," as a result of an eightfold increase in accessions while administrators were "unable or unwilling to come to grips with this situation." The underlying problem was the library's failure to find "competent administrators within its own ranks or . . . from other libraries. And as administration deteriorated the inevitable result was the supremacy of the technicians, who demanded completeness and perfection in method at all times and at all costs. . . . [T]here is an evident lack of discipline." So in the end, the solution was to recruit (male) executives to discipline the (mostly female) technicians.

Adelaide Hasse would have found bitter amusement in these men's discovery of issues she had tried to address decades earlier. She might have asked why their mentor, Edwin Anderson, hadn't considered the questions that now needed careful study. But since their report on matters of concern to all American libraries was classified "confidential" and would remain so for the next thirty years, she had no opportunity to comment on it.

Notes

1. Alfred Grunberg, "How to Make Your Public Library a Business Asset," *American Magazine* (May 1919): 61.

2. *New York Times*, 1 March 1909.

3. Catherine Shanley, *The Library Employees Union of Greater New York, 1917-1929* (Diss., Columbia University, 1992), 118-54.

4. *Margaret Sanger: An Autobiography*, excerpted in Jill Ker Conway, ed., *Written by Herself: Autobiographies of American Women: An Anthology* (New York: Vintage Books, 1992), 570.

5. *Woman's Who's Who of America*, 371. This directory included each entrant's position on suffrage, and according to Dee Garrison, *Apostles of Culture* (New York: Free Press, 1979), 225, only 6 percent of the librarians favored it, the lowest of any occupational group, making Hasse's mild statement of support bolder than it seems.

6. *New York Evening Mail*, 17 Sept. 1915.

7. AH to Dana, 3 Nov. 1915, AH-NY; Dana to AH, 23 Nov. 1915, AH-LC.

8. Adelaide Hasse, "Library Work as a Profession for Women," *Hunter College Bulletin* (5 April 1916): 2 (also typescript, 24 March 1916, AH-NY).

9. AH to Mrs. R. Valentine Webster, 5 May 1916, AH-NY.

10. Jean Bethke Elshtain, *Jane Addams and the Dream of American Democracy: A Life* (New York: Basic Books, 2002), 226-44.

11. Robert Hug to AH, 7 May 1917, AH-CB.

12. Hewins to AH, 27 April 1915, AH-NY; Hill to Lummis, 20 March 1918, Lummis papers, Braun Library, Southwest Museum, Los Angeles. FBI File 62-329 (1922) mentions the report to the Secret Service, but an inquiry to the National Archives did not locate the original in the Secret Service records.

13. Gertrude Matthews to AH, 5 Aug. 1917, AH-NY; *New York Evening Mail*, 17 Sept. 1915; AH to Lydenberg, 1 Sept. 1916, AH-CB; Ariel Fielding to the author, 12 Nov. 2004; Adelaide Fielding Kerr to David Laughlin, 3 Oct. 1990, in possession of the author.

14. H. Halper to Elsie Rushmore, 15 Aug. 1918, AH-CB; AH to Alice Holden, 4 Aug. 1917, AH-NY; information about Joanna Strange from *New York State Library School Register, 1887-1926*, others from LJ's column of news about librarians.

15. Shoninger to AH, 5 May 1916, AH-CB; AH to Municipal Civil Service Commission, 25 Sept. 1913, AH-CB.

16. AH-Friedel correspondence, Jan.-Oct. 1917, AH-CB; Dana-AH exchange, 20, 21, 26 July 1917, AH-CB. Friedel later left library work and prospered in business, ending his days as a leading citizen of Beverly Hills, California (*National Cyclopedia of American Biography* 36:298-99).

17. Ahern quoted in Garrison, *Apostles*, 183; Plummer's memorial service was published as a pamphlet and "A Library Life," LJ 41 (Dec. 1916): 865-81.

18. AH to Everett Perry, 5 Nov. 1917, AH-CB.

19. AH to Lydenberg, 5 Oct. 1915, AH-CB; AH to Anderson, 31 Aug. 1915, AH-CB.

20. Adelaide Hasse, "A Practical Clipping Collection for a Public Library," *New Hampshire Library Bulletin* 11 (1915): 150-52; Dana to AH, 22 Dec. 1915, AH-CB.

21. AH to Lydenberg, 20 May 1915, AH-CB.

22. AH exchange with Federal Trade Commission, 10 Nov., 12 Dec. 1915; AH exchange with *Coal Age*, 3, 5 Nov. 1915; AH exchange with *Economic World*, 27 Nov. 1915, 25 Feb., 3, 13, 15, 16 March, 1, 17 April 1916, 20 Feb. 1917, all AH-NY.

23. AH to Walter Swingle, 5 June 1917, AH-CB.

24. Adelaide Hasse, "Library Preparedness in the Fields of Economics and Sociology," *ALA Bulletin* 10 (1916 conference proceedings): 202-5; also LJ 41 (Aug. 1916): 557-60.

25. *ALA Bulletin* 10 (1916 conference proceedings): 422-29; Dana to AH, 15 Sept. 1916, AH-CB.

26. AH to Anderson, 15 June 1915, AH-CB.

27. Metcalf, McCombs, and Waite to Anderson, 21 June 1915, AH-CB.

28. AH memo, n.d., AH-CB.

29. Lydenberg, Burns, and AH exchange, Oct. 1915, AH-CB.

30. AH -Lydenberg exchange, 12, 25 Oct. 1915, AH-CB; Metcalf, *Random Recollection of an Anachronism* (New York: Reade Books, 1980), 119.

31. Metcalf, *Random*, 146, 181-84, 189.

32. Ibid., 183-84, 198-99.

33. AH-Moth exchange, 30 Sept., 2, 5 Oct. 1915, AH-CB.

34. "Entries from the Documents Catalog which show that even Miss Hasse could make mistakes," n.d., AH-CB; AH to Lydenberg, 18 Nov. 1915, AH-CB.

35. Lydenberg to Anderson, 26 Jan. 1916, AH-CB. The vertical file seems to have become one of the main grievances against Hasse, with much material about it in AH-CB, including an undated typescript "The Documents Clipping Collection" and letters from AH seeking material.

36. Waite to Anderson, n.d., AH-CB.

37. Phyllis Dain, *The New York Public Library: A History of Its Founding and Early Years* (New York: NYPL, 1972), 123.

38. AH to Lydenberg, 12 Feb. 1916, AH-CB.

39. Lydenberg to AH, 16 Feb. 1916, AH-CB.

40. AH to Lydenberg, 16 Feb. 1916, AH-CB.

41. Lydenberg to AH, 16 Feb. 1916, AH reply, n.d., AH-CB.

42. AH-Lydenberg exchange, 25 March 1916, AH-CB.

43. AH-Anderson-Lydenberg exchange, 10, 12, 13 April 1916, AH-CB; LJ 41 (June 1916):401-2; *New York Mail*, 6 April 1916.

44. AH-Anderson-Lydenberg exchange, 12 July 1916, AH-CB.

45. Adelaide Hasse, *The Compensations of Librarianship* (privately printed, 1919), 13; Fanny Bandelier to Lummis, 6 July 1916, Lummis papers, Braun Library, Southwest Museum, Los Angeles; AH to Lydenberg, 1 Sept. 1916, AH-CB.

46. AH to Rose Feld, 13 Sept. 1916, AH-NY.

47. AH to Anderson, 30 Sept. 1916, AH-CB.

48. AH-division chiefs exchange, Oct. 1916, AH-CB; AH to Lydenberg, 27 July 1918, AH-CB.

49. LJ 44 (Jan. 1919): 4; LJ 32 (Dec. 1907): 551.

50. Carnegie Institution of Washington, *Yearbook* 14 (1915) 110, 15 (1916) 98-102, 16 (1917) 14.

51. "Comments of Mr. Lydenberg, Chief Reference Librarian," n.d., AH-CB. AH's version of the transfer is in *Compensations* and "A Statement in Behalf of Miss Adelaide R. Hasse . . . ," [Dec. 1918], AH-CB.

52. Moth to Anderson, n.d. [1916], RG 7, Economics Division, Cataloging box, NYPL archives.

53. Sears, report on documents cataloging requested by Lydenberg, n.d., RG 7, Economics Division, Cataloging box, NYPL archives.

54. Excerpt from minutes of Executive Committee, 8 Dec. 1916.

55. Lydenberg note on interview with AH, 13 Jan. 1917.

56. "Mr. Lydenberg's statement," n.d., AH-CB.

57. AH-Lydenberg exchanges, 16, 17, 18, 21, 22, 24, 25 Jan. 1917, AH-CB.

58. Hasse, *Compensations*, 16; "Comments of the Director on Miss Hasse's Statement," n.d., AH-CB.

59. Hasse, *Compensations*, 16.

60. Moth to Rice, 5 Nov. 1920, RG 7, Economics Division, Cataloging box, NYPL Archives.

61. Metcalf, *Random*, 199, 210-14; LJ 45 (Dec. 1920): 1000; "Work of the Document Section," 1 Jan. 1929, RG 7, Economics Division, Cataloging box, NYPL Archives.

62. Quoted in Michael Carpenter, *Corporate Authorship: Its Role in Library Cataloging* (Westport, CT: Greenwood Press, 1981), 23-25.

Chapter 8

Economics Division, 1917-1918

However painful the cataloging situation might be, Hasse was determined to press on with development of the Economics Division. She increased her emphasis on special services for business, her involvement in civic affairs, and her publication of controversial commentary, making 1917-18 an ever more frenetic whirl of activity. At the same time, she believed that Anderson's animosity made it a question of "how long I could hold out" under "almost unbearable conditions." The tensions between them became more open, and in the gossipy atmosphere of the library, awareness that Hasse was "persona non grata" with the director encouraged others to show hostility, especially as anti-German feeling made it easy to identify her with the forces of evil. Hasse persevered with the support of her "exceptionally devoted and enthusiastic staff" and a clientele that "grew more and more appreciative." Added to her workload, the stress, the sleepless nights and "bitterness and utter loneliness in my heart" affected her emotionally and physically. She had health problems in 1916 and, an indication that she suffered from headaches, mastoid surgery in the spring of 1917.[1]

With her Carnegie bibliographies in doubt, she also dropped her bibliography in the *National Municipal Review*, saying that she "felt it necessary to retire from all duties outside of her official ones" at NYPL. Since she actually kept on with many outside activities, her real motive may have been unwillingness to accept direction from Charles Williamson, who became associate editor for publications, responsible for the book review and bibliography sections. This was a repeat of her experience with Williamson's hiring at NYPL: after a year at the Municipal Reference Library, he was given a position superior to her at the *National Municipal Review*, despite her years of bibliographic and reference work for the journal. The editor took the opportunity "to say publicly what he has many times said privately, that Miss Hasse has been one of the most effective of the regular contributors." The National Municipal League also eliminated her civic bibliography committee, whose failure to report Hasse attributed to her ill

health, and combined its functions with another committee of which Williamson was a member.[2]

Though concentrating on her division's service to business and war-related
research, Hasse also became more vocal in writing and speaking on the need for
change in public libraries. With her documents expertise apparently devalued at
NYPL, the always forward-looking Hasse turned to new priorities (though she
somehow found time to give a thirty-lecture course on U.S. documents at Columbia that summer).[3] The day after Christmas 1916, shortly after the shock of
the cataloging change, she returned from holiday to contact a businessman for
advice on how to make the Economics Division more useful to business, telling
him that she was trying to find new ways to get at the content of the vast numbers of publications that NYPL received from around the world.[4] In January,
one of her most widely read articles, "Public Libraries and Business Men," appeared in a leading business magazine, taking her message directly to the business community. Hasse urged businessmen to look on the public library as a
partner in their enterprises and make their needs known to these public institutions supported by their taxes. "It's your library," she advised, so make it a
"workable, efficient, up-to-date business laboratory for your city" instead of developing private business libraries while leaving the public library to women
and children. Hasse acknowledged that many libraries' budgets were not adequate to meet the needs of business, but she argued that it was more cost effective for business to fund better public libraries than to support individual special
libraries. While asking businessmen to think of librarians as "experts" eager to
work with them and "alert to the returns you should have on your money," she
couldn't resist some digs likely to raise blood pressure at NYPL, calling for
"live cataloguers, who are human beings and not just machines," and library
staff with expertise, rather than "dead wood, in library work because they 'love
to read'" or were related to a trustee.[5]

The article was reprinted in several library periodicals, Hasse distributed six
thousand copies, and there were requests for many more from libraries all over
the country. She also sent copies to the ten New York newspapers, leading
magazines, and various prominent men with an interest in the subject, including
Charles Beard and Magnus Alexander. A Hunter College professor sent encouragement typical of what Hasse heard from outsiders: "There is no question
whatever about the enormous social waste of energy and expense in our present
unorganized condition of library work."[6]

One recipient, George W. Lee, a prominent special librarian with a Boston
engineering firm, sent an encouraging but questioning letter about the difficult
underlying issue of how much free reference service public libraries could provide. Could they develop "measured service," which might involve charging for
some work?[7] Public librarians knew that their clientele needed assistance to find
information, but most saw their service as advising and guiding people in using
the library, not doing the research for them. Special librarians did much more
for their limited, often private, clientele. This was a crucial issue Hasse didn't
address, other than suggesting that businesses might hire librarians who would
use public libraries rather than incurring the costs of their own on-site libraries.

At NYPL, there was growing resentment of Hasse for doing too much; as the Economics Division staff eagerly took on research requests, she was seen as "doing favors" that went beyond what other staff could or would do for the public. Hasse argued that if libraries became more efficient and effective in providing expert information service, their communities would be willing to pay for quality. This probably seemed naive or simply foolish to Edwin Anderson, who was struggling with budget deficits and, after 1917, with a hostile new mayor, nor was he enthusiastic about special service to business. When Hasse sent him some recent letters of appreciation for her division's help, he commented in regard to a Wall Street firm, "Haven't they a library of their own where they pay better than we?"[8]

A few months later, Hasse made an appeal to librarians in a *Library Journal* special issue on service to business. In "Making a Market in Libraries," she called for fundamental change in the attitude of librarians, who were urged to see themselves as a business dependent on creating a market, going beyond "the immature, the leisure and the handicapped classes" to provide services needed by businessmen. Hasse was scathing about "'old-fashioned librarians' . . . their old-time catalogs, their shaky statistics and their petty decisions" and the "slow, unprogressive, sit by the fire and spin" profession with its "fear of change" and "'world without end, amen' point of view." Librarians must meet changing conditions with marketing campaigns, advertising, special services, and expert staff. "One of these days there is going to be a Library Revolution," she proclaimed, perhaps thinking of events in Russia, "and from that time on library executives are going to be captains of industry, lined up shoulder to shoulder with the only salvation of our country—sound business. The library industry will then be as well organized, as well manned, as efficient in service as any successful industry." To those who said their libraries already were stretched to the limit while city officials gave no increase in funds, she again insisted, without citing any evidence, that good service would get support: "Money can be had for anything in this world that is worth while." Too many libraries failed to make a market and were effectively dead:

> But the library death rate is tragically high. With your eyes wide open for once, see the exhibition of library corpses strewing this country! Dead! Killed by neglect! Died, from lack of exercise! Succumbed, because of too little fresh air! Drowned in a sea of petty jealousies! Smothered to death under their own cloud of dust! Not from overwork have they passed away! Not from excessive usage!

Turn away from terminal self-satisfaction, Hasse urged, "for we must compare ourselves with the real builders of business, and make our libraries, from the point of view of service at least, rank with the best of them." She quoted railroad titan James J. Hill: "Every man who has really lived has had some time in his life the Great Adventure. The Great Northern Railroad has been mine." Where was such spirit in libraries? "Where is the man, librarian or not, who will . . . take for his Great Adventure the revolutionizing of Public Libraries?"[9]

Thoughts of life's Great Adventure, business giants, revolutionary change, all came naturally to Hasse's messianic temperament. Such rhetoric was not inspiring to her colleagues at NYPL, where her portrayal of libraries as a land of the living dead was seen as demeaning the profession to promote herself with outsiders. Billings had made his career a great adventure, but Anderson and Lydenberg were not inclined to see life in such terms. (Indeed, Lydenberg was so unadventurous that he declined Metcalf's invitation to join the men who went hiking on the Columbus Day long weekend, because he wouldn't spend more than one night away from home; Metcalf finally arranged to pick him up on Saturday morning for the drive to the Catskills and then return him on Sunday afternoon.)[10] As resentment grew and Hasse felt herself more a prophet without honor in the library, her language became more radical, though she was a revolutionary finding salvation in the American businessman. As she wrote to Walter Swingle, a pioneer in photostat use in libraries, "I am not losing faith in my convictions, although I find the more I give expression to them the colder the shoulder of my associates becomes." Swingle had commended her for "Making a Market," wishing her success in the "great venture in libraries" and agreeing that the problem was "largely the fault of the librarians . . . and there must first of all be a change in their attitude."[11]

The *Library Journal* issue on service to business must have been particularly irritating to Anderson. Besides Hasse, the librarian contributors were two old foes, Dana and Bostwick, and one of the business contributors praised Hasse's ideas. The table of contents showed still more of her visibility: "Miss Hasse to Give Course in United States Documents at Columbia." Then there was the news report "New York Librarians Ask for More Pay," evidence of the restiveness of his staff, which he hoped to control by approving the recent establishment of a staff association as an alternative to agitation for a union or civil service. Adding to his annoyance was a follow-up letter to LJ from Ernest Bradford, statistician of U.S. Rubber (one of the most innovative companies of the day), who praised the Economics Division as "under the direction of Miss Hasse, a service station of very great assistance." He went on to complain that much NYPL material did not circulate and to suggest purchasing more circulating business books, establishing a business collection downtown, issuing fee-based cards with special privileges for business users, and hiring a "trained fact extractor and statistician" who would give business service similar to legislative reference (though conceding that library salaries were too low for those with such skills but hoping that adequate pay "should be forthcoming"). Hasse promptly wrote to Bradford that she wished all his suggestions could be acted on at once, but to Anderson, who was given space to reply in the same issue, Bradford's assumptions were exasperating as he struggled with budget deficits and the inadequate endowment, made worse by the economic upheaval of wartime. In his reply, he pointed out that the library had equipment to provide photostat copies from noncirculating material, which did have the advantage of being always in the building. He explained the "crying need" for funds and suggested that business raise money for development of a business section instead of seeking special privileges that were contrary to the spirit of a free public library. Anderson's annoyance was palpable in regard to the "trained fact extractor," where he complained of the "unbusinesslike" assumption that a better salary would somehow appear, and the Economics Division:

> We are glad to have Mr. Bradford's testimony to the assistance rendered . . . by our economics division. He seems, however, to be under the impression that business men use none of the other sixteen divisions. . . . They use nearly all of them. More readers, for instance, use our divisions of technology, art, or current periodicals than use the economics division, which has only 2 1/2 per cent of the average number of readers in the reference department each day. It would be easy to get from the readers in these other divisions letters setting forth their special needs. . . . It is the business of the administration to see that one class of readers does not run away with the whole appropriation, and that a due balance is maintained between the various divisions.

But Bradford had not written that business men used only the Economics Division. He had said that NYPL's "collection" contained valuable materials and the Economics Division was "perhaps" the most consulted by business. Either Anderson was so upset by praise for Hasse that he couldn't think straight, or he deliberately distorted Bradford's words in order to belittle the Economics Division.[12]

Hasse's promotion of business service may have been the last straw to Anderson for fear that it represented another step in her strategy to succeed him or Lydenberg if their positions became open. Hasse knew everyone who was anyone in New York, in the arts, journalism, government, reform, scholarship, and women's organizations. She had an outstanding record of achievement as a bibliographer and librarian, recognized in the press. If she now established a reputation for specialized service to the city's business community, she would be perfectly positioned to campaign for a higher position. This fundamentally threatened both Anderson's intense need for secrecy and his strategy of hiring and promoting men in library management. Such anxiety was not something he could acknowledge; instead, he complained that Hasse exaggerated the importance of her division and demanded more than its fair share of resources, evidence of her egotism and selfishness, while he, as an executive, had to strive for balance among all parts of the organization. When the Economics Division was established, however, Billings had described it to Cadwalader as "one of the most important in the Library in its influence for the public welfare," and Dain's official history refers to it as "one of the Reference Department's most important and heavily used divisions."[13]

~ ~ ~

Service to business was a priority but far from the only thing on Hasse's mind in the stormy early months of 1917, which began with suffragists picketing the White House (Maud Malone was among those arrested), followed by news of the Russian Revolution, which was initially seen as a hopeful sign of the coming reconstruction of all that was backward and undemocratic. There were also alarming reports about Germany: Americans were angered by the German policy of unrestricted submarine warfare and the sensational discovery of Germany's efforts to form an alliance with Mexico to take back the southwestern states in the event of war. President Wilson had kept out of the European nightmare for three years, but finally, on April 2, he asked Congress for a declaration of war that was overwhelmingly approved.

To the shock of German Americans and others who opposed war, there was an immediate onslaught against both everything German and Americans' basic civil liberties. Within a week of Wilson's call for war, Hasse had been reported to the Secret Service by a man who found her "suspicious in her actions at the library and needs watching."[14] Such suspicion was encouraged by the president's Flag Day address denouncing subversion and warning that Germany had "filled our unsuspecting communities with vicious spies and conspirators" who had "diligently spread sedition among us." He called on the citizenry to report disloyalty, while Congress would pass draconian legislation against espionage and sedition that effectively banned free speech. At the same time, the government organized an unprecedented mobilization of public opinion, orchestrating an atmosphere of patriotic frenzy in which those who lacked enthusiasm for the war stood out, the more easily to be labeled dangerous. Pacifists, Socialists, "highbrows," and unions were suspect, along with those of German ancestry. Many Americans proved all too eager to report suspicions of neighbors and co-workers for investigation by federal, state, or local law enforcement as well as by various vigilante groups. German Americans were investigated, fired, harassed, imprisoned, even lynched. The first object of suspicion was the German American press—many cities had a German-language newspaper—but soon there were efforts to ban every aspect of German culture, even performance of the music of the great German composers. German Americans, long regarded as the good immigrants, favorably contrasted with the Irish and other ethnic groups, now found themselves stereotyped as arrogant, aggressive, domineering, "Prussian," as well as secretly loyal to Germany and plotting to subvert the American war effort.

All this would have been bad enough for Hasse with her German ancestry, but in the hysterical atmosphere, suspicion was aroused by her presence in Germany during the first months of the war and by her family connection to Ernst Hasse of the Pan-German League, which now was the subject of sensational allegations that its rhetoric revealed Germany's intentions to conquer the world with the help of German migrants in other countries. Hasse had never met Ernst Hasse, who was long dead anyway, and their family relationship was not close (half first cousins once removed), but unfortunately she had donated his Hasse family genealogy to the library, and sometime in 1917-18, in his tiny handwriting, Lydenberg copied the exact lines of descent to show the cousins' familial connection for Anderson and the trustees.[15]

In this tumultuous atmosphere, Hasse kept up her busy pace. In February, she went up to Vassar College for an afternoon speech on library careers for women, and, instead of going directly home to Tuckahoe, she returned to the library to work late and send a note to Lydenberg that she would be late on Satur-

day because of an early meeting of the Women's Municipal League Civics
Committee. Her work with the committee led Hasse to plan an exhibit of library
materials on civic education, but she had to appeal for Anderson's approval to
use an exhibit room, because Victor Paltsits, who was responsible for library
exhibits, "does not care to say that he may or may not require the small exhibi-
tion room," apparently an instance of more pettiness towards Hasse.[16] The matter was referred to Lydenberg, who consulted with Paltsits and approved the exhibit, which opened on May 1. Civic education had become a popular concern
of the day, partly as a reaction to the huge number of immigrants and the increasing enfranchisement of women, but also as an expression of the era's hopes
that Americans could be educated to a "civic vision" and a "new American
spirit" that would be both ethical and efficient. *Library Journal* reported on libraries that were developing civic education rooms, and Hasse added it to her
many interests and soon became involved with Alissa Franc, a recent immigrant
who had been inspired to write a popular guide, *Your Government: What the
Government Does for You*. Hasse praised Franc's manuscript to E. P. Dutton
and even suggested a cover blurb for which the publisher paid her $30: "You
means men of business, farmer, exporter, home maker, school boy or school
girl. In some way, the GOVERNMENT HELPS each one of you. This book
tells you how. The government needs your help. You cannot give it unless you
know how the government operates. This book tells you how." Hasse also
wrote the introduction, which was mentioned in a *New York Times* review that
also quoted her cover blurb. Soon she and Franc were at work on a book about
teaching civics in the schools.[17]

Hasse also promoted civic involvement with an article about the Women's
Legislative Council she had observed in Los Angeles, offering it to the *Evening
Mail* and the magazine of the General Federation of Women's Clubs, where it
appeared in an issue that also featured a denunciation of Pan-Germanism as a
symptom of the German conspiracy to rule the world, just the sort of attitude
that was causing Hasse problems.[18] At the same time, she was busy with professional speaking, with spring engagements at the Syracuse University library
school and the meeting of the American Association of Museums.[19] She also
was planning both a speech and an exhibit of trade papers at the ALA convention in June, followed by her course at Columbia. Just when Hasse's schedule
was most hectic, her first assistant Joanna Strange was lost to a serious illness.

The civics exhibit soon brought an enthusiastic letter from a young man
named Lewis Mumford, an admirer of the Scottish thinker Patrick Geddes,
whose work was included in the display. Hasse replied gratefully, encouraging
Mumford to visit her in the library. The record of their encounter takes on significance in light of accusations Anderson soon would make that Hasse was
only interested in important people and received letters of praise only because
she solicited them. Mumford's letter was unsolicited, and Hasse responded
warmly, though he was an obscure and unpromising college dropout whose future prominence as a public intellectual she could not have foreseen.[20]

Hasse did work with important people in this period, but they were not the
sort to impress Anderson, who especially valued his association with the trus-

tees and his membership in the Century Association, the elite men's club where he often had lunch. She referred Sidney Zimand to John Commons, the leading progressive economist, who needed someone to check the notes in his history of American labor. She sent a friendly note to W. E. B. DuBois, the boldest voice for African Americans, about "our conversation yesterday in Bellport regarding clippings on the Colored Question. . . . Our department has a collection of clippings on this subject, and we shall be very glad to have you use them." She hopefully reminded him of his offer to donate his own clippings, which would "be of great value." That summer, she was a member of the Women's Municipal League Committee of One Hundred for Non-Partisan Government, a group of the city's leading women that prepared a platform of the reforms wanted from the next mayor.[21]

Another prominent New Yorker involved Hasse in the "New York harbor case" that led to the establishment of the intergovernmental Port Authority of New York. Julius Henry Cohen, a politically connected attorney active in reform circles, sought help in researching his brief to the Interstate Commerce Commission; he represented the Chamber of Commerce, the Merchants Association, and the state of New York in a case considered vital to the city's economy. Hasse gave him intensive assistance, preparing a bibliography of over 350 items related to his research in "interstate relations of New York and New Jersey, history of the Erie Canal, and history of American railroad rate structures, etc." Cohen sent letters of appreciation to Hasse and Anderson, but when she later cited them as evidence of her good work, Anderson told the trustees that she had done too much for Cohen and was "willing that the entire institution should be put at his service as his personal secretary if she could gain his favor thereby." In reality, it is inconceivable that a library director would not expect an extra effort to help a well-connected lawyer representing state government and leading business organizations on a matter important to the city. Yet even in these circumstances, Anderson found fault with Hasse.[22]

Hasse turned more to Dana for the support that was lacking at NYPL. He readily contributed to the civics exhibit and worked with Hasse for months on her trade papers exhibit for ALA. Educating librarians about the potential of trade publications as an information source was a priority for Hasse, but she also saw the exhibit as a way to promote libraries to business. As she wrote to Dana, "a few of us who know what we want pulling together can make this a smashing good thing and obtain the interest of the business community more quickly than any amount of library talk will ever do. . . . Let us pull together . . . and get the A.L.A. out of its cultured cult into a world of real things."[23]

Reinforcing the exhibit's message, Hasse also gave a talk that appeared in *Library Journal* as "Public vs. Special Libraries." Addressing the special librarians, she proclaimed that the 1917 ALA conference would "go down in library history as marking a new era" in which public libraries recognized their responsibility to serve business in the way special libraries did. Public libraries were about to make their most brilliant success, she was sure, but businessmen would be a demanding clientele, and librarians must be sure they could match the expertise of the special libraries before they advertised business service. Urging SLA to develop a standard course of study for business library work, she again complained that library schools produced people qualified to do "filing and similar work." Serving business required "supplying current information promptly," which meant using "material not ordinarily found in public libraries," such as trade papers, market letters, and foreign journals, or telephoning or telegraphing to a source, in the spirit that "nothing in the world is so important to us" as making the report for the client. "Lunches are missed, dinners are missed, trains are missed until we 'get over the top' with that report," said Hasse of the spirit of the Economics Division, linking its work with the best-selling account of the war as an adventure in male bonding, *Over the Top by an American Soldier Who Went* (1917). She was "extremely punctilious" in dealing with business, describing how she interviewed clients, recorded their requests, and called to check if the work was satisfactory, "as tho we were actually making a business transaction delivering goods." It would be well worth the effort for libraries, however, because nothing was more important for them than "to organize a thorogoing campaign to perfect and standardize thruout the Union the public library service to the business man." As she listened to the talk of library service to soldiers, she thought that librarians "have not realized that every business man is a soldier for his country. Eliminate the business man and you have a stricken country."[24]

All her achievements in the first half of 1917 brought no commendation at NYPL. The administration later complained that her SLA speech had included an anecdote about sending a telegram to get the answer to a question, when the information was already available in the library, but this is another of the allegations made when Hasse had no opportunity to reply. What is clear is that Hasse returned from ALA to a peculiar imbroglio that gave more evidence of Anderson's hostility. The day before her departure, Hasse had posted an announcement, "Mr. Schwenson is detailed as floor and stock superintendent," responsible for scheduling, supervising pages, and "care of stock." After she left, Rollin Sawyer furiously complained to Anderson that Hasse had removed his responsibility for staff scheduling. Anderson was so disturbed that he fired off a telegram to Lydenberg at ALA asking if he had authorized the "transfer of Sawyer's usual duties to Schwenson" and directing him to reply at once. Hearing that Lydenberg had not been consulted, he told Sawyer to remove Hasse's notice and replace it with a statement that the work would remain Sawyer's. He also reported Hasse's action to a board member, Lewis Cass Ledyard, as evidence of insubordination, though the record does not explain how it was insubordinate. When Hasse returned on June 29, she found Anderson's notice and asked to meet with him, but he was unavailable, having left on a month's vacation. She sent an account of her side of the story to Anderson and Lydenberg, who later dismissed it as "craftily specious." Hasse said she had been worried that the division's bibliography on the cost of living, scheduled for three fall issues of the *Bulletin,* needed intensive work to meet the deadline, so she asked Sawyer to give all his time to it, while giving Schwenson experience in scheduling at a time when she was planning to change the structure of the evening schedule. She ended by remarking that she had told Sawyer to prepare the schedule according to her new plan and continue the bibliographic project, but "he has not, so far as I know, done any work on the bibliography." With remarkable restraint, Hasse said nothing of the impropriety of hastily and publicly reversing a division chief's staff assignment without consulting her, nor did she point to the double standard by which Sawyer was rewarded for going over her head to the director with an angry protest while she was criticized for sharply worded memos about errors. Such demeaning treatment could only reinforce Hasse's perception that she was the object of a vendetta by Anderson and his young men. The division staff shared her sense of injustice, and Sawyer soon decided to transfer to the Technology Division.[25]

This incident is one of the most mystifying among Hasse's troubles. It had great significance to Anderson, who carefully documented it as evidence of Hasse's bad behavior, but even if Hasse was unfair to Sawyer, Anderson's reaction seems disproportionate, particularly in an organization in which, according to Metcalf, another division chief's harsh treatment was tolerated as a good test of Charles McCombs. Lydenberg later tried to explain it as an instance of Hasse's temperamental behavior with those who disagreed with her; he said that Hasse thought well enough of Sawyer to recommend a raise for him in the 1917 budget, but "differences of opinion arose" that caused Hasse to suggest his transfer, which was refused when Sawyer objected. No documentation of this was provided. Hasse's few references to Sawyer in memos to the administration suggest that she regarded him as a weak link because of his absences due to heart trouble and his ineffectiveness when sent to make contacts and gather materials at a conference on Latin America, but there is no evidence of strong feelings pro or con, and she apparently did encourage his bibliographic work in the *Bulletin*. Sawyer had joined NYPL from the Albany library school and seems to have been determined to have the rank of "first assistant," first at the Municipal Reference Library (where Seaver thought he was first assistant) and then in the Economics Division.[26] (Perhaps the difference of opinion with Hasse was about who would become first assistant in place of Joanna Strange, who became ill in May.) That the petty power over staff schedules meant so much to Sawyer suggests an intense need for status, and Anderson's intervention was an indication of favoritism that Hasse naturally resented. Perhaps Sawyer's connections (his father and grandfather were prominent clergymen, and his aunt was married to Arthur Bostwick) won him favored treatment, or perhaps Anderson had moved him to the Economics Division as a spy and possible successor to Hasse. In fact, Sawyer did become chief of the division a few years later.

When Anderson returned from vacation, there was more evidence of hostility, this time about Hasse's request for reimbursement of her ALA conference expenses. He sent a frosty note complaining that her request for permission to attend had arrived in his office the day she left, and when he telephoned her division, he was told she was already gone. "I should like an explanation of your attitude in this matter," he wrote, to which Hasse apologetically explained that she had discussed the trip with Lydenberg well in advance but forgot to send a note to Anderson until the day before she left. When he called, she was still in the building and tried to reach him before leaving, erroneously assuming she would see him at the conference to explain.[27]

Unless Hasse feared that Anderson would refuse permission, she would have had no reason to delay her request, but she easily could have forgotten about it in such a busy period. This correspondence went into Anderson's file along with various innocuous notes from Hasse to Lydenberg about absences to speak or attend meetings, suggesting that the underlying issue was resentment of her outside activities, seen as more evidence of self-importance and self-promotion by a woman who should have been content to stay at her post in the library. Anderson, who didn't share Kelso's view that librarians should be visible outside the library, had conveyed his skepticism about meetings in 1916, telling Hasse that he didn't want to spend money on her attending a conference of businessmen on the "mere chance" of benefits when the library was struggling with inadequate income and a shortage of staff. She failed to take the hint and continued to send notes informing Lydenberg that she was off to this or that meeting, not realizing that they would go into the file of evidence against her.[28]

Despite the tensions with Anderson, Hasse persisted in her efforts to interest him in developing her division. In March, with the cataloging transfer behind them, she reminded him that he had ended "one of our late interviews with the remark that I bring up the subject of the reorganization of the Economics Division in March." She heard from Lydenberg that the director didn't recall the matter but would be glad to have her bring it up. Hasse replied that she thought Anderson had something to say: "You were present when he said he had 'something big' in mind which he was not ready to discuss but to 'bring it up again in March.'" Lydenberg noted only that he spoke to her about it, and there is no further record of "something big." In July, just after the Sawyer incident and Anderson's letter to Library Journal had demonstrated his hostility, Hasse again wrote a memo prodding the administration to formulate policy for the future of the division. Trying to show that it was not only her idea, she suggested consultation with potential users through "a conference of persons representing economic interests," such as banks, the business press, and academic institutions. She assured them that she would have no part in shaping the policy, but she would find it inspiring to have the consensus of economic researchers, while such an effort at consultation would make a favorable impression on the public. She gave the memo to Lydenberg with the understanding that he would take it to Anderson, but he did nothing for four months, finally sending it to Anderson in November with only a comment that he had promised to pass it on. By then, the tension between Anderson and Hasse was even worse.[29]

Hasse was more successful with Lydenberg that summer when she suggested that the division install a blackboard to post the bill status of high-interest legislation. But such small improvements were not enough to satisfy her at a time when the nation was swept up in the war effort. Many of her New York acquaintances were off to Washington to join the Council of National Defense or other wartime agencies. Sometimes they sent requests for help to Hasse: Ida Tarbell's assistant sought advice on organizing information for the Women's Committee of the Council of National Defense, and the Council also contacted her for references to the reconstruction of Britain.[30]

In September, press reports alerted Hasse to a great opportunity to use her expertise in national service: President Wilson had directed his close associate, Colonel Edward House, to collect and organize the information that would be needed for the eventual peace conference. This secret project, known simply as the Inquiry, later would be seen as a precursor of the Central Intelligence Agency and the Council on Foreign Relations. House established the Inquiry in New York, entirely outside of government, and designated as director his brother-in-law, President Mezes of City College, with Walter Lippmann as general secretary of the project that would recruit more than a hundred experts to put together the information needed to reorganize the world as Wilson hoped. As soon as word of the Inquiry leaked to the press, Hasse wrote to House, asking to be appointed its librarian. When House, who had been inundated by job seekers, made only a perfunctory acknowledgment, she wrote to Mezes to offer her assistance in making use of NYPL's resources.[31] Eventually, to her shock and embarrassment, she learned that the Inquiry was already working in an office in the basement of NYPL, but Anderson and Lydenberg had kept it secret from her and told the group to seek assistance at the Information Desk. Hasse understandably took this as another insult from Anderson (who had been told to keep the Inquiry's presence confidential but seems to have taken it to an extreme), but she didn't realize that he now regarded her as a security risk. The Inquiry's director finally did seek her help, and the Economics Division was able to assist with some research, but the group soon moved far uptown to the American Geographical Society, which must have been maddening to Hasse.[32] Although she would continue to help some of the Inquiry's researchers, NYPL had lost the chance to identify itself as the center of a historic effort to gather information for America's new role in world affairs. Adding to her distress, she suspected, probably accurately, that Isadore Mudge, the Columbia reference librarian and companion of Minnie Sears, was warning the Inquiry's researchers to avoid the disloyal Hasse. One prominent economist told Williamson that "we have not been able, for obvious reasons, to avail ourselves of the full assistance" of the Economics Division.[33]

The following year, *Library Journal* published a report from the ALA conference that paid tribute to the help provided to the Inquiry by various librarians, especially Mudge and other librarians at Columbia, Putnam at LC, Richardson of Princeton, and that "so cheerfully given" by Anderson, Lydenberg, and "others" at NYPL. No one was disturbed by these men's eagerness to help important people, but Hasse's interest in the Inquiry was suspect to Anderson. Soon he would report her to the government, citing as evidence against her that when the Inquiry's researchers used the Economics Division, "Miss Hasse takes pains to assist them in securing all information, books, papers, etc., that they may desire." Hasse could hardly have been in a more impossible position, suspect for the same assistance to the Inquiry that brought praise to other librarians, including the man who reported her, at the ALA conference and in the pages of *Library Journal*.[34]

~ ~ ~

Not realizing that Anderson now suspected her of being some sort of German agent or stooge as well as a troublemaker in the library, Hasse continued to try to develop a working relationship with him, but several of her actions in the fall of 1917 could only intensify his animosity. She seemed ambivalent, sometimes hopeful of improving the situation but not willing to deny her professional values or disappear into the woodwork to avoid Anderson's wrath. She was in a classic double bind, in that the public activity that brought her approval and advanced her reputation would have seemed a way to protect herself, even as it intensified Anderson's hostility.

In October, Hasse managed to offend not only Anderson but much of the library power structure with her thoughts on women librarians in the Journal of the Association of Collegiate Alumnae, the organization of women college graduates. It was her most vigorous attack on everything she found objectionable in libraries: narrowly technical training producing stunted graduates who "stop learning when they leave school," "undeveloped" reference work with "archaic catalogues and sporadic indexes" instead of fully developed information service, low wages for the rank and file while the highest salaries were "secured as often thru favoritism as thru any inherent ability," frustration for "ambitious, intelligent women" with the "lack of initiative" in administration. Instead of trying to draw women to an attractively presented career, Hasse appealed to her readers to rescue a failed idea with the "tremendously brilliant organizing power" shown in the suffrage movement. "The Inez Milholland type is sadly needed among us to vivify the inertia of existing conditions," she wrote, calling up the image of the dynamic, Vassar-educated, young orator of the suffrage campaign. Echoing Dana's private comments, she publicly complained of librarians mired in mediocrity: "The situation as it exists today presents a dead level of mediocrity. . . . With one or two exceptions I do not remember any unusual work being done by library school graduates. But it is difficult to see how an occupation sought by the great majority of those engaged in it as a refuge rather than a career, could be other than the grave it is."[5]

Though library school graduates might privately agree on the need for improvement, they could hardly accept such public scorn for their special educational credential, the source of their claim to professional status. And writing for the Association of Collegiate Alumnae was offensive to women library school graduates, who resented the organization's policy that library schools were non-academic technical training whose graduates did not qualify for membership. Yet there was a historic connection between women librarians and the association, the group to which Melvil Dewey had appealed in 1886 for educated women to enter library work and attend the school he was about to open. Thus, thirty years on, Hasse might be seen as following in the footsteps of Dewey, addressing the new generation of college women with a call to revitalize the library movement.

As if her remarks about library schools were not infuriating enough to Anderson, Hasse went on with implied criticism of his administration of NYPL that must have seemed unforgivable. She compared the annual expenditure of NYPL with "the great techno-professional service institutions of the federal government," such as the Geological Survey and the Weather Bureau, finding that the government agencies that produced superb information service operated at about the same or less expenditure and with much smaller payrolls than NYPL. While there could be useful comparisons between libraries and such information agencies, Hasse's sweeping generalization about budgets left her open to accusations of making an apples-and-oranges analogy. NYPL simply wasn't the same as the Geological Survey, and Hasse only worsened her situation by asking, "Why is it that the same amount of money which produced such tremendous results in the Government bureaus . . . produces such pitifully negligible results when spent for public libraries?" And she could only alienate the library establishment when she described public libraries as "a dead weight on the spirit of progress." Of course the comments were marked on the copy that went into Anderson's file. But Hasse was desperate to warn, accurately as it turned out, that if libraries did not become more active, "a middleman agency will be developed which will simply rework the library resources to meet the public requirements and sell the new product back to the library and to the public." Her hope was to recruit energetic young women "in favor of libraries as public service plants" to make public libraries more like special libraries in providing information.

Public libraries owed much of their growth to the efforts of civic-minded women who wanted to raise the cultural level of their communities, provide moral and social uplift, and create educational centers. Now women were half the enrollment in higher education, and Hasse was trying to interest the younger generation in taking libraries to a new level. She was publicly calling attention to problems that also were recognized by some influential insiders. At the same time that her article appeared, the Carnegie Corporation ended its grants for library buildings on the grounds that too many towns failed to support their libraries, which was blamed on "untrained and inefficient librarians" rather than the indifference or limited resources of the residents. In Dee Garrison's analysis, this was a sign of the underlying crisis of the public library, which had failed to fulfill hopes that it would be a major force in society and was sliding back "to its essential core: a generalist collection of books, chiefly fiction, read by middle-class patrons, chiefly female," plus an expanded children's section.[36] This was what Hasse suggested at the time. She had aimed to make public libraries relevant from the beginning of her career, and now she was striving to establish them as essential to business, to the world of men with economic and political power.

Library historians have disputed Garrison's interpretation as unfair to women librarians and unrealistic about the potential of public libraries. Suzanne Hildenbrand has suggested that the period of feminization was actually a golden age in the development of American libraries.[37] It could be argued that American public libraries had been notably successful in a country with little tradition of publicly supported institutions and a culture that was profoundly anti-intellectual. In a short period, libraries had become established in cities and towns across the nation, "free to all," with standards for cataloging, classification, reference, and children's service. They had attracted the support of the nation's richest man and leading philanthropist. They had recruited a workforce of dedicated, albeit low-paid, women and developed professional training, methods, associations, and publications. If the public library remained marginal amid the noisy commercial bustle of American life, it hardly deserved to be labeled a failure. But to Hasse, having lived through a half century of political, economic, and technological change, in the midst of a war that was going to complete the Progressive Era by reorganizing the world to make it safe for democracy, libraries seemed to be losing their vision and sinking into a swamp of irrelevance. Her aim was to inspire younger women to take up the cause that had drawn so many able women in the decade after Dewey's original appeal.

At NYPL, Hasse was continually reminded of Edwin Anderson's very different attitude towards the recruitment of future library leaders. Shortly after her article appeared, she received a reminder that Anderson's preference for hiring young men was not unusual among library directors. Everett Perry wrote from Los Angeles to ask if she could suggest a man for the technology department with the ability to fill in as director in his absence. He emphasized that it must be a man, "because we shall eventually need an Assistant Librarian, and it is my plan to get a man good enough to act in that capacity" after a tryout in technology work. This was a remarkably insensitive remark to a woman who had been assistant to a woman director at LAPL, where there had been only women directors from 1880 to 1905. That Perry happened to write soon after Hasse's appeal to college women suggests an intention, perhaps unconscious, to send her a message.[38]

Hasse's feeling that the library movement needed new energy was not unique among the pioneer women librarians of her generation. Lutie Stearns had recently left the Wisconsin Free Library Commission for a more stimulating career as a freelance lecturer, though she would continue to comment on library issues, "often to the discomfiture of her erstwhile colleagues," denouncing "public librarians for their complacency and timid loyalty to the established order." Emma Baldwin would soon leave her longtime position as Frank Hill's assistant in Brooklyn with the hope of starting a training program in library administration. Cornelia Marvin was feeling the disillusion she would later describe to Mary Eileen Ahern: "Twenty-five years ago . . . the mechanical things which were done were accomplished to clear the way for the great work which was to come. Everyone was hopeful. I do not know just what has happened."[39]

As usual, Hasse received favorable response from outsiders. Susan Ball of U.S. Rubber wrote that she and Ernest Bradford had enjoyed the article, but "I tremble for the fate of the library school students." The League for Business Opportunities for Women, another group of New York's elite reforming women, asked for something similar, discussing "librarians' struggle to get higher wages and better conditions of work," since Hasse and her division "are right in the thick of it and have all the information right at hand." Hasse was indeed in the thick of issues of women's pay and working conditions, within both NYPL and the profession, as the war expanded women's opportunities and raised their expectations, serving as a "catalyst to the feminist movement" that "greatly increased the confidence and self-image of American women. It demonstrated what they might do if given the chance." With young men in the military, women often were able to move into what had been male work, seeming to fulfill the hopes for women's economic advancement. As Mary Dreier Robins exulted to the 1917 conference of the Women's Trade Union League, "This is the woman's age! At last after centuries of disabilities and discriminations, women are coming into the labor and festival of life on equal terms with men."[40]

A sign of women's rising expectations appeared in an unusual outbreak of assertiveness among some librarians over the exclusion of women from the work of the Library War Service Committee, particularly from the libraries of military camps. Indignant letters appeared in *Public Libraries* from women who wished to remain anonymous. Led by Beatrice Winser, Dana's associate, and urged on by Tessa Kelso, a small group of prominent women challenged Herbert Putnam, director of the Library War Service and Librarian of Congress. He tried to blame the War Department, which turned out to have no official policy against women librarians. Winser accused Putnam of deceit, warning, "The fundamental mistake made by you, . . . seems to have been the usual one of thinking that men are better qualified than women for work in the world. . . . Let us not forget that women form a half of all democracies."[41]

Putnam had made public statements about women librarians' inferiority, their lack of "manliness," in the past without drawing protest, but the wartime atmosphere emboldened the women to pursue the matter with a public inquiry at the 1918 ALA conference, where James Wyer, Frank Hill, and Putnam assured them that there was no discrimination, only various factors making it impractical for women librarians to work in military camps. They admonished women for wanting adventure away from home when they could support the war effort just as well by staying at their posts and filling in for absent men. What men said privately, however, was reported in *Public Libraries* in an account of a conversation overheard at ALA, where some young men discussed their preference for keeping it "all in the hands of men"; one remarked that there was "only one woman in the profession who was big enough for the place." This lone woman was not identified, leaving open the possibility that he referred to Hasse, one of the few women librarians prominent in public life.[42]

Putnam even raised the familiar obsession with women librarians' sacred service to children, expressing shock that there were children's librarians willing to leave their work to become government file clerks in Washington. He could not name a man in war service in Washington, said the Librarian of Congress and director of the Library War Service, "who can do for the future of this country what the librarian of a children's department can do at this very moment." Apparently the women were too polite to ask Putnam why he didn't give up his work in Washington to become a children's librarian. In fact, Winser had made that very point in a recent *Public Libraries*. In reply to a man who had defended Wyer's statement that work in camp libraries was "a man's job" with the assertion that no man would "pout if told that the management of a children's room is a 'woman's job,'" Winser wrote that "it would be a very good idea to have men serve as children's librarians," though the writer "evidently feels that a man would be belittled if he were selected to be a children's librarian."[43]

As it happened, one of the group challenging Putnam was a children's librarian, Anne Carroll Moore of NYPL's Children's Services, and it was she who warned most strongly of a general problem of which the camp libraries issue was a symptom, the lack of appeal of library work to younger women:

> But we are losing right and left . . . promising young women who have given five, ten or more years to library work and have distinct contributions to make. These young women have been eagerly welcomed and readily placed by . . . groups of war workers or in government service. I believe we . . . are already in the midst of the gravest crisis in library service with which we have ever been confronted. . . . We have got to meet the questions of the younger women with something responsive to their appeal if we are to hold their interest."

Moore was especially aware of the problem at NYPL, where dissatisfied employees were leaving for better pay and opportunity, even in typing and filing jobs. In 1917, fifty-four staff of the Reference Department (19 percent) left for better paid work, and more, 27 percent, left the Circulation Department for unspecified reasons. Given the nature of the workforce, many of these would have been young women.

~ ~ ~

The women who remained at NYPL had neither equal opportunity nor anything else to celebrate. One thing Hasse and Metcalf agreed on was the existence of considerable "unrest" among library employees. It had long been recognized that NYPL paid less than comparable libraries, and the situation had worsened with high wartime inflation. Besides lacking pensions, the Reference Department had no personnel policies or salary schedules to alleviate perceptions of unfairness. With so much turnover, the workload of those who remained increased, and Metcalf recalled, "Each year during the war, staff unrest in the library increased." Anderson's official response was to deny any special problem, telling *Library Journal* that employee turnover was common in libraries and throughout the economy, but privately he was increasingly desperate.[45]

In the spring of 1917, Anderson agreed to the formation of the NYPL Staff Association, which would give employees a voice in their "social, professional, and economic betterment" without resort to a union. Not everyone agreed that the Staff Association, with its ties to the administration, was the best approach to their problems. The irrepressible suffrage campaigner Maud Malone promptly took the lead in forming the New York Library Employees Union. In New York, site of the garment workers' strikes and the women teachers' campaign for pay equity, home of the Women's Trade Union League, there was obvious potential for a union of the large, mostly female workforce of the public libraries. A year earlier the city's teachers had formed a union that would be a vigorous advocate of intellectual freedom and due process; Leonora O'Reilly of the Women's Trade Union League had advised the teachers to "stop thinking they were better than ordinary workers and . . . join a real trade union."[46] This was the message Maud Malone would promote with her usual flair, arguing that library workers were as much "sweated labor" as the women in garment factories. With their experience in suffrage and other reform movements, Malone and her sister Marcella, who worked for the Queens library system, saw a union of library workers as a way to organize women and address fundamental issues of gender discrimination underlying the problems of pay and working conditions.[47]

Hasse initially was hopeful that the Staff Association would provide a way to improve the situation. In June, she was a candidate for president against Franklin Hopper of the Order Department. He won the election, but Hasse believed that she would have been elected if Anderson had not intervened by directing Hopper not to withdraw his candidacy and then spreading the rumor that Hasse was unfit for the office because she was the real instigator of the union.[48] Anderson denied this, but he does seem to have been eager to connect Hasse with the union. Hasse sympathized with the LEU, but there is no evidence that she was behind it, and certainly Maud Malone would never be anyone's puppet. Malone had vigorously protested elitist attitudes within the suffrage movement; she would not have allowed the union to be dominated or manipulated by a division chief when her aim was to empower the women in the lower ranks.

After losing the election, Hasse was made chair of the Economic Committee of the Reference Department, charged to promote the staff's economic welfare. In November, she discussed the committee's ideas with Anderson and then sent him the written statement he requested. It concluded that "much of the unrest now known to exist throughout the Reference Department staff is due largely to the unsatisfactory adjustment of employment, of salaries and of promotion." The committee sought only to investigate further, asking for Anderson's approval of "efforts to ascertain the validity of and to substantiate its conclusion," a seemingly reasonable suggestion that threatened to bring up matters Anderson did not want discussed. He tried his usual method of no reply; after three weeks, Hasse sent a second copy with a note that she feared the original had been lost. Anderson stalled further with the reply that he had presented the matter to the Executive Committee, which "would be glad to receive and consider the statement of any facts which, in the opinion of the committee, justify its conclusion that the unrest, etc." Six months earlier, however, Anderson had himself warned the Executive Committee about unrest that he admitted was due to failure of the administration and the trustees to deal with the pay problem.[49]

It took the committee more than a month to compose a response to the director's cryptic message. In January, as Hasse was about to take leave to teach in California, the committee sent a letter assuring Anderson of its "spirit of friendly cooperation" and agreeing that the current labor situation was abnormal, noting that it did not know if the unrest had caused the high turnover. At the same time, perhaps hoping that the Staff Association's Executive Board could deal better with Anderson, it sent the board a proposal for a "Personnel Board" of at least five staff to serve as intermediary with the administration on employment matters, particularly the need to standardize salaries. It also suggested a system of rotating staff among divisions to provide varied experience and better working relationships.[50]

~ ~ ~

Just before her departure for California, Hasse had the pleasure of another publication aimed at influential people outside libraries when "Why Not?" appeared in a leading Progressive journal, *The New Republic.* It was another *cri-de-coeur* of the librarian who longed to be part of the real world: "Outside of these beautiful buildings, the great world goes swirling, an occasional spray comes spattering in and we on the inside are refreshed, we are 'in touch' with the great swirling world. Every year millions of dollars are spent to maintain these beautiful buildings and to provide for us a milieu in which we may sit and think we think. Our immolated self-contemplation almost suggests the traditional Oriental."

Hasse pointed to the Council of National Defense as one example of the great forces that needed the help of librarians, who instead "are withering into a useless cult for want of contact with these forces, into shadows in a No-man's land." The library's potential was being destroyed "by prolonged over-emphasis on . . . mechanical values, by a vision-less acceptance of mechanical values as ultimate factors." Repeatedly she asked why libraries couldn't galvanize "the present inert mass into a pulsating service plant" and seek out "market relations with the great outside world."[51]

Hasse illustrated with her usual anecdotes from her own experience, referring to the Inquiry and a typical problem of dealing with assistants rather than the person who needed the information: a young woman had been sent to gather statistics on European merchant marines and had "floundered over the catalog" until Hasse explained that the data were within general statistical reference books that were not to be found under subjects in the catalog "in the present stage of our cataloging development." (Anderson would later claim that the woman had complained of being publicly insulted.) Another case involved a Columbia professor who sought Hasse's help in locating information on European free ports for the Tariff Commission. Hasse argued that it didn't occur to those needing information to contact a librarian directly because the library "consistently declines to function as a public service organization." Hasse was articulating a common frustration among reference librarians, but blaming the problem on the failings of library service overlooked other factors influencing "principals," such as ignorance, anxiety, time pressures, and status needs. Her use of personal references, asking why hadn't the Tariff Commission "appealed directly to me" and admitting "a certain professional resentment not to be in more direct relations with the principal," was part of her theme of the librarian frustrated at not being directly connected with the work of the world, but to Anderson, as he marked the personal references in a copy for his files, it was evidence of megalomania that required him to take action.

~ ~ ~

As usual with Anderson, taking action meant a secret maneuver that could not be traced to him, and Hasse inadvertently had provided him with an excuse to report her to the government as a possible subversive. In planning her trip to California, she suggested that it would be a good chance to go to Mexico to obtain documents that the library had not received for more than four years, during a period of civil war and general turmoil. Mexican public documents had been a strong area of the collection, subject of a thirty-page bibliography in the NYPL *Bulletin* in 1909, but now something had to be done to retrieve the missing materials. Her proposal was that the library pay her salary and train fare during the travel in Mexico, while she would be responsible for living expenses. Anderson replied that the Executive Committee "seem to think it unwise," an understandable reaction after years of civil war in Mexico, with Pancho Villa still on the loose and anti-American feeling lingering from President Wilson's military interventions and the American ambassador's meddling in Mexican affairs. By 1918, however, the central government was in control of the cities and railroads, and a new constitution had been established, so Hasse saw an opportunity to locate the missing documents and make connections to ensure continued receipt. To Anderson, however, her suggestion was so alarming that he decided to inform the Secret Service (then competing with the Justice Department to investigate German agents). His suspicions were encouraged by a report from Charles Williamson of an occurrence in the Economics Division that indicated a German sympathizer on its staff.[52]

On January 18, a few days before Hasse's departure, Anderson went to the local office of the Secret Service to report the proposed Mexican trip, which he said was too costly to be worthwhile in obtaining documents. He explained that he had refused permission because of Hasse's pro-German sympathies. If he had given approval, he would have had to provide letters of introduction that would have made her seem "an accredited and official person," putting her in "a splendid position to help the German cause if she had been so inclined." Other than speculating that Hasse would engage in some sort of propaganda, he had little to offer. He reported misleadingly that she was born to "German parents" and had been in Germany when the war began, where he suspected "she was played up to" by the Germans, who recognized that she was "the ideal type of person for [German ambassador] von Bernstorff to have used in his work here." He explained that Hasse was an authority on government information from all over the world and was making great efforts to assist the Inquiry, in which her "knowledge and ability render her able to be of material assistance." Since this was both her patriotic duty and a basic job responsibility, it didn't make compelling evidence against her. He left a copy of Hasse's *New Republic* piece, perhaps as evidence of her interest in the Inquiry or her dangerous attitude, and then followed up with a letter about his suspicions and a call to report Hasse's exact departure date and the information that she was traveling with a friend, rather than her son, which he seemed to regard as suspect. The vagueness of his allegations shows more about Anderson than Hasse, and perhaps it reveals the real source of his anxiety: "Informant believes her personality as well as her sympathies render her dangerous. She is a very forceful, arrogant woman of decided views."[53]

In the end, Hasse did not go to Mexico, but Anderson continued to harbor suspicions that he was still eager to report four years later to the Justice Department's Bureau of Investigation. By then, he had obtained some correspondence from Hasse's files that showed she had offered to write about the situation in Mexico for the *Evening Mail* just before making her proposal to him. On her return, she told the editor she had been unable to get information on Mexico, other than observing in Los Angeles "a very tense feeling . . . about being the first to get hold of the Mexican market as soon as that country is opened up." She mentioned press reports on "German activities for catching the Mexican trade which led me to make the opening I did." Oddly, the file makes no mention of the most suspicious aspect of this: in 1915, the *Mail* had been secretly purchased by the German government to serve its interests in the struggle for American public opinion. This made headlines in July 1918, when the editor, Edward Rumely, was indicted for not informing the United States government. There is no sign that Hasse knew this, however, and she would hardly have kept her correspondence with Rumely if she were part of a conspiracy. Everyone connected with the *Mail* claimed to be horrified by the discovery of Rumely's secret arrangement. Hasse's proposal to write "a series of letters from Mexico describing in a popular way business and commercial conditions" was made first to Edwin Clapp, an economics professor at New York University who also wrote editorials for the *Mail*. Like so many American scholars, Clapp had received his doctorate from a German university, and he had written a book on economic aspects of the war. Hasse had helped him with research and praised some of his editorial commentary, which had vigorously criticized the British blockade of Germany as harmful to American commerce and contrary to the principle, long defended by the United States, of freedom of the seas. Clapp had referred her inquiry to Rumely, who expressed interest.[54]

The most likely explanation is that Hasse was interested in economic issues that many saw as the real reason for international conflict; competition for Latin American markets and resources was high among these. (In a sign of government interest, the secretary of state would soon ask the Inquiry to give special attention to the region, even though it was not expected to be part of any peace negotiations.) At a time when she was contributing to general periodicals, Hasse saw a chance for more visibility by writing for a New York newspaper on an important economic topic. She may even have had hopes of developing a writing career, thinking of the women who were pressing to be war correspondents in Europe and perhaps of John Reed, whose celebrity as a journalist began with his reporting on the turmoil in Mexico. And writing could help pay for her travel to obtain documents she had been unable to provide researchers at a time of high interest in Mexico. In any event, she did not make much effort to pursue what seems to have been an impulse reflecting her adventurous spirit as well as her collector's urge to track down missing documents.

Those who had sympathized with Germany became circumspect about expressing their views, but Hasse was one of the few tough enough to resist the intense pressure to buy war bonds. Some correspondence that ended up in Anderson's Hasse file showed her to have been in contact with researchers who had been most active in countering anti-German propaganda, but this was mostly before the declaration of war. She had helped men like Edwin Clapp, Edmund von Mach, Frank Illesley, and Otto Merkel locate official documents and statistics, but she does not seem to have done more for them than for any library users. Illesley regarded her as someone who could be trusted in a dangerous environment, warning not to mention his name in a way that might connect him with "suspicion of propaganda." Merkel, who was under observation for disseminating information favorable to Germany as director of an organization of Americans who had attended German universities, was arrested in the library in December 1917. With the simultaneous arrest of Hans von Stengel, a cartoonist whose work was disrespectful of President Wilson and the war effort, the *Times* reported that the internment of "two of the brainiest and most important German propagandists" was a blow to their friend Ambassador von Bernstorff and other "German agents." Merkel was said to be a friend of the "large number of pro-Germans who are employed as instructors in American colleges and universities" and had been mailing them pro-German materials, especially about the "alleged disclosures of the Russian Bolsheviki" of diplomatic correspondence showing secret agreements among the Allies. Merkel responded he had broken no laws and was no longer connected with German universities.[55]

In such an atmosphere, with more than fifteen hundred Americans arrested for "disloyal utterances," Hasse must have been acutely aware of the dangers of being connected with German propaganda or expressing opinions that might seem subversive. Women were less likely to come under suspicion, but those women who were charged tended to be unmarried professionals whose attitudes "violated both wartime prescriptions of loyalty and middle-class definitions of gender-appropriate behavior." New York City led the nation in firing teachers; several were women who personally opposed the war but had not said so in their classrooms. William Allen wrote to Hasse as a member of a Committee of One Hundred to denounce the loyalty testing of teachers and their dismissal "on the basis of private interviews of which not even stenographic notes are taken. . . . Prussia never saw Prussianism of a more dangerous type." His defense of civil liberties and due process ended up in Anderson's file of evidence against Hasse.[56]

Under intense public pressure, librarians joined the patriotic fervor, competing to report their removal of subversive books, such as those written in German or advocating pacifism; letters reporting the discovery of a page or two of pro-German material in seemingly innocuous volumes regularly appeared in *Public Libraries*. At the same time, they readily accepted gifts of British propaganda donated by front organizations, for the library press advised that libraries were part of the war effort and "to be neutral now is disloyal."[57] The always skeptical Dana was one of the few to challenge acceptance of wartime propaganda and censorship. The more common attitude was demonstrated cruelly at ALA in the summer of 1918, when Richard Bowker, whose blindness made him especially dependent on the solace of music, expressed the hope that peace would come soon, so that the music of Mozart and Beethoven could once again be enjoyed; the ALA audience reacted with a "chorus of boos" for the aged blind man who had done so much for libraries. Even in Wisconsin, with its large German American population, Charles McCarthy came under attack because his books had praised German policies in city planning, forest conservation, and old age pensions.[58] If people like Bowker, McCarthy, and Jane Addams, with their work to improve American life, could be subject to such abuse, Hasse was frighteningly vulnerable.

~ ~ ~

Six weeks in Southern California gave Hasse a good respite from her troubles in New York. Besides teaching in Riverside, she visited Los Angeles to see her family and be entertained at LAPL by Everett Perry. She and Charles Lummis were eager to meet, but Hasse found she didn't have enough time between seeing her mother in Santa Monica and the LAPL schedule of an evening party followed by a morning speech to the staff and a tour of the branches. She assured Lummis that she had committed to teach again at Riverside in 1919 and would see him then. It was a disappointment to Lummis, who had noted in his diary, "a beautiful astonishment this morning, a letter from Adelaide Hasse, . . . now one of the Stars of NYPL. . . . I surely want to see her. For she surely is one of the redeeming features in the Public Library system of the U.S." He was bewildered to hear from Frank Hill that he hadn't missed much if Hasse couldn't see him: "Of course you knew her in Los Angeles and probably still have a high opinion of her." In cryptic insider style, Hill offered no explanation of why opinions of Hasse had changed and further puzzled Lummis with the remark, "I wonder if her children were with her." Hill was a friend of Anderson's, and his letter indicated that Hasse's demonization was well under way in eastern library circles and was not limited to her German connections and controversial statements. Even her adoptive motherhood had become some kind of evidence against her.[59]

In California, however, there was only warmth, both physical and emotional, with the success of being hired for a return engagement, treated as an honored guest at LAPL, welcomed by Lummis, and having a last visit with her mother. She also had encouraging words from her enthusiastic staff back in the Economics Division. Rose Eichenbaum wrote that she had turned down a job offer from a Federal Reserve bank solely to continue working with Hasse's "personal inspiration." "You have a way of getting the best there is out of a person," she said, "so that one cannot help but growing." Alice Ramsburg reported outreach efforts, with a talk to the League of Advertising Women and a visit to George Frederick of the Business Bourse, a researcher and consultant who had read "Why Not?" From Elsie Rushmore, who had taken Joanna Strange's place as first assistant, came word that, as a result of "Why Not?" in *The New Republic*, an employee of Treasury Secretary McAdoo had brought in a list of four hundred industries for which he wanted statistics of increase since 1914: "I told him we lived to do jobs like that and we are all at work on it."[60]

"Why Not?" also brought appreciative letters from librarians. A Philadelphia woman complained of the organizations that came to the library for information but never thought to put librarians on their boards, "and then the time wasted giving casual instruction to incompetent secretaries!" A former librarian who had switched to business described herself as "an ardent feminist" and regretted women librarians' interest in the "petty details rather than the broad view of the work." Dana sent his hearty approval. Not realizing the danger Hasse was in, he urged her to be even more outspoken: "I wish you would do this kind of thing oftener and I wish you were more addicted to getting up on your feet at Association meetings, once in awhile, and turning loose. . . . I have been almost alone in my d----d activities in these matters for many years."[61]

Surprisingly, there also was a letter from Mary Eileen Ahern of *Public Libraries* asking for two thousand words on a subject of Hasse's choice, preferably "constructive criticism." Ahern feared that there was "something akin to staleness in the output of library writing," with movements coming in "waves, which do nothing more than to wash up and back, and each new wave brings other things in no way related," without "the spirit of coordination." After consulting Cornelia Marvin, she contacted Hasse as one of the women librarians who had done important work, as "it has seemed that there is lacking an expression or articulation of the opinions and views of the women in the work." Though a notably independent and tough-minded woman, Ahern was always concerned with unity and careful in speaking of gender, but in 1918 she and her readers were disturbed about the Library War Service and its implications for women librarians. The majority of library workers were women, she wrote, but added that it would be "a deplorable thing to emphasize this fact or give it undue weight in our cooperative work for the benefit of all." Hasse replied that there was "an immense opportunity to demonstrate the existence of organized cooperative library effort," especially since the "suffragists have demonstrated that women have brilliant organizing ability." But she felt some uncertainty "that what I say will meet with your approval." Ahern assured her that she would be grateful for Hasse's contribution (presumably "This Business of Ours," the lead article in the July issue) and pledged, "I, of all people, am a strong advocate of free press, free speech." Such encouragement from the cautious Ahern (an opponent of the suffrage amendment) must have reassured Hasse that she was making an impression among influential women librarians, but Ahern's words of support for free speech ended up in Anderson's file of evidence against her.[62]

Hasse returned home to more appreciation. John Cornell wrote, "At present a library is the refuge of love sick maidens and broken down old men. If you can reach the men in the market place instead of the nursery, the asylum, and the harem, here's to your success." There was recognition from the New York newspapers as well. Hasse was "walking on air" to find that the *Evening Mail* had published an editorial praising "Why Not?" for calling upon librarians "to come out from their medieval haunts of monastic seclusion and join in modern progress." It reiterated Hasse's warning that, with vast changes coming, libraries needed "a 'live' force capable of keeping abreast of the march of the sciences of economics and business." Quoting her extensively, the *Mail* concluded, "Miss Hasse makes us realize that there are forces in our libraries capable and willing to make the readjustment required." The same message soon appeared in a story about Hasse in the *Evening Sun,* "Average American Library Merely a Storehouse of Good but Unused Material." "What ails the library?" the reporter asked

Hasse, "one of the foremost librarians of America." "Just this, that they are not getting across," she said. "Libraries should be doing wonderful public service, but they are not making good in this capacity." Moreover, libraries regard books and magazines as "simply objects of inventory, instead of material to sell. . . . The idea of salesmanship has never occurred to us." To other librarians, particularly some at NYPL, nothing could be more infuriating than Hasse's encouragement of such hated stereotypes.[63]

~ ~ ~

Buoyed by so much approval, Hasse returned to old and new problems with her coworkers. While she was in California, government agents had searched her house four times, and her housekeeper got the impression that someone at NYPL had reported her. Hasse suspected Rollin Sawyer; much as she distrusted Anderson, she seems never to have thought he would do such a thing. She also heard that Dorothy Miller of the American History Division was accusing her of pro-German activity. Hasse reported all this to Lydenberg, telling him that she had threatened Miller with libel action, though only as a bluff. Lydenberg wrote a long verbatim account of their conversation, quoting Hasse as being particularly indignant that anyone would think her foolish enough to be involved in German propaganda or "to leave traces around if I were doing such things!" Several times she said, "Germany doesn't need me," exasperated at the absurdity of suspecting that she could have any value as a German agent. Lydenberg, who showed no awareness that Anderson had reported Hasse to the government, seemed to regard her protestations as suspect, but he soothingly told her that he had not heard of any allegations by library staff. He then contacted Miller, who had said that the California trip "had been encouraged by the Library as a means of getting rid of Miss Hasse because of her pro-German attitude." Her only evidence was an incident in which a woman mistook another librarian for Hasse and commended her for doing fine work among the Germans. Lydenberg then sent for that librarian, who had left NYPL but came in to explain that a woman with a German accent had smilingly said she had seen her picture in the *Staatszeitung* and expressed appreciation along the lines of "you've been so very good to us." When she realized the woman had mistaken her for Hasse, she sent her to 229 without further discussion, "nor did she say anything to connect Miss Hasse with any . . . propaganda." Having written up the conversations in great detail, Lydenberg sent them to Anderson without comment.[64]

While Lydenberg was investigating her loyalty, Hasse had an exasperating report from Sidney Zimand about Lydenberg's attitude towards the Economics Division. Zimand had managed to promote the division's service in the *New York World*, encouraging information requests by phone or mail. In March, he received a letter from a businessman who complained that he had sent a request for the procedure for filing chattel mortgages in various states, only to hear from Lydenberg that the information was in the library but there was no one to seek it out for him. Zimand promptly sent the man several pages of typed excerpts from a book on chattel mortgages. For Lydenberg to undo Zimand's publicity efforts without telling him or making any apparent effort to establish service policy could only further alienate the Economics Division's eager staff. It must have seemed a particular slap to Zimand, who had tried to interest Lydenberg in the division's work by sending him a list of recent reference questions with explanations of what had been involved in finding the information; it went into the file of evidence against Hasse.[65]

Hasse also returned to another petty insult from Anderson. Before leaving for California, she had submitted her division's annual report for 1917, having checked with Lydenberg as to the desired length and been told to write what she wanted, though it might be shortened for publication. She wrote only three paragraphs, briefly discussing the service demands on the division from 22,542 registered researchers, the need for better facilities, and the value of the clipping file, which now numbered seventy-five thousand pieces. Making no reference to business service, she assured the administration that scholarly research and government inquiries were served. Again emphasizing the need for staff meetings, and perhaps also appealing to Anderson for acceptance, she pointed with pride to the inauguration of monthly division staff meetings which promised to create "a spirit of unity and participation and 'belonging' which is the very basis of corporate success." When the director's annual report was published, however, there was not a word about the Economics Division, which Hasse regarded as a denigration of her staff's dedication and success in advancing NYPL's reputation. Anderson later said that the wartime paper shortage forced him to omit divisional reports, but when he had omitted them from the previous year's report, he did include several sentences about the Economics Division. In the 1917 report, he mentioned the other divisions and devoted a page to information about war research in the Science and Technology Divisions, pointing to the heavy demand for "statistics of production and manufacture in many industries . . . probably greater than in any other library" because of the many journalists in the city. In this context, the absence of any mention of the Economics Division does seem a glaring omission.[66]

Hasse also found that Anderson had co-opted the staff Economics Committee in her absence. The acting chair, Nelson Nichols, had informed him that the committee had been studying staff unrest and unanimously recommended that the committee itself become a personnel board, "not in any way to bring a barrier between individuals and Director, but to effect better coordination." Anderson called Nichols in for a "frank and friendly" chat and explained that he had already been planning to hire an executive assistant "with the hope that members of the staff, especially the women, would feel entirely free to bring their problems to the Executive Office." Alone with the director, who seemed to be suggesting that staff unrest was mostly female troubles, Nichols agreed to Anderson's alternative, although it didn't appear to offer a solution to the problems of pay and promotion.

Anderson did hire such an assistant that summer, when Rebecca Rankin came looking for a temporary job while she was in New York to help her sick mother. Rankin already had another job being held for her, which gave Anderson a convenient chance to try out the new position. Rankin's recollection was that her job was not well defined, and she seems not to have been aware that she was supposed to be a confidant with whom female staff could discuss problems. An ambitious college and library school graduate with high standards of businesslike behavior, Rankin probably didn't strike other women as someone in whom they would confide. She was given a desk outside Anderson's office, where she screened job applications and worked on publications while the editor was on war service, but she seems mostly to have been sent to various departments to "help out" and then report her observations to Anderson.[67]

Meanwhile, the staff unrest grew worse, with demands for civil service status and other public agitation by the Library Employees Union. Unfortunately for Hasse, the president of the LEU was close to her both professionally and personally, which encouraged suspicions that she was intriguing with the union. Tilloah Squires had joined NYPL originally to work on the inventory. In the spring of 1918, Hasse hired her for the foreign relations index, which meant she was paid by the Carnegie Institution, a technicality that didn't constrain her work for a union of library employees.[68] Working on the Carnegie index had the advantage of allowing her to work in the library without being a library employee, thus protecting against retaliation for her union activity. Hasse also provided her with a home in Tuckahoe, which was seen as further evidence that they were conspiring against the administration.

Hasse's imprudence in providing a union activist with a job and a home suggests emotional involvement, and there may have been suspicions of lesbianism at a time when backlash against the New Woman often took the form of anxiety that older "mannish lesbians" were seducing young women away from a healthy heterosexual life.[69] Tilloah Squires was much younger than Hasse, and, in later life at least, she had a "butch" style of short hair and masculine clothing. Whether Hasse and Squires were lovers is unknown, but their rapport was such that they became lifelong companions. Anderson added information about their connection to his file and later made a point of telling at least one prominent librarian that they had lived together.[70]

Squires certainly would have been aware of Hasse's problems in the library. As one of the idealistic young women who admired Hasse, Squires adopted her employer's ideas to her rhetoric in publicizing the union's cause, but there is no reason to think the LEU's message would have been different without Hasse's presence. Hasse did support the union as an organization that was trying to improve working conditions, and she even became a member in 1918 (though, as a department head, her eligibility was questionable), but there is no proof that she was directly involved in the LEU's activity. For Anderson and his allies, however, there was enough circumstantial evidence to support conspiracy theories about Hasse and the hated union. While it is possible that, consciously or unconsciously, Hasse aimed to use the union to undermine the administration, it also is possible that Anderson projected his own deviousness onto her open sympathy for the LEU and Squires. And, if Hasse was seen as plotting with the union, which had the ear of the mayor, on top of currying favor with important people in business, journalism, and government, that made her threat to male hegemony even greater.

As always, Hasse was too busy to spend much time brooding, working on more publications, planning special projects, again teaching at Columbia, along with her normal workload in the library, but the cumulative impact of the anti-German frenzy, investigation by the government, and hostility from some colleagues was deeply stressful. Hasse relied on the moral support of her staff: "One of the compensations of those trying months was the long walks in beautiful Westchester County, which I took with some of my young co-workers, who were as keenly irritated as I was by the stupid attitude obtaining in the library. During these walks we dreamed wonderful dreams of what a real library might accomplish in New York City. The only disappointment in that was the very grayness of the actuality of the next day."[71] Hasse thus admitted that the Economics Division staff regarded itself as a breed apart, which could only add to perceptions of disloyalty. Hasse saw herself as loyal to the best values of her country, the library movement, and NYPL as planned by Billings, but in an atmosphere of obsession with disloyalty, she easily became a target for the resentment and anxiety simmering within the library.

Anderson reported his suspicions to the chair of the Executive Committee, Elihu Root, who, far from being a calming influence, had his own reasons to view Hasse with alarm. Root had been a leading opponent of both women's suffrage and everything German, even wanting to ban the teaching of German in New York's public schools. No defender of civil liberties, he warned Americans not to ask questions about the causes or conduct of the war, and, late in 1917, he remarked that there were men walking the streets "who ought to be taken out at sunrise and shot for treason."[72] Then there was another factor that would have made Root wary of this woman who spoke of unrest among the workers, wanted to create a "personnel board" to mediate between labor and management, and was suspected of plotting with the radical feminist union. In the summer of 1917, President Wilson had sent Root to Russia as head of a delegation to evaluate the postrevolutionary situation and keep the provisional Kerensky government in the war effort. When Root delivered the message that further American aid was dependent on continuing in the war, the desperate Kerensky told him what he wanted to hear. Root then followed his usual routine of meetings and banquets, not noticing that Russian society was disintegrating around him. He returned with an optimistic report that looked ridiculous a few months later when the Russian military collapsed and the Bolsheviks seized power. For a man nearing the end of his distinguished career, this was a major embarrassment. Renowned for his shrewdness, Elihu Root had failed to see the danger of a band of Marxist revolutionaries who preached class war of the workers and peasants against the capitalist system.[73]

November was a particularly bad month for Root. Not only did the Bolsheviks come to power in Russia but the New York elections were won by two forces he despised. The state's voters finally approved women's suffrage, which opponents blamed on Socialists (who elected seven aldermen and ten state assemblymen in the city) and pro-German forces united in a "triumph of disloyal groups."[74] At the same time, the incumbent reform mayor, John Purroy Mitchel, was defeated by the Tammany Hall candidate, a previously obscure Brooklyn magistrate who had been essentially created by Root's bitterest enemy, William Randolph Hearst. The new mayor, "Honest John" Hylan, had been presented in the Hearst press as a fighter for the ordinary man against "predatory interests" and "agents of great wealth." Hearst had hated Root since the election of 1906, when his candidacy for governor was defeated in the last days of the campaign by Root's accusation that the assassination of President McKinley had been caused by the violent language in Hearst's newspapers. Their enmity had intensified during the fight over neutrality, in which Root advocated support for Britain, while Hearst was a vehement proponent of the view that Wall Street was maneuvering the nation into war to protect its financial interests. In 1917, the Hearst press charged that Root was willing to send young Americans to die for Britain but had himself avoided service in the Civil War, "did not enlist WHEN THE NATION'S LIFE WAS AT STAKE. . . . We protest against war being forced on the nation by men who had neither the patriotism nor the courage to fight for the nation in their own youth."[75] The Mitchel campaign hit back with accusations that Hylan and Hearst were pro-German, and Root proclaimed that "all true Americans must vote for Mayor Mitchel," which naturally won him the enmity of the new mayor.[76] Hylan and Hearst shared a visceral hostility to Root and the other eminent rich men who made up the NYPL Board of Trustees. Soon the mayor would cut the library's funding and open a decade-long war on the trustees and administration, and soon *Library Journal* would complain of his "thoroly Bolshevik attitude" for saying that if the city had full control of the library, he would reduce the salaries of the top administrators and raise the pay of "those who do the work."[77] For Elihu Root, the barbarians were at the gate. He was not inclined to take a tolerant view of Adelaide Hasse, this dangerous, disloyal woman warning of unrest and calling for change, especially when she was of German ancestry and praised the suffragists. The more obvious target of his ire would have been Maud Malone, but the LEU's noisiest spokesperson was untouchable in a city where organized labor was powerful. Malone gleefully enraged her opponents and gained additional protection by allying herself with Mayor Hylan, feeding him allegations about the library's mismanagement.

Hasse further disturbed Anderson by working with Charles Beard on a plan for a new division of business service. This put Anderson in the awkward position of having to fend off a proposal from the influential director of the Municipal Research Bureau, but there were other reasons why contact with Beard added to suspicion of Hasse. Beard was famous for the shocking theory that the authors of the Constitution, the Founding Fathers, had been motivated by economic self-interest, and he had recently resigned from the faculty of Columbia to protest the dismissal of two colleagues, one of whom had participated in peace organizations, while the other had signed a petition asking Congress not to send conscripts overseas (which many regarded as unconstitutional). Demonstrating that not even the Ivy League elite would resist demands for total loyalty, Columbia's president Nicholas Murray Butler asserted that dissent that was tolerable in peacetime became sedition and treason in war. Though Beard's principled resignation, which included a scathing denunciation of the Columbia trustees, would be remembered as a rare defense of civil liberties and academic freedom, it was more guilt by association in the eyes of Edwin Anderson, whose file of letters between Hasse and Beard included a newspaper clipping about his resignation from Columbia.[78]

In May 1918, with no sign of government action against Hasse, Anderson returned to accusations of bad behavior in the library. The roots of this controversy lay in Metcalf's complaints about the Economics Division staff taking volumes directly from the stacks, which he renewed when he returned from leave in 1917. Metcalf was particularly annoyed that Hasse's article for the Association of Collegiate Alumnae included an anecdote about a library school graduate so obsessed with tidiness that she cleared a table of material held for a longtime researcher and returned it to the shelves. Hasse described this as "an orderly piece of vandalism," but Metcalf said the books were mostly from the stacks and had been held in 229 for months without any record, one of many examples of "a single division without thought of the rest of the library." Hasse replied that she would consult the "reference workers" and meanwhile pointed to her own problems with errors by Metcalf's staff. Without addressing his point, she vaguely agreed "to do what we can as I have always said before." The Economics Division reference staff then agreed to a statement written by Morris Kolchin, who said the real problem was the inefficiency of the stack service; they couldn't expect readers to wait an hour to get books through channels, and when "every minute counts" they couldn't always take time to fill out cards. He repeated Hasse's theme that the use of the books was what mattered, even if "not absolutely orderly." Metcalf admitted that there were problems with his "green staff" and said he was ready to hear Hasse's suggestions, but he insisted that they get back to the point, that the Economics Division had to do "a very simple thing . . . that we learned the importance of long before we thought of going to library school. It is simply this, a record of some kind, of all books taken from their regular places for any length of time."[79]

At the same time, another Russian immigrant on Hasse's staff complained about a reader sent from the third floor just before closing and the frequency with which the Information Desk sent readers to the Economics Division "no matter what the time is or whatever the subject may be." This brought a furious response from Charles McCombs about "lack of cooperation" and the slow, undependable service in 229, which was "evidently without responsible supervision." McCombs had recently made other complaints about the Economics Division; he and Metcalf seem to have become Hasse's chief critics in 1917-18.[80]

Hasse conceded that there were problems and suggested a solution that was responsive to Metcalf, included elements of her ideas for reorganization, and was acceptable to the other divisions. After much consultation, there was shifting aimed at moving volumes most used in Room 228 there while some most likely to be called for in the Main Reading Room went to the stacks. Hasse thought the Economics Division was adhering to policy by sending people needing, for example, Geological Survey reports to the Science Division rather than removing volumes from other locations and by retrieving volumes from the stacks via the official tube system rather than going into the stacks to get them (even though the building was designed to give the division direct access to the stacks). She then was frustrated to find readers being sent to the Economics Division for documents that were in the stacks, wasting the time of both readers and her staff in having to call for volumes that could have been obtained at the Information Desk. She sent a suggestion to Lydenberg that the staff newsletter carry a reminder that the staff in Room 229 "did not handle documents as such." Instead of discussing this, Lydenberg asked Anderson if he had "given any instruction that documents are not to be handled 'as such' in 229." A few days later, Hasse sent another note about the problem, in this case a reader sent from the third floor for a compilation of state laws that was in the stacks. She pointed out that her staff was "religiously" complying with the policy of sending those wanting a known item upstairs to get it through channels and asked that other librarians "cooperate at least to the extent of not sending readers to us for books plainly not economics and which moreover are in the stacks."[81]

Lydenberg's only response was a brusque note: "The Director tells me he has never authorized you to rule that 'documents as such' are not to be handled by your staff." Behind the scenes, he and Anderson were exchanging memos and drafts of messages to Hasse as though she had brought on a major crisis. Yet there is evidence that supports Hasse's understanding in a memo to Lydenberg from Paul North Rice. More than a year before, Rice had written that "if the Information Desk rather than the Economics Division is supposed to serve the public all documents other than economics ones," it was urgent to push through the recataloging of documents and locate duplicate sets of documents indexes "near enough to the Information Desk so that assistants supposed to cope with the intricacies of documents may have easy access to them."[82] For Lydenberg to act as though he never heard of such a policy is puzzling, as it clearly had been at least under consideration in 1917. If a decision had been made not to adopt the policy referred to by Rice, why didn't Lydenberg mention it? Hasse's suggestion that the policy be stated in the staff newsletter seems another attempt to get the administration to put things in writing, a sensible approach to a situation in which none of the librarians involved in these disputes cited policy statements, memoranda of understanding, or meeting minutes.

Hasse replied that it was not a question of authority but a practical issue of service in sending readers from the third floor to the second for documents located in the stacks, citing the second case of a reader who had requested New York state laws being sent to 229. While noneconomic documents in 229 "are served unquestioningly to readers," she explained, "there is no reason, however, in sending a reader who applies upstairs for say an army register located in Stack III, to 229. That was the only point." She assured Lydenberg that the Economics Division was "trying our best to get a coordinated service in operation" and appealed for help in communicating to the other divisions. Here also, a memo from Lydenberg himself supports Hasse's position. As far back as 1912, he had warned the staff of an increase in complaints from "readers who have been sent aimlessly from one room to another," and urged "in no case should a reader or visitor be sent to another room or part of the building unless we are sure that the information . . . can without doubt be secured in that room."

Meanwhile, Hasse received an icy memorandum from Anderson, informing her of a complaint that on the previous day, a Sunday, a reader was made to wait forty minutes for a volume in 229 that he had requested at the Information Desk, and when Miss Fullerton finally went to 229, Miss Eichenbaum said she was "forbidden by you to handle public documents unless they were of economic interest." Without getting Hasse's side of the story, he threatened dismissal for insubordination: "This is but one of several instances which indicate an unwillingness on your part to cooperate in the orderly work of the Library and to accept the organization and distribution of duties which have been determined upon. I regret that it is my duty to say that the effect of such conduct on your part is very demoralizing to the service and that it cannot be permitted."[83]

Hasse promptly replied that there is "evidently a misunderstanding as to an alleged order of mine," adding that she would "be glad to be examined on that score." She had asked Rose Eichenbaum for a written report on the incident, which "came as a surprise because in our weekly Division Staff meetings the discussions have been largely on cooperation to secure 100% service." She then sent him Eichenbaum's precise account of a minor misunderstanding concerning a call slip stamped 2:49 p.m. that arrived before 3 p.m. A page was looking for the book when Pauline Fullerton came in to inquire, and Eichenbaum went with her to look, finding the item by 3:10 p.m.

> The conversation from which Miss Fullerton understood that we handled no material other than economic was as follows verbatim:
> Miss Fullerton, "Miss Eichenbaum, haven't you the Navy Estimate?"
> Miss Eichenbaum (without looking at slip), "If it is a Department report of any kind—you know we work only with Economic Documents."—(looking at slip) "Oh! That's in here. Come, I'll help you find it."

Fullerton then provided her version, which was fuzzy about the conversation. She too claimed to be seeking clarification of policy:

> The matter was reported to Mr Waite, simply to ascertain if possible just what our attempted responsibility in the matter of non-economic document material is to be. Am I to understand that we are not to depend at all upon the document indexes in Room 229, nor upon the cooperation the department might give us? I certainly understood from Miss Eichenbaum that the reader had not been served in Room 229, because of Miss Hasse's ruling that documents were not to be served readers in the Economics Division unless the material were distinctly economic in character.

Anderson's reaction was to send another hostile letter, warning Hasse that various incidents concerning documents service "and your general attitude convince me that you have assumed to decide administrative questions which are not in your province to decide." Again attributing all authority to the Executive Committee, he said that in its decisions to merge the Economics and Documents Divisions and then transfer documents cataloging, "there was certainly on the part of the committee no intention to alienate the public documents from the combined division; and you therefore have no authority to state to anyone that the Economics Division does not handle documents as such."

> Please to understand that you and your staff are to give readers public documents when they call for them, whether shelved in your room or not. Your staff are to give information from the documents catalogue in your room at night and on Sundays and holidays, when the cataloguers are not working there. Your attempts to throw upon others the responsibility for the handling of public documents, except when they are of economic interest or are shelved in your rooms, must cease.
>
> You say you are trying to give "100 percent. cooperation," that you are trying "to get coordinated service" in operation. . . . Prove these fair words by giving other divisions the cooperation they seek and fail to get now. The general impression throughout the Library . . . is that you lose no opportunity to show your resentment at the transfer of cataloguing routine with reference to public documents. Sixteen months is a long time to cherish such resentment; and I must insist that you show a desire cordially to cooperate with all divisions of the Library, and coordinate your service with the rest of the Library and not merely within your own Division.

This was a milder version of a message Anderson had been struggling to compose for a week. In an earlier canceled draft, he threatened, "Unless you are prepared to cooperate with the administration and the other divisions . . . with sincere good-will, as do the Chiefs of all the other divisions, I would suggest that you make way for someone who will."

Having received two letters within a week in which Anderson was harshly critical and seemed to be accusing her of insubordination, Hasse took several days to compose a reply. She began by reviewing the history of discussions about the Economics Division taking volumes directly from the stacks, which she had "admitted . . . led to difficulties," the acceptance of her compromise solution, "many conferences" leading to the redistribution of books located in Room 228 and Stack 5, which had "worked out to the satisfaction" of all concerned, the effort of the division "to call for books from the Stacks by the tube service . . . under the impression that we were thus working towards the wishes of all concerned as expressed at the reference chief meetings." She then reminded him, "and I daresay the Executive Committee is aware of the fact as well," that documents were located all over the building, in the stacks and the special collections.

> Since the gradual development of the plan above referred to we have conscientiously, believing we were carrying out a policy of the administration, referred readers calling for say Geological Reports to 225, etc. etc.
>
> For twenty-odd years I have served this Library to the very best of my ability. They were the best years of my life. I have no intention of receding one iota from the quality of my past service. . . . It may reasonably be assumed that I have attained to some judgment as to public service within that time. Guided by that judgment it has seemed wisest to refer a reader who calls for Geological Reports to the Division where they are located.

She also pointed out that, with the turnover in staff, "there is no one on the Economic Staff now who has any experience with documents," except herself and Edna Gearhart. This may be a reference to the documents catalog, as the listed staff had all begun work after the cataloging transfer, except for Gearhart, whose service went back to the beginning of 1916; the other six had been in the division from seven to seventeen months. Hasse ended with another reference to her long service and an appeal for "support and cooperation in making the Economics Collection . . . the best, the strongest in the country."

Anderson had the eleven memos typed as a set to be used as more evidence against Hasse, though it is hard to see that they proved anything except the muddled state of management at NYPL. Lydenberg and Anderson made no response to Hasse's apparently reasonable understanding that she was following a policy that had been extensively discussed and represented the wishes of the administration. There was no reply to her example of Geological Survey reports or her point about criticism of her division taking books directly from the stacks, nor was there any effort to develop a policy on documents reference that dealt with such issues. Anderson was apparently disingenuous in his reference to the Executive Committee's intentions, as it is unlikely that the committee had ever considered the matter; when it approved the transfer of documents cataloging, it apparently wasn't even informed that documents were the issue. Lydenberg seemed to have nothing to say about whatever had been so extensively discussed among the Reference Department chiefs, and Anderson seemed only to want to attack Hasse, not clarify a situation in which some readers were being sent to the Economics Division for volumes that weren't there, but, in the case of the Fullerton complaint, not sent to the division for a report that was there. Anderson's language in repeatedly accusing Hasse of making administrative decisions that were not within her authority suggests not only determination to find her insubordinate but also an anxiety that his authority was being undermined by a woman who didn't know her place.

Hasse may have been maneuvering to get elements of her reorganization plan, which had included elimination of the Documents Division, and she probably enjoyed pointing out that the Information Desk wasn't always able to deal with legal reference questions, which she had wanted to make part of a new public affairs division. She may even have been manipulating the situation in revenge for the cataloging transfer or had some other motivation, but that is all speculation. What is clear is that her division had been criticized for taking documents directly from the stacks (which Billings' plan had intended), but now, in more double bind, when she cited efforts to cooperate in correcting the problem, she was accused of failing to cooperate anyway.

Hasse made no reference to the continued presence of the documents catalog, which might seem to indicate some expectation of reference service for all documents, except that Anderson's memo shows that it was available only on evenings and weekends, and Moth's memo says that the cards were constantly being revised and removed, making it difficult for Hasse and her staff to use it effectively. And as she pointed out, given the level of turnover, her staff did not have expertise with documents and their various locations in the library. Part of the problem seemed to be a state of uncertainty about government documents, a chronic condition in American libraries for reasons that Billings had grasped twenty years earlier when he told Hasse that a large library needed two sets of documents, one to be held as a separate collection, one to be integrated with the books and periodicals. Billings had planned a compromise solution, with documents included in the subject classification and the main catalog's subject entries, while Hasse's expertise was used in a division responsible for cataloging and specialized reference service, with a unique catalog and many documents located in its reading room or the adjacent stacks. With elements of that system changed, Hasse found herself in a library that seemed simultaneously to want government documents to be treated like any other material while also being able to refer readers to a specialized reference desk with questions about documents and law. Hasse wanted to avoid the frustrations inherent in the situation and concentrate on developing the Economics Division as a new phase of her career, but Anderson was even more infuriated at the prospect of her making a new reputation for service to business.

~ ~ ~

At the time, there seems to have been a reaction among public libraries against the specialization in government publications that was the basis of Hasse's reputation as an expert. Indeed, LAPL would soon dismantle the separate documents collection she had organized in the 1890s and reclassify it among the books. In 1922, Congress finally allowed selectivity that would enable most depositories to reduce the volume of documents received. As many public libraries in the program cut their selections, however, the expansion of higher education created more interest in government information for research in academic libraries, which gradually became predominant in collecting documents.

In the aftermath of the wartime drive to mobilize the citizenry, public libraries were interested in promoting popular documents and campaigning for publication of simplified government information. This interest was pursued by a group of women who formed a subcommittee of the ALA Public Documents Committee and by Edith Guerrier, whose experience with wartime government work inspired her to seek a library information service in the federal government. It would serve as a "clearing house through which information in hundreds of offices will be made available to librarians who have . . . no satisfactory means of knowing in which . . . a particular piece of information is located" and prepare "comprehensive digests" of government publications. In effect, these women rejected Hasse's career model of the woman librarian with expertise in the complexities of government information and instead asked the government to provide an easily understandable digest of its mysteries. Guerrier pursued this energetically but futilely throughout the 1920s, a period when Republican administrations were more interested in eliminating publications to save money than in establishing a new information bureau.[84]

An authoritative advocate for treating documents like books was none other than Hasse's long-ago associate at GPO, Edith Clarke, who seems to have retired and decided to cap her career by asserting her expertise as a writer and speaker on public documents. In 1916, Clarke addressed the ALA documents program on her vision of how government publications should be "made easy to understand, easy to handle." Her suggested reforms were mostly what librarians, including Hasse, had been urging for years, and Richard Bowker's long-winded remarks pointed to the relevance of his committee's report on needed changes at the 1891 conference (further emphasized by reprinting it in LJ). That must have sent Hasse's memory back to the meeting in San Francisco where she had first encountered Bowker and the policy issues of government publications. Asked to comment, she said only that she too once had a dream of reforming the cataloging and distribution of documents but had "got over it." Instead of hoping for simplification, Hasse emphasized documents' usefulness for sophisticated information service, calling attention to the importance of a provision in the pending printing bill that would provide depository distribution of the congressional committee hearings that could be so useful for "advanced reference work."[85]

Two years later, Clarke published a guide to government publications in which she pooh-poohed the notion of special treatment for public documents, even while issuing a three-hundred-page manual on their idiosyncrasies:

> It is a popular notion that government publications are a class apart from every other kind of literature, to be placed all together in a group by themselves in a library; that special codes of cataloging rules, and separate classification systems, and different library practice generally must be devised for them; and that they can be understood only by specialists. In the making of this little work this notion is regarded as an error that is to be counteracted by the spread of clear, accurate, and full information. . . . The keynote . . . is that government publications should be given the same footing and treatment as any other works; and that their publishing should be conducted on the same principles and methods as publishing business in private hands.[86]

Reviewing for *Library Journal*, James Wyer approved Clarke's "very sensible basic premise . . . that government publications in libraries are no different from other books and are not a sacro-sanct class of books calling for separate and peculiar esoteric treatment," but he found the book as a whole lacking "logical arrangement and clear and unencumbered exposition."[87]

Despite her confidence that documents could be readily explained, Clarke included a long chapter, "Why Bewildering," that identified some of their special difficulties:

> The publications of our national government have been . . . very bewildering, an entanglement in the mass, and a hard nut to crack in the individual document. The difficulties in their use are various. Some of them can be remedied; others inhere in the documents themselves. Their difficulty exists in, first, their subject matter, and in the ill-digested manner of its presentation, i.e. lack of competent editing; second, in the bad and all but useless indexes which before 1895 were given them; third, in their corpo-

rate authorship . . . that is, in the fact that their authors are not persons, but government or official bodies and . . . that these bodies are in constant process of change; fourth, in their involved titles with excessive verbiage . . . ; fifth, in the way the publications of Congress are arranged and gathered into volumes, without grouping by subject or source . . .; sixth, in being reprinted and reprinted to make up various series, in which works already separately published and dissimilar in subject and length are arbitrarily tied together . . .; seventh, in their being reprinted, also, as parts of larger works, an inferior officer's report being reprinted in that of the next higher officer, and so on till it reaches the top of the ladder; these reprints or editions being in most cases each the same in text as the original print.

Clarke's lengthy exposition of the problems of agency entries and unclear titles was just what Hasse had been explaining for years, and her detailed account of the "mess" of the "Document problem" going on "forever" was not likely to encourage confidence that documents could be treated like any other library materials. At several points, Clarke essentially repeated Hasse's constant theme, that to use documents effectively, "it is essential to learn to think in terms of government bodies, to know them by name, to distinguish between two bodies with names identical or differing only slightly, but which are distinct and in different departments, etc.; to know the functions of each and its relations with other higher and lower units of the government organization."[88]

In keeping with her keystone premise, Clarke warned against use of the Documents Office classification, "originated by Miss A. R. Hasse," despite the "huge saving in time and brain work" it offered as the classification that came on the invoices in depository shipments. Although its value was "indisputable" for GPO's collection of federal documents, she could not endorse its use to create a separate collection in a library otherwise arranged by subject. Clarke supported her position with reference to the "axiom among librarians" that gifts should not be accepted if required to be kept together as a special collection and to the problem of breaks in series when agencies were reorganized.[89]

Clarke was confident that her own decisions in the *Document Catalogue* remained valid, and she questioned LC's different policies for congressional report titles and agency entries. Still defending her decision to invert agency names, Clarke also suggested that libraries adapt their LC cards by filing in inverted name order or at least by making cross references from inverted names to the LC form. Clarke had spent her career as a cataloger, and she approached the issues much as Sears had, as problems of catalog records, seemingly without much concern for either costs or subject access to the content of documents, though these were the crucial issues for libraries. For all her detailed knowledge, there was a confusion underlying her work, similar to that at NYPL, on the issues of cataloging and reference for documents. At NYPL, the result was to lay blame on Hasse, who was somehow supposed to satisfy everyone's needs in an atmosphere of constant criticism. Hasse seems to have been ready and willing to focus on developing her division and promoting her vision of library service, but success with these goals only intensified her coworkers' resentment.

~ ~ ~

In the same month as Anderson's hostile letters, the indomitable Hasse kept up her outreach to influential New Yorkers. To Bruce Calvert of the Advertising Club, she sent an invitation to try her division's services, while Julius Henry Cohen received a four-page list of international commissions and their powers, along with an offer of a fuller list that he was eager to have.[90] She was quoted with more criticism of library training by Babette Deutsch, an LEU sympathizer and friend of Tilloah Squires, for an article in *The Dial*, a leading Progressive journal. Deutsch accused library schools of producing "a combination filing clerk and social uplifter" when library reference work really needed men and women "capable of scholarly research and sympathetic collaboration." (Deutsch may have had her own agenda there, since her future husband, the scholarly Avrahm Yarmolinsky, joined NYPL as head of the Slavonic Division in 1918.) She feared that the public library "like a sinking ship . . . provided for women and children first," though Dana's branch library for business in Newark was cited as an exception. Deutsch acknowledged the funding problem and its connection to low salaries, to which she attributed the founding of the LEU, but she saw a possible solution in "standardization" of all aspects of library organization and staffing, leading to the certification of librarians and perhaps even to a "nationalized" library system, like national banks in drawing on a "federal reserve of information." Deutsch's eager and earnest but rather vague concern with the condition of libraries, like the *New Republic*'s publication of "Why Not?" reflected a perception among Progressives that libraries were not modernizing with the energy that was reshaping other aspects of American civic life. An admirer mentioned the *Dial* article when he wrote to praise Hasse's ideas as being just of the moment, "in the air the need of it . . . so simple and necessary and yet no one has thought of it."[91]

Hasse was busily propagating her ideas with more publications throughout the spring and summer. The editor of *Special Libraries,* her friend J. H. Friedel, asked for more contributions: "You know how eagerly everyone reads whatever you say." To the members of the General Federation of Women's Clubs, Hasse urged understanding of "The Business of Being a Librarian," especially of libraries' potential to serve their husbands' businesses by disseminating the information they collected. She again argued that businessmen were not getting their tax money's worth from public libraries focused on women and children. Attributing the "backwardness" of libraries to the traditional attitude of the "custodian," she again called on librarians to provide expert business information service and advertise it.[92]

A few months later, Hasse vigorously criticized "our alleged profession" in the lead article in *Public Libraries.* Her complaint was again the mediocrity of both library schools and the work given their graduates, whose years of postsecondary education qualified them for routine processing work that could be learned quickly by "a bright high school girl." Attachment to "elementary processes" and "mechanical formulas" obscured "the real raison d'etre of a public library, viz. service to the public—the whole public, not only women and children—to such a degree that now the records and not the service constitute the sum and substance of 'professional' activity." Hasse contrasted the limited development of American libraries over forty years of professionalization with the amazing growth and impact of the automobile industry in half the time. She blamed the "unfortunate failure of the public library system to adjust itself to modern requirements" on the "inadequate curriculum of the training schools" and again warned that the public demanded expert service, while the typical library school graduate "can make a perfect catalog card, she can shelf-list and file and typewrite, she is a trained library worker, yes, but she cannot tell you where to get a table showing the effect of wars on security value fluctuations." The solution she urged was a new curriculum, with record keeping and book preparation taught in short courses, while quite different education, which she didn't describe, was given for truly professional library careers.[93]

The summer of 1918 was the usual bustle of activity that must have seemed a lifeline as hostility intensified within the library. Hasse's inner turmoil matched the world outside. The suffrage movement was at fever pitch, demanding a constitutional amendment as part of the war effort, in recognition of the work of women in supporting the war and filling the jobs of men in military service. The war frenzy was inescapable, with NYPL's front terrace often serving as the reviewing stand for military parades, bond sale rallies, and other patriotic demonstrations, "military and naval bands of all degrees of excellence and loudness, firing squads of soldiers or sailors or marines giving salutes . . . troops of performing elephants, singers from the opera, stage celebrities, tanks, airplanes, wooden ships, canvas tents, wooden huts, ambulances and a bewildering succession of other evidences to martial activity."[94]

Having used her vacation time for the California trip, Hasse had no escape but her suburban home and her civic and professional activities. She again taught a class on documents at Columbia from 8:30 to 9:30 in the morning, and she was working with Alissa Franc on their book about civics education, as well as on the book about American libraries she had begun with Joanna Strange (whose death in August added to Hasse's sense of loss) and a proposal for a major new bibliographic project that would index economic materials. She also contacted Bernard Baruch, who, as chairman of the War Industries Board, was coordinating much of the American economy, to suggest mobilizing the resources of large libraries for the board's work. "This library has a very considerable store of current economic information lying idle," she told him, adding a pointed appeal to the man nicknamed "Dr. Facts" by the president, "By information I mean not books but facts." She offered to submit a proposal to mobilize and mine these resources "according to a well defined plan." Meanwhile, at the request of Adolph Ochs of the *New York Times*, she wrote a proposal for an index to the paper's encyclopedia of the war; she had been recommended by another of her admirers, New Orleans librarian William Beer, who wrote that he always gained fresh energy from contact with her.[95]

In July, there was another incident involving suspicion of disloyalty, when two policemen came to Lydenberg's office with questions about various employees. Lydenberg sent Anderson a detailed account of what he seemed to regard as a rather droll encounter with dim police who asked about a lecture by a Dr. Shapiro, said to be an associate of Trotsky, and the location of the "anarchist room." Lydenberg told them that no Dr. Shapiro had worked or lectured there, but, as the name was common among Jews, many Shapiros would have used the library, and Trotsky probably had used it when he lived in New York. There was no "anarchist room," he explained, but then helpfully volunteered that the Jewish and Slavonic divisions "were used by people who might be expected to have anarchist leanings," and the Economics Division held materials on the subject. When asked about Hasse, he encouraged their interest by telling them she was already under investigation by federal agents and "on her return from Germany was not reticent in expressing her sympathies for Germany." They proceeded to interview Hasse, who learned there had been an anonymous note about her. She suggested who might have sent it and reported to Lydenberg that they thought it "a false alarm." In the library gossip mill, the police inquiry was fuel to the flames of suspicion and hostility around Hasse, whose feeling of being surrounded by enemies could only be exacerbated by another anonymous accusation.[96]

At the same time, there was more confusion and frustration concerning Hasse's ambitions for new projects. Her assistant Elsie Rushmore sent a memo to Lydenberg about transferring more materials to Room 229 and issuing a bulletin of economic books. Lydenberg replied to Hasse that he knew nothing about these matters and wondered if Rushmore had consulted her. Hasse explained that Rushmore wrote as the "Service Section Chief" after consultation with Hasse and Metcalf, who wanted a written request for any shifting. The bulletin of economic books had long been planned, and both she and Sawyer had discussed it with him. Lydenberg had no recollection, and Sawyer said he had discussed it only with the publications director, who had not been enthusiastic. Lydenberg told her that shifting had to be deferred because of staff shortages, and the new bulletin, which neither he nor Anderson recalled approving, could not be published when paper was in short supply. Uneasy about the Economics Division, he asked for a statement of its organization and procedure, which Hasse promptly supplied. Room 229 was for readers and 228 for special researchers with assigned tables and typewriting permitted, and the staff of the division was divided into three sections: filing, service, and reference.[97]

On top of this, Hasse had to deal with a complaint to Lydenberg from William Gamble of the Technology Division that her division had been holding one of his division's volumes too long. Reporting that the volume was back on the shelf, she took the opportunity to urge a different attitude, since what mattered was that books were used, not where a volume was at any given moment (not what she had told Williamson six years earlier):

> May I trouble you to advise Mr. Gamble that I by no means consider that I have lien on books in any part of the building, least of all those in 228 or 229. I should feel a slacker if I saw them always on the shelves. My feeling is that I am being paid to see that books are used. For the past few months, we have been seriously inconvenienced by the large number of SDG books taken from 228 to 225. We have not asked Dr. Arctowski to interrupt his re-

searches in order that these books may be in orderly disposition in 228. . . .
We have instead gone to 225 ourselves to use them.

The volume had been used by a government agent, and "we are doing all we can
to make the N.Y.P.L. indispensable to him as we did in the case of the Doheny
commission and as we are trying to do in the case of the Latin American
Inquiry." And since Gamble had complained about her, Hasse felt entitled to
point out the failings of reference service in his division. When Gamble had demanded the return of another volume, she personally took it to the reader, who
turned out to be seeking recent data on the production of atmospheric nitrogen.
Hasse immediately explained the best information sources, converting the reader
to "a daily worker in 229," although "there is no reason why this information
should not have been given in 115." Again prodding Lydenberg to improve reference service, Hasse added that the problem was the failure to invoke "the principle of salesmanship." She feared that "the feeling of suspicion, of unwillingness to share our work with each other, and of misunderstanding will obtain as
long as the present policy of keeping the workers from getting together and talking over their problems and interests exists."[98]

Hasse was not alone in her concern about interdepartmental tensions. In the
same month, Charles McCombs, now chair of the Economic Committee, asked
the staff for ideas to "promote better understanding and cooperation between different departments." When Elsie Rushmore suggested a committee of representatives of each division "to meet weekly for discussion of interdepartment interests and affairs," her memo ended up in Anderson's Hasse file, as though such
innocuous ideas were part of Hasse's conspiracies. (Rushmore also suggested
employing a publicity agent to increase awareness of the salary problem and hiring boys from the Henry Street Settlement House, with opportunities for promotion.) Talk of meetings and salesmanship was much in the air of the time,
but it made no impression on Lydenberg, who once glumly told Metcalf that
"human nature has not changed very much in the last 3000 years." His only reaction was to check further on the disputed volume and note Gamble's claim
that it had not returned to the shelf until four days after its absence was noted.[99]

Even had the administration been more receptive, salesmanship and better
communication would hardly have solved the overwhelming problems of reference service in a complex organization with many diverse users and an underpaid, inexperienced staff, but Hasse always sought solutions to fundamental
problems. Lydenberg, who had not worked as a reference librarian, didn't seem
to understand how irritating the lack of coordination was to someone with
Hasse's high standards as she dealt with researchers. The criticism implicit in
her comments apparently made him defensive, so that he began to suspect that,
once again, the real problem was her attitude, that she and her staff were too full
of their own importance to serve the "little people." As he had once listed examples of cataloging errors, now he made notes of service problems, though there
seemed to be even less to record in this case. In an undated note on three complaints about the Economics Division, he found that "there is little in the way
of charging actual indifference or insolence" but rather "an indifferent attitude to-

wards the public, an unwillingness to be bothered by trifles while big matters are under consideration." While finding "little one can put one's finger on," Lydenberg somehow concluded that "there is ample indication of a different attitude than that of any other division." He seemed to have forgotten that when the library opened Billings had emphasized that the divisions were to serve serious, substantive research, not minor queries that could be handled at the Information Desk or the branches, a point even made in the pages of LJ by William Gamble.

~ ~ ~

In this atmosphere, Hasse must have enjoyed Tilloah Squires' success in publicizing the Library Employees Union in the summer of 1918. In July, she had a letter in the *Evening Post* in which, reflecting the union's interest in broader women's issues, she raised matters that were not so widely acknowledged as the pay problem. Squires described library workers as "underestimated and consequently undeveloped and underpaid." Librarians had been "especially shy and backward" about calling attention to their problems, primarily from fears that administrators opposed any labor agitation, which also was "undignified and unprofessional." She complained of the appointment and promotion of library school graduates over those with long experience, one of the union's chief grievances, and urged that the Circulation Department staff be classed as civil service and the library school transferred to the Board of Education, proposals that were endorsed by the local Federation of Women's Civil Service Organizations and the Federation of Women's Clubs.[100]

Squires' letter brought a reply from Isabella Cooper of the Staff Association, who argued that inadequate pay was the fundamental problem for such demanding work, pointing to the "difficulty encountered by workers in being adequately educated, physically fit and essentially courteous at $50 per month."[101] The Staff Association had been assigned by Anderson to answer the LEU's charges, because he and the trustees might be labeled antiunion if they publicly replied. This might seem to be a form of divide-and-conquer, but the Staff Association's leaders, mostly middle managers, showed no hesitancy in serving as the administration's proxy in fighting the union that aimed to speak primarily for the lower ranks of the clerical staff. Although the two groups agreed on many issues, the Staff Association became increasingly bitter towards the union and eventually would urge that Maud Malone be fired. Since the LEU kept its membership secret, the antiunion forces suspected it of being only a front for the Malones and a few other agitators. The Staff Association claimed that most employees preferred its cooperative approach in working with the administration, but since staff might join for reasons unrelated to the union issue, its large membership did not prove the point.

Squires also appeared at the ALA conference in Saratoga Springs, where she handed out flyers in an unsuccessful effort to get consideration of a resolution on civil service; the flyers were added to the file on Hasse, who had no visible connection with them. What must have really alarmed Anderson was the wording of the resolution, which argued that sex discrimination was the real reason for low pay in libraries:

> Whereas, low and inadequate salaries are paid to librarians solely due to the fact that the majority of rank and file in the work are women, and
> Whereas, all the highest salaried positions are given to men . . . , and
> Whereas, this discrimination is based solely on sex lines and not on any superiority of intelligence, ability, or knowledge, therefore,
> Be It Resolved, That we are in favor of throwing open all positions in library work . . . from the position of Librarian of Congress to that of a page, to men and women equally and for equal pay.[102]

Anderson agreed that low pay was related to a feminized workforce, but his solution was to bring in more men with college and library school education, a proposition now challenged by the LEU. Following Hasse's published statements about discrimination, it stirred fears of a campaign, like that of the suffragists or the city's women teachers, that could limit his control of pay and other aspects of employment. At the same time, the complaints about the Library War Service were another warning that feminist insurgency might be developing among women library workers.

The *Civil Service Chronicle* had been giving much sympathetic attention to library workers and the efforts of the LEU. At the end of the summer, it published Squires' comments on NYPL working conditions, in which she went beyond the pay issue to criticize management, particularly in the Reference Department, for "an entire absence of coordination." There was no interdepartmental cooperation, and the division chiefs were "mere figureheads," with the smallest decisions made by "a central authority which has no direct contact with divisional details." The result was "much conflict and duplication," and finally "there is waste, and waste is expensive." As for the workers, there would be no abatement of the widespread dissatisfaction so long as there was "no consciousness of 'esprit de corps.'" Squires complained particularly about the "entire lack of system" for wages, hiring, and promotion, ending with some vigorous union rhetoric: "no self-respecting employe should be asked to sign a payroll and have the amount of his salary added after his signature has been made. This form of exploiting labor is a commentary on the value the Library administration places upon professional work. For here it has absolute control and here it is lacking administrative ability and justice and fair play to its employes."[103]

Squires' criticism would be blamed on Hasse. The two friends must have influenced each other to some unknown extent, but Squires was capable of reaching her own conclusions from what she observed in the library and learned as union president. To some librarians, however, there was no doubt who was really to blame, and their anger would be turned on Hasse, to shatter her career even as she seemed at a peak of prestige and achievement.

Notes

1. Adelaide Hasse, *The Compensations of Librarianship* (privately printed, 1919), 15-16; AH toLydenberg, 29 April 1917, AH-CB.

2. *National Municipal Review* 6 (Jan. 1917): 104, 175-76.

3. LJ 42 (April 1917): 309.

4. AH to W. B. Walker, 26 Dec. 1916, AH-NY.

5. Adelaide Hasse, "Public Libraries and Business Men," *American Industries* (Jan. 1917): 23-25.

6. Edgar Dawson to AH, 28 Feb. 1917, AH-LC.

7. Lee to AH, 26 Feb. 1917, AH-NY.

8. Anderson to AH, 10 Oct. 1917, AH-CB.

9. Adelaide Hasse, "Making a Market in Libraries," LJ 42 (April 1917): 270-72.

10. Keyes Metcalf, *Random Recollections of an Anachronism* (New York: Readex Books, 1980), 133-34.

11. Swingle-AH exchange, 4, 5 June 1917, AH-CB.

12. "What More Can the Library Do?" [Bradford-Anderson exchange] LJ 42 (June 1917): 447-49.

13. Phyllis Dain, *The New York Public Library: A History of Its Founding and Early Years* (New York: NYPL, 1972), 327-28.

14. U.S. Federal Bureau of Investigation File 62-329 (1922) mentions the report as in the possession of the Secret Service, but it cannot be located in the Secret Service records now in the National Archives.

15. Undated Hasse family tree in Lydenberg's handwriting, AH-CB.

16. AH to Lydenberg, 22, 23 Feb. 1917, AH-CB; AH -- Anderson, 22 March 1917, AH-CB.

17. AH correspondence with John McCrae of E. P. Dutton, 15, 16, 20, 22, 24 Dec. 1917, AH-CB, along with various AH notes to Lydenberg about working on the book with Franc in 1918; review, *New York Times*, 12 May 1918.

18. Adelaide Hasse, "Women's Legislative Council of Los Angeles," *General Federation Magazine* (Aug. 1918): 24-25.

19. AH toLydenberg, 16 May 1917, AH-CB; AH to Dana, 28 March 1917, AH-CB; Adelaide Hasse, "Extent of the Trade Paper Press in the United States," in American Association of Museums, *Proceedings* (1917 conference), 88-90.

20. Mumford-AH exchanges, 10 May, 17 Sept. 1917, Lewis Mumford papers, Special Collections, Van Pelt Library, University of Pennsylvania, Philadelphia.

21. AH to Commons, 1 May 1917, AH-NY; AH to DuBois, 24 Sept. 1917, AH-NY; *New York Times*, 12 Aug. 1917.

22. Cohen to AH and Anderson, 26 Feb. 1917, AH-NY; "Comments of the Director on Miss Hasse's Statement . . . ," n.d., AH-CB.

23. AH to Dana, 28 March 1917, AH-CB. The term "cultured cult" had been around at least since 1899, when it appeared in a poem that mocked the debate over how much librarians should direct readers to worthy books in place of the popular fiction they wanted, Carolyn Welles, "The Problem," LJ 29 (1899): 618. Other letters about the trade papers exhibit with Dana and F. M. Feiker of *Electrical World*, AH-NY. The exhibit is described in *ALA Bulletin* 11 (1917 conference proceedings): 245 and LJ 42 (Aug. 1917): 629.

24. Adelaide Hasse, "Public vs. Special Libraries," LJ 42 (Oct. 1917): 798-80.

25. The notices, telegrams, and AH's memo, 5 July 1917, were typed as a single document, AH-CB.

26. Sawyer identified himself as "first assistant" of the Municipal Reference Library in *Who's Who in Library Service* (1933).

27. Anderson-AH exchange, 2 Aug. 1917, also retyped with the record of the Sawyer incident, AH-CB.

28. AH-Anderson exchange, 22 March 1916, and various AH notes about meetings, AH-CB.

29. AH-Anderson-Lydenberg exchange, 16, 17 March 1917, AH-CB; AH memo on "Future Policy of Economics Division," 10 July 1917, with cover note from Lydenberg to Anderson, 3 Nov. 1917, AH-CB.

30. AH-Lydenberg exchange, 13 Aug. 1917, AH-CB; Gertrude Matthews to AH, 5 Aug. 1917, AH-NY; AH to E. M. Friedman, Sept. 1917, AH-NY.

31. AH to House, 29 Sept. 1917, AH-NY; House to AH, 3 Oct. 1917, AH-CB; AH to S. E. Mezes, 4 Oct. 1917, AH-CB.

32. Hasse, *Compensations*, 17.

33. Allyn Young to Charles Williamson, 8 Oct. 1918, AH-CB. Anderson noted on the letter that Young was "one of the most important men" in the Inquiry.

34. Andrew Keogh, "Our Library Resources as Shown by Some Government Needs in the War," LJ 44 (Aug. 1919): 505; U.S. Secret Service (1918) Report on Adelhaid [sic] R. Hasse, p. 3, RG 87, U.S. National Archives.

35. Adelaide Hasse, "Women in Libraries," *Journal of the Association of Collegiate Alumnae* 11 (Oct. 1917): 74-80.

36. Dee Garrison, *Apostles of Culture: The Public Librarian and American Society, 1876-1920* (New York: Free Press, 1979): 224. For a fuller discussion of the implications of the Carnegie building program, see Abigail Van Slyck, *Free to All: Carnegie Libraries and American Culture, 1890-1920* (Chicago: University of Chicago Press, 1995).

37. Suzanne Hildenbrand, "A Historical Perspective on Gender Issues in American Librarianship," *Canadian Journal of Information Science* 17 (Sept. 1992): 25.

38. Perry to AH, 30 Oct. 1917, AH-CB.

39. John Calvin Colson, "Lutie Stearns," *DALB*, 504-5; Marvin quoted in Joanne Passett, *Cultural Crusaders: Women Librarians in the American West, 1900-1917* (Albuquerque: University of New Mexico Press, 1994), 122.

40. Ball to AH, n.d., AH-CB; Eva vom Baur Hansl-AH exchange, 26, 29 Oct. 1917, AH-CB; J. Stanley Lemons, *The Woman Citizen: Social Feminism in the 1920s* (Charlottesville: University Press of Virginia, 1990), 4-5, 20.

41. Quoted in Garrison, *Apostles*, 221.

42. *ALA Bulletin* 12 (1918 conference proceedings): 283-87; "Heard on the Train," PL 23 (Oct. 1918): 388.

43. PL 23 (July 1918): 316.

44. *ALA Bulletin* 12 (1918 conference proceedings): 285-86.

45. Metcalf, *Random*, 181; LJ 43 (June 1918): 464.

46. *New York Times*, 11 March 1916.

47. Catherine Shanley, *The Library Employees Union of Greater New York, 1917-1929* (Diss., Columbia University, 1992) is the fullest treatment of the LEU, the Malone sisters, and the situation in NYPL and city government. Unless otherwise cited, it is the source of references to the LEU in this and the following chapter.

48. "A Statement in Behalf of Miss Adelaide R. Hasse" [1918], 4, AH-CB.

49. AH-Anderson exchange, 9 Nov., 3, 8 Dec. 1917, RG 6, Director's Office, NYPL archives; Shanley, *LEU*, 87-88.

50. AH to Anderson, 18 Jan. 1918, AH-CB.

51. Adelaide Hasse, "Why Not?" *New Republic* (19 Jan. 1918), 341.

52. AH-Anderson exchange, AH-CB; Williamson's report (10 Jan. 1918) has been lost, but a note in AH-CB refers to it having once been in the file.

53. U.S. Secret Service (1918), Report on Adelhaid [sic] R. Hasse, RG 87, U.S. National Archives.

54. U.S. Federal Bureau of Investigation File 62-329 (1922). AH exchange with Clapp and Rumely, AH-CB; on ownership of *Evening Mail*, see *New York Times*, 10 July 1918; Kevin O'Keefe, *A Thousand Deadlines: The New York City Press and American Neutrality, 1914-17* (The Hague: Nijoff, 1972), 116; Ferdinand Lundberg, *Imperial Hearst: A Social Biography* (Westport, CT: Greenwood Press, 1936; repr.), 243.

55. J. F. Harris, National War Savings Committee, to AH, 5 Aug. 1918; AH to von Mach, 28 June, 22 Sept. 1916; AH to Merkel, 25 May 1917; AH-Illesley exchange, n.d., 18 Oct., 8 Nov. 1916, all AH-CB; *New York Times*, 7 Dec. 1917.

56. Kathleen Kennedy, *Disloyal Mothers and Scurrilous Citizens: Women and Subversion during World War I* (Bloomington: Indiana University Press, 1999), xv, 100-107; Allen to AH, 19 Nov. 1917, AH-CB. It is not clear which of the various Committees of One Hundred Allen alluded to; Hasse was a member of the Women's Municipal League Committee of One Hundred but may have belonged to others, perhaps one supportive of Germany.

57. Quoted in Garrison, *Apostles*, 220.

58. Wayne Wiegand, *"An Active Instrument for Propaganda": The American Public Library during World War I* (New York: Greenwood Press, 1989) covers all aspects, including the attack on a prominent woman librarian in Portland, Oregon, for refusing to buy war bonds (55-58) and the booing of Bowker (58); Marian Casey, *Charles McCarthy: Librarianship and Reform* (Chicago: ALA, 1981), 128-30.

59. AH-Lummis exchange, 18, 20, 26 Feb. 1918; Lummis journal 20 Feb. 1918; Hill to Lummis, 20 March 1918, all Lummis papers, Braun Library, Southwest Museum, Los Angeles.

60. Eichenbaum, Ramsburg, Rushmore to AH, all Feb. 1918, AH-CB.

61. Ada Livright, Ada McCarthy, and Dana to AH, all Feb. 1918, AH-CB.

62. Ahern-AH exchange, 18, 28 Feb., 18 March 1918, AH-CB.

63. John Cornell to AH, 2 March 1918, AH-CB; *New York Evening Mail*, 28 Jan. 1918; AH to E. A. Rumely, 16 March 1918, AH-CB; *New York Evening Sun*, 26 March 1918.

64. Lydenberg memoranda, 26, 28 March 1918, AH-CB.

65. H. Schlachters to Zimand, 16 March 1918, AH-CB; Zimand to Lydenberg, 26 Jan. 1918, AH-CB.

66. AH -Lydenberg exchange, 29, 31 Dec. 1917, AH-CB; Hasse, *Compensations*, 14-15; NYPL 1917 Annual Report.

67. L. Nelson Nichols to Anderson, 18 Feb. 1918 and Anderson note on their conversation, 7 March 1918, RG 6, Director's Office, NYPL Archives; Barry Seaver, *The Career of Rebecca Browning Rankin* (Diss., University of North Carolina, Chapel Hill, 1997), 12-18.

68. AH to Lydenberg, 13 June 1918, AH-CB.

69. Carroll Smith-Rosenberg, "The New Woman as Androgyne," in *Disorderly Conduct: Visions of Gender in Victorian America* (New York: Oxford University Press, 1986), 280-89.

70. Ariel Fielding to the author, 12 Sept. 2004; Anderson to Edith Guerrier, 10 March 1919, RG 6, Director's Office, New York Public Library Archives.

71. Hasse, *Compensations*, 17.

72. Kennedy, *Disloyal Mothers*, 71; "shot for treason" quoted in Frederick Luebke, *Bonds of Loyalty: German-Americans and World War I* (Dekalb: Northern Illinois University Press, 1974), 241.

73. George Kennan, *Russia and the West under Lenin and Stalin* (Boston: Little, Brown, 1961), 25-26.

74. Lemons, *Woman Citizen*, 11. Suffrage demonstrations at the White House were also blamed on pro-German, disloyal elements.

75. Quoted in David Nasaw, *The Chief: The Life of William Randolph Hearst* (Boston: Houghton Mifflin, 2000), 258-59.

76. Quoted in Shanley, *LEU*, 347-48.

77. LJ 44 (May 1919): 276.

78. AH-Beard correspondence, March-May 1918, AH-CB.

79. Metcalf-AH exchanges through Lydenberg, 17, 21, 22 Nov. 1917, AH-CB.

80. H. Halper to AH, 22 Nov. 1917, McCombs to Lydenberg, 27 Nov. 1917, AH-CB.

81. AH-Lydenberg-Anderson exchange, May 1918, AH-CB.

82. Rice to Lydenberg, n.d. [March 1917], AH-CB.

83. The numerous memos on this incident are all AH-CB.

84. LJ 49 (15 Jan. 1924): 80; Susan Lee Grabler, "Government Information Of, By, and For the People: The Changing Mission of the American Library Association's Public Documents Committee, 1876-1956," *Journal of Government Information* 22 (Jan.-Feb. 1995): 50-53; LJ 49 (15 Jan. 1924): 80.

85. *ALA Bulletin* 10 (1916 conference proceedings): 446.

86. Edith Clarke, *Guide to the Use of United States Government Publications* (Boston: Boston Book Company, 1918), 8-9.

87. LJ 43 (Aug. 1918): 623-25.

88. Clarke, *Guide*, 63-64, 68.

89. Ibid., 237-40.

90. AH to Calvert, 13 May 1918, AH-CB; Lurene McDonald to Cohen, 27 May 1918, AH-CB.

91. Babette Deutsch, "The Public Library and the Public Need," *The Dial* 64 (23 May1918): 475-77; Maurice Magnus to AH, 12 June 1918, AH-CB.

92. Friedel to AH, 18 Sept. 1918, AH-CB; Adelaide Hasse, "The Business of Being a Librarian," *General Federation Magazine* 17 (April 1918): 33-34.

93. Adelaide Hasse, "This Business of Ours," PL 23 (July 1918): 303-5.

94. Harry Lydenberg, *History of the New York Public Library* (New York: NYPL, 1923), 435.

95. AH to Baruch, 27 June 1918, AH-CB; William Beer-AH exchange, 2, 7 Aug. 1918, AH-CB.

96. Lydenberg to Anderson, 24 July 1918, RG 6, Director's Office, Enemy Aliens file, NYPL Archives; AH to Lydenberg, 23 July 1918, AH-CB.

97. Rushmore-Lydenberg-AH exchange, 17, 20, 22 July, 26 Aug. 1918, RG 6, Director's Office, Economics Division file, NYPL Archives.

98. AH to Lydenberg, 27 July 1918, AH-CB.

99. Rushmore to McCombs, 17 July 1918, AH-CB; Metcalf, *Random*, 127.

100. *New York Evening Post*, 26 July 1918, clipping in AH-CB.

101. *New York Evening Post*, 5 Aug. 1918, clipping in AH-CB.

102. Two LEU flyers, AH-CB, with a note that Squires distributed them at ALA.

103. *Civil Service Chronicle*, 23 Aug., 26 Sept. 1918, clippings in AH-CB, with a note from Squires to trustee WilliamAppleton, calling his attention to them.

Chapter 9

Crisis, 1918-1919

In September, the patriotic demonstrations blared on around the library, and no one expected that the war would end early in November. The government continued its zealous investigations of disloyalty, raiding the office of the newly formed National Civil Liberties Bureau (later, American Civil Liberties Union) to seize its files. By the end of the month, New Yorkers had a new fear, as the influenza epidemic grew out of control while the health authorities denied the danger. In Washington, the suffrage movement pressed hard for its constitutional amendment, and finally, on September 30, President Wilson went before the Senate to urge passage. The next day, the senators rejected it by only two votes. With the fall elections approaching, women able to vote in many states, and senators now elected by popular vote, the suffrage amendment was within striking distance of passage in Congress.

September seemed to go on as usual for Hasse in the duality of praise outside and hostility within the library. Under the title "Do Libraries Impede Research?", *Special Libraries* published more of her criticism of library cataloging, the poor quality of which she blamed on "overweening concentration on methodology." Challenging conventional attitudes was especially important, she wrote, when "not only are new enterprises under contemplation but absolute revolution in the management of old enterprises is taking place." This brought an enthusiastic letter from George Frederick of the Business Bourse, secretary of the National Research Council, who complained that conservative management prevented the library from becoming "a real haven for vital information of the hour—which should be the ideal of a truly modern library." Frederick's pet idea was for NYPL to set up a special room for information on a current hot topic, postwar reconstruction, just as *The Dial* was planning a special reconstruction issue. Such simplistic calls for special collections on current interests might be a headache to library directors, but to Hasse it was reinforcement of her desire to make the Economics Division "indispensable" for information needed in the war effort and the reordering expected to follow.[1]

The conflicts in the library continued, with more exchanges about books from other divisions used in 229 and disputes about classification and location. Hasse had to appeal to Lydenberg about a problem with William Gamble over books on free ports incorrectly classed with works on the engineering of harbors in the Technology Division rather than as economics. Free ports were a much discussed topic of the day, and such an obvious error in classification would not have improved Hasse's mood. Behind her back, Frank Waite and Rob Henderson complained about her doing too much for a professor preparing a reading list. He had been given names of staff who might assist his rush job on personal time, but then another professor referred him to Hasse, "who directed one of her assistants to do the work during library hours," with payment by the professor only for work that couldn't be finished on work time. Lydenberg discussed it with Anderson, who added the report to his Hasse file, apparently as evidence of her "doing favors" for users. There is no record that Hasse was given a chance to present her side of the story.[2]

Charles McCombs was particularly venomous, complaining to Lydenberg that when the Economics Division failed to send a journal volume upstairs, the staff was observed "chatting" by the person who went looking for it. Hasse explained that the volume had been put on the carrier but had gone back and forth due to faulty service elsewhere. She apologized profusely for the chatting girls, explaining that it was the last day celebration of the summer substitutes, some of whom had brought in a box of candy. A week later, when a reader was sent to 229 from the main reading room for a volume of New York laws that was in the stacks, Hasse retaliated with a note to McCombs asking, "What is the meaning of this?" McCombs told Lydenberg that he would not waste further time on Hasse's "trivial complaints," and besides, "I do not propose to answer directly so rude and peremptory a demand as 'What is the meaning of this?'!!" He went on incoherently that it should be clear to Hasse that her division serviced requests for statutes, although "an inexperienced or careless assistant may have sent the reader to 229," which seems to imply that the request should have been filled on the third floor, as Hasse thought. When Hasse reported to Lydenberg that delay in sending a requested book to her division caused a reader to leave before it arrived, McCombs replied that there was no evidence that the book had been called for, and furthermore, "If I chose to report all unreasonable delays in service from 229 . . . the Economics Division would waste quite a bit of time in investigating." McCombs' notes were in his microscopically tiny handwriting, even more constricted than Lydenberg's, while Hasse's swift, flowing script became bigger and bolder in this period of increasing tension.[3]

Even a friendly gesture to Lydenberg seemed to be held against Hasse. When she sent him thanks for the "prompt replacement" of a "Marx book," it too went into Anderson's file, for reasons that are unclear, perhaps because she mentioned that Morris Kolchin of her staff knew Glick, a newspaper reporter working on his thesis while serving in the navy; her note is not clear on Glick's connection with the book. Kolchin was an immigrant from Russia, and acquaintance with someone somehow connected with a "Marx book" may have linked him—and Hasse—in Anderson's mind with the Bolsheviks.[4]

While Hasse bickered with Gamble and McCombs, she didn't realize that more dangerous hostility was seething in Keyes Metcalf. Life had been difficult for Metcalf that summer. Early in July, he was taken ill with a high fever, perhaps an early case of the influenza epidemic that would kill more than twelve thousand in the city. Pale and thin, he pushed himself to return to work before being fully recovered. In August, during a heat wave, his wife gave birth to their second child in their apartment. It was a difficult labor that left her with injuries that would require surgery, and she also suffered from severe migraine headaches. The baby's heat rash became infected, causing him to cry so hard that he ruptured himself and had to wear a truss for months. Metcalf worried about how he would care for an invalid wife and two small children on his salary, and sometime in this period he developed a nervous twitch he was unaware of until a coworker mentioned it.[5]

In September, when he saw Tilloah Squires' comments about the Reference Department in the *Civil Service Chronicle,* he was furiously certain that "Miss Hasse was responsible for it," because Squires was her "protégé," an interesting assumption from one who was himself the protégé of prominent librarians. In a remarkable omission even for Metcalf, he made no mention of the union and Squires' position as president, thus avoiding the awkward fact that it is routine for union leaders to criticize management. Omitting the information that Squires' comments appeared in the *Civil Service Chronicle* as the views of the president of a union seeking civil service for library employees, Metcalf said only that "letters appeared" attacking NYPL and Lydenberg, as though Hasse and Squires had taken to writing to newspapers out of sheer malice. He claimed to have been deeply offended by criticism of Lydenberg, to the point that he "did not want to work in a place where such statements were published about the person under whom I was working." This gives the impression that Squires, guided by Hasse, made offensive allegations about Lydenberg, but actually she mostly criticized aspects of management without naming who was responsible. Squires did complain about the inconsistent salaries established at the discretion of the Chief of the Reference Department, but that was exactly what had so infuriated Metcalf when he was hired by Lydenberg. Metcalf condemned Squires' intolerable insults in the same book in which he presented an unflattering portrait of Lydenberg and confirmed much of what she said about the Reference Department. Lydenberg was no longer alive to complain when Metcalf, while claiming to be an admirer, described him as "ultra conservative, to put it mildly," having little interest in administration and giving it "less time than it required," often disagreeing with Anderson but silently bowing to his decisions, and subjecting his staff to unpleasant secret tests. Metcalf did not even acknowledge any connection between Squires' complaint about pay inequities and his own anger at the way Lydenberg handled his original salary or his discovery that the women in his class all had lower salaries than the men. Ignoring the existence of the union and the validity of Squires' criticism, Metcalf presented himself as rushing to the defense of Lydenberg in the culmination of his narrative of men abused by the shrewish Hasse. What really seemed to infuriate him, however, was public criticism of the library administration by women. Presumably his anger was compounded by the stress in his personal life, but its immediate projection onto Hasse as responsible for the words of her "protégé" suggests a particular fear of her mentoring of energetic, publicity-minded young feminists whose criticism of NYPL's management threatened the advantaged status of men like himself.[6]

The furious Metcalf immediately went to Lydenberg's office to tell him that the staff "had complete confidence in him and that something must be done to prevent this kind of abuse." His recollection was that Lydenberg "quietly said that he was not in a position to defend himself and nothing could be done unless the staff agreed with my attitude." From Metcalf's account, it is unclear what Lydenberg meant by this or if he even understood that Metcalf blamed Hasse for what the union said. He might have been referring to another reply from the Staff Association or intended only to calm the angry Metcalf, but subsequent events suggest that the conversation was more pointed than Metcalf admits. Repeating that something must be done, Metcalf returned to his desk and drafted a call for Hasse's dismissal. McCombs "revised and strengthened" it, and they obtained signatures from eighteen other staff, mostly male division chiefs but also including four women, before submitting it to Anderson.

In just four paragraphs, Metcalf and McCombs did a masterful job of suggesting that Hasse was "detrimental to the work and usefulness of the whole library" without actually providing evidence or examples of their accusations:

> The Chief of the Economics Division, Miss Adelaide R. Hasse, has been conducting through newspapers and periodicals a campaign which is injuring the Library, misrepresenting the library profession, and is definitely calculated to bring discredit upon us as librarians.
>
> Furthermore we believe that she is systematically working to undermine your administration and to cause discord and dissatisfaction among the staff, and . . . that ample proof of these activities exists.
>
> We are convinced that her conception of library service and its practice as exemplified in the administration of the Economics Division, her frequent refusal to cooperate fairly with other divisions, her frequent disregard of the interests of other divisions and of the rights of her colleagues, and her habitual rudeness to members of the staff, interfere seriously with the work of the division chiefs, and are detrimental to the work and usefulness of the whole Library and to the spirit and welfare of the staff.
>
> Considering the harm that she is doing to the Library, we protest against the continuance of Miss Hasse as an employee . . . , and place ourselves on record as ready to support you in any steps which you think it wise and necessary to take in regard to her, for the good of the service.[7]

These allegations raise more questions than they answer. Just what was the "campaign" Hasse was conducting in the press? If it was her articles and interviews critical of library education, cataloging, and management, all commonplace views within the library world but seldom expressed to outsiders, were they grounds for dismissal? Perhaps not by the later standards of a profession that claims to defend intellectual freedom or some opinions of the Supreme Court on the First Amendment rights of public employees, but in the atmosphere of the time, anything that smacked of disloyalty was intolerable. If they referred to the statements of Tilloah Squires as LEU president, there is no proof that Hasse was responsible, and firing her for friendship with a union leader was a particularly nasty form of guilt by association. Nor is there any specificity about how she was working to "cause discord and dissatisfaction" in the staff, while there is ample proof, including Metcalf's own memoir, that staff unrest existed for reasons that had nothing to do with Hasse. Then there is the reference to "her conception of library service." What was this and how was it problematic? Was she violating policy, or was the problem only resentment that her division did more for readers? Explaining this would have been awkward when Hasse was so well known for extensive, much-appreciated service, and outsiders might ask why others couldn't do as much as her division did. Equally awkward would have been specifics about Hasse's "disregard" for the "interests" and "rights" of other divisions. What were they, and how was a department head expected to respect them? As for "habitual rudeness," Hasse had admitted to being "disagreeable" as the alternative to being "ineffectual," but was she really exceptionally rude, to the point of damaging the organization, or was it a case of the double standard, judging her differently as a woman? The latter interpretation is supported by a memo in which William Gamble told Anderson that he had not encountered Hasse's rudeness. Conflicts between Hasse and Gamble are on record, so if he didn't find her rude, other men may have been overreacting to a forceful woman.

The letters that Gamble and Heryk Arctowski sent to Anderson were less discreet in articulating what disturbed Hasse's coworkers. To Gamble, it was not rudeness but her "disloyalty," which he mentioned three times, and her "attitude of defiance" towards the administration, as shown by her "lamentable attempt" to organize the reference staff. It is unclear what this meant, perhaps a reference to her calls for staff meetings or to the union or the Economic Committee's proposals—or something else that Gamble didn't explain. Gamble repeated four times that "I resent" Hasse's behavior, citing her "campaign for what seems to be her own aggrandizement . . . her poisoning the public mind into the belief that the Economic Division is the only efficient section . . . her advertisement of the Library as a fount of favors which have nothing to do with legitimate library work thereby placing the other divisions in the awkward position of explaining why they cannot 'deliver the goods.'" Hasse's successful promotion of her division and herself infuriated Gamble, who felt no hesitation in expressing his anger to the director.[8]

Arctowski explained that, although he had refused to sign on the grounds that he did not agree with all of the letter, his real reason was fear of making a "'public martyr' of a person whose motives are or may be purely political and anti-patriotic." He wanted the matter handled secretly by "proper authorities and not discussed, neither privately nor publicly." It is unclear whether he referred only to Hasse's dismissal or to some government action, but his emphasis on secrecy is more alarmingly contrary to American values than anything Hasse ever said.[9]

Metcalf's brief and smoothly worded accusation avoided the pitfalls of such individual complaints, but its true brilliance as bureaucratic backstabbing was the number of signatures. The trustees would be unlikely to spend much time analyzing the text, but certainly they would be impressed by the weight of twenty signatures. Workers in any organization may spend a good deal of time complaining about each other, but, if only from enlightened self-interest, they are unlikely to sign a call for the dismissal of a coworker. If twenty NYPL librarians wanted Hasse fired "for the good of the service," the natural assumption would be that she was utterly impossible. An alternative interpretation might suggest that this was an unhealthy organization whose administration failed in its responsibility to deal with organizational conflict and, at a time of unrest within and without the library, encouraged the scapegoating of a high-ranking German American woman. The trustees were not inclined to ask questions, however. Busy and important men (there were no women on the board and would be none for another thirty years), they agreed that a troublesome employee should be fired, and the times did not encourage careful consideration.

The signers included men who had dealings with Hasse (Metcalf, McCombs, Sawyer, Waite, Taylor, Gamble, Paltsits, and Moth) and some who were close to the administration (Franklin Hopper, soon to be made head of the Circulation Department, and Robert Finster, Secretary to the Director and Clerk of the Board). Other signers, such as the heads of Art, Genealogy, and Orientalia, seem unlikely to have had much contact with Hasse, but presumably they shared the perception of her disloyalty. Freidus of the Jewish Division, whose problems in the library were similar to Hasse's, was not a signatory, nor was Wilberforce Eames; there is no record of whether they refused to sign or were not asked. Other chiefs not among the signers were away on war service. The four women, whose signatures provided cover against accusations of sex discrimination, were Minnie Sears and Bertha Eger of Cataloging and Maria Leavitt and Gertrude Hill of the Order Department, all of whom had contact with Hasse in their work. The signers ranged from younger men (Metcalf, McCombs, Sawyer) to the longest serving (Bjerregaard and Frank Weitenkampf, both approaching forty years at NYPL), and included some of Hasse's contemporaries hired by Billings. Such a representative group of twenty could not be dismissed as a mere clique. Nothing is known about the circumstances in which the signatures were gathered, but obviously the signers understood that the administration would be receptive to their petition. Hasse would claim that some of them had second thoughts when they saw the result of their action. Since the statement was slightly ambiguous about what they wanted done, it is possible that not all of them intended that she be fired, but clearly they wanted her punished for her public criticism of librarians. Nor can it be known to what extent their desire to purge Hasse was affected by the fear and anger swirling around and within them, from the war and its patriotic frenzy, the hatred of all things German, the demands of the suffragists, the inflation that more than doubled prices, even the invisible threat of the influenza that became virulent that month. Certainly it was not an atmosphere conducive to calm and reason.

In the last week of September, Metcalf presented the letter to Anderson, who followed his usual course of referring it to the Executive Committee at its meeting on October 4, reminding the members that "the case of Miss Hasse had been brought to their attention several times before, either formally or informally." After "full discussion," the nature of which Anderson did not record in the minutes, the committee voted unanimously to inform Hasse that her services "are no longer desired," that she be "given the opportunity to resign her position at once," and that "in view of her long connection with the Library," Anderson be authorized to pay her through the end of the year, at his discretion.[10]

Conveniently for Anderson, Charles Williamson, who was working temporarily on the Carnegie Corporation's Americanization study, needed a job and immediately accepted an offer to return to the Economics Division. Since leaving the Municipal Reference Library in May, Williamson had been unsuccessfully seeking academic library positions, including the directorship at Yale. With a replacement found, on October 7 Anderson sent Hasse a two-sentence note announcing the decision of the Executive Committee that her services were no longer wanted. She was given an opportunity to resign and pressured to go quietly with the warning, "I am authorized to deal with you in the matter of salary after today as generously as your attitude may warrant."[11]

The stunned Hasse immediately requested an explanation. The next day, she arrived at work to find a notice posted that Williamson had been reappointed chief of the division, with Metcalf supervising until his arrival and Dorothy Miller in charge of reference. The division's staff convened and drafted a protest, which Hasse said she discouraged for fear it would "jeopardize their positions."[12] Then she received a letter from Anderson at his most cryptic, telling her that he was "not authorized to give the reasons" for the Executive Committee's decision, but "you know those reasons better than anyone else, and that they are sufficient."

For several days, Hasse tried to see Anderson, finally writing again on October 12 to assure him that she did not know the reasons and was "utterly at a loss as to what it is to which you refer." She denied any suggestion that there was anything in her long record with the library that she would want kept from public view, ending with a request that she be "informed of the exact imputations or charges, if they are such, pending against me, and that I be granted a hearing or some opportunity to meet such imputations or charges." Two days later, she sent her request for a hearing to Elihu Root, explaining that disclosure of anything brought before the Executive Committee "would be a relief as against the implied discredit inhering in the situation as it rests today." There was precedent for such hearings, which the trustees had occasionally granted in the past. She received no reply, and the full board held a special meeting to confirm her dismissal. Anderson then informed her that there were "no imputations or charges" against her (thus evading the fundamental American principle that an accused be informed of the charges and permitted to confront her accusers). He said that the Executive Committee had had her under observation and concluded "that the way in which you have performed these duties and your failure to cooperate cordially with other divisions . . . have been such as to impair the efficiency" of the service, requiring her dismissal "in the best interests of the Library." He added that since she had failed to resign, her employment was terminated with three months' severance pay. Thus ended Hasse's twenty-one years at the New York Public Library.[13]

While Hasse had been seeking an explanation, Metcalf had taken a seat about fifteen feet in front of her desk. He recalled "feeling that Miss Hasse's eyes were boring holes through my back," which may have reflected some pangs of conscience, as he much later conceded that "the whole thing left a bad taste in my mouth." He thought it "a shame to have Miss Hasse's library career end in this way," but nevertheless, "I am convinced that I did the right thing."[14] This righteous certainty must have been reinforced by his appointment in December to be Anderson's executive assistant. Rebecca Rankin, who had decided she wanted to stay in New York after all, transferred to the Municipal Reference Library to replace William Seaver, who had gone on ALA war service.

Guilty conscience may also account for Metcalf's faulty recollection of how long he sat under Hasse's hostile gaze, which he says lasted until the end of the year. Williamson's contemporary account is that she "held her desk and had full access to the letter files" for no more than ten days, until he arrived to take charge. When Hasse continued to come in to collect personal belongings and use the library, Williamson made things unpleasant. Seeing Hasse talking to a woman with whom she had mutual friends, he intervened to announce that "readers are not allowed to speak to Miss Hasse." When the woman objected, Williamson took her aside for a whispered discussion that she declined to discuss afterwards. Williamson immediately brought back Rollin Sawyer and fired two of the staff, while five others resigned. All sources acknowledged that her staff remained "loyal and vociferous in support" of Hasse, but Lydenberg explained that she had driven out anyone who disagreed with her.[15]

As if the turmoil in her life were not enough, the atmosphere in the city added to Hasse's sense of being caught in a nightmare. In October, the flu epidemic became so severe, with thousands of deaths, that the library was among the public places closed for a week. Then, early in November, the city went wild twice, first at a false report that the war had ended, and then when there really was an armistice on the eleventh, exactly four years after Hasse had returned from the trip to Germany that did her so much damage. The celebration went on from sunrise into the night, with Fifth Avenue in front of the library packed with cheering, singing, weeping crowds who hung the Kaiser in effigy.

Anderson sent Hasse a deadline for removing her personal property from the library and told her that Squires now was regarded as her employee and barred from entering the stacks. Hasse replied politely, but in December she complained to the postal authorities that her personal mail was being opened; Lydenberg replied that, because she had declined an opportunity to give instructions about her mail, letters addressed to her as division chief were being opened. Whatever Williamson may have done with Hasse's incoming mail, it is clear that he went through her files in search of evidence for Anderson's collection, including her inquiry about joining the LEU, on which Anderson noted that Williamson found it in December, and letters from Dana, Friedel, Ahern, Beard, and many others.[16]

~ ~ ~

Although Hasse soon had a new job with the government in Washington, she was not inclined to fade away. For almost a year, she would continue to seek an explanation and an opportunity to clear her name of the suspicions created by her sudden, unexplained firing. In seeking a hearing, she may have had some faint hope of getting her job back (and also of exposing Anderson and the conditions he created), but her main concerns were the protection of her reputation and the principle that a public servant of long service should not be dismissed without a hearing. Almost immediately, she began to hear rumors spread by Anderson's allies that she had been taken from the library by a federal officer and interned as a German agent. Hasse would suffer lasting harm from vague allegations that she had been fired for "some want of loyalty or . . . pro-German sympathy," as New York's education commissioner heard, probably from James Wyer. Anderson would continue to stoke such suspicions behind the scenes as a way to damage her reputation and confuse the issue of why she was fired. Though Hasse never saw what he said and apparently never knew that at various times he told the Secret Service, the Federal Bureau of Investigation, and the Civil Service Commission that she was a disloyal German sympathizer, she knew all too well how Anderson operated, "by whispered words, by lifting of eyebrows, by a deftly turned phrase." She understood that these were "the easiest and the most effective means . . . to assassinate me professionally as well as to justify having kicked me out of the library." The option to resign was not much of a choice under the circumstances, as a sudden resignation would have sent the library world's gossips into a frenzy of suspicion. In making her dismissal public and demanding a hearing, Hasse was showing that she had nothing to hide and trying to shift attention to the actions of an administration that refused to state any reasons for its action or provide the basic due process of a hearing.[17]

On November 2, Hasse sent a letter to each member of the board explaining that her requests for a hearing had been ignored by Anderson and Root, so that she now repeated it formally to each of them. She warned that unless given a hearing, she would "appeal to the citizens of the City of New York whom I have served."[18] She then informed prominent New Yorkers of her dismissal, receiving letters praising her work and expressing shock at what H. W. Kent of the Metropolitan Museum called "deeply regrettable and not understandable." Julius Henry Cohen wrote to a trustee of his "amazement that . . . Miss Hasse has been summarily dismissed without any hearing and without any statement of the reasons for her dismissal." Cohen suggested that "it does not seem in the public interest that so valuable a servant should be lost, nor would it seem to be encouraging to other employees . . . of the Library to have such an example of summary dismissal set before them." Hasse also sought support from women's organizations. Squires wrote on behalf of the LEU, of course, to urge a hearing and reconsideration. She also informed a fellow union activist, Henry Linville, president of the new teachers union, who was struggling with similar dismissals of his members, telling him, "There are no grounds here for even a 'loyalty' case, so heaven knows what has been 'cooked up.' I believe it is the vindictive action of a little clique in the library, so pernicious in its activities that no one could realize it unless through personal observation on the inside." She and Hasse called on a leader of the local Federation of Women's Clubs to discuss the firing and the need for women trustees, which prominent women did eventually advocate, without success. In November, letters calling for reconsideration came from women leaders of the Public Education Association, the League of Advertising Women, and the Consumers League. Florence Kelley wrote of Hasse's "invaluable assistance," but that was hardly likely to move the trustees. At the December 11 meeting, their only reaction was to note that they had approved the dismissal in October.[19]

Soon after, the board heard from a man who caused them more concern, the prominent and politically connected attorney George Gordon Battle, who represented Hasse at the same time that he helped the Civil Liberties Bureau retrieve its files from the government. Battle was an eminent trial lawyer, active in numerous civic causes; he also represented the Tammany Hall organization and was a prominent supporter of the newly elected governor, Al Smith. A Virginian of considerable charm, he had come north in search of opportunity not available in the post Civil War South and retained a lifelong sympathy for outsiders. Battle assured the board that he acted only in the interest of justice, with no expectation of compensation, and implied no criticism, suggesting only that a mistake had been made. He asked that Hasse be given a hearing by one of the trustees.[20]

Battle enclosed an eleven-page statement by Hasse in which she described her long career and many publications and quoted praise from researchers, anonymous Economics Division staff, and Anderson himself in four commendatory notes. She insisted that she had "never any difficulty with associates or superiors" at LAPL and GPO, and she called on Billings' secretary to testify that her relations with him had been "always cordial in the extreme." (Anderson said that the secretary denied any knowledge of their relationship; he offered no recollection of Billings' opinion of Hasse from his own six years as associate director or Lydenberg's many years as Billings' assistant.) Hasse was handicapped by not having any charges to answer nor knowing what had been said about her, with the result that her statement was not very effective as a defense, and her stronger points tended to be outweighed by confusing attempts to explain the situation in the library. She made the mistake of trying to describe her problems with the subtle Anderson, which sounded like a fuss over minor matters, such as the Staff Association, the 1917 annual report, and the complexities of documents cataloging and reference. Emphasizing her long work with documents, with no mention of her wider interests, she claimed that the sudden cataloging transfer had revealed Anderson's hostility and "deliberate policy of exclusion," which seemed to support Anderson's charge that she was embittered by his cataloging decision. Trying to explain the hostility of her coworkers, she blamed their tendency to take personally her calls for change and their resentment "that I was the only woman Division Chief, that my Division was receiving considerable public recognition, that my Division was one of the largest and most active in the Reference Department, that I was the highest salaried woman in the Reference Department." She might seem to have a reasonable claim of sex discrimination, but the all-male board was unlikely to understand or care. Only on the last page did she raise another strong point, the lack of due process for a public employee of more than twenty years' service, ending with a "protest against a proceeding so undemocratic, so unprofessional as the manner of my dismissal" and, "believing in the just intentions of the Board," requesting a hearing.[21]

Battle received an immediate reply from one of the trustees, Henry Fairfield Osborn, president of the American Museum of Natural History, who explained that he saw Hasse's case as simply an "instance of incompatibility," a common situation in which "an otherwise very valuable and trusted employee acquired or developed an incapacity to work amicably with his or her associates." Employees might rank high in character, energy, and ability but lack the required compatibility. Battle, careful not to alienate a trustee who at least communicated, assured Osborn that he understood his point and was sure that "any action which you have taken or may take in this matter will be dictated by the highest motives."[22] Osborn's reasonable tone showed the difficulty of Hasse's situation. The "incompatible" label is conveniently applied to those who differ with administrators or whose temperament, values, gender, ethnicity, or other characteristics don't blend into the organizational culture, and the statement signed by twenty coworkers surely established the existence of some form of incompatibility. By later standards of employment law, such allegations may not be used as a rationalization for sex discrimination or violation of public employees' First Amendment rights, but in 1918 that was not a concern of Henry Fairfield Osborn, a notoriously pompous example of old New York, a nephew of J. P. Morgan, and an opponent of women being allowed to vote or use birth control.[23]

Osborn sent a copy of his letter to Anderson, who replied with a suggestion that Hasse was both Germanic and deranged: "The 'incompatibility' arises from a truly Prussian arrogance and a megalomania which many people here think borders on dementia." While Hasse was denied a hearing or any statement of the reason for her dismissal, Anderson could provide the trustees with written comment on anything she or her supporters said, which he did with considerable venom, meanwhile maintaining his dignified public silence. Anderson was under considerable strain as Hasse persisted in challenging her dismissal. Metcalf remembered the period as the only time when Anderson spoke harshly to him, which he attributed to the director's pain from an attack of lumbago, apparently not suspecting that Anderson might be venting his irritation at the turmoil Metcalf's petition had brought down on him.[24]

In November, apparently in response to letters praising Hasse's service, he presented "a few illustrative instances of unsatisfactory service rendered to readers by the former Chief of the Economics Division." Using comments Lydenberg had written for him, Anderson essentially admitted absence of specific evidence, but, though there was "little anyone can put a finger on," somehow there was "ample indication of a different attitude" in the Economics Division. He conceded that Hasse might counter such accusations "with instances of unsatisfactory service in other parts of the Library remedied through her skill, insight, knowledge, and kindly interest," but he would have no knowledge of what really happened in such cases, because the library's practice was to get what a complaining reader wanted without taking time to investigate "apparent lapses in service." (This is at variance with a letter he had sent to the *Times* a few months earlier, in response to an allegation of censorship by an anonymous "Inquirer" who claimed to have been told "rather scornfully and rather haughtily" that an unspecified New York library did not and would not have the title he requested, *The Unpardonable Sin*. Anderson said that NYPL had approved the book for all branches and asked that "Inquirer" send him information to identify the branch and library assistant in question.) He listed seven comments by users indicative of faulty service in the Economics Division; most were reported second- or thirdhand, and none was documented or examined in detail. Isadore Mudge was quoted as saying that Economics was the only division with which Columbia students had difficulty, and she herself refused to have any telephone contact with it, instead calling the Information Desk "with certainty of accurate and sympathetic response." No specifics were given, and the allegation didn't jibe with Lydenberg's earlier statement that users appreciated the enthusiasm and effort of the division's staff. Possibly Mudge was venting her resentment of Hasse's criticism of library school graduates or her differences with Minnie Sears, or she may have been overcome with suspicion of Hasse as pro-German, or there may have been tensions between the division's staff and the young men from Columbia, at the time resistant to pressure for admission by Jews and women. Without documentation, one can endlessly speculate, but seven vague reports out of thousands of users of the division do not reveal a pattern. The wording of one allegation was particularly telling about the nature of the problem, however: an encyclopedia researcher was reported to have told Waite and Lydenberg that Hasse "gave him to understand that she had no time to wait on him. . . . He is a quiet, inoffensive, self-effacing, mild-mannered man, not impressive." Here was the essence of the complaint against Hasse: she didn't show respect for self-effacing, mild-mannered, unimpressive men.[25]

In response to Hasse's statement to the trustees, Anderson provided comments by himself, Lydenberg, and Williamson. He condemned Hasse for having "always been more efficient as a publicity agent for herself than as a practical library worker," who made it a practice to "coddle" and "give an inordinate amount of time" to important people "to the neglect of the general public, and then get letters of appreciation for so doing." She had "an arrogance which is truly Prussian, an exaggerated idea of her own importance which amounts almost to megalomania, a total disregard of the rights, opinions, and feelings of her fellow workers, and . . . utter inability to understand why they should resent this." To top it off, she lacked a sense of humor. For those who might wonder why such a fiend hadn't been dismissed earlier, Anderson explained that he had wanted to fire her in 1916 for her "childish, ill-natured, and insulting" behavior over the cataloging transfer but deferred to Lydenberg's hope "to try to bring her around and get her to work harmoniously with her associates."[26]

Anderson ended with an example of his readiness to take offense at anything Hasse did or, in this case, didn't do. Lydenberg "bore the brunt" of the trouble Hasse caused, he said, and now, "His reward is that Miss Hasse in her statement passes him by with silent contempt." The man "who tried to put her *en rapport* with the rest of the staff, and who probably suffered most from her arrogance and petulance, is not even honored in her statement by a condemnation." If Hasse had condemned Lydenberg, that would have been evidence of her disloyalty and other sins, but not mentioning him was somehow just as wicked, "silent contempt." Hasse may have regarded Lydenberg with silent contempt, but it is equally possible that Anderson and Metcalf were projecting their own contempt for him. In a kind of emotional displacement, both men seemed determined to create narratives of themselves as defenders of Lydenberg, the quiet man attacked by an angry, disorderly female. Hasse never made any public comment about Lydenberg, perhaps because she regarded him as a doormat for Anderson, but his defense served as a handy weapon to attack the woman whose real threat was to the status quo, particularly the gendered hierarchy of libraries.

The tone of Lydenberg's statement was more sorrow than anger, without Anderson's cold fury, but supporting the account of "angularities, contentiousness, inflexibility, insistence on her own point of view, lack of sympathy for fellow workers or appreciation of their point of view" which were documented in the "large bundle of notes, memoranda, and letters on file in the Director's office." He rejected Hasse's claims of mistreatment, quoted her admission "I know I am disagreeable" as evidence that she was the real problem, and cited her treatment of Rollin Sawyer to show she couldn't tolerate differences of opinion (without explaining what their differences were). Though mostly sticking to specifics about library conflicts, Lydenberg showed that he too could wield a stiletto, when he denied that Hasse was fired for German sympathies but added the convoluted suggestion that "the fact that Ernst Hasse, founder of the Pan German Society, is a relative may be not without interest in that connection." The most prejudicial war-related remark in his statement was actually inserted by Anderson: quoting a snide note Hasse wrote about Carl Cannon's ineptitude with the *Congressional Record*, Lydenberg said only that Cannon was one of the "most valuable" reference assistants, but Anderson inserted the information that he "is now in France with a German bullet in his hip," as though Hasse had attacked a wounded soldier.[27]

Charles Williamson's comments were scathing in portraying Hasse as incompetent, unreasonable, stubborn, self-righteous, professionally unethical, self-aggrandizing, egotistical, and dishonest. In his eagerness to condemn Hasse, Anderson didn't seem to notice the flagrant conflict of interest in Williamson's justifying Hasse's dismissal when he had benefited by obtaining her job. Had Hasse been given a formal hearing, the administration would not have dared to present such testimony, but in the secret proceedings of the trustees, the impropriety apparently went unchallenged.

Williamson did cite three incidents that had some documentation: Hasse's hostile 1912 memo to him and two examples of what he said was faulty reference service (though it is not clear that she really erred in either case). Apparently realizing that this didn't amount to much, he claimed that many similar incidents were known but "not matters of record." In Hasse's papers, however, there is evidence that Williamson did not always have such a low opinion of her reference work. As late as 1917, he referred an inquiry about foreign bonds to Hasse as "the best person for you to see. . . . If she does not have the information you need, I have no doubt that she will make a serious effort to get it."²⁸

Most of what he wrote was vehement in utterly rejecting everything in Hasse's statement, to the point of exaggeration in claiming that turnover at NYPL "was not at all exceptional" and that Hasse's bibliographical work was "of the past," while her recent publications "all show an effort to undermine and attack the Director." Her complaint about the 1917 annual report was evidence of her obsession with self-promotion, though "a librarian who is not willing to do her work without getting instant recognition and publicity is unfitted for the business." Williamson portrayed Hasse as a complete fraud who excelled only at publicity and had been difficult to work with before his arrival in 1911, as he said he had heard from Billings and other division chiefs. Neither Anderson nor Lydenberg went back that far, perhaps recognizing that it would raise questions about why Hasse hadn't been dealt with earlier. Anderson pointed to having made her chief of the Economics Division as evidence of his goodwill and implied that she had become impossible in recent years, since the cataloging transfer. Lydenberg mostly discussed her behavior in the period 1916-17. (By focusing on Hasse's late forties, they also may have played to the belief of the time that women were prone to "menopausal insanity.") They were careful to deny that there was any discrimination against her as the only woman division chief or that she was fired for being a union member or a German sympathizer, although Anderson's file and Metcalf's memoir show that all three were contributing factors. They concentrated on their portrayal of a madwoman, bad-tempered, selfish, disrespectful of authority, disloyal, and crazed with her "peculiar passion for commendation and recognition." To the elderly men of the board, it was a monstrous picture, a projection of their deepest anxieties about angry, demanding females out to "rule or ruin," in the phrase Anderson applied to both Hasse and Maud Malone.

The picture of Hasse as demented with antagonism and egomania had been raised by her coworkers and endorsed by her superiors. Now Elihu Root drew on his vast authority to confirm it further. The trustees were sufficiently concerned about the involvement of George Gordon Battle to ask Root to review the case at their meeting on January 8. He "presented a detailed and thorough review of the evidence . . . with copious quotations from correspondence" between Hasse and the administration, from Hasse's published articles, "and from other documents and correspondence." The details of his presentation were not recorded, but Root apparently relied on material from Anderson's file, which has survived in the NYPL archives. It shows the extent to which the case against Hasse depended on Anderson's interpretation, since few of the papers by themselves reveal anything damaging. Indeed, many of them praise Hasse, but since Anderson apparently assumed such praise to be empty flattery that she had solicited to feed her omnivorous ego, it added to the evidence against her. By later standards, the file would be good evidence for a lawsuit by Hasse against the board and administration, and by any standards, it was profoundly unfair that the case against her was made by one of the nation's leading lawyers while she was neither present nor represented by counsel. This didn't bother the board, which concluded that Hasse "was fully advised of the reasons which led . . . to the conclusion that the good of the service required the termination . . . and that she had full opportunity to controvert those reasons or to explain her relation thereto." That was patently untrue, but the trustees were determined to stonewall. Admitting the possibility of error, either procedural or substantive, was too awkward, particularly if it meant challenging the authority of Elihu Root. Battle was informed that there would be no hearing.[29]

It remains unclear why the trustees would not agree to Battle's request for a hearing by just one of them, which would have given them some defense against accusations of unfair treatment of a prominent woman with long service. If they believed Anderson's account, a hearing could be an opportunity to expose Hasse. Even without the distortions of her enemies, there remained at least some evidence that she was incompatible with the organizational culture to use as justification for going ahead with the dismissal after giving her a chance to be heard. Probably Root was unwilling to make any concessions to an uppity woman, and as the man who chaired the 1912 Republican Convention, notorious for its "steamroller" over the Roosevelt forces, dominating the trustees was child's play. And, even with only one trustee present, a hearing implied a formal proceeding with stated charges, witnesses, and counsel for Hasse. With his long legal experience, Root could see the danger of a hearing on a case so vague, subjective, and related to calls for change in the library by Hasse and the union. It could be a trap by Battle to provide more ammunition for unions, feminists, reformers, the press, the mayor, all the forces Root loathed. Better to take a firm stand to end the matter—and make it clear to troublesome women that men were still in control.

Meanwhile, Hasse was in Washington with exciting new government work, and, feeling elated to be out of the NYPL atmosphere, she couldn't resist sending Anderson a holiday message: "A happy Christmas! It may please you to know that my earning power has trebled since October."[30] After that she was too busy to pursue the matter for awhile, other than to warn Isadore Mudge about spreading false rumors. She had heard from several sources that "in some way a rumor was spread" among Columbia faculty and students working for the Inquiry to avoid the Economics Division because the chief was pro-German, so she wanted Mudge to know that she had been approved for confidential government work. Those responsible for unfounded rumors might come to the attention of a section of the Justice Department concerned with the "protection of loyal Americans," she advised, so should Mudge "happen to know who had been spreading such rumors in your Department," she might want to warn them. Mudge hastened to report to Anderson, and the letter went into his files.[31]

In the spring, Hasse returned to the fray, inspired by an Easter visit to Billings' grave at Arlington, where she contemplated the "scrapping" of her work of sixteen years under Billings in the six years of the Anderson regime. Al Smith, the new governor of New York, had connections with several Hasse sympathizers and was persuaded to write to his contact on the board, Morgan O'Brien, who finally became the only member to meet with her. Though a member of the Executive Committee, O'Brien, as a Democrat and an Irish Catholic, was regarded as an outsider by the other trustees; he had joined the board at the insistence of the city government, chronically unhappy about the public library's private, self-perpetuating, and unrepresentative board. He told Hasse that the trustees knew of her good work and had no "charges" against her but had been swayed by the letter signed by other staff. He could only suggest that Hasse write her own statement for the board. She had already tried that but took advantage of his suggestion to put a final word on record, probably for use in a pamphlet she was writing about her experience. Also, the LEU found her case useful in its campaign for civil service, and it was planning to seek resolutions of support from several organizations, including ALA. Hasse was back in Tuckahoe in May and may have decided to press the NYPL board further partly to provide more ammunition for the union, which was so persistently making her a cause célèbre.[32]

Early in May, the union again presented resolutions to the Federation of Women's Clubs. Maud Malone spoke with her usual eloquence, holding up Hasse's summary dismissal as a warning of what could happen even to a woman with many years' service and an "international reputation": "She came to the office one morning and found a letter dismissing her. . . . Miss Hasse from that time to this has been trying to get the charges against her and we can not get them. . . . Miss Hasse has not been able to get that and none of the other women are able to get it."[33] Malone impressed the group but not enough to pass the resolution, which Anderson had been fighting behind the scenes. He had called on the help of Richard Bowker, who used his reputation as a reformer to assure the federation that civil service was not needed in the library.

The spring of 1919 was not a good time for a union to appeal to middle-class club women, as the wartime hysteria of 1917-18 had turned into the Red Scare of 1919-20. Following the Bolsheviks' coup in Russia, there were other Communist attempts to seize power in Europe, and even American Progressives were discouraged by signs of "class warfare" undermining their hopes for cooperation and social harmony. In February, there had been a brief, peaceful general strike in Seattle, where, despite the strikers' orderly behavior and continuation of essential services, the mayor denounced them as revolutionaries threatening to bring on Red Russian anarchy. In April, a bomb arrived by mail at the mayor's office, followed by another that blew off the hands of a senator's maid, and then the discovery by postal inspectors of thirty-four more bombs. The evil Hun was replaced by the evil Bolshevik in the public mind, and a union, the International Workers of the World (IWW), was the object of national fear and loathing, accused of disloyalty during the war and Bolshevism after.

As he fought off the LEU on one front, Anderson was confronted with a new Hasse nightmare. The May issue of *American Magazine* appeared with a glowing tribute to Hasse as a library miracle worker who had used marketing to transform the somnolent Economics Division into a busy, crowded research center. Bizarrely, the article made no mention of her dismissal and gave the impression she was still in charge of the division. Hasse was quoted extensively on some of her favorite themes: "The library, instead of going after its market, has always waited for the market to come to it. . . . A library is a utility, not a monument, and the sooner the business men of this country realize that they have an unused asset within their reach the better it will be for their business and for the libraries." It featured a picture of Hasse relaxing in a lawn chair, come back to haunt the men who so detested her knack for publicity.[34]

With that praise in the public mind, Hasse wrote again to the board, bluntly reiterating her protest at the manner of her dismissal "without notice, without charges, and without a hearing." She told them of her pride in the work she had done with Billings' "cordial cooperation and intelligent direction" and of her contempt for Anderson's "personal antagonism" and "degrading spy system." If the board attributed her dismissal to failure to cooperate cordially, she would protest that such cooperation with the conditions in the Reference Department "is not compatible with loyalty either to the Library or the public." In a pointed dig at Anderson and Root, she wrote of her "devotion to the memory" of Billings and her "gratitude for the ever gracious interest" of Cadwalader, concluding that the board's action "could never have taken place in the lifetime of those gentlemen." The board coldly replied that it had considered her case fully. That was the end of Hasse's efforts to communicate with the trustees, but the drama of her battle continued through the summer of 1919.[35]

Replying to an inquiry from Bowker about how libraries could best appeal to business, she warned that the kind of men she had been working with in Washington deplored "the inefficiency of the service, not the potentialities" of libraries. It was such men that *Library Journal* should consult, for "they, and not librarians, are the beneficiaries of the service. Because I have dared to dilate upon this point I have been 'retired' from the New York Public Library." Soon she would have reason to wonder if she should have been milder, but Bowker already had taken sides by serving as a stand-in for Anderson and using his stature as a reformer to influence the club women against the LEU's resolution. Then, in May, *Library Journal* denounced Mayor Hylan for two offenses: encouraging the union "in abuse of the library administration and library authorities" and appointing trustees of the Queens Public Library who abolished the office of chief librarian and dismissed Jessie Hume, who had been in the post even longer than Hasse had been at NYPL. Most galling to Hasse, Bowker went all out in protesting the "outrageous manner" of Hume's summary dismissal, noting that she had requested a hearing on the charges against her "but no charges were forthcoming." Ignoring Hasse's identical predicament, he fumed, "Nothing more disgraceful than this removal is to be found in the history of the library profession and we cannot make too earnest protest against it." While Bowker said nothing about Hasse's dismissal but fulminated against Hume's, the LEU denounced Hasse's treatment while ignoring Hume's firing by appointees of its ally, Mayor Hylan.[36]

In June, the LEU obtained approval of a civil service resolution from the American Federation of Labor convention. It immediately moved on to the ALA conference, determined that ALA would not again evade consideration of its resolution, which went beyond the civil service question to raise larger issues of discrimination against women. ALA was not receptive to a resolution from Maud Malone, who was not a member (though her sister Marcella was). In June, *Library Journal* had warned against unions and accused the LEU of making false statements. Bowker argued that the NYPL Staff Association could be as effective as a union in influencing city funding, without the "dangers of unionization . . . closed shop, sympathetic strikes, the dictation of labor leaders, and the rival administration which they inevitably seek to set up," which he knew all too well from experience with the printing trades. What was needed, he concluded with his unfailingly high-minded hopefulness, was better understanding between workers, trustees, and administrators.[37]

Despite his opposition to the LEU, Bowker was not inclined to suppress discussion, and he encouraged a program on civil service at ALA, explaining that the question was "rather acute in New York now . . . and I thought it was about time for librarians to have a thorough posting on it." The program featured Bowker, Arthur Bostwick of St. Louis, who warned against revolution with allusions to the situation in Russia, and George Bowerman of the District of Columbia library, which had a union. Bowerman urged ALA not to condemn unions, which were not "bolshevistic" in America and represented "the best in public librarianship" in his library. Several women spoke briefly about the DC union and the NYPL Staff Association, and Mary Eileen Ahern disputed the LEU's claim that civil service had raised library salaries in Chicago.[38]

Since Maud Malone was present, she was invited to speak about the LEU and its resolution. Malone made a witty and impassioned analysis of the nature of library work that challenged basic assumptions of the ALA establishment about professional status and the position of women. Low salaries were "interchangeable" with "intolerable working conditions" she argued, because the salaries made librarians "sweated labor" as much as garment workers. Those who formed the union wanted to be part of the power of the labor movement, but they also believed that "after all the talk about 'professional' you know librarians are workers." Classifying librarians as professional was an undemocratic and un-American idea that served only to provide superior status, for Malone had "never found a librarian who could tell me what she understands by being a 'professional.'" The aim of the LEU was not only to raise salaries but "to leaven the whole mass of the library movement, to try to bring it more in contact with the great modern movements; for until our public libraries become more democratic they will not do much good."

Malone also proclaimed the union's intention to change the treatment of the women who were 90 percent of the workforce while "all the large, more important positions in the library world have been cornered by men." She argued that women always entered through the lower grades while men never did, that women could not rise above branch libraries to central administration, and that at NYPL, where all department heads, administrators, and trustees were men, "selection of these upper officers is not made on the basis of superiority of intelligence or ability; it is simply made on the basis of sex." She ended by reiterating that the union opposed the "un-American spirit of caste" among librarians, who were "industrial workers" as much as any of the skilled trades, but she backtracked somewhat on professionalism, saying that the LEU was not against the "professional idea" so much as it was for on-the-job training being considered in promotion and appointment on the same basis as library school education.

After Malone's speech, there was some discussion of discrimination against women, but the *ALA Bulletin*'s otherwise detailed account of the meeting did not report what was said on the subject, and *Library Journal* did not even mention it. The issue was on the mind of Richard Bowker, however, when he unexpectedly found himself following Malone and put aside his prepared remarks on library salaries for an impromptu and somewhat rambling rebuttal. He was most alarmed by the "spirit of antagonism" that unions represented and the LEU's expression of that spirit in its claim of discrimination against women. To Bowker, "there was no profession in which women were more honored, or had a larger place, had more democratic control of their professional organization." When Bowker disputed Malone on the need for unions and civil service, he had the authority of a notable career in business and reform movements, including work for civil service reform of political patronage as far back as the 1870s, and he also had long experience of the library world in ALA, as a trustee of Brooklyn Public Library, and as publisher of *Library Journal*. But when he tried to address the subject of women in library work, he could muster only high-minded banality. Malone's "spirit of antagonism" disturbed Bowker, because "the spirit of the library profession is one of abounding desire that we should all work together . . . in the ranks alike of labor and of professional men, every man and every woman, to bring about that highest ideal of thorough unity, Americanization, and uplift of the American people." Bowker had spent more than fifty years in the tumult of conflicting American interests. He had fought for free trade and civil service, two of the most contentious political battles of his time. He had been told by none other than Samuel Gompers, leader of the American Federation of Labor, that there was a state of war between employers and employees. He was old enough to remember the Civil War, and only a year before he had been booed by ALA members for hoping for an end to the Great War. Yet after a lifetime of experience with human conflict, he seemed unable to cope with the idea of conflict in libraries, whether between the interests of men and women, management and labor, or professional and clerical ranks.

After further discussion, the meeting adjourned at a late hour, with "animated conversation" continuing in the hall and hotel. There was more to come from Malone, however, for the LEU still had its real bombshell to present to the membership meeting in its resolution on sex discrimination, the strongest feminist resolution ever presented to ALA. While mentioning no names, it clearly referred to Hasse with a reference to the removal of women librarians from the best-paid positions:

Whereas, The present low and inadequate salaries paid to librarians in public libraries are due solely to the fact that all of the rank and file in the work are women; and
Whereas, All the highest salaried positions are given to men by the boards

of trustees; and

Whereas, The present policy of library boards is to remove women from all positions of responsibility and largest financial returns, and replace them with men only, and

Whereas, This discrimination is based on sex, and not on any superiority of intelligence, ability, or knowledge on the part of the men appointed; therefore,

BE IT RESOLVED, that we are against this system of removing women without cause and are in favor of throwing open all positions in library work, from Librarian of Congress down to that of page, to men and women equally, and for equal pay.

After some confusion with the Resolutions Committee, which had decided not to present the resolution, the text was located and offered to the membership. There was little discussion; no one spoke for it, and two ALA leaders criticized the suggestion of sex discrimination. Bowker registered his objection as a trustee to the statement that library boards discriminated against women. Alice Tyler protested that women held important positions and were treated equally. She created some confusion with the obfuscating remark that women were "carrying their fair share of responsibility" and understood that men had "no thought of crowding women out of the profession." As head of a library school, Tyler was one of the high-status women who trained the poorly paid (but "professional") women workers in the male-headed library hierarchies. She would be elected president of ALA the following year (1920-21), the third woman to hold the post. After her comments, the resolution was defeated by a vote of 121 to 1 in a meeting that was four-fifths women. These women "knew they were not down-trodden," *Library Journal* proclaimed, and they understood that there was "no calling in which working conditions are more tolerable and happy." The union argued that women were afraid to show public support for "an insurrectionary idea" and were confused by Tyler's statement.[39] Probably both were correct. The resolution's link with unions and the notorious Maud Malone was too alarming for cautious ALA members, but, as Anne Carroll Moore had warned, it was a time of widespread dissatisfaction among library workers, and probably more than one would have voted for the resolution on a secret ballot. As Anderson told the trustees that fall, employees were not eager for a union, but "discontent and unrest [were] rife throughout all grades."[40]

In the aftermath of the war's patriotic fervor, ALA simmered with frustrated zeal, and the issues raised by Hasse and the LEU were related to a yearning for change that produced the movement for the "Enlarged Program," a plan to expand library service, provide more publicity, improve education, develop certification, and establish closer relations with related organizations, particularly SLA and the National Education Association (which, unlike ALA, had already been through a battle by feminists to take power from the male old guard). There was also an effort to establish a new organization, the Library Workers Association, to serve the needs of those who had not attended library school, but without the worrisome connotations of unions. Throughout 1919-20, the professional journals were marked by impatient commentary and calls for change in letters, editorials, and papers such as Marjory Doud's "The Inarticulate Library Assistant," another warning that educated women were leaving libraries for more interesting work in less autocratic organizations, and Ida Kidder's "The Creative Impulse in the Library," which urged her fellow directors to develop staff creativity, with the result that "we shall not only have secured better service for our public but we shall have aroused the creative impulse in these young women (most of our assistants are young women) and added to their joy in life; we shall not only have given them an interest in their work and principles to apply to it, but we shall have enlarged their vision of all life and equipped them better to meet its problems."[41] In reaction, the uneasy Mary Eileen Ahern editorialized against the divisiveness of the young men pushing the Enlarged Program (J. H. Friedel was an SLA representative on the committee) and the young women organizing the Library Workers Association, while Anderson was one of a group of library directors who publicly questioned whether the membership really wanted the ambitious and costly Enlarged Program. The unfortunate Alice Tyler, her presidential year in turmoil, pleaded for tolerance. In the end, both movements failed, as the Enlarged Program fund drive came nowhere near its goal, and the Library Workers Association quietly disappeared.

That left the Special Libraries Association as the organization with appeal for librarians who wanted change, as was vividly expressed in its 1920 presidential address by Maud Carabin, who delivered some of the most scathing comments since Dana's 1896 ALA inaugural. After discussing special librarians' role in supporting business and research, Carabin turned to the condition of librarianship and how to improve it. She described her conversations with various professional men, all of whom saw librarians as limited in intellect, the women able to do detail work for long periods but lacking the capacity to "pinch hit" outside their routines, while the men usually were misfits in any situation. Such perceptions must be cause for reflection, Carabin said in language similar to Hasse's: "Does librarianship make the individual a misfit? Or does the misfit gravitate to librarianship? Does the preparation for librarianship so prune and stultify him as to make of him a negative factor, a revert from accepted social and business type, a person for whom many allowances should be made?"[42]

Carabin called for a higher idea of service by librarians with wider knowledge and deeper understanding: "service with scholarship, service with poise, service which commands recognition, . . . not alone a knowledge of the 'sources' but a knowledge of the subjects themselves." Like Hasse, she saw a need for new forms of education that would combine apprenticeship, perhaps starting in high school, with higher education that would develop specialized knowledge in librarians, who would have "depth, scholarship, and a genuine grasp of the subject," avoiding "the provincialism, the superficiality which results from trying to be 'all things to all men.'" In a series of damning questions, Carabin directed blame not on the personal limitations of librarians but rather on the repressive system in which they worked, suggesting that the "short-comings of the vast army of library workers is attributable to the autocracy within the library system" which had made librarians "as the serfs of the feudal era; . . . identity suppressed, and escape from his caste inconceivable."

Does the American library system breed a spirit of genuine good fellow-
ship? Is it broad enough to accord us all the right to breathe? Is it large
enough to afford us all a place to stand and grow? Is it high-minded
enough to be aloof from demagoguery and dictatorship? Are initiative and
ambition encouraged by the system, or does it interpret these qualities as
being a menace, . . . a mark of incipient insubordination? Does its ethical
code sanction . . . pigeon-holing and cramping . . . the aspiring?

To some extent, Carabin must have been thinking of what happened at
NYPL and reacting to Hasse's published commentary, particularly the grenade
she had lobbed into the volatile atmosphere of 1919 in the form of her autobiographical pamphlet, *The Compensations of Librarianship*. There Hasse frankly
expressed her scorn for Anderson, the trustees, and some NYPL librarians, while
raising questions similar to Carabin's about the work environment of libraries.
The first half offered a lively account of her career up to 1913, emphasizing the
"fostering encouragement" she received from her employers. Kelso and Billings
were held up as ideal library administrators, with their wide experience in the
world, energetic and innovative spirits, and encouragement of a young librarian.
Appealing to the frustrated young, Hasse said she would "never cease to appreciate" her mentors' interest in her development:

> There must be many young people in library work . . . to whom opportuni-
> ties such as I was so generously shown how to utilize, are lost, merely be-
> cause an employer or executive is self-centered, indifferent, otherwise en-
> grossed or just blind. And yet what more valuable asset can an employer or
> executive choose than a servant hungry for expression in service? I have
> often wondered if the excessive turnover in library work might not be due
> to this hunger seeking sustenance denied by oblivious employers.[43]

She emphasized that she and Billings, fellow workaholics, had shared the
goal of a great international collection of government documents.

> I wish all the young people in the library world, ofttimes discouraged by
> conditions which stultify real professional development, could experience
> some of that feeling of opportunity which Dr. Billings so richly dispensed.
> The realization that your employer believes you are going to make good is
> a wonderful impetus. The art of the employer is indeed a rare one. Dr. Bill-
> ings was more than an employer. He was co-worker, and anything but nig-
> gardly in assigning work either for himself or his fellow workmen.[44]

There could hardly be a greater contrast to the enigmatic Anderson as Hasse
described him: "The sacred presence is never seen among the workers. One never
hears of it at public functions. Indeed, barring its almost automatic 'No funds. I
can not run this library on nearly two million dollars a year,' now become notoriously familiar, one never hears of it at all." Since Billings' death, she had
never received "a single constructive direction," and she felt disgusted by the atmosphere Anderson created: "The total lack of inspiration, the sordid discrimi-

nation, the vicious clique system were all abhorrent to me, and offended my deep affection for this particular library, and my ideal for any library." Gradually she was ostracized, "subject to childish persecutions," such as omitting the Economics Division from the 1917 annual report. The sudden, unexplained transfer of documents cataloging was a "feint" at getting rid of her by prodding her into a "demonstration on my part which would warrant dismissal." Her colleagues were encouraged "to entertain open hostility," and her German name was used against her. Finally came the letter of dismissal, which the administration had continued to swath in secrecy. Hasse covered her dismissal and its aftermath by reprinting some of the correspondence with which she tried to get an explanation. She acknowledged hearing that twenty staff signed a call for her removal, but this raised the question of how such an unusual occurrence should have been handled: "I can believe that those individuals would do such a thing, but that an administrator and a body of Trustees would lend themselves to act peremptorily on such material against one of the oldest servants in the library, without . . . observing the most perfunctory courtesy towards that servant, that is a matter which I can not understand."⁴⁵

After recounting some of the rumors and other petty nastiness surrounding her dismissal, Hasse finished on a happier note with the satisfactions of her new job in Washington. Now she had a "glorious opportunity to serve the Government and to work," and of course it was work that would always matter most, "work into which I can throw myself with zest, to which I can give myself," with "the joy of work for work's sake [which] is almost as holy and quite as absorbing as the creative impulse." Her final words were a hope for library work's "immense and . . . quite unrealized possibilities." Librarianship, "peculiarly suited to women," would receive better monetary reward when its leadership improved. Meanwhile, she urged the young not to lose faith, to keep up hope, courage, and the "true spirit of workmanship."⁴⁶

Though hardly on the scale of Metcalf's much longer memoir, *Compensations of Librarianship* has its share of self-serving exaggerations and simplifications. Hasse's statement that there was "almost no turnover" in her division conflicts with her memo showing that only one of seven reference workers had been there more than two years. Her account of the cataloging transfer was disputed by Lydenberg, though without documentation, and her version of how Billings hired her bears slight resemblance to the story told by his letters. Perhaps aiming to appeal to readers who knew her primarily for work with documents, she gave the impression that Anderson destroyed her efforts to carry out Billings' plans for a great documents collection, with no mention of her wish to build a broader division of public affairs or business. The hostility of her coworkers she blamed on Anderson's manipulation, with no acknowledgment of the part played by her criticisms of individuals, library school graduates, and the profession generally. While Metcalf, Anderson, and Williamson laid blame on the monstrous Hasse, her narrative made Anderson a villain in the style of Iago or Richard III, focusing as much on his personality as he did on hers. Her version was as vague as his about how their conflict developed, suggesting that Anderson's petty personal animosity became unbearable in the years 1916-18.

The emphasis was on the shocking circumstances of her dismissal, including the text of the brusque notes with which Anderson ended her two decades of distinguished service and refused her a hearing.

Compensations of Librarianship is one document among many that tell the story of Adelaide Hasse, but in the history of American librarianship, it has—or should have—a notable place as an expression of the turmoil of 1918-20, a rare instance of autobiographical writing by a woman librarian, and an equally rare expression of anger in women's writing generally. As Jill Ker Conway has noted, "The library movement inspired far less autobiographical writing . . . from women" than the other feminized fields of social work and nursing.[47] As a very personal account of the career of one of the most prominent of the first generation of women librarians, Compensations ought to be much cited and analyzed, but it has been ignored, aside from occasional quotation of Hasse's more high-minded statements.

Even women who did write about their lives rarely permitted themselves the indignation that Hasse expressed with such force and frankness. According to Carolyn Heilbrun, women writing autobiographies have felt forbidden to express anger until recently, but Hasse did not hesitate to denounce Anderson for "pseudo-administration" that was "nothing less than contemptible." Hasse's memoir cannot be said to suffer from the "flatness" that Conway and Heilbrun see as characteristic of the narratives of that generation of achieving women, nor is there difficulty, which Conway attributes to such women, in making herself the subject or object of her own story.[48] Hasse tells a vivid tale of a mission to improve public access to government information, of her growth with mentors like Kelso and Billings and her misery when Edwin Anderson created a poisonous environment in the library she would "never cease to love." She identifies with heroes: her Forty-Eighter grandfather, driven from Germany to a new life in America; Tessa Kelso, making LAPL "one of the livest, most progressive libraries I have known"; Billings, a leader of "great gentle manliness . . . an ideal person to direct the destinies of an educational public service institution." In the crisis of her career, she fights against "professional assassination," refusing to go quietly, demanding to see the charges and be given a hearing, then moving on to important new work. She is the heroine of the drama, with a supporting cast of generous, large-spirited mentors, enthusiastic young followers, and a devious, despicable villain. As Public Libraries discreetly summed up, "The kaleidoscopic light and shadows of the story shows that the author has touched the depths as well as the heights in her long experience."[49]

Such emotional openness was bewildering to some readers. The proper Bostonian George W. Lee responded with the fatuous advice that Hasse should love her enemies and the improbable hope that she would someday have an ALA position in which her "ability and consecration to work will be appreciated." He infuriated Hasse with the pious admonition that if she was as pro-German as he had heard, it would be "cause for repentance," and he even suggested that the government had hired her so that she could be more easily watched. Lee was shocked to receive Hasse's scornful reply: "I feel justified in calling you a contemptible ass." He sent her note to Anderson, wondering, "What is the matter with her anyway?" He regretted the loss of "a Niagara Falls of power . . . for the benefit of the library world," but perhaps "she suffers from an impulsive nature which prevents her from fitting in with the rest of the world" or perhaps "her biggest trouble is that she has no sense of humor." Anderson responded with his usual hint that Hasse was mad, that her letter and pamphlet were "excellent illustration of what is the matter with the lady," and he did not care to have further controversy with her.[50]

As usual, Anderson could avoid public reply because he had a proxy, again in the person of Richard Bowker. Already drawn into serving as Anderson's agent against the LEU and shaken by Malone's agitation at ALA, Bowker lashed out at Hasse after what Squires said was a secret meeting with Anderson. In August, *Library Journal* devoted almost a full page to an editorial that effectively supported Anderson in blaming Hasse's dismissal on her personality with its "'temperamental idiosyncrasies' which made it difficult to see facts and people in their real relation." The "plain truth" was that Hasse's "temperament and perspective created an impossible situation," and finally other department heads requested her removal because "cooperation with herself and her department was impracticable." He meant "not the least impeachment of Miss Hasse's excellent character," and regretted to speak thus of someone of such "fine industry and splendid achievement," but "in fairness to all concerned, the facts should be made known to the profession." Yet Bowker essentially supported Hasse's main concerns, agreeing that her government employment "disposed of . . . annoying and exaggerated suspicions" about her German ancestry and that the trustees should have given a hearing to "an employee of such standing and length of service." Apparently unaware of the extent to which her firing was connected to the LEU, he stated firmly that if Hasse was a union member, it "has had no bearing, for that must be a matter of individual right and choice." He also made an error that reinforced the image of an irrational Hasse, quoting her as saying that her work under Billings was undone in six months with Anderson, rather than six years.[51]

Bowker's editorial must have been almost as much a blow to Hasse as the dismissal itself. To be attacked so personally and publicly, in the most widely read professional journal, was enormously damaging, especially coming from a man who had known her for most of her career and had so often praised her work. Indeed, the same issue quoted Bowker telling an ALA documents meeting how much he regretted the termination of Hasse's "remarkable . . . invaluable" state documents index, and LJ had invited her to contribute a paper to a symposium on library education that appeared the next month. Yet Bowker not only validated Anderson's claim that the problem was Hasse's personality, not the other issues he brushed aside, he also enabled Anderson to maintain the dignified silence that made Hasse's public indignation seem even more alarming, the strident raving of a madwoman. Being blind, Bowker could not examine the written record himself, and he seemed unaware of the extent to which Hasse was fired for published opinions, association with the union's president, and vaguely suspected disloyalty. He did not meet with Hasse before attacking her, and if he did meet with Anderson, he would have heard a practiced presentation of what impressed the trustees. Bowker knew from experience that Hasse could be outspoken and insistent in pressing her views, and, like the trustees, he found the number of those calling for her removal to be compelling evidence that she was a problem damaging to the library's functioning.

Bowker claimed that Hasse's pamphlet had "dared" *Library Journal* to "speak out," but he could have ignored it, noted it noncommittally, as *Public Libraries* did, or reported it as news, with Anderson given the opportunity to present his side. Bowker used editorials to comment freely on library issues, but, always the gentlemanly reformer, he generally took a positive tone and avoided personal attacks; it was extraordinary for LJ to assert that a prominent librarian deserved to be fired because of her personality. He had expressed blunt disapproval of Mayor Hylan and the LEU, but he also gave the union two pages for a report on its activities in the same issue in which he denounced Hasse. LJ also published Tilloah Squires' letter accusing it of bias in "acceptance of the opinions of one group as the 'facts' and the 'truth'" about Hasse. Squires pointed out that Bowker, like the NYPL Executive Committee, could be misled by Anderson's selective presentation of "evidence," and she contrasted his indignation at the lack of a hearing for Jessie Hume with his tolerance for the secret proceedings against Hasse. Squires called again for civil service as the only way to obtain "a hearing for library employees before an unbiased board."[52]

Squires' letter was the only published criticism of the editorial, at a time when being defended by a union was not helpful, even in New York. Throughout the summer, there had been raids on radical organizations by the state police and the U.S. Justice Department, and the infamous Lusk Committee of the state legislature warned of an impending Bolshevik revolution that would join blacks with alien radicals from Europe. In September, there were strikes by the steelworkers and, particularly alarming, by the Boston police, and with winter approaching, there was the frightening threat of a coal miners' strike that the mine owners said had been ordered by Lenin and Trotsky. Even Mayor Hylan expressed alarm at union excesses.

Hasse was busy in Washington and said nothing more publicly, but in October, still not willing to fade away, she sent a taunting letter to Anderson, with copies to several trustees, division chiefs, and Bowker, announcing that in the year since her "abrupt removal" she was better off financially, "congenially employed" in work that brought her in contact with members of the Cabinet, and had several unsolicited job offers, all of which she mentioned "to ease your mind against any mortification that you may have entertained because of the execrable form observed in the manner of my removal." Anderson sneered that she ought therefore to be grateful for being fired, but Bowker kindly assured her that he rejoiced in her success "if not in the tone and spirit of your letter" and was pleased that "good library work throughout your long years of service have thus fulfilled themselves in giving you abounding opportunity." He asked her to keep *Library Journal* informed, "as its readers are sure to be interested in your success and continuing welfare."[53]

In the month since his editorial, Bowker had had an experience with Anderson that may have given him second thoughts about the situation at NYPL. In a courtesy not extended to Hasse, he had sent Anderson the galleys of a piece about librarians' pay that mentioned the amount of his salary as "common knowledge." Anderson objected, "I must insist that my salary is confidential," as were all of the salaries in the Reference Department. Bowker took the opportunity to give a friendly warning that his salary was "common knowledge throughout the profession, and I do not see why it should have secrecy about it." He suggested that it was a mistake to consider NYPL "a more or less private affair, with which the city has no concern," adding, in apparent reference to Hasse, that there was an "impression abroad that the trustees have been rather secret and secretive . . . and I think this might be the cloud as large as a man's hand—or a woman's." Anderson replied coldly that he was aware of the perception that the trustees were secretive, but they were "men of large affairs who have learned to be suspicious of people who are always talking about their business." Showing his disdain for open discussion, Anderson said that he had "seen too many evidences of their quiet wisdom to make me favor bill-board and newspaper publicity methods." The article would be "more dignified if less were said about the salaries of chief librarians everywhere." Bowker acquiesced, but after forty-five years with *Library Journal*, he must have found it a shock to be instructed on the proper level of dignity and discretion.[54]

Whether from uneasiness about NYPL or guilt feelings, Bowker showed some consideration for Hasse in the year after his attack, though always with ambivalence towards a woman whose work he admired even as her persona disturbed him. In December, LJ reported that confusion about the death of Hasse's mother had caused "the painful rumor of the death of Miss Adelaide Hasse," but "the entire profession" would be glad to learn that she was alive. (Hasse kept a copy of an erroneous newspaper report of her death, which identified her as "one of the most prominent librarians in the country.")[55] The next year, still trying to show that there was no sex discrimination, Bowker wrote three articles profiling prominent women librarians. The last woman mentioned was Hasse, of whom he concluded ambiguously: "No one has won a more distinctive position or made more stir in the library profession." Now he was mild on *Compensations*: "The story of her early life is most interestingly told in an autobiographical pamphlet which records also the differences which caused her retirement . . . after twenty-one years of service."

In most of his profiles, Bowker summed up the subjects' personalities: "vigorous" Mary Eileen Ahern, "vivacious" Sallie Askew, and so on. For Hasse, Bowker found the word that expressed his ambivalence: "Her virile personality has made her both friends and foes, but the tender side is shown in her adoption of the little child who visitors . . . would sometimes see spending the day with her among her beloved documents." In his uneasiness, Bowker labeled Hasse's personality masculine, "virile," an adjective sometimes applied to the New Woman as a sign that she was unnatural. Yet, always struggling to be fair, he recognized that her temperament made friends as well as enemies and even encompassed motherhood, the most sacred sign of the True Woman. Bowker recognized her devotion to work, but it was not enough for him to say that she had an assertive personality and loved her work; he had to define her in gender concepts that reflected the anxiety of a man who had lived through vast change in the lives of women and now feared that it had gone too far.[56]

~ ~ ~

Hasse never again discussed her dismissal in public and kept no papers connected with it, but Anderson's file survived in the NYPL Archives. Since little in it constitutes clear evidence against Hasse, and Anderson left no explanatory notes, it effectively illustrates the enigmatic style of the man she described as a "collector of mystery." Tilloah Squires soon joined Hasse in Washington, but she remained active in the LEU for several years and further harassed Anderson with a letter to *Public Libraries* in which she pointed out that men in well-paid directorships often were, like Anderson, dropouts from other work, as if "a dash into law, engineering, newspaper work, business, school teaching or zinc and lead mining gives just the proper experience needed to manage or organize a large library. There is no reason why ex-newspaper men, ex-principals, mediocre lawyers, tired businessmen and etc. should be appointed to the 'chiefships' while women remain—faithful, tireless, efficient, indispensable adjuncts—drawing their rewards from those 'many other than salary compensations' which have been for so long the chief solace of the 'weaker sex.' There is no reason for this condition except sex discrimination in the library profession."[57]

The LEU and Mayor Hylan continued to plague Anderson and the trustees throughout the 1920s. The Staff Association repeatedly called for the dismissal of Maud Malone, and Anderson privately raged at her "rule or ruin" attitude, but she was safe so long as she remained connected with the union movement. Maintaining his usual public silence, Anderson vented his anger further at Hasse, attacking her viciously to both the federal Civil Service Commission and the Bureau of Investigation in 1921. When Hasse applied for a civil service position, Anderson replied to an inquiry in a way that was most damaging. He stated that he did not believe she was "absolutely loyal" to the government, and of her general reputation, he said that she "was so pro-German during the war" that she was repeatedly investigated (not mentioning his own role in trying to get a Secret Service investigation). To the question whether the applicant had ever "been discharged for inefficiency, neglect of duty or moral unfitness," he answered yes, although Hasse had not been fired for any of those causes, and added that she was so "temperamentally . . . impossible" that the division chiefs called for her dismissal. Then, when the Bureau of Investigation, where J. Edgar Hoover was eager to investigate anyone whose loyalty was questioned, inquired about Hasse, Anderson brought up every bit of trivia with a German connection, now expanded by letters from Hasse's files about the proposed Mexican trip and her research help to Edmund Von Mach, Frank Illesley, and Otto Merkel. There was her letter to Isadore Mudge, her connection to Ernst Hasse, her presence in Germany in 1914, even her wearing "German peasant costume" to a library reception, plus a recent development, a holiday greeting card sent to Hasse from none other than Otto Merkel in Berlin, where he was head of the Red Cross. The agent reported that Hasse had been fired for insubordination and pro-German activities, particularly her correspondence with Clapp and Rumely, though it is unlikely that those letters were known to Anderson before Hasse's dismissal.[58]

As Anderson's health declined in the late twenties, Lydenberg was appointed Assistant Director and then succeeded as director from 1934 to 1941. Both men were bequeathed $40,000 by a trustee, J. P. Morgan's attorney Lewis Cass Ledyard, while employees continued without pensions. At least salaries had improved in the postwar years, for which the LEU and the Staff Association both claimed credit.

Keyes Metcalf became Chief of the Reference Department in 1928, but by then, according to his memoir, his position as executive assistant already had enabled him to take over much of the administration from the passive Lydenberg and the remote Anderson. Metcalf explained his appointment as the result of a fortuitous suggestion to a Staff Association committee chaired by Charles McCombs. It had decided to investigate the staff unrest, Metcalf says (ignoring Hasse's effort with the same committee earlier in the same year), and he wrote a proposal for a personnel officer in the director's office that came to Anderson's attention and inspired him to appoint Metcalf to that very position, as well as to be "generally useful . . . in any tasks that came up."[59] Metcalf conveniently forgot that the position already existed in the person of Rebecca Rankin, who had decided to stay in New York after all. She suddenly received an offer to move to the Municipal Reference Library, which Anderson encouraged her to accept. Rankin agreed to become assistant to Dorsey Hyde, whose free-wheeling, free-spending ways alarmed Anderson. Hyde had Hasse-like ambitions for bibliographic and civic education projects, which brought warnings from Anderson about costs and the danger of becoming "more journalistic than library." Hyde soon departed, and Rankin was promoted to his position, where she had a long and successful career in the job Anderson had once considered unsuitable for a woman. She prospered particularly after the election of the reform mayor Fiorello La Guardia, who encouraged women in responsible positions; Rankin had made a favorable impression on La Guardia and his secretary, who had become his wife.[60] Neither Metcalf's memoir nor Rankin's biography suggest a link between Metcalf's role in getting rid of Hasse and the convenient availability of the executive assistant position that began his rise to eminence as a "giant of the profession." His career culminated in the library directorship at Harvard, where the halo effect of the university cast its glow over his otherwise unremarkable achievements. ALA honored him with election to both its presidency and honorary membership.

One of Metcalf's main responsibilities was in the area of personnel, where he implemented Anderson's constant urging to improve the quality of the staff by hiring new library school graduates, "making a special effort to bring men into research library work." In his memoir, Metcalf was careful to note that Anderson also wanted to hire capable women, but somehow they preferred the Circulation Department. Thus Metcalf could devote an entire chapter to listing the prominent male librarians who began their careers when he and Anderson hired them for the Reference Department, creating a classic old boy network of men who moved on a "glass escalator" into the best-paid and highest-status positions in American libraries.[61] Their network was a key factor in reaffirming a gendered hierarchy in large libraries, in which male executives directed the mostly female workforce. At NYPL, with Hasse and Sears gone and the younger women going to the branch libraries, there was no challenge to the assumption that men should have the more prestigious managerial positions. In the profession generally, the second generation of women librarians, far from finding expanding opportunities, was kept below the glass ceiling; the women who had struggled to develop the impoverished library schools and the libraries of agricultural and normal colleges usually were succeeded by men as the institutions became larger. Women were a majority of ALA members, but it was understood that there was a limit to how often they were allowed to be president, usually as an end-of-career reward, and the Association of Research Libraries (ARL) was established as the exclusive preserve of the elite male executives of large libraries serving an elite clientele. When Mary Eileen Ahern retired, *Public Libraries* went out of business, and no longer was there a strong woman speaking for those who worked in small public libraries.

According to a tribute in the NYPL *Bulletin*, Metcalf is remembered for his "bold solutions" to administrative problems. One of these must have come as a shock to Isadore Mudge at Columbia, when he restricted college students' access to the research collections. Perhaps their experiences with Metcalf gave Mudge and her companion Minnie Sears second thoughts about their readiness to join his attack on Hasse. Despite their cooperation in signing the statement against Hasse, Sears and Gertrude Hill were pushed out soon after for the offense of being "perfectionist," Metcalf's favorite pejorative for women who supervised complex, detailed work. As discussed earlier, Sears left in 1920 when she lost her authority over cataloging, while Hill was pressed into retirement in 1919 because her serial subscription records were too complex for new staff to learn quickly. Metcalf wondered if she could afford to retire, but Lydenberg persuaded her "that it was time for her to retire, which she did without tears or other complications." (This may be another of Metcalf's memory lapses; Hill had no pension, and her library training at Pratt was in 1894, twenty-five years earlier, which would not make her retirement age unless she went to library school in middle age.) Another woman signer, Maria Leavitt, remained in their favor for being "always easy to work with," especially since she had "taken on the responsibility for being the leader of the older women on the staff and worked well with Mr. Lydenberg." Metcalf recalled that her "cheerful ways had much to do with keeping the women of the reference department staff happy and contented," surely a remarkable achievement with women who were underpaid, overworked, and had no pensions. Perhaps the summary dismissal of Adelaide Hasse, at age fifty with twenty-one years of service, soon followed by the departures of Hill and Sears, also influenced the older women.[62]

Charles Williamson returned as chief of the Economics Division, with a salary higher than Hasse's. Seven of Hasse's staff quit or were fired, and Rollin Sawyer returned with the status of first assistant. Within a year, Williamson was able to obtain the additional space that had been denied Hasse. He appealed to Anderson for the addition of Rooms 225 and 227 to provide for shifting from the stacks and to give him an office, for "an endeavor to make the Economics Division what it ought to be will be too hard a task without a satisfactory room separated from the public reading rooms to be used as an office. A very distressingly large part of my time is wasted by having to do all my work in a reading room where the public feels free to interrupt at any moment and take hours of my time when there is no particular service that I can give." If Hasse had said this, it would have been cited as evidence of her grandiosity, indifference to the interests of others, and unwillingness to help ordinary people. For Williamson, the administration promptly decided to merge the Science Division into the Technology Division on the first floor (resulting in the departure of Heryk Arctowski) and give the space on the second floor to the Economics Division. This was followed by extensive shifting of documents and economics books, arranged by Metcalf as weekend work he would supervise for the extra money needed for his invalid wife.[63]

Despite the ease with which his wishes were granted, Williamson stayed less than two years. He became head of the Rockefeller Foundation's Information Service for a few years and then finally landed an academic post as director of libraries and head of the new library school at Columbia in 1926. There he soon became involved in a long and increasingly nasty conflict with Roger Howson, who had been in the library since 1913. The tensions between the two seem to have been due to an extreme lack of clarity about their respective responsibilities, with Williamson having the title Director of Libraries, while Howson was Librarian of the University, as well as differing ideas about library work, Williamson's long absence due to ill health in the 1930s, and basically incompatible personalities. Howson, a Briton with a Cambridge education, was similar to Hasse in temperament: "an extrovert, outspoken, with a ready answer to everything—traits extremely annoying to Williamson. . . . Howson was extremely popular with the university faculty, while Williamson never really cultivated them." Eventually, after Williamson's repeated threats to resign and repeated investigations by committees and administrators, Howson was given a year's paid leave and moved to a new job in the history department.[64]

Williamson is remembered mainly for his influence in shifting library education from library-based training schools to university graduate programs, which began soon after he returned to NYPL, when the Carnegie Corporation (its board chaired by Elihu Root) asked him to study the education of librarians. His confidential report was similar to but more scathing than Hasse's criticism of the existing library schools, which he accused of "a certain deadening of initiative and imagination . . . from an excessive attention to detail." He proposed a distinct separation of technical and professional training, the latter to be provided in universities to college graduates. Williamson was vague about the curriculum of such a professional school, but he confidently urged it as the path to improved quality and higher status, sure to bring librarians respect as experts in library management, prepared by graduate education for executive responsibilities. Privately, he acknowledged to the Carnegie board that his hidden agenda was to reverse the feminization of the profession.[65]

Paul North Rice, Carl Cannon, Frank Waite, Rob Henderson, Charles

McCombs, and Rollin Sawyer had successful careers as department heads at NYPL. In 1937, Rice succeeded Metcalf as Chief of the Reference Department; both men were elected president of ALA. Sawyer was Chief of the Economics Division for thirty years, guiding its expansion with the aim "to build up a reference library . . . that will be a Mecca for every person interested in any branch of the Social Sciences." On his retirement, Sawyer told the press that during his service the division grew from "one small room to four large rooms, any one of which is larger than the original one," giving the impression that this was solely his achievement. He also served briefly as chair of the ALA Public Documents Committee (1930-32), where he took it upon himself to urge that the government save money by ending the free distribution of documents to depository libraries. Since this was contrary to ALA policy, he was discreetly replaced with Frederick Kuhlman of the University of Chicago, who revived the committee with members from the growing academic libraries that wanted the depository library program expanded to serve research.[66]

Metcalf and the other Anderson protégés were diligent in promoting the man who hired them as a genius at identifying talent. As one NYPL alumnus wrote, Anderson "was always on the watch, particularly for able young men, so that the New York Public Library became the training ground for many of the great librarians of America." The contrary view of Adelaide Hasse went unmentioned, as did Anderson's treatment of three of the giants of the first generation of women librarians, Hasse and Sears at NYPL and May Seymour at the New York State Library. The influence of Anderson's old boy network established the conventional wisdom of his "unique strength" in staff development. No one seemed to notice a certain comic pomposity in these men praising Anderson's wisdom in recognizing their great ability.[67]

Hasse's Economics Division staff went on to work in special libraries or other fields where their experience proved useful. Elsie Rushmore joined the library of the Russell Sage Foundation, dedicated to research in support of social reform, where she edited a guide to serials of social agencies that was praised by *Library Journal*. She then moved to the J. Walter Thompson advertising agency, making a last appearance in LJ as a speaker on library publicity in which she, like Hasse, warned librarians that promoting their methodology would not impress the public. Edna Gearhart joined the library at McGraw-Hill, while Lurene McDonald went to the library of the Canadian Department of Labor and then returned to the city as librarian at the New School for Social Research, founded by Charles Beard and other Progressives as an alternative approach to higher education. Alice Ramsburg rejoined NYPL after serving with the Red Cross in France but transferred to the Technology Division. Morris Kolchin worked as a researcher for the governor's commission on problems in the coat and suit industry and then served for twenty-five years as executive director of the association of dress manufacturers, a major industry group in New York. Sidney Zimand, who dropped the Anglicized version of his name to become Savel Zimand, was a researcher and writer on economics and international affairs in the 1920s; he then moved into a second career organizing public health campaigns. Both men merited obituaries in the *New York Times*, where there was no mention of their experience with NYPL.[68]

After the publication of Hasse's pamphlet and Bowker's editorial, silence descended on the distressing subject. The LEU continued to point to her firing as an example of the need for reform, but the union ceased to exist in the late twenties, and the Malone sisters were fired a few years later. Maud Malone then became a Communist; at her death in 1951, the *Daily Worker* eulogized her under the headline, "She Always Set a Lofty Goal."[69]

The dismissal of Adelaide Hasse became a kind of repressed memory, but there was one last occasion when Hasse showed that she had not forgotten or forgiven. The 1936 American Library Association conference in Richmond, Virginia, now is regarded as an embarrassment because of the association's acceptance of the segregation of its African American members. It should also be known as the occasion of Adelaide Hasse's revenge, when ALA inadvertently provided her an opportunity for a last shot at Elihu Root. The great man had been nominated for honorary membership, the association's highest honor, which required unanimous approval of the ALA Council. Hasse, who was president-elect of the District of Columbia Library Association, arranged for its president, John Vance, to appoint her a chapter representative to the Council, and when Root's honorary membership came up, Hasse, Vance, and a third member voted against it, making ALA probably the only organization ever to reject a proposal to honor Elihu Root. (More typically, a few months earlier, the Carnegie Corporation had presented the Council on Foreign Relations with a bust of Root, accompanied by much praise for his wisdom.)

Although some of those present knew the underlying story, the *ALA Bulletin* provided only the opponents' bland explanation that "other distinguished Americans, closer to the library profession, should be recognized." In a puzzled tone, the *New York Times* reported that Root's honorary membership had been blocked "on the ground that he was not eminent in library pursuits," although he had long served on the NYPL board, and others who were not librarians had been so honored. Hasse mounted the clipping on cardboard to keep permanently, along with Vance's letter appointing her to the Council. With the story in the *Times*, ALA could not cover up and keep it from Root. At ninety-one, having received innumerable honors, he probably wasn't much interested in honorary membership in ALA anyway, but at least he would know that he had not destroyed Adelaide Hasse, that she was still in the field, still fighting.[70]

The scene made a great impression on Keyes Metcalf, but once again he muddled the story to reflect badly on Hasse, reporting that she alone vetoed the honorary membership, not of Root, but of Frederick Keppel of the Carnegie Corporation, a "good friend" of NYPL and Harry Lydenberg. Again his narrative was of Hasse, always the angry, disorderly woman, attacking a man who had done her no harm, just because he happened to be a friend of Lydenberg. While erasing Root and his significance from the story, Metcalf vividly recalled the council members standing to vote in favor and then the shock of the "tall, stately" figure of Hasse rising in opposition. Adelaide Hasse, he realized, "had the last word."[71]

Notes

1. Adelaide Hasse, "Do Libraries Impede Research?" SL 9 (Sept.-Oct. 1918): 155-56; J. George Frederick to AH, 23 Sept. 1918, AH-CB.

2. AH to Lydenberg, 18 Sept. 1918, AH-CB; Lydenberg to Anderson transmitting Waite and Henderson memo, 27 Sept. 1918, AH-CB.

3. AH-Lydenberg-McCombs exchanges, 7, 11, 16, 17, 21 Sept. 1918, AH-CB.

4. AH to Lydenberg, 20 Sept. 1918, AH-CB.

5. Keyes Metcalf, Random Recollections of an Anachronism (New York: Readex Books, 1980), 191-92.

6. Ibid., 134-35, 184.

7. Ibid., 184-85. The original letter is in AH-CB.

8. Ibid., 186-87.

9. Ibid., 186.

10. Minutes of Executive Committee meeting, 4 Oct. 1918, excerpt in AH-CB.

11. Adelaide Hasse, The Compensations of Librarianship (privately printed, 1919), 17.

12. "Statement in Behalf of Miss Adelaide R. Hasse . . .," n.d. 1918, p. 5, AH-CB.

13. Hasse, Compensations, 18-19.

14. Metcalf, Random, 188.

15. "Comments of Dr. Williamson," AH-CB; Hasse, Compensations, 23; "Comments of Mr. Lydenberg," AH-CB.

16. Anderson-AH exchange, 25, 27 Oct., 1 Nov. 1918, AH-CB; "Comments of Dr. Williamson," AH-CB.

17. Hasse, Compensations, 21-23.

18. AH to each trustee, 2 Nov. 1918, AH-CB.

19. Squires to Linville, 27 Oct. 1918, Henry Richardson Linville papers, Walter P. Reuther Library, Wayne State University, Detroit; letters to board from Squires, 30 Oct. 1918, and three civic organizations, 25 Nov. 1918, AH-CB.

20. Battle to Root, 24 Dec. 1918, AH-CB.

21. "Statement in Behalf of Miss Adelaide R. Hasse," AH-CB.

22. Osborn-Battle exchange, 27, 30 Dec. 1918, AH-CB.

23. Daniel Kevles, In the Name of Eugenics: Genetics and the Uses of Human Heredity (New York: Knopf, 1985), 88-89. Osborn was a leading advocate of eugenics and restrictions on immigration.

24. Anderson to Osborn, 30 Dec. 1918, AH-CB; Metcalf, Random, 118-19.

25. Anderson, "A few illustrative instances of unsatisfactory service rendered to readers by the former Chief of the Economics Division," 13 Nov. 1918, AH-CB; his letter to the New York Times, 4 Sept. 1918.

26. "Comments of the Director on Miss Hasse's statement sent to the trustees by Mr. Battle . . .," n.d., AH-CB.

27. "Comments of Mr. Lydenberg," AH-CB. The point about Cannon's wound is noted on Lydenberg's draft in Anderson's handwriting and included in the final typescript.

28. "Comments of Dr. Williamson," AH-CB; Williamson to Ida Fingerhut, 6 April 1917, AH-NY.

29. Extract from minutes of the Board meeting, 8 Jan. 1919, AH-CB.

30. "Comments of the Director," AH-CB.

31. AH to Mudge, 15 Feb. 1919, Mudge to Anderson, 22 Feb. 1919, AH-CB.

32. Hasse, *Compensations*, 13, 20.

33. Quoted in NYPL Circulation Committee meeting minutes, 7 May 1919.

34. Alfred Grunberg, "How to Make Your Public Library a Business Asset," *American Magazine* (May 1919): 61-62.

35. Hasse, *Compensations*, 20-21.

36. AH to Bowker, 31 May 1919, Bowker papers, NYPL; LJ 44 (May 1919): 276.

37. LJ 44 (June 1919): 349-50.

38. Bowker to George Utley, 8 May 1919, Bowker papers, NYPL; *ALA Bulletin* 13 (1919 conference proceedings): 358-59, 376-86; LJ 44 (Aug. 1919): 521-22, 528-29.

39. LJ 44 (Aug. 1919): 487; Catherine Shanley, *The Library Employees Union of Greater New York, 1917-1929* (Diss., Columbia University, 1992), 173.

40. Quoted in Shanley, *LEU*, 299.

41. Marjory Doud, "The Inarticulate Library Assistant," LJ 45 15 June 1920 : 540-43; Ida Kidder, "The Creative Impulse in the Library," PL 24 (May 1919): 156.

42. Maud Carabin, "Looking Forward with the S.L.A.," LJ 45 (1 May 1920): 391-95.

43. Hasse, *Compensations*, 4.

44. Ibid., 11.

45. Ibid., 13-21.

46. Ibid., 23-24.

47. Jill Ker Conway, *The Female Experience in 18th and 19th Century America: A Guide to the History of American Women* (New York: Garland, 1982), 109.

48. Carolyn Heilbrun, *Writing a Woman's Life* (New York: Norton, 1988), 12-16, 24-25; Jill Ker Conway, *When Memory Speaks: Reflections on Autobiography* (New York: Knopf, 1998), 88.

49. PL 24 (Oct. 1919): 306.

50. Lee-AH exchange, 16, 19 July 1919, AH-CB; Lee-Anderson exchange, 22, 23 July 1919, AH-CB.

51. LJ 44 (Aug. 1919): 488.

52. LJ 44 (Aug. 1919): 512-13; LJ 44 (Oct. 1919): 672.

53. AH to Anderson, 7 Oct. 1918, AH-CB; Bowker to AH, 8 Oct. 1919, Bowker papers, NYPL.

54. Anderson-Bowker exchange, 17, 19, 23 Sept. 1919, Bowker papers, NYPL.

55. LJ 44 (Dec. 1919): 804; "Miss Adelaide Hasse Dies in Los Angeles," newspaper clipping, AH-LC.

56. Richard Bowker, "Women in the Library Profession," LJ 45 (Aug. 1920): 640. On the "virile" New Woman, see Carroll Smith-Rosenberg, "The New Woman as Androgyne: Social Disorder and Gender Crisis, 1870-1936," in her *Disorderly Conduct: Visions of Gender in Victorian America* (New York: Oxford University Press, 1986), 280.

57. PL 25 (Oct. 1920): 435-36. The 1920 census shows Squires and Hasse at the same address in Washington.

58. Civil Service inquiry, 11 March 1921, AH-CB; U.S. Federal Bureau of Investigation File 62-329 (1922).

59. Metcalf, *Random*, 181-8, 346.

60. Barry Seaver, *The Career of Rebecca Browning Rankin* (Diss., University of North Carolina, Chapel Hill, 1997), 21-22, 39-48.

61. Metcalf, *Random*, 225-26, 240; on the "glass escalator," see Christine L. Williams, *Still a Man's World: Men Who Do Women's Work* (Berkeley: University of California Press, 1995).

62. "Keyes DeWitt Metcalf," NYPL *Bulletin* 65 (June 1961): 345-46; Metcalf, *Random*, 200-201.

63. Williamson to Anderson, 29 Sept. 1919, RG 6, Director's Office, Economics Division file, NYPL archives; Metcalf, *Random*, 205.

64. Paul Winkler, *The Greatest of Greatness: The Life and Work of Charles C. Williamson* (Metuchen, NJ: Scarecrow Press, 1992), 214.

65. Barbara Brand, "Pratt Institute Library School: The Perils of Professionalization," in Suzanne Hildenbrand, ed., *Reclaiming the American Library Past: Writing the Women In* (Norwood, NJ: Ablex, 1996), 262-63.

66. Sawyer quoted in Phyllis Dain, *The New York Public Library, A History of its Founding and Early Years* (New York: NYPL, 1972), 328, and *New York Times*, 4 May 1953; Susan Lee Grabler, "Government Information Of, By, and For the People: The Changing Mission of the American Library Association's Public Documents Committee, 1876-1956," *Journal of Government Information* 22 (Jan.-Feb. 1995): 53-55, n88.

67. Wayne Shirley, "An American Librarian's Heritage," in Louis Shores, ed., *Challenges to Librarianship* (Dubuque, IA: William C. Brown Co., 1953), 149; Phyllis Dain, "Edwin Hatfield Anderson" in DALB, 9.

68. Information about women staff from news notes in LJ and SL. The *New York Times* contains many references to Zimand and Kolchin, including their obituaries, 19 Dec. 1967 and 7 March 1955.

69. Shanley, *LEU*, 154, 365-7.

70. *ALA Bulletin* 30 (June 1936): 512; Vance to AH, 27 April 1936, and *New York Times* clipping, 16 May 1936, AH-LC.

71. Metcalf, *Random*, 188-89.

PART III

WASHINGTON

Chapter 10

War Agencies, 1919-1923

Hasse's career continued for more than thirty years after she left New York, but never again would she have the stable, prominent library base the New York Public Library had provided. Instead, her career became more that of the consultant or independent contractor, sometimes a mix of short-term and part-time jobs, sometimes two jobs at once. This gave her interesting opportunities that suited her enterprising spirit, but it also meant periods of uncertainty and financial strain. No matter what her employment, Hasse remained focused on government information, for as she wrote in 1919, "I shall never lose interest in any effort to make the contents of documents accessible."[1]

The pattern of temporary work began with her job as a researcher for the War Labor Policies Board, one of the wartime agencies that had drawn the best and brightest to emergency service in Washington. Its chairman was Felix Frankfurter, a Harvard Law School professor noted for his dazzling combination of intellect and networking. Though only in his thirties, he was established as a leader among Progressives, much involved with *The New Republic* and the Consumers League. Frankfurter was always alert to hire good people, women as well as men, and advance the careers of his many friends and protégés. He had rescued Charles McCarthy from a frustrating job with the Food Administration and sent him to Europe to study worker training and labor relations. Frankfurter, McCarthy, and others among the "band of brothers" in wartime Washington —men like Bernard Baruch, Herbert Hoover, and Robert Brookings—shared the dream of a government-guided postwar world with a more rational, coordinated economic and political system. Others in the Wilson administration were eager to abandon regulation and dismantle the special agencies after the armistice, but Frankfurter hoped to keep his agency alive and anticipated the need for research work at least for the treaty negotiations in Paris and perhaps into the postwar adjustment. So it was that Hasse was hired to do research in December, when she received a phone call from Frankfurter and left for Washington on the midnight train. Her hiring had been recommended by Josephine Goldmark of the

Consumers League in a telephone call and letter to Max Lowenthal, Frank-furter's assistant. She described Hasse as "an exceptionally well qualified person for any research work," but said nothing in writing about her dismissal and referred Lowenthal to Walter Weyl for judgment of Hasse's "discretion."[2]

Weyl was a scholarly economist and a leading Progressive intellectual, one of the founders of *The New Republic*. In the same period when he joined with Goldmark to aid Hasse, he apparently also helped Sidney Zimand get work in New York for the War Labor Policies Board and a contract with his publisher for the timely publication of translations of the antiwar speeches of the heroic German Socialist, Karl Liebknecht, leader of the revolution that ended the German monarchy. Before immigrating to the United States in 1913, Zimand had been close to Liebknecht and Rosa Luxemburg. In their prefaces to the book, Weyl and Zimand expressed hopes for a wonderful new era in Germany, but Liebknecht and Luxemburg were murdered early in 1919.[3]

Frankfurter, Lowenthal, Goldmark, and Weyl all were of German Jewish ancestry; the latter two were children of Forty-Eighters, while Frankfurter had come from Vienna to New York as a child. With their German names and Jewish sensitivities, they were well aware of how the anti-German and anti-union hysteria was further poisoning what they already saw as a society rife with injustice. Frankfurter was a founder of the American Civil Liberties Union and would be a passionate defender of Sacco and Vanzetti, while Lowenthal would be one of the very few Americans willing to challenge J. Edgar Hoover at the peak of his power. Frankfurter later described Lowenthal as "a very sensitive fellow, particularly responsive to cruelty and hardship," a man who "literally became ill" with distress while investigating the brutal mistreatment of striking miners and their families in Arizona in 1916.[4] Thus they were ready to sympathize with Hasse, whom they knew to be highly capable (Goldmark and Frankfurter having worked with her on the Oregon labor law cases, while Weyl was involved with the Latin American aspect of the Inquiry, which made use of the Economics Division), and they were not the kind of people who would defer to Elihu Root and the other rich WASPs on the NYPL board. As for Edwin Anderson, Frankfurter's view of library administration was shown years later when he encouraged President Franklin Roosevelt to appoint a non-librarian, Archibald MacLeish, Librarian of Congress, warning that the technically trained librarian saw only "the merely mechanical side of the library—and fails to see the library as the gateway to the development of culture."[5]

Though Hasse's work for the War Labor Policies Board lasted only a few months, it gave her an escape from the painful situation in New York to government work with Progressive activists. (It also provided a convenient explanation for her departure from NYPL; in future job applications, she would give "called to Washington" as her reason for leaving NYPL, as though she had been one of the many Americans who left their jobs for wartime service.) Frankfurter was soon off to the peace treaty negotiations in Paris, but Lowenthal remained to supervise the researchers who were preparing reports on labor conditions in European countries for the American delegation. With her knowledge of languages and information sources, Hasse was a resource for the staff while herself writing the reports on Austria and Holland. One of those she worked with was another of Frankfurter's brainy young men, Harold Laski, then at Harvard, later long associated with the Labour Party and the London School of Economics. They worked long hours under pressure, but for Hasse it was a joy: "I like to have work into which I can throw myself with zest, to which I can give myself. Some people work for money, some for the boss, but the joy of work for work's sake is almost as holy and quite as absorbing as is the creative impulse."[6]

Such an environment was just what Hasse needed after the toxic atmosphere in New York. She often thought of the "irony of fate" that had brought her from rejection by NYPL to work for the president and his peace treaty negotiators. "For the first time in six years, I felt clean inside," she wrote of a period of renewal when she often recalled Simon Newcombe's feeling of finding a "world of sweetness and light" in his work. Released from the anguish of her last years at NYPL, she wrote "The Great Release," an impassioned call for the public library to release itself from the blight of bureaucracy, undemocratic attitudes, and thoughtless, joyless methodology, lest it be "released as a vital factor in community service to be replaced by the special library."[7]

At Easter, she went to Billings' grave at Arlington to mourn all she had lost with his death. Although she remained tangled in her battle with NYPL through much of the year, she now could enjoy work with people she respected. That spring, Hasse told Bowker she dealt with men who were enthusiastic about the potential of libraries while "deploring the inefficiency of service." Hasse's reputation among such men was burnished by the appearance of the *American Magazine* article that lavished praise on her marketing the Economics Division while saying nothing of her dismissal. Already in her first month in Washington, she had been identified as "probably the best person in the country" for a major new job that seemed "quite overwhelming but a glorious opportunity to serve the government and to work." She was hired to organize the records of the War Industries Board (WIB), whose more than seven hundred file cabinets held the most extensive data on American industry ever collected by the government. The board had been responsible for the wartime mobilization of industry and thus for managing much of the American economy.[8]

The chairman of the War Industries Board was Bernard Baruch, like Frankfurter an outsider turned insider who managed to know everyone who was anyone as he continuously invented new phases of his brilliant career. A Jew from the South, he had made a fortune on Wall Street as a speculator with shrewd instincts and a grasp of information such that his friend Woodrow Wilson dubbed him "Dr. Facts." An unremitting self-promoter, Baruch cultivated an image of wealth and power that was exaggerated but self-fulfilling, as awareness of his closeness to the president gave him more power than the legal authorization of the WIB. The crisis of war was his opportunity to shine as a statesman, skillfully maneuvering to use the board's broad but ambiguous powers to bring order to the economy. The Progressive Era's longing for efficiency and central control seemed to be fulfilled as Baruch imposed drastic simplification and standardization on the manufacture of practically everything, reducing 232 kinds of buggy wheels to four and 150 colors of typewriter ribbon to five. This was only part of the all-encompassing effort described by an admiring journalist:

But these comparative trivialities give a too small-faceted picture of what the War Industries Board was, and of American industry under the Board's co-ordinating control. One could visualize it, the stream of materials, minutely intricate in detail, massive in the aggregate, which from the finished shell on the front, ran back to the ultimate mines and factories in which they were produced . . . the flow of each, and their junction-points regulated as nearly watch-like as was attainable by Baruch and his aides at Washington.[9]

Baruch cultivated a mystique, not just for himself, but also for the organization he led. He inspired esprit de corps from the typists to the wealthy dollar-a-year men who surrounded him, and many regarded their work with him as the high point of their lives. The alumni of the War Industries Board formed a network whose political and economic power would continue for decades. In the hectic atmosphere of wartime Washington, Baruch and his lieutenants had wielded power with panache, relying on high spirits, mastery of information, and teamwork to accomplish their goals, with minimal direct exercise of authority.

Like Wilson's other wartime managers, Baruch wanted to extend his agency into the hoped-for postwar reconstruction or at least keep it alive to mobilize for future crises. That was not to be, but as the board was closed down, Baruch fought to keep its records together and organize them for access to the vast amount of data that was in disorder as the various subdivisions deposited their files. More than most men, Baruch knew the value of economic information, and he also understood that the records could provide guidance in future crises. Probably he also wanted to preserve them as a monument to his own achievement and a source of the history that he and an associate, Grosvenor Clarkson, would write. With no national archives, he had to maneuver with a Congress that had no enthusiasm for maintaining the records and the agencies that wanted to take portions of them. He staved them off by obtaining an executive order that the records and files of the War Industries Board be turned over to the Council of National Defense to be cataloged to provide a permanent record before distributing them to the departments that wanted them. The Council of National Defense, the longest lived of the wartime agencies, was composed of five members of the cabinet; its director was Grosvenor Clarkson, a New York advertising man close to Baruch.

In July 1919, Hasse was appointed an expert in the Council of National Defense. Her salary was $3,000, the same as at NYPL, but her employer was more congenial. In September, Clarkson acknowledged her "excellent memorandum" which "gave me the first intelligently comprehensive view of the situation." The following month, when she informed him that she had offered to spend one day a month working with documents at Boston Public Library, he assured her that he left matters "entirely to your judgment, on which I have great reliance."[10]

In working on the WIB project, Hasse became acquainted with Baruch, a gregarious charmer who spent little time with his family and often socialized with his staff. Besides their mutual appreciation of information, they had similar family backgrounds: Baruch's father had emigrated to avoid military service in Prussia, became a doctor, and served as an army surgeon for the Confederacy. Hasse later told her niece that Baruch had said she would have great success operating a Washington boarding house that charged a premium for the combination of her good cooking and good conversation.[11] A man who appreciated intelligent women and promoted their careers, he may have helped her obtain subsequent jobs in organizations with which he had connections. Baruch and the other men she worked with in Washington must have reminded her of Billings and validated her ideal of the career she had tried to create at NYPL. Baruch's understanding of the value of information, publicity, and esprit de corps had brought him wealth and power in the world of men, while her similar values as a woman librarian had led to disaster.

Even as she moved into her new environment, Hasse issued the pamphlet about her career that brought on the shock of Bowker's personal attack. Fortunately, the men she worked for now weren't readers of *Library Journal*, but every librarian in America would see the allegation that Adelaide Hasse deserved to be fired for her "temperamental idiosyncrasies." It confirmed her fears of the poison Anderson was spreading and the futility of trying to make her case openly. She left it to Squires to send a letter of protest, while she made no further public reference to NYPL and never again published the kind of controversial commentary with which she had tried to rouse librarians in 1916-19.

On the anniversary of her dismissal, she couldn't resist sending a taunting letter to Anderson, Bowker, and other men at NYPL, reporting that she was "congenially employed in government work," where she sometimes came in contact with members of the cabinet, and had received unsolicited offers of work from NYPL clients, including two New York financial houses, and from a western library seeking an executive with "social sympathy." Bowker sent a conciliatory if rather patronizing reply, urging her to keep *Library Journal* informed of her career developments. After his blast in August, LJ published her paper on education for reference work in September and Squires' indignant letter in October, and in the following year it reported news of her career and included her in Bowker's series on women librarians. Hasse's profile was the last in the series, perhaps reflecting the author's uncertainty as to how to deal with such an awkward subject, but he somewhat made amends by praising her achievements, saying little about her "retirement" from NYPL, and struggling to provide a balanced view of the "virile personality" that he regarded with such ambivalence. When he concluded, "No one has won a more distinctive position or made more stir in the library profession," readers would understand the delicacy of his reference to the unpleasantness that he and Hasse wanted to put behind them.[12]

In her first year in Washington, Hasse seems to have had some hope of remaining involved with leading public libraries. In October, when she wrote to Boston Public Library to recommend a former NYPL librarian for documents work, Hasse offered herself as well, volunteering to come to Boston one day a month to help organize the documents department and collection.[13] Boston was NYPL's rival for prestige among large public libraries, and Hasse may have hoped to revive her ideas about documents there, but she never again would work for a public library. Instead, she shifted her focus to special libraries, library education, and various indexing and bibliography projects, eventually identifying herself as a bibliographer, not a librarian, in *Who's Who in America*. The death of her mother in December, soon followed by the death in childbirth of her sister Jessie Fielding, was a reminder of time swiftly passing, and her new life in Washington gradually distanced her from the twenty years she had devoted to the ideal of the great urban public library.

Certainly the War Industries Board's records were enough to consume even Hasse's energy, at least for the first year. Besides starting on the organization of what she estimated as almost three million pieces, Hasse reported that she and her staff had to deal with 1,616 inquiries involving pending litigation, various government reports, inquiries by congressional committees, and claims cases involving the Justice and Interior Departments. The board might be extinct, but "its files are still active."[14]

Hasse immediately realized that the War Industries Board "represented an amazingly far-reaching experiment in Government regulation" that would be of interest for research far into the future. Its many important rulings had not been published, so one of her first actions was to reclaim all rulings from various files, and arrange "every official publication, declaration, circular, and order . . . in a coherent collection." She also saw enormous potential in the economic information that she planned to put "into one standardized arrangement." The wealth of statistical data could be utilized "when the time comes, as undoubtedly it will come, that the Government of this country will follow the custom of other Governments and establish a national centralized statistical organization." There were the "studies, compilations, and formulas" prepared by the "ablest industrialists, economists, statisticians, and scientists of this country" that must be preserved "for future as well as present requirements." Hasse was in information heaven, and as always, her goal was ambitious, to make it possible "to produce with certainty all the information in the files on any one transaction or commodity."[15]

She interpreted her charge to catalog all board records to mean the "effecting of such coordination that all correspondence, reports, etc., concerning a given matter might be located by means of segregation and a card file." That is, she would reorganize the records, not just leave them as they were while preparing a catalog record of what was there. The problem in developing any system of access was the sheer volume of the records and their lack of standardization:

> Each of the eighty-odd units of the War Industries Board kept its files in its own way, and there was no central file for the board organization as a whole. Some papers were filed alphabetically, others were filed numerically. Some units kept a subject file; others kept a combination of alphabetic, numerical, and subject files. In the alphabetic files sometimes the writer and sometimes the addressee supplied the file key. In the performance of their functions there was frequently a complicated inter-relation between finished products and raw materials, commodity units and functional units, and as a consequence of this inter-relation there was reference of correspondence from one unit to another until the papers constituting contributory evidence in a particular case were scattered through the files of many units. However satisfactorily the records may have operated while under the jurisdiction of the individual units, they became an incoherent

mass of approximately 3,000,000 pieces when those units ceased functioning and the file operators had departed.[16]

Hasse's consolidated system had three main groups of records: the administrative, the technical or commodity, and the company files. Her goal was to group together everything on a particular commodity or company, regardless of which organizational unit had originated the records. The large commodity groups had more than five thousand subject headings, with cross references within the files, and there was a master list of the subjects and cross references. The survey of the records that Hasse prepared for *Official Sources of War History* required thirty pages just to outline the contents of the unit and general administrative files.

Though Hasse devoted more than three years to the WIB records, the project was never entirely completed. At various times, other refiling was done to assemble papers for use by Senate committees, the Justice Department, and the Army Industrial College. When the National Archives finally was established, the records were transferred there in 1937. The archivists decided to restore them to their original provenance according to the units that created them, and Hasse's fourteen thousand commodity files were reduced to less than half that number. Hasse's subject plan was undone in favor of the archival system based on government organization that she would be identified with (and criticized for) in her documents classification. The irony was compounded soon after, when the approach of another war revived interest in the work of the War Industries Board, but those who came to the archives seeking commodity information found it no longer conveniently available.[17]

~ ~ ~

Once the War Industries Board project was under way, Hasse showed her usual tendency to take on additional work. By the fall of 1920, she had two new undertakings, either of which would have been a full-time job for most people: operating a school for business librarians and editing *Special Libraries*. With these enterprises, Hasse was plugged into the zeitgeist of the twenties, when American business was admired for its dynamism in producing exciting, affordable new products, and confidence in the "new economy" was reflected in the booming stock market.

In September, Hasse became director of the School for Business Librarians, a section of the Washington School for Secretaries. She sent announcements to library periodicals and placed display ads to proclaim that the school was under her "personal direction" and was unique in training for special libraries work. The library press reported this as the opening of a new school, but Hasse actually was taking over a program that had been initiated by Ralph Power, a business librarian and proponent of the opportunities special libraries offered women. By promoting it as a new school under her direction, Hasse gave the program higher status than merely some courses in a secretarial school.

Admission to the school required a high school diploma, then a relatively elite credential and the minimum requirement for the majority of existing library schools. All applicants were interviewed by Hasse. Graded certificates were awarded to graduates, but students not seeking credentials also could be admitted. Applicants were warned that those with poor work or attendance would not be allowed to take the exams at the end of each course. The school's information circular seemed to be aimed at a more sophisticated student than the average high school graduate, perhaps college women, government workers, or public librarians seeking practical training for a new field, just as they might go to secretarial school to gain employment skills. The circular identified six "directors" and eight members of an "Advisory Council" that included prominent academics as well as men and women in the business world. Though these outside advisers were named, and two pages were devoted to listing companies that had business libraries, the circular was oddly short on specific information about courses, class times, credits needed for graduation, and faculty other than Hasse. The school's tuition, $180 for nine months in 1921 and $25 per month for a four-month term in 1922-23, indicated a fairly substantial program; in contrast, when Hasse taught a two-nights-per-week YWCA course in business library work in 1922, the cost was only $30 for the term.[18]

Hasse said students were prepared "to equip and manage the library of large business houses and industrial plants—to undertake business research—and to qualify as data file executives." The course of study described in the circular was extensive, focused on specialized information resources, from trade journals to congressional hearings, and "processes for displaying information," such as statistical tabulations, graphics, indexes, abstracts, and digests. On the apparent assumption that librarians would be preparing bibliographies and reports, manuscript preparation and proofreading were included. Study of cataloging and classification completed the curriculum.

There was no mention of clerical tasks or the physical organization of libraries. In her 1918-19 commentary on library education, Hasse had criticized over-emphasis on "the physical care of the book, including its charging and discharging, reading of the shelves, etc." Instead, library schools should teach the specialized literature of the disciplines for librarians who would be truly professional experts in "information centers." The curriculum she outlined in *Library Journal* in 1919 was more extensive, lasting two or three years, than her business library program, but she was consistent in emphasizing a broad view of the literature of a field as a range of sources with which the would-be librarian must be familiar. The goal was better librarians providing better service and rewarded with better pay, she argued: "The service . . . by persons prepared in this way would be of such a grade that it would be recognized as professional service. There would be fewer employees and these would have better pay. Administrators could no longer confuse messenger service with reference work."[19]

What became of the School for Business Librarians is unclear. There is nothing about it in Hasse's papers, although she kept the flyer for the YWCA course, and she made no mention of it in later summaries of her career, where she tended to downplay her library connections. Either it was not successful or she gave it up when she moved on to other jobs. When Hasse began her program, ALA had a committee to develop certification standards for those who had not graduated from library school, but soon interest shifted to university graduate programs in library science, due largely to the influence of Charles Williamson's reports to the Carnegie Corporation. Williamson's ideas were challenged by a few women leaders of library schools, particularly Josephine Rathbone of Pratt, who disputed Williamson's assumption "that the choice is between college graduates and relatively uneducated persons fresh from high schools," when in reality, "there are in the profession many women who have been unable to attend college but who have gained by reading, study, and contacts all that college can give—cultured, trained minds, broad outlook." Alice Tyler of Western Reserve, who had ridiculed Maud Malone's comments about sex discrimination, now complained that Williamson didn't take into account the limited resources of schools like hers. But the trend of the time was away from apprenticeship to university-based education for the professions, and, always hopeful of more Carnegie money, most library leaders accepted the idea of graduate schools to prepare managerial experts with a theoretical base in library science. The theory and the science remained fuzzy, but the Carnegie Corporation did support establishment of graduate library schools at two leading universities, Chicago and Columbia.

Williamson's idea of two distinct types of training for executives and technicians did not develop, but the gendered hierarchy of the field was reinforced as more men were drawn to graduate programs that gave them professional status and entry to administrative positions. In his original secret report to the Carnegie Corporation, Williamson had pointed to the need for educational standards that would halt the feminization of the profession. Women continued to be drawn to the field, however, and entered the graduate programs with the hope of professional status, despite being essentially barred from the highest-ranking, better-paid administrative positions. Women without library school degrees were limited to clerking in large libraries or operating public libraries in small towns, with little chance of developing a career as Hasse had. The library workforce remained overwhelmingly female, but the divide between women claiming professional status and those categorized as clerical deterred development of the kind of solidarity sought by the LEU. Hasse's program in a secretarial school was aimed at bright, ambitious women who might not have college degrees, the kind of women Rathbone described, but by 1924, the local library association was discussing the need for a graduate program in Washington.[20]

In a sad irony of this period when Hasse was trying to develop new education for business librarians, Library Journal published a history of the LAPL training school that never mentioned her name. The course Hasse designed was described as "amazingly modern in its scope," but the only credit given was to Kelso, "whose ideas in regard to library training, government documents and the relation of the library to the community were twenty-five years ahead of her time." The erasure of Adelaide Hasse from the history of American public libraries and the education of librarians was well under way by 1923.[21]

An unexpected result of the School for Business Librarians was a letter from Melvil Dewey, who had received the 1922-23 circular and congratulated Hasse on "yur admirabl skeme for business librarians and . . . the good work yu do in whatever yu turn your hand to." He went on to express his sympathy for her experience with their mutual enemy, Edwin Anderson, who "had the long arm of the lever becauz of his official position but everyone who knew yu and him knew wher the fault lay." Dewey, who had been widowed six months earlier, urged Hasse to visit the Lake Placid Club to see all that he had built there. There is no record of Hasse's reply, but Dewey's flattery and invitation to visit may have been a factor in the campaign against his alleged sexual harassment of women librarians waged by Tessa Kelso in 1924. She vigorously protested to the New York Library Association that its plan to meet at Lake Placid was unacceptable, given Dewey's history of offenses that were "of a vicious type of sexual depravity and criminal in the eyes of the law." Kelso provided no specific examples or evidence, but, after some confused consideration, with Edwin Anderson probably involved behind the scenes, the association decided to avoid Lake Placid. Dewey indignantly complained: "It is really pathetic when an unbalanst smoking drinking swearing caracter can stampede a lot of sensible people."[22]

~ ~ ~

Also in the fall of 1920, Hasse took on another big responsibility as the editor of *Special Libraries*, the monthly journal of the Special Libraries Association, beginning with the November issue. "There is hardly an opportunity in library work . . . which holds the possibilities of the Editorship of *Special Libraries*," she proclaimed.[23] With typical self-promotion, Hasse displayed her name at the head of the new editorial page, just below the title. The journal had been gradually improved by various editors, but Hasse's immediate predecessor, her friend J. H. Friedel, had been unable to get the issues out on schedule. Hasse produced it on time and quickly revamped the publication procedure, format, and content. She moved its office to Washington, changed the typographic appearance with a new printer, and held frequent meetings to consult SLA leaders, including President Dorsey Hyde, another refugee from the Anderson regime at NYPL. In her first year, Hasse added regular features on government services and libraries. "Timely Bibliographical Topics" was given a catchier title, "The Data File." She worked to make the journal known to a wider audience, sending out news releases to the business press about features of interest to businessmen, such as a list of trade directories.

Encouraging a sense of great opportunities for special librarians, she gave the first page of the April issue to a message from Secretary of Commerce Herbert Hoover, one of the men who had come to prominence as a wartime manager, first of Belgian relief and then the U.S. Food Administration. He was seen as the epitome of the efficient, forward-looking managers who would guide the great enterprises of twentieth-century America, and even Bernard "Dr. Facts" Baruch praised his ability to absorb and analyze information. Hoover was an engineer of limited imagination, however, and his banal message only advised that to the extent "information is promptly received and accurately compiled the business will tend to prosper and the organization to function smoothly," while "the business librarian who can make his service an integral part of his firm's organization may become a positive factor, both in the increase of profit and in the development of constructive business standards."

With more enthusiasm and rhetorical flourish, this was the message that Hasse repeated in cheerleading editorials about the special library "movement." Every month, the journal's editorials urged special librarians to seize their opportunities in a postwar world that recognized the value of information, to become full participants in their employers—"banks, public utility companies, commercial houses, manufacturing plants, . . . newspapers, . . . technical, scientific and civic institutions." "We have won recognition," Hasse assured her readers. "We must now work to make good . . . and to win for ourselves the same indispensable position in the world of affairs which our employers . . . have labored for and won." The librarian must know her organization and its information needs, thinking of "my company" or "my bank" rather than "my library," seeing herself as a manager of information crucial to the success of the organization. The successful special librarian's job was to "control the fact information structure just as the financier controls the credit structure, by knowledge, experience and intuition; to know where it is wise and profitable to invest research capacity, where it is useful and wasteful to do so, where fact resources are latent, awaiting explication, and to maintain continual contact with the always fluctuating store of bankable information." *Special Libraries'* editorial page gave Hasse a vehicle for her favorite theme, that libraries must offer coordinated, active information service that would track down facts, regardless of their source.[24]

Hasse also sought to inspire with praise for librarians who had inspired her. Of Dana, she wrote that the Special Libraries Association was "the child of a man of vision." An editorial note with an article on the National Medical Library spoke of Billings: "The amazing faith of one man in the efficacy of the printed page brought into being in this country two of the greatest library systems of their kind, the Surgeon General's Library and the New York Public Library organization." When Charles McCarthy and Eunice Oberly both died in 1921, Hasse published tributes that said much about her own ideals. McCarthy's story "would bear re-telling again and again . . . inalienably a part of special library history," she said of his dedication to the Wisconsin Legislative Reference Library. As for Oberly, Hasse might have been thinking of her own career: "Miss Oberly was that rare combination—a scholar and a good executive. Her bibliographical enterprises are clearly the work of one who has not only mastered her subject but mastered it through reverence and understanding. Neither in Miss Oberly's bibliographical labors nor in her executive work was there anything perfunctory. Not only did she strive to perfect her work but she succeeded in doing so."[25]

When Hasse resigned the editorship after two years, SLA regretted the loss of her "splendid services." The Executive Board noted that she had "given generously of her time, capability, and energy," with the result that *Special Libraries* had shown "continuous improvement . . . both in content and physical appearance . . . due to the painstaking efforts of its Editor-in-Chief."[26]

~ ~ ~

By 1921, Hasse could feel the satisfaction of having reinvented her career after the NYPL disaster, finding new outlets for her commitment to government information, active reference service, and library training, but the events of 1918 continued to cast shadows over her new life.

With the new Republican administration taking office in March, Hasse's thoughts turned to finding a permanent job. She applied for a civil service appointment as a division chief (in an agency not identified in the archival document). Unfortunately, an inquiry went to Edwin Anderson, who went out of his way to make damaging allegations about her disloyalty and "impossible" personality, and Hasse did not get the job.[27]

In July, the Council of National Defense was abolished, but Hasse continued the WIB records project in the Statistical Office of the Assistant Secretary of War. Later that year, an employee of the State Department went to the Justice Department's Bureau of Investigation (later the Federal Bureau of Investigation or FBI) to warn that the loyalty of a War Department employee, Adelaide Hasse, was suspect because New York Public Library had dismissed her for "disloyal utterances and conduct." In a stunning betrayal, the informant was Bertha Pierce, one of the three graduates in the first class of the library training school taught by Hasse in 1891. Pierce had been employed at LAPL for five years and had worked for Hasse again on the state documents index in 1907-08.[28]

Since only six of twenty applicants had been admitted to the first class, and only three of them passed, Pierce would seem to have had reason for gratitude to Hasse for starting her on a career and later giving her another job on a prestigious indexing project. Instead, she tried to destroy the new life Hasse had salvaged. Nothing is known about the nature of their relationship, but the suspicion is unavoidable that Pierce had resented Hasse's success for thirty years and finally saw a chance to deliver a stab in the back. At each point where their lives intersected, in Los Angeles, New York, and Washington, Hasse was Somebody, her name in print, her achievements praised, while Pierce, only two years younger, was a nobody who labored in obscurity. Her sneak attack in 1921 raises the question of whether Pierce was Kelso's anonymous critic in 1895; the content of those letters indicated that the writer was a resentful library employee who had attended the training school. As a literature cataloger with knowledge of French, she may also have been involved in the storm over *Le Cadet*.

From her government personnel record, Pierce seems to have been capable but emotionally unstable. In 1921 she was beginning a sad descent into "marked nervous difficulties" that included breakdowns and finally complete disability. Though she said her nervous problems began around 1920, she probably had been troubled long before; her work history shows gaps and frequent job changes. Her longest employment had been her first job at LAPL, which she left soon after Kelso and Hasse; the 1900 census showed her living with her family and unemployed. Her biggest achievement was going to college in her thirties, obtaining a bachelor's degree from the University of Chicago in 1906. She then worked briefly for Hasse and a New York publisher before returning to Los Angeles. From 1910 to 1917, she claimed to have been settling her father's estate and managing his business, which she did not identify. The war gave her an opportunity to join the War Trade Board as a clerk and then a librarian. In *Compensations of Librarianship*, Hasse had proudly mentioned that one of her former students managed an important war agency library.

In 1919, Pierce was able to transfer to civil service status as a librarian in the State Department, a position that would have seemed ideal to most women, using her education and experience in a major government agency in Washington. There a series of supervisors evaluated her work as good to excellent, but most expressed varying degrees of dissatisfaction with her personal qualities in regard to cooperation and relations with coworkers. The most vehement criticism came from Tyler Dennett of the Publications Division, a prolific writer on the history of foreign relations, who was exasperated with Pierce for "frequently . . . making statements which she must have known to be untrue." He described her as having superior ability but a completely unsatisfactory attitude, "wholly lacking loyalty toward her superiors . . . appears to seek opportunities to make trouble . . . emotionally unbalanced and . . . her statements of facts are not trustworthy." Her problems were "somewhat pathological," he concluded. A year later, her behavior had improved but still caused problems because of her suspicion that if others learned about her job, someone would take it away from her (not an unreasonable fear after Dennett's criticism).

As an aging woman in a man's world, Pierce may have had reason for anger and suspicion, and some men may have overreacted to a woman who, as one complained, "is not cheerful," but the repeated criticism from supervisors and her continuing deterioration in what apparently was an attractive situation —interesting work with increases in pay and rank and no suggestion of dismissal—indicates emotional problems, as does the seemingly motiveless malignity of her attack on Hasse. Her civil service status and capable performance enabled her to remain in the State Department, but several times she was transferred to a different division, doing the same kind of work. Her last stop was in Indexing and Archives, where her supervisor rated her weak in attitude and cooperation but didn't make an issue of it. Despite the tolerant boss, her instability worsened, and her nervous breakdowns caused long absences. Her problems were compounded by a radical mastectomy in 1931 that made it difficult to use one arm and by brittle bones that affected her mobility. Even with all this ill health and the resulting absences, she formally complained of being in a dead-end job and requested a more responsible position. She was found to be completely unable to work in 1936 and retired at sixty-five.

Since Pierce was accused of some of the same failings as Hasse, the records of her government employment make an interesting contrast with Hasse's experience at NYPL, one that validates the LEU's claims for the advantages of civil service, at least from the employee's perspective. Pierce could not be summarily dismissed, and she was regularly, formally evaluated on a standardized form that required rating all aspects of her job performance. Her supervisors could openly warn that they were unhappy with aspects of her behavior, but they also had to acknowledge that she was good at her job and performed most aspects of it well. Instead of the festering animosity and conspiratorial atmosphere at NYPL, there was an open, orderly process of identifying strengths and weaknesses on the record. Dismissal would have required a formal proceeding to demonstrate by the preponderance of evidence that she was detrimental to the service, a sensitive undertaking at a time when activist feminists were particularly interested in the opportunities civil service offered women, and government officials were wary of offending newly enfranchised female voters.

It is not clear from the FBI file, some of which is blacked out, whether Pierce revealed that she had known Hasse since 1891. Though she had no direct knowledge of the reasons for Hasse's dismissal, and the war with Germany had been over for three years, J. Edgar Hoover, head of the section to investigate subversives, was eager to inquire into Hasse's "loyalty and integrity," and Military Intelligence was advised that a War Department employee was under investigation.

Mysteriously, agents were assigned to look into Hasse's life as far back as her GPO and LAPL work in the 1890s, which had no connection with disloyalty in the 1917-18 war. The inquiries about her early career were not productive. The chief clerk at GPO checked the files and found "nothing against Miss Hasse either as to her loyalty or integrity," with the possible exception of the allegation that she had taken a government record when she left. In Los Angeles, an informant remembered her but, having had no contact for many years, could only report the hearsay that Hasse had left NYPL because she was pro-German. Showing the lasting damage done by the *Library Journal* editorial, the informant produced a copy, which the agent found "very interesting," apparently not noticing that it rejected suggestions of disloyalty.

At NYPL, Anderson was happy to dredge up anything that might show Hasse's pro-German views. Correspondence about the Mexican trip and with Frank Illesley and Otto Merkel was provided, along with the story of Merkel's arrest in the library and the news that he recently had sent Hasse a holiday card from Berlin, where he was head of the Red Cross. Her family relation to Ernst Hasse was again reported without explaining that she had no contact with him, as was the tale of her attending a staff party in "German peasant dress" in 1915. The agent recorded all this but apparently did no further investigation in New York. Checks with the Secret Service and the Protective League turned up reports of wartime suspicions but no evidence worth pursuing.

Meanwhile, back in Los Angeles, an agent found someone who had known Hasse casually sixteen years earlier. She firmly stated, "Miss Hasse is altogether pure American, as far as sentiment and loyalty are concerned," adding that she knew "absolutely nothing detrimental to Miss Hasse and . . . understood her to be a person of the highest honor and integrity." That apparently was the end of the matter, but since the Justice Department has refused to release five pages of the file, there may have been additional investigation that is still being kept secret.

~ ~ ~

Whatever suspicions might lurk among librarians, they didn't prevent Hasse's appearance on a program at the 1922 joint ALA-SLA conference in Detroit. There she made remarks that would be cited as evidence of the alienation between the special librarians and the public librarians who were the majority of ALA membership. Hasse was on a panel assembled by the ALA Publishing Board to discuss what it could do for various library interest groups, such as academic and special librarians. At present, Hasse said, ALA could do "nothing in the way of publications" for special libraries, because of its dominant public library perspective and lack of understanding of "just what a special library is." Though the tenor of her remarks was thoughtful and conciliatory towards public libraries, then and later she was inaccurately reported to have answered "a very abrupt 'Nothing'" that reflected the tension between ALA and SLA. After some discussion of the nature of special libraries and how ALA might promote their information service, she ended her remarks on a note of what may have been annoyance with ALA slights of SLA or perhaps with the presence of Harry Lydenberg on the program: "I think it takes a good deal of nerve on the part of the A.L.A. at this late date to ask what it can do for special library work, when there is a well organized association . . . doing what the A.L.A. has not done, maintaining a magazine of its own to serve its special interests, to get into touch as much as it can, with the employers, with the market of its constituents."

The attention to these tart remarks has distracted from Hasse's stimulating comments about reference service, where she offered a catchy definition of special libraries as "information factories," explaining, "I am not talking about journals or pamphlets or books. I am talking about information,—the specific fact." If ALA could advertise library information service to business groups, that would be useful, but she warned not to try to promote libraries on the basis of their professional procedures and methods: "Of course we have got to be proficient in procedure and method, but do not try to sell it because it is not saleable." What mattered was the quality of information service, not just claims of professionalism.[29]

Despite her enthusiasm for SLA, Hasse abruptly resigned as editor of *Special Libraries* at the end of 1922; no reason was given in the announcement. In later summaries of her career, Hasse said she was called to New York in 1923 to serve as consultant to the financial editor of Hearst's *New York American* but left on his "demise." Other than saying she did research at $70 per week, she did not provide specific information about her work, the dates, or the name of the editor. In fact, the paper's financial editor in 1922-23 was Edwin Clapp, an acquaintance from her NYPL days, when he had taught economics at New York University and written editorials for the *Evening Mail* that put him under suspicion of being pro-German. It is certainly possible that Clapp would have hired Hasse to do research, but since he died in 1930, not 1923, she may have been covering up something about her work history, unless her reference to Clapp's "demise" meant only his move to another job at the paper in 1924. Whatever happened, by the end of the year Hasse was back in Washington to take a new position that seemed ideally suited to her interests and experience.[30]

Notes

1. AH to Charles Belden, 14 Oct. 1919, AH-LC.
2. Michael Parish, *Felix Frankfurter and HisTimes*, v. 1, *The Reform Years* (New York: Free Press, 1982), 107-17; Goldmark to Lowenthal, 15 Nov. 1918, RG 61, War Labor Policies Board, U.S. National Archives.
3. Savel Zimand, ed. and trans., *"The Future Belongs to the People," by Karl Liebknecht* (New York: Macmillan, 1918); *New York Times*, 18 Jan. 1919; *Nation*, 25 Jan. 1919.
4. *Felix Frankfurter Reminisces* (New York: Reynal, 1960), 136.
5. David Streeter, "Judging Librarianship: Are Library Leaders Trained—or Born?" *American Libraries* 26 (May 1995): 408-11.
6. Adelaide Hasse, *Compensations of Librarianship* (privately printed, 1919), 23-24.
7. Ibid., 23; Adelaide Hasse, "The Great Release," SL 10 (Jan.-Feb. 1919): 2-3.
8. AH to Bowker, 31 May 1919, Bowker papers, NYPL; memo to Harold Clark, 8 Jan. 1919, AH-LC; Hasse, *Compensations*, 23.
9. Mark Sullivan, *Our Times: Over Here, 1914-1918* (New York: Scribner's, 1933), 384. On Baruch and the War Industries Board, see also David M. Kennedy, *Over Here: The First World War and American Society* (Oxford & New York: Oxford University Press, 1980), 126-43, and Jordan Schwarz, *The Speculator: Bernard M. Baruch in Washington, 1917-65* (Chapel Hill: University of North Carolina Press, 1981).
10. Appointment notice, 22 July 1919, AH-LC; Clarkson to AH, 6 Sept., 14 Oct. 1919, AH-LC.
11. Adelaide Fielding Kerr to David Laughlin, 3 Oct. 1990, in possession of the author.
12. Bowker to AH, 8 Oct. 1919, Bowker papers, NYPL; Richard Bowker, "Women in the Library Profession," LJ 45 (Aug. 1920): 640.
13. AH to Charles Belden, 14 Oct. 1919, AH-LC.
14. U.S. Council of National Defense, 4th Annual Report (Washington: GPO, 1920), 75.
15. Ibid., 75-76.
16. Waldo Leland and Newton Mereness, *Introduction to the American Official Sources for the Economic and Social History of the War* (New Haven: Yale University Press, 1926), 346.
17. U.S. National Archives, *Preliminary Inventory of the War Industries Board Records* (Washington: National Archives, 1941), ix-x.
18. There is nothing about the school in AH-LC, which does contain a flyer for the YWCA course. Its 1922-23 circular is in the Dewey papers, Rare Book and Manuscript Library, Columbia University. Some information is in the comparative chart of library schools in J. H. Friedel, *Training for Librarianship* (Philadelphia: Lippincott, 1921), the District of Columbia Library Association Committee on Library Training, *Washington's Facilities for Training in Library Science* (Washington: DCLA, 1923), and "A Training School for Business Librarians," SL 11 (Sept.-Oct. 1920): 167.

19. Adelaide Hasse, "The Teaching of Reference Work in Library Schools," LJ 44 (Sept. 1919): 582-84. This is part of an LJ symposium that also includes a piece by J. H. Friedel, whose comments about inadequate reference service in public libraries probably refer back to the tensions at NYPL between the Economics Division and other departments.

20. Barbara Brand, "Pratt Institute Library School: The Perils of Professionalization," in Suzanne Hildenbrand, ed., *Reclaiming the American Library Past: Writing the Women In* (Norwood, NJ: Ablex, 1996); John Y. Cole, *Capital Libraries and Librarians: A Brief History of the District of Columbia Library Association, 1894-1994* (Washington: Library of Congress, 1994), 29.

21. Marion Horton, "The Los Angeles Library School," LJ 48 (15 Nov. 1923): 959.

22. Dewey to AH, 13 Feb. 1923, Kelso to John Lowe, 18 April 1924, Dewey to Frank Hill, 27 May 1924, all Dewey papers, Rare Book and Manuscript Library, Columbia University.

23. SL 11 (Sept.-Oct. 1920): 172.

24. The editorials were not signed, but most that appeared during AH's editorship read as if written by her. Such enthusiastic editorials had not appeared under the previous editors. Those quoted are from Nov. 1921, May 1922, Jan. 1922.

25. SL 12 (May 1921): 97; SL 12 (Dec. 1921): 236.

26. SL 14 (Feb. 1923): 26.

27. U.S. Civil Service Commission form 2224, 11 March 1921, AH-CB.

28. U.S. Federal Bureau of Investigation File 62-329 (1922). Information about Bertha Pierce is from the 1892-96 LAPL Annual Reports and her federal employment file, U.S. National Archives and Records Administration, Civilian Personnel Records, St. Louis.

29. Adelaide Hasse, "ALA Publications for the Special Library," *ALA Bulletin* 16 (1922 conference proceedings): 105-6. AH answering "Nothing" is in PL 27 (July 1922): 412, and Dennis Thomison, *A History of the American Library Association* (Chicago: ALA, 1975), 67.

30. "Biographical Record" [1939], AH-LC, and SEC employment application, 1941, AH federal employment file, U.S. National Archives and Records Administration, Civilian Personnel Records, St. Louis. Information about Edwin Clapp, *Who Was Who in America*.

Chapter 11

Brookings Institution, 1923-1932

In the fall of 1923, Hasse received a message that opened a new phase of her career. After five years of instability, she would have a base for the next decade in a unique new organization devoted to research on public policy. It was being developed by Robert S. Brookings, a wealthy businessman from St. Louis who had come to Washington to serve on the War Industries Board.

Brookings' experience in government intensified his interest in the Institute for Government Research (IGR), a nonpartisan research organization founded in 1916 by a group of business leaders seeking to improve government administration. In St. Louis, Brookings' faith in education had inspired him to develop a failing college into the well-endowed Washington University. Now, as a trustee of the IGR, he was equally determined to rescue another institution on the brink of failure, with its initial funding almost exhausted. The institute had proved its worth, playing a key role in establishing systems for the federal budget, civil service classification, and government employee pensions. At seventy, Brookings set out to raise the money to continue the IGR and also establish the Institute for Economic Policy, which the Carnegie Institution agreed to support for ten years. It opened in 1922, sharing quarters with the IGR in a building Brookings erected on Jackson Place across from the White House. The next year, he added a pioneering graduate school in public administration. Within a few years, his tripartite creation would be reorganized into simply the Brookings Institution, the model for a new force in Washington, the "think tank" dedicated to the study and analysis of public policy.[1]

The head of the economic institute was a University of Chicago economist, Harold Moulton, who accepted appointment only with provision in the by-laws that the trustees would support research, not express their opinions on issues. Moulton established an initial program of a dozen economists working in international economic reconstruction, international commercial policies, agriculture, and industrial labor. His own interest was war debts and reparations, particularly the problem of German recovery while burdened with heavy reparations.

Hasse had been aware of the institute from its founding, reporting in *Special Libraries* that Karoline Klager of the Labor Department had been appointed its librarian. In October 1923, she received a note from Moulton asking to see her, as "the Institute very much needs your kind assistance."[2] Hasse responded immediately and was appointed to the position of Bibliographer, serving as a research guide and information resource for the staff and graduate students, while Klager operated the library. The government institute had its own librarian and bibliographer.

Little record of Hasse's work has survived. Among her personal papers, she kept a three-hundred-page bibliography for the institute, "Some Recent Studies on Statistical Methods and their Application; Tentative Draft List," done in April 1925. At the request of Robert Brookings, she wrote a memo on the research problems in Washington when the government had neither a national archives nor a true national library. In it, she demonstrated her wide knowledge of factors that included individual staff members and bibliographic projects in various agencies and the ever-changing structure of government departments. The Library of Congress and agency libraries all had limited hours and facilities, and the lack of coordination of the government's libraries resulted in duplication and underutilization of specialized materials. Hasse also discussed the needs of the graduate students, who might have little knowledge of reference works, and the researchers without contacts to help locate government information in "a large mass of materials, the extent, scope, even the location of which is indefinite."[3]

For archival material, Hasse suggested obtaining access to the information collected by the congressional committee studying an archives building and inviting officials from key agency archival collections to address the Brookings students. For published information, she called for improved access to some Library of Congress collections, such as the Law Library, Documents Division, and Smithsonian Collection, where hours were much shorter than for the Main Reading Room and the Periodical Room. Hasse emphasized the need for centralized reference centers to provide coordinated access to the resources of government libraries. The many agency libraries often suffered from limited space and haphazard development in an environment of perennial government reorganizations and turf battles; to identify holdings and reduce duplication of little-used materials, Congress ought to authorize a "clearing house survey." An advisory research committee of agency representatives was needed to develop more projects like the Bureau of Efficiency's card file of agency activities by subject, the union list of serials under development, and the bibliography of scientific research coordinated by the National Research Council. Coordination of libraries for efficiency had always been Hasse's concern, and she would continue to call for communication and cooperation among the many special libraries in Washington.

As always, Hasse had ideas for developing research tools. She told Brookings that she was preparing a memorandum on the "function of bibliography in economic research," in which she would suggest the "authorization on the part of the Institute of various aids to economic research," perhaps prepared with the

assistance of the graduate students. The records indicate that Hasse unsuccessfully suggested bibliographic and other reference publications throughout her
decade at Brookings, not seeming to realize that the men who employed her
wanted only a research assistant who would locate and fetch whatever information they needed whenever they wanted it.

In 1928, there was some turmoil as the two institutes and the graduate
school were merged into the single Brookings Institution, with Moulton as
president. This became a heated public controversy when the graduate school
objected to the changes approved by the trustees, who persisted in their decision
to eliminate the school as a degree-granting institution. In the midst of the upheaval, Karoline Klager departed, and Hasse was appointed to replace her as librarian with the title Chief of the Library and Bibliography Division and a salary of $4,000 for the 1929-30 fiscal year. Despite the good salary and impres-
sive title, the library was a one-woman operation that lacked clear goals and
policies. Hasse's return to library management soon involved her in problems
that were all too familiar: limited resources, undefined objectives, and criticism
from men sure that they knew best.[4]

The library was located in the basement, with no separate staff work space
and so few tables that Hasse sometimes worked on the floor. She was expected
to meet the needs of varying numbers of staff working on various projects and
to merge the collections of the two institutes while maintaining a second collection in the graduate school's residence on Eye Street. (Though the school was
closing, students already in the midst of degree programs would continue their
work.) Hasse soon complained of the "folly" of expecting one librarian to be responsible for both sites.

In September 1928, Hasse wrote a detailed memorandum on library policy
issues that needed clarification. No copy has survived, but it apparently suggested ambitious plans for developing the library as a resource for Brookings research while also undertaking a large bibliographic project. The Brookings Advisory Council replied with guidance so general as to be essentially meaning-
less. Hasse should "so arrange the administration of the library that her time
will be free from routine tasks." Secondly, "all materials of permanent value"
owned by the institute should be identified and Hasse then inform the Library
Committee "in her judgment the most desirable alternative plan for cataloging
and physically distributing" them. It was not the time to pursue a "large bibliographic undertaking" when priorities should be "such planning and reorganization of the library as is necessary" and developing a plan for improved collecting
and access to fugitive materials, such as pamphlets.[5]

Hasse spent the next year trying to implement these general directions, but
she soon found that there was little support or understanding behind them, and
the issue of the pamphlets would become a major headache. She was provided
with one assistant who largely determined her own hours, working only certain
days and never before nine, so that Hasse often had to sort the mail, answer the
phone, and label materials herself. As she worked on the collection, she found
problems far worse than she had expected, to the point that she told Moulton
she would not have attempted the job had she realized the library's condition.

There was no shelflist to make an inventory, and apparently many books had been passed on to researchers on arrival, without classification or record of disposition; a manuscript card had been made for each new book, but contact had been lost with many of the volumes recorded. Cataloging had fallen far behind, and even when Library of Congress cards had been purchased, they had not been processed. There were piles of pamphlets and other ephemera, with more continually being requested or arriving from staff offices, but no cabinets were available for a vertical file. The periodical collection needed review, and there had been no binding for a year. While faced with this morass, Hasse was expected to continue to acquire new material and provide reference service to both current Brookings researchers and former staff who wrote for information.

In what she described as an "utterly discouraging year," Hasse made some headway. A large quantity of government documents duplicated in both institutes was consolidated, with fourteen mailbags of duplicates sent to GPO, and the requisite shifting done. Periodical binding was brought up to date. Congressional hearings were organized and updated. With no file cabinets, the pamphlets were given a quick, provisional arrangement, grouped in general classes on the shelves (a standard practice in special libraries), to make them available pending further work. Hasse often worked late at night and on weekends; her suggestion that the library be closed temporarily to give her uninterrupted time to catch up was rejected. When she urged consolidation of the H and J classes from the graduate residence in the main library, the reason given for not making such a simple efficiency was that it would leave "bare and unsightly shelves" behind. To top it off, in the summer of 1929, she was asked to make indexes for Census Bureau publications and then learned that there "was no provision for a vacation" for her.

In this frustrating situation, the always enterprising Hasse found a new career opportunity. In September 1929, she obtained Moulton's permission to work half-time at Brookings for $2,500 and half-time as chief indexer of the *United States Daily* for $2,500. It would be a flexible arrangement whereby she could be practically full-time at one or the other, depending on the workload. For Hasse, this had the advantage of increasing her total earnings while reducing the time spent in the frustrating Brookings library and providing an opportunity in the work she preferred, improving access to government information by indexing an innovative new publication. In at least one later job application, she reconstructed her history at Brookings as having been mostly administrative work as librarian from 1923 to 1928, when she resigned to do indexing work she preferred at *United States Daily*. Her reasons for lying are unclear; she may have been covering up her age or simplifying the two-jobs arrangement, but she also was expressing the emotional truth that she had come to see administrative responsibility in libraries as a thankless, hopeless task. Henceforth, she would concentrate on in-depth bibliographies and indexes of government publications that gave her the satisfaction of providing access to content, with the ultimate goal that the information be useful to decision makers.[6]

United States Daily had been founded by David Lawrence, a journalist with connections to leading political figures. In 1926, he obtained financing from his friend Bernard Baruch and other prominent Americans, including Robert Brookings, for a daily paper that would consist entirely of material from official federal and state government sources, thus serving as a kind of official gazette that the federal government did not then publish. As a daily, it generated a volume of material that especially needed an index, and Hasse was uniquely qualified to do such specialized work with government information. She again plunged into a major indexing project that would produce large folio volumes of annual cumulated indexes to *United States Daily*'s thousands of pages of laws, court opinions, administrative rulings, research reports, press releases, and official statements. The cover title was *Annual Index-Digest*, described as "A Key to the Activities of the Federal and State Governments," suggesting that it might be acquired as a stand-alone guide to government. The *Daily* also operated a service for those seeking particular types of publications, aiming to be a complete government information service.

It is not clear why Moulton approved Hasse's half-time schedule when the library had such pressing needs. Perhaps he intended to deal with library staffing when the results of the new arrangement were clear, and perhaps Hasse hoped that the money she was giving up could be used to hire more clerical staff. The Brookings Institution was a sponsor of the *Daily*, and the need for an index would have been obvious to him. The promising new arrangement had barely begun, however, when the library and Hasse's work came under attack from a member of the Brookings library committee, Charles Hardy, in a memo on the "inadequacy of the library service" to the committee's chairman, Lawrence Schmeckebier, with copies to Moulton and Hasse. There was no indication that he had discussed his complaints with Hasse, but he had consulted with Schmeckebier, who advised him to put his suggestions in writing.[7]

Hardy began with a three-page memo, "Work of the Library." He acknowledged that the "present staff is much smaller than the minimum staff which could possibly keep up with the work as at present organized." It would be necessary to curtail the work or increase the staff, and either was feasible financially, since expenditures were below the amount budgeted. In Hardy's view, however, "certain of the present activities of the library could be greatly curtailed," primarily by disposing of the "great mass of pamphlets, corporation reports, and other fugitive material which is now being indexed and filed by number on the shelves." (He apparently assumed erroneously that assigning classes to the pamphlets meant they had been fully cataloged.) Hardy doubted that most of this served Brookings' needs, pointing to advance releases of data published later in monthly or annual serials and to corporation annual reports, whose essential data was available in *Poors Corporation Service*. He complained about the "very untidy appearance" of such material on the shelves and urged that the small number of needed items be arranged by subject in file cabinets. His sarcastic conclusion, which Hasse underlined on her copy, was that "the library's greatest need at the present moment is a larger waste basket." He also wanted a review of the periodical collection by the Library Committee, a reduction in binding periodicals, and the elimination of a collection of college catalogs, since they could be obtained from the American Council of Education, which was housed in the building. He wanted more attention to the appearance of the library and provision of reading room space "isolated from the working quarters of the library staff." He did acknowledge the need for "adequate assistance" to allow the librarian to make research trips to other libraries, but he also wanted the cataloging of books to have higher priority, and assistance to researchers should take precedence over "routine operations," not specifying what routine matters could be set aside.

His rather mysterious conclusion was that no portion of the budget should remain unexpended "while the present conditions of disorder and the inadequacy of service in the library continue." Since most of his memo seemed aimed at curtailing expenditure and eliminating inefficiency, the overall impression was negative, with an undercurrent of hostility towards Hasse, but, at the same time, his complaints effectively supported her account of the library's problems. He seems not to have discussed his ideas with her or tried to learn about her efforts. Hasse had always been alert to keeping her superiors informed, and her reply pointed to instances of communicating with Moulton, Schmeckebier, and "the several Library committees" about issues raised by Hardy. Now she found herself in the position of having to respond to uninformed criticism from a micromanaging member of the Library Committee, which Moulton had earlier told her was to be concerned only with "such general questions of library and bibliographical policy as may be raised by you," not with "routine matters of library administration."[8]

Hasse wrote an immediate reply, briefly answering Hardy's allegations in seven points. She recalled her 1928 memo about the "folly" of expecting one librarian to provide service for two sites. In regard to the pamphlets, she firmly stated that Hardy was "under an entire misapprehension as to the whole procedure" in assuming that they were fully cataloged. This wasn't the first time she had been hired to organize chaos, Hasse said, but never had she been required to deal with so many activities in such difficult conditions. She agreed that the "pitiful" selection of periodicals needed review. The college catalogs had been acquired to meet the needs of a Brookings researcher for lists of faculty not available elsewhere, including at the American Council of Education, which sometimes used the Brookings collection. As for the separation of the reading room from the staff work area, of course she would like to have better space. Hasse made it clear that she was exasperated, but she was careful to make her points "respectfully" and emphasize the need for positive policies and plans for library development. The real problem was the absence of "an adequate library policy . . . one which does not make the Library a warehouse for tenants' property, a corridor for workmen, a storage place for personal property, an employees' welfare center. Nor does it mean that the librarian be positioned as a combination moron, porter, messenger, and policeman." She called for a development plan to make the library a "research center for scholars" and offered her "wholehearted cooperation" and readiness to submit such a plan.[9]

Hardy ignored this and instead expanded on his criticisms, particularly of the pamphlets, in three more memos in which he listed what should be discarded and how a vertical file should be organized.[10] Why Hardy took it upon himself to make such an issue of the library is unclear. Perhaps Hasse, under stress, had said something that offended him, or perhaps he wanted to slap down a woman librarian who proposed ambitious plans. He seems to have been a fussy, irritable personality, disturbed by the untidy appearance of the pamphlets on the shelves, jumping to the erroneous conclusion that they had been cataloged, and quick to blame Hasse for whatever he didn't like. (A few years later, he would be denouncing the New Deal for aiming "to substitute centralized authority . . . for what is left of free competitive enterprise.") Schmeckebier's role in the contretemps is also mysterious; though all of Hardy's and Hasse's memos were addressed to him as committee chair, there is no evidence that he did anything to resolve the matter. Schmeckebier's career would be based on his extremely detailed guides to government publications, notably the standard manual *Government Publications and Their Use*. He had already published a book on the Government Printing Office that made no mention of Hasse, his Brookings colleague, in the section on the library she created. Also, he had recently addressed government documents librarians at ALA, making criticisms similar to Hasse's of twenty years earlier; like her, he argued that population was not a suitable basis for designating depository libraries and proposed a better-defined system of three classes of depositories. Perhaps he and Hasse had feelings of rivalry, or she may have annoyed him by demonstrating her expertise—or perhaps he just didn't want to get involved in conflict.

On November 1, Hasse had gone to Philadelphia to speak at an SLA meeting about her hopes for the future of bibliography. She returned to find Hardy's further complaints, to which she replied in four memos on November 6, 7, and 8, making detailed refutation of the allegations in each of his memos, while also emphasizing how much work she had done under difficult conditions. In twelve pages that might be titled "The Librarian's Lament," she articulated the complexity of the work of the library, the difficulty of determining what was needed by staff for varied research projects, and the sheer impossibility of one person providing all the on-demand reference service while also operating the library, especially when she sometimes didn't even have a table for her work.[11]

Hasse emphasized again that shelving the pamphlet collection was a provisional solution to piles of material and more arriving from staff offices. "If it is wastebasket material, it should not be sent to the library," she suggested. Without going into detail about her work at NYPL, she explained that she had long experience with vertical files in cabinets, but, as should have been obvious to Hardy, the library had no cabinets available and no space for any that might be acquired. Selecting examples from Hardy's list of "worthless" items, she pointed out that many had been requested by Brookings fellows, and some contained the only issuance of essential information. The agricultural bulletins, which Hardy dismissed as "of no possible use to us," actually were among the most used material, "a carefully selected lot of statistical bulletins collected with a view to supplying continuing runs of statistical data." (The Department of Agriculture was then a major source of economic data and analysis.) Hardy's complaint about daily releases from the Silk Exchange would be valid if less frequent reports were available, but the dailies were all that was issued. Some issuances from government agencies were kept as the only detailed record of administrative actions; Hasse reminded Schmeckebier that she had sent him a memo on this type of material and had his approval for keeping it.

Hasse devoted five pages to explaining the value of some of the titles on Hardy's four-page discard list, including anecdotes of their use by Brookings researchers, the difficulty or impossibility of obtaining them elsewhere, and the high cost of staff time searching for them compared to the cost of retaining them in the library. She concluded with a summary of key points about such "ephemeral" publications, trying to clarify in general terms how useful such material might be and how difficult it was for any librarian to make decisions on acquisitions and processing, since "no matter how carefully done, it is never satisfactory to everybody concerned." Her final point was that Hardy's assumption that materials should be obtained from other libraries was "debatable . . . and good arguments can be offered for either side."

The matter then moved to the Library Committee (Schmeckebier, Hardy, and Louis Lorwin), which issued an eight-point report in the form of minutes; no copy is available, but it apparently largely supported Hardy's views. In what seems a further insult to Hasse, Hardy added a supplemental recommendation "that the person employed to look after routine work of the library should have full responsibility for that work." The recommendation was sent to the Brookings Council, with no copy to Hasse.

On November 26, the council "approved in principle" most of the committee's points, vaguely concluding that duplicate files of ephemera "readily available" in Washington not be acquired and material "not desired to keep permanently shall, if possible, be disposed of before we move to the new building." It did agree that the library could have a shared messenger boy, a cataloger to clear out the backlog, and a clerk to look after the routine work. The cataloging "should be greatly restricted," however, with only author and shelflist cards, no pamphlets cataloged individually, and, in a final bit of micromanaging, the pocket and charge card omitted from books "not likely to have extensive circulation." Its general policy conclusion was that the library should be primarily a service "assisting the staff and research fellows to utilize efficiently the library resources of Washington," while "reducing to a minimum the amount expended for general books not needed in connection with specific projects." Having essentially rejected Hasse's interest in developing the collection, the council also rejected Hardy's reports, at least for the remainder of the fiscal year, which was to be "a test period for the improvement of the administration of the library."[12]

Moulton reviewed the situation with Hasse, who appreciated his providing her with copies of the minutes and Hardy's comments. Afterwards, she sent a note of thanks for his courtesy and assurances of her "sincere desire to meet your wishes at all times" and her "utmost regret that I should have been the cause of this unpleasant situation for you." As for Hardy, she didn't hide her scorn: "I was horrified at the so evidently deliberate misrepresentation on the part of Mr. Hardy." Recognizing the futility of further debate, she told Moulton she would not "be adolescent about it." He replied that he appreciated her note and the spirit behind it and held a "sincere hope that we can work this thing out to the satisfaction of everybody concerned."[13]

Hasse returned to full-time work at Brookings until the fall of 1930, when she again worked part-time on the index of *United States Daily*, whose circulation was growing, reaching 41,000 in 1930. From England, F. R. Cowell of H.M. Stationery Office sent his congratulations on the quality of the index, "a magnificent achievement . . . unique in political literature." By then a new librarian had been hired at Brookings, and Hasse was again the bibliographer. In 1931, Brookings moved into its impressive new building on Jackson Place, where Hasse took advantage of the dining room for a weekly library lunch group to encourage communication among Washington librarians.[14]

Always interested in developing reference works, Hasse reviewed and corrected Inez Mcfee's *How Our Government Is Run* for the publisher Crowell. She proposed to Moulton that Brookings publish an encyclopedia of American government that would be continued by yearbooks. This was vetoed by W. F. Willoughby, former head of the Institute for Government Research, who wanted it understood that he had proposed such yearbooks himself but now doubted that "funds and resources" were available. (Eventually, in better economic times, Congressional Quarterly would publish yearbooks of Congress, which became essential reference works for libraries.)[15]

Hasse no longer did much speaking and writing, but she occasionally published an expression of her faith in bibliography and her conviction that business and serious researchers needed more information service than libraries typically provided. In 1929, in the midst of Hardy's petty complaints, she spoke to an SLA chapter about her ever hopeful vision, "Bibliography: Today and Tomorrow." Here she summarized her experience in moving from classical bibliography, with its emphasis on physical characteristics, and library processing of books as "containers" to recognition of the need to get at the contents of the containers. Modeling her talk on the British series "Today and Tomorrow," she reminisced about her long-ago search in the Public Record Office and then turned to her vision of a "research service of tomorrow . . . composed of affiliated but separately functioning bureaus" that would somehow provide any current or historical data, by means of "card indexes . . . so arranged that any possible approach would be facilitated." She was confident, "It is only a question of time when it will be possible for a research worker in Copenhagen to call Philadelphia, New York or Washington, and when by television there will be flashed back to him the requested references in reply." Hasse was still hoping for the Holy Grail, "a central agency of information," now using the telephone and the recently invented television. Though not quite futurist enough to foresee computer networks and search engines, she came remarkably close to a vision of the Internet in 1929.[16]

While Hasse struggled with problems at Brookings, her son Leslie added to her stress. In October 1928, he had obtained a discharge from the Naval Reserve to enlist in the Coast Guard, but by March he was already in trouble as a deserter. In a wire from Texas asking for money, he explained that a car breakdown had prevented him from returning on time from leave. This involved Hasse in correspondence with the authorities, trying to help Leslie in what was a pattern with a son who was often in scrapes and in need of money, which Hasse gave him. At some point he married a woman whose barely literate letter in Hasse's papers asks if and when they had been divorced.[17]

Aside from the problems with her son, Hasse seemed to have settled into an ideal situation, both professionally and personally. She bought a car and a house in suburban Silver Spring, probably with the help of a loan from her sister Elsa, secured by her share of the Los Angeles real estate inherited from their parents. At some point, Hasse acquired two more lots in the Silver Spring subdivision and some lots at the Maryland shore, putting most of her savings into real property. She shared her home with Tilloah Squires, who worked as a bookkeeper, helped with the housework, and did the driving for shopping and errands. Hasse cooked their hearty breakfast, followed by coffee and a cigarette as she scanned the paper, occasionally chuckling and commenting on the background of some item about the government. Though always obsessed with her work, Hasse found time to enjoy gardening and cooking in the tidy house at 806 Islington Street, where she accumulated a collection of ten thousand books. She also was active in the group that started a public library in Silver Spring.[18]

Ironically, on the very days in 1929 when Hasse and Hardy had tangled over the details of library policy, events in the outside world set off an economic earthquake that would shake the Brookings Institution as it shattered the lives of many Americans. The stock market crash on October 29 did not alone cause the Great Depression, nor was it immediately apparent that the nation was headed for disaster. By the following April, the stock market seemed to have recovered, but then its erratic decline resumed, reaching a bottom 86 percent below the 1929 peak in 1932, as a complex series of events in Europe and America led to global economic paralysis.

Hasse continued her dual employment, earning $2,692 from Brookings in 1931, but the spreading depression was affecting everything and everyone. *United States Daily*'s 1930 circulation was a peak that fell with the economy; in May 1933, Lawrence closed it at a loss to Baruch and started a weekly news magazine, *United States News*. The Brookings Institution was finding it increasingly difficult to operate as foundation and individual support declined with stock values, and it lost its chief fund-raiser with Robert Brookings' death in 1932. Many plans had to be canceled, and the staff was asked to take a 10 percent pay cut. Hasse earned only $1,003 from Brookings in 1932, the year her employment ended. The records give no reason for her departure on July 1, taking her pension accumulation with her. She was unlikely to have quit her job at a time of high unemployment, but a part-time bibliographer was vulnerable to being laid off or retired when funds were tight, research projects curtailed, and the last graduate degrees granted. The following year, she sought to be rehired, and she gave Moulton as a reference in her job hunting, indicating that there was no dissatisfaction with her job performance. Whatever the reason, Hasse now was in a dire situation, without a job or a pension at age sixty-four, as the nation sank into the Great Depression.

Notes

1. *The Brookings Institution: A Fifty-Year History* (Washington: Brookings Institution, 1966) is the source of background information for this chapter.

2. Moulton to AH, Oct. 1923, AH-LC.

3. AH to Robert Brookings, 8 Nov. 1924, Brookings Institution archives.

4. AH's problems with the library were described in her memoranda to Lawrence Schmeckebier, 26 Oct., 6, 7, 8 Nov. 1929, AH-LC.

5. Quoted in Charles Hardy to Schmeckebier, 31 Oct. 1929, AH-LC.

6. Moulton to AH and David Lawrence, both 19 Sept. 1929, AH-LC. Records of her shifting between the two employers in the next three years are in AH-LC and the Brookings archives. The job application is in her federal employment file, U.S. National Archives and Records Administration, Civilian Personnel Records, St. Louis.

7. Hardy to Schmeckebier, 24 Oct. 1929, AH-LC.

8. Moulton to AH, 23 May 1929, Brookings Institution archives.

9. AH to Schmeckebier, 26 Oct. 1929, AH-LC.

10. Hardy to Schmeckebier, 30, 31 Oct. 1929, AH-LC.

11. AH to Schmeckebier, 6, 7, 8 Nov. 1929, AH-LC.

12. Minutes of Council meeting, 26 Nov. 1929, Brookings Institution archives.

13. AH to Moulton, 7 Dec. 1929, Brookings Institution archives; Moulton to AH, 7 Dec. 1929, AH-LC.

14. Cowell to AH, 17 Dec. 1931, AH-LC; AH invitation to library lunch group, 16 Oct. 1931, AH-LC.

15. AH to Moulton, 14 Dec. 1930, Willoughby to Moulton, 17 Jan. 1931, AH-LC.

16. Adelaide Hasse, "Bibliography: Today and Tomorrow," SL 21 (March 1930): 75-80.

17. Correspondence about problems of Leslie Maynard, AH-LC.

18. AH's personal life, Adelaide Fielding Kerr to David Laughlin, 3 Oct. 1990, in possession of the author, and correspondence in AH-LC and in AH's federal employment file.

Chapter 12

New Deal and After, 1933-1953

The year 1933 opened as one of the bleakest in American history. A quarter of the labor force was unemployed, and thousands of banks and businesses had failed. Farmers and the urban jobless were equally desperate. The national mood was ugly, and President-elect Franklin Delano Roosevelt narrowly escaped assassination.

Hasse was among the barely employed, and the job prospects for a woman in her sixties were not promising. That summer, she updated the guide to the federal government for Crowell, and George Washington University hired her to teach a night class on government documents in the fall, but her efforts to find other employment were futile. Though prompt in the past, she had trouble with her house payments. Even after she found work, this remained a chronic problem until the mortgage was paid off in 1940. Hasse vaguely offered the bank apologies for the "muddle" and assurances that she was "not given to this sort of thing." The $2,500 loan from her sister effectively became a gift, as first the interest payment was dropped, and then the loan was repeatedly renewed by Elsa's lawyers.[1]

Hasse pursued various hopes for employment. She tried to interest ALA and the Carnegie Institution in reviving the state documents index; Frederick Kuhlman, the chair of the Public Documents Committee, was research-oriented and had mentioned the need for more systematic and standardized state records, but as he looked into the problem, he realized it would take "a rather handsome sum, because there is an enormous amount of work to be done in some states," something Hasse knew all too well. She sought appointment as indexer of the *Congressional Record*, obtaining the support of her local Democratic Party organization, and applied for a research position with the new Tennessee Valley Authority. She approached the Business Historical Association with a project on "a new source for the history of American Business Information." Told that the society was financially precluded from new undertakings, Hasse wrote back rather desperately that conditions were "bound to change" and while she had "some extra time," the work could be done "at a very nominal figure" and could even be started "with the understanding that payment be made when conditions ease up."[2]

During the summer, she heard that the Brookings librarian was "very fed up with Brookings" and looking for another job. Immediately, Hasse contacted Levrett Lyons and her old nemesis Charles Hardy, who now had authority over the library, to ask that she be considered for the position she had found so frustrating a few years earlier. Lyons was polite but not encouraging, and eventually someone else was hired. In September, Moulton sent congratulations on her teaching appointment, which had been announced in the press. Hasse replied that she had plenty of time for other work and was interested in returning to the Brookings library, but she admitted what Moulton already knew, "I am not terribly keen about administrative work, much preferring research." She even asked if he had any ideas of how she could obtain funding for her current research interest.[3]

Adding to the gloom of the year, Tessa Kelso died in August in Santa Barbara, where she had spent her last years, a sad reminder of the high hopes they had shared so long ago. *Library Journal* gave a full page to Marian Manley's tribute to the special warmth and vitality Kelso had brought to the library world. Hasse told Emma Baldwin that she didn't like the piece, because it didn't say enough about how Kelso's personal qualities had contributed to her success in Los Angeles. She probably also was annoyed that in mentioning her work with Kelso, LJ misspelled her name as Haase, a sign of how long it had been since she was familiar to the editors.[4]

Hasse's twenty-three-year-old niece, Adelaide Fielding, came from California for a six-month stay while unsuccessfully seeking work in journalism. Fielding seems not to have realized that her aunt was underemployed. Squires warned that Hasse was devoted to her work, which was not to be disturbed, and Fielding had the impression that Hasse was sought out for various government jobs for which she sometimes had difficulty getting paid, due to congressional or bureaucratic delays. She regarded her aunt as a workaholic who was content with brief morning and evening conversations and devoted most of her time to her unspecified work, but she enjoyed Hasse's company, describing a "serious yet friendly manner . . . a keen sense of humor and loved a good story." Hasse's determination to preserve the image of a successful career is particularly poignant as she passed by the opportunity to spend time with her motherless niece. The little that Fielding learned about her aunt came mainly from conversation with Tilloah Squires, who had "enormous respect" for Hasse and her work. It was Squires who told her of the problems with Leslie and of Hasse's connections with prominent people like Bernard Baruch and Frances Perkins, the new Secretary of Labor, though giving the impression that Hasse would never seek their help and always received unsolicited job offers. Although she didn't feel close to her aunt, Fielding enjoyed the visit and appreciated Hasse's gift of a seat in the stands for Roosevelt's inauguration and her suggestion of the "lame duck" period as the subject of one of the few articles she sold. There were a few awkward moments, as when Hasse prepared an elaborate dinner as a birthday surprise, but Fielding, not knowing that her aunt had spent the day working on a feast, came home so late that the meal was spoiled. On one occasion, Fielding encountered Hasse's touchiness at any sign of male condescension, when a friend of hers came to the house with an offer to clean the furnace and basement. His help was indignantly refused by Hasse, who complained to Fielding that a man would think she couldn't clean her own furnace. (Every inch of the house was spotless.)[5]

While Hasse and her niece looked for work, vast change came to the federal government with the inauguration of Franklin D. Roosevelt. The president soon proved to be a governmental activist committed to "bold, persistent experimentation." The atmosphere of the capital changed to a spirit of using government aggressively to deal with the nation's problems, and Hasse's old acquaintances from the Progressive Era in New York and Wisconsin were pouring into town to work in the New Deal's agencies and programs. Her former employers, Baruch and Frankfurter, were close to Roosevelt and his energetic wife, Eleanor. Frances Perkins, who had begun her career as a social worker with the Consumers League and then risen in the New York state administrations of Al Smith and Franklin Roosevelt, became the first woman cabinet member, but she was only the most prominent of the many women from the social work and reform movements who were finding jobs in the new administration. These were people who believed that government could solve problems on the basis of rational analysis, which, fortunately for Hasse, would require a great deal of information.[6]

Of course Hasse was keeping up with developments in the government. In the summer of 1933, Crowell hired her to update *How Our Government Is Run*, a tricky job, as the publisher couldn't afford to reset it and required the revised text to fit exactly where the old text was deleted. An additional section on the New Deal was wanted, and Hasse found that no one office, not even the White House press secretary, had all the documentation on the president's initiatives, so she spent three days tracking it down in various departments. She advised Crowell to promote the book as the first to provide a schedule of New Deal actions and to issue a volume of documentation with connecting narrative, "in view of the world-wide interest this experiment is arousing."[7]

In July, a friend at the Interstate Commerce Commission urged her to seek a place in the new administration: "How you would shine as a special investigator to the National Industrial Recovery Administration. I should think you would make a big connection with one of the new Boards." By the end of the year, that was just what Hasse had done. When Brookings sent out a request for information on former staff in regard to "many changes of position," she could triumphantly report that she was "Research Consultant, FERA Library."[8]

~ ~ ~

FERA, the Federal Emergency Relief Administration, was seen as the heart and soul of the New Deal. Most federal agencies had a part in the activist, reforming approach to the national crisis, but FERA had been created in the spring of 1933 specifically to provide immediate help to the millions of unemployed. From a shabby office building on New York Avenue, the small staff tackled the initial job of distributing relief funds to the states, but increasingly the agency would aim to develop projects that enabled Americans to earn their government relief payments and perhaps learn new skills in the process. Its 1935 name change to Works Progress Administration (WPA) reflected a broader approach to recovery and reconstruction through public works projects, not just provision of the dole that further demoralized the unemployed. Much of FERA's energy and innovation came from its administrator, Harry Hopkins, a New York social worker with drive, idealism, and the ear of Eleanor Roosevelt. Hopkins was a vivid personality, energetic, decisive, and blunt, the kind of dynamic leader who would have reminded Hasse of Kelso and Billings. He also was more open to hiring women in his agency than other men in the administration, most of whom needed continual prodding from Mrs. Roosevelt.

Hasse was initially hired as a Research Consultant at a $6 per diem in January 1934. Two months later, she was changed to an annual salary of $2,600, raised to $2,900 in 1935. Responsible for reference and bibliography in the FERA library, she plunged into the preparation of mimeographed bibliographies on such topics as recovery planning, noninstitutional relief measures of the states, transients, and demolition in blighted areas, while also gathering the information resources needed as the New Deal tackled such complex issues as old age and unemployment insurance, housing, and recovery plans. By her third month on the job, Hasse was issuing a weekly accessions list, and she soon was maintaining a set of thirty looseleaf binders, one for each division, of all current relief and social security measures (fully indexed, of course). Her knowledge of Washington libraries was useful for the many interlibrary loans the staff wanted, and her persistence was needed to get even thirty-two of the states to send reports of their relief work for the library. All of this was reported in a *Washington News* feature "Experts Head FERA Research Library, Grows Big After Two Years in Operation." Hasse must have been pleased to be prominently mentioned as one of the experts and by congratulations from a former student, now librarian of the Forest Service, "You certainly deserve every bit of praise that was given you, and we, who had the opportunity of studying under you, are indeed fortunate."[9]

When the 1934 elections confirmed the Democrats' control of Congress, 1935 became the great year of reform, with more social legislation than any year before or since. Hopkins told his staff, "This is our hour. . . . Get your minds to work on developing a complete ticket to provide security for all the folks in this country up and down and across the board."[10] The WPA began spending on unprecedented work projects to employ millions. Soon Hasse was preparing bibliographies on a subject that was a priority for New Deal action. The president had appointed the Committee on Economic Security, chaired by Frances Perkins and including Harry Hopkins, to determine how to provide retirement and unemployment insurance. The executive director was Edwin Witte, a University of Wisconsin professor whose background was similar to Hasse's: a Wisconsin native of German ancestry, he had been deeply influenced by Charles McCarthy when he worked for the Legislative Reference Library as a student, and after McCarthy's death, he became the library's director. During the year the committee grappled with formulating a social insurance system, Hasse provided bibliographies: *Summary of American Old Age Security Legislation, 1879-1934; American Federation of Labor: Social Security Commitments, 1904-1934; Old Age Security in the United States, a Selected List of References; Selected List of References on Old Age Security, Pt. 1 Foreign Countries, Pt. 2 United States, Pt. 3 U.S. States*. As always, her work was thorough, including books, theses, articles, and government reports, with extensive annotations and cross references to explain what plans were discussed, provide key quotations, and show connections among publications.

After her first two years at FERA/WPA, Hasse tended to title her work "digest" or "synopsis" rather than "list" or "bibliography," reflecting her long-standing aim to make content accessible, not merely list publications. Her greatest pride was the semi-monthly *Housing Index-Digest,* prepared for the Central Housing Committee, a coordinating group of the eight agencies concerned with housing construction and finance. Housing was a New Deal priority, leading to establishment of the Federal Housing Authority in 1934 and the U.S. Housing Authority in 1937 to distribute $800 million for slum clearance, construction of low-cost housing, and repair of existing housing. Urban planning was encouraged, as were model greenbelt towns built by WPA labor. Such large-scale government involvement in housing was entirely new, and Hasse was determined to provide information on all the issues. Her expertise was recognized when she was selected to contribute to the special housing issue of the prestigious *Annals of the American Academy*.[11]

In the summer of 1936, she sailed to Europe on the Queen Mary, intending to make contacts and gather information on European housing policies and programs. In her excitement about the trip, Hasse showed she was as intense as ever about the importance of bibliographic work. A week before her departure, she wrote to Eleanor Roosevelt to ask for a letter of introduction from the first lady or the president, in order to open doors and save time in Europe. Hasse enclosed a copy of the *Housing Index-Digest* and explained, "I am anxious to make it the outstanding source of basic information on the subject of Housing both in the United States and abroad." She conceded that she "should have gone about this in a formal manner," but she knew both Roosevelts were intensely concerned with housing, and she reminded the first lady that they had met at the speakers' table at the DC Library Association dinner in April. This appeal was not as eccentric as it might seem, since Mrs. Roosevelt was well known for taking an interest in all sorts of people, and thousands of Americans wrote to her for aid and advice. The ever-helpful first lady promptly passed the letter on to the president with the query, "Could this be done?" Her secretary then had to inform Hasse that neither "the President nor she can ever give a letter such as you wish," suggesting that she instead ask the State Department for a letter. Hasse dashed off an apology for having "blundered," and managed, at the last minute, to obtain a letter from State, along with the privilege of using diplomatic pouches to send back material collected on the eight-week journey that took her to France, Germany, Poland, the Soviet Union, Scandinavia, and Britain.[12]

On her return, she corresponded with the director of the Swedish Stadshe-
rut, who wanted to receive the *Housing Index-Digest* and exchange materials.
"All the housing people in America are on edge waiting for the introduction of
the new housing authority legislation," she reported, adding that the 1936 meeting of the American Economic Association had a program on housing for the
first time. She explained that the next issue of the *Housing Index-Digest* would
be delayed "owing to its size" and would include a summary of all pending
housing legislation. Hasse aimed to make it more than an index to the literature;
some issues of volumes 2 and 3 were devoted to annotated statistics of European housing, while others provided data on cities. An issue on city research
data was so wide-ranging that *Special Libraries* described it as "a most useful
compendium of general statistical information." Along with editing the *Housing
Index-Digest*, Hasse chaired the bibliography section of the Central Housing
Committee and produced more bibliographies, including one on urban real estate appraisal for a committee of government and private agencies and an index
to the building operation statistics of the Bureau of Labor Statistics for the Central Statistical Board.[13]

Hasse was fortunate to have good rapport with her boss in the FERA/WPA
years. The head of the library, Ellen Commons, was the daughter-in-law of John
Commons, the influential Wisconsin economist whose acquaintance with Hasse
went back to Astor Library days. John Commons had greatly admired Charles
McCarthy, and Ellen Commons became an admirer of Hasse, whom she called
"my Pilot" and credited with inspiring her to remain a librarian when she was
considering a change to social work.[14] This was a real tribute to Hasse at a time
when social work had become a path to power and reform for such New Deal
leaders as Hopkins and Perkins, while librarians were more than ever seen as
dull, limited plodders. FDR appointed social workers to key positions, but he
didn't consider librarians capable even of serving as Librarian of Congress, as
was made painfully clear when he ignored ALA's offers of advice and gave the
job to an energetic renaissance man, Archibald MacLeish, poet, journalist, and
Harvard Law graduate recommended by Felix Frankfurter. The ALA establishment protested that MacLeish had no experience in library administration and
was not "professionally trained," but the president sneered that such qualifications produced only "professionally trained seals." Harry Lydenberg, now director of NYPL, was designated to testify against the appointment (because he was
available, not for his powers of persuasion). He warned the Senate committee
that MacLeish couldn't manage the library and continue writing at the same
time, but few senators bothered to attend the hearing, and MacLeish immediately received unanimous approval. *Library Journal* conceded that librarians
should feel "chastened when we realize how our 'training for librarians' has
failed to produce or develop obviously outstanding leaders in the profession."
To which Hasse was entitled to say, "I told you so." She must have found some
amusement, though tinged with sadness, in the ineffectual testimony of Lydenberg, who himself had neither library school training nor interest in administration, and in the changed values of the NYPL Staff Association, which endorsed
MacLeish's appointment. Unfortunately, with the president's negative reaction

to the persistent advisory efforts of the ALA male in-group, he didn't realize that there were qualified women librarians available within the New Deal, such as Hasse at the WPA and Cornelia Marvin, now the wife and chief assistant of a Democratic congressman.[15]

By then, Hasse had little contact with ALA. Though working in a library, she avoided the title "librarian" and minimized reference to her library career. Still the old faith in libraries as centers of information, education, and research sometimes stirred, as when she wrote to the head of the Carnegie Institution of a "vision of the expansion of the great library into a community of scientists, engineers, and forward-looking students of social and economic problems."[16] She did remain active in SLA and the District of Columbia Library Association, speaking on programs and serving as DCLA vice-president and president for 1937-1938. This enabled her to arrange for the president, LC law librarian John Vance, to appoint her a chapter representative to the ALA Council, where she vetoed honorary membership for Elihu Root in 1936. Besides getting a bit of revenge, Hasse must have enjoyed stirring up some trouble at a conference that was a symbol of conservatism and ineptitude. At the peak of one of the most progressive periods in American history, ALA chose to meet in the segregated South and informed its African American members that they could not use the same hotels and restaurants as white members. When the blacks protested, ALA replied that so long as meeting rooms were open to all members, the association had no concern with "social discrimination" in accommodations.[17]

Six weeks earlier, Hasse had sat proudly at the head table and given the opening address at the DCLA banquet where Eleanor Roosevelt spoke on the value of libraries.[18] ALA might be so backward as to accept segregation, choose an ancient Republican who had fought woman's suffrage for its highest honor, oppose unions, and endlessly debate whether even to seek federal funds for libraries, but with Hasse as president-elect, DCLA would connect with the dynamic first lady, who could have been speaking for Hasse when she told the press, "Peace can be as exciting to the daredevil as wartime. There is nothing so exciting as creating a new social order."[19] In November, that new order was overwhelmingly endorsed by the voters, with Roosevelt carrying all but two states and large majorities for the Democrats in Congress.

The following year, Hasse learned that her career was not entirely forgotten among librarians, when the Buffalo public library included her in an exhibit, "Outstanding Women of Achievement in America."[20] That summer, one of the most famous women of achievement, Amelia Earhart, disappeared on a flight across the Pacific. Earhart, the second person to fly alone across the Atlantic, had been an inspiration to American women, and her death was felt as a profound loss that inspired eulogies from Mrs. Roosevelt and many others. Hasse was so moved by one poem that she wrote to the author, Nathalia Crane, of her appreciation for its words about Earhart's courage.

A sudden courage plucks us from ourselves
Bids us be heroine though death the price
. . . .

Count her among the beautiful and brave,
Her turquoise mausoleum in each wave.

Crane replied, "Your letter 'was a beautiful thing to do and beautifully done,'
and therein lies the expression of another heroine." Hasse kept the poem and letter for the rest of her life, an expression of the courage it had taken to live as the
heroine of a story of achievement.[21]

For five exhilarating years, Hasse was part of the effort to reform the social
order and transform the role of government while preserving the basic system of
democratic capitalism, but by the late 1930s the New Deal was in decline, only
a few years after it had seemed triumphant. The economy fell into recession in
1937, and Roosevelt's attempt to pack the Supreme Court stirred fears that he
sought to become a dictator. The president's attention shifted to foreign affairs,
and Harry Hopkins, considered a possible heir to Roosevelt, moved to the
Commerce Department. The Republicans gained in the 1938 election, and the
WPA was one of their favorite targets. Its budget was slashed, and all those who
had been working on projects for more than eighteen months had to be dismissed. Reduced to a shell, the WPA merged with two other agencies as the
Federal Works Agency. In the uncertainty, Hasse kept up her visibility, working
on an "asset survey of library facilities and resources" for the new agency, con-
vening a meeting of the housing bibliography group, and addressing the librarians at the Federal Security Agency, where Ellen Commons now worked, but it
was not enough to save her job. She was furloughed in the fall of 1939.[22]

Hasse had continued her networking and been alert to new job opportunities
throughout her FERA/WPA years, so she was not unprepared for another turn in
her long career path. Besides her housing committee work and her involvement
in SLA and DCLA, she had continued to teach at George Washington University, offering a new course in 1935 on research methods for government information in Washington. (A student remembered her as "strict . . . but very
pleasant.")[23] She had done two more revisions of *How Our Government Is Run.*
When the Federal Register Act finally established a national gazette in 1935,
Hasse contacted Rep. Emmanuel Cellar about her experience and interest. She
continued to seek a sponsor for more work on indexing diplomatic papers, encouraged by the praise for her index in Samuel Flagg Bemis's guide to United
States diplomatic history. Bemis had said that a continuation of her index after
1861 was much needed, so Hasse sent him a proposal which he suggested she
take up with a committee on historical sources. In 1938, she announced that
WPA had authorized her to resume the foreign affairs index at the invitation of
the American Association of International Law, but this never came to fruition,
nor did her efforts to revive the state documents index. She was called on to index various Senate hearings, and in 1937 the WPA gave permission for her to
work for Senator Harry Byrd's Select Committee on Investigation of the Executive Agencies of the Government, a project that again involved her with the
Brookings Institution in indexing its report on reorganization of the executive
branch. Once an advocate of a stronger executive, Brookings had become
alarmed at the expansion of government, and the conservative Senator Byrd

chose it for expert analysis free of New Deal inclinations. The report differed from the administration's proposal for reorganization and played a part in influencing opinion against the president's plan. For Hasse, with the New Deal under fire, it was prudent to keep a hand in with its opponents, renewing her connection with Brookings and cultivating Byrd's staff, but her next employment would be very much part of the economic reform spirit of the WPA.

At seventy-one, Hasse wasn't financially able to retire, with no pension income, and she probably wasn't inclined to do so anyway. Nothing dulled her dedication to work with government information, and with her skill as a specialized indexer well known in Washington, the 1940s would be almost as busy as the previous decades. Hasse adapted to a pattern of temporary jobs variously titled consultant, editor, or editorial analyst, while keeping up with her usual round of teaching, speaking, and office holding. Realizing that her age could be a problem to potential employers, she subtracted six years on several Civil Service forms, changing her birth date from 1868 to 1874, and in one case even subtracted twenty-one years by giving 1889 as her year of birth. The lie about her age required omission of her years at LAPL, and she avoided awkward subjects with other falsifications of her employment history.[24]

From the WPA, she moved to an equally vital enterprise as an editorial analyst for the Temporary National Economic Committee (TNEC), a joint congressional-executive study of the American economy in search of the ultimate goal of stable prosperity and full employment in a capitalist system without extremes of boom and bust. It was charged to investigate economic concentration, the price system, and public policy, but the chair, Senator Joseph O'Mahoney of Wyoming, and New Dealers like Hopkins were particularly concerned about the monopoly power of big business. Large corporations prepared to defend themselves with presentations of sophisticated statistical data, and various agencies were called on for data and analysis. Besides its own staff, the TNEC could turn to support units in each department, with the Securities and Exchange Commission (SEC) particularly active in gathering information for what became one of the largest government inquiries in American history. Over eighteen months of hearings, the committee generated seventeen thousand pages of testimony and exhibits, while the staff produced forty-three volumes of monographs on major economic topics. Never before had the government made such a comprehensive attempt to gather information on the economy, and Hasse's expertise on data sources and indexing was much appreciated. By the time the TNEC's final report was issued in 1941, the nation was being drawn towards war, and interest in the economy seemed less urgent. In a sense, the TNEC was the New Deal's last hurrah, validating the fiscal and regulatory policies it established. Senator O'Mahoney arranged for Hasse to prepare an overall index to the entire set of hearings and monographs (for which she had already done individual indexes), hoping to make the information useful in shaping the postwar economy, just as Baruch as once hoped the War Industry Board's information would be of long-term value. After "three years of grinding work," she turned in seventy-five thousand index cards in 1947, only to find that the Republicans now controlling Congress were not interested in publishing the index, which was relegated to "gathering dust in the attic of the Senate office building."[25]

As a result of her "splendid job" at the TNEC, Hasse was hired for indexing work as editorial analyst for the Securities and Exchange Commission (SEC), an aggressive investigator of business practices affecting the stock market. Hasse prepared index-digests for reports on investment trusts and protective and reorganization committees. These indexes were so thorough and detailed as to form digests of the contents, demonstrating her mastery of the terminology and other details of the subject, as well as her grasp of the importance of cross references. A grateful business librarian wrote of how much easier her life would be if only there were more such indexes. When Hasse began, the SEC hoped to continue the indexing, but by the time she finished the initial project in 1943, war was the government's priority, and the commission's headquarters had been transferred to Philadelphia, where Hasse did not care to move.[26]

Hasse next had a temporary war service appointment in the library of the Civil Service Commission, which wanted a thorough index of the Ramsbeck hearings, followed by an indexing assignment for the State Department. In 1944-45, there was a part-time appointment as a consultant to the Census Bureau, where she developed subject guides that brought more appreciation from special librarians. From New York, Linda Morley wrote that when she saw the census subject guide, she could have guessed Hasse's connection "because of your long time interest in promoting this type of service. . . . One of the things I like particularly is the practice of including explanatory notes and the liberal references. . . . Somehow or other you escaped the attitude so prevalent among librarians that results in formalizing and impersonalizing to the extent that the product loses much of its usefulness!" Another librarian rejoiced, "Can you imagine the joy in Israel over the Census Bureau Experimental Bulletin for November 1944? A subject guide! Bless your heart!"[27]

When Washington finally got a graduate program in library science at Catholic University, Hasse quickly became involved, addressing the first students and receiving teaching appointments from 1940 through 1943.[28] She continued active in the Special Libraries Association, serving as vice-president of the Baltimore chapter and then leading the movement finally to establish a Washington chapter in 1940. In calling for the new chapter, Hasse was as messianic as ever about the "important opportunities . . . beckoning" special librarians and her hope that the status of librarians would finally improve: "New terminologies, new processes, new industries, new industrial integrations are daily experience. As a matter of fact, the frontiers of the economic universe loom new and strange, and this phenomenon very closely touches a revised special libraries status. These changing frontiers are . . . reflected in the flood of data pouring out of Washington, which reaches some of our colleagues some of the time but not all of our colleagues all the time. And here lies the unique function of the organization you are here to create, viz.: to plan and execute a system of superhighways through this maze of data."[29]

If the Washington SLA chapter could achieve her dream of bringing order out of the chaos of government information, it would be not only of practical service, but it might bring special librarians closer to equal status with other staff in their organizations. After fifty years in the field, Hasse still had faith that librarians could solve the information explosion, now by building information superhighways, and thus finally raise their perpetually low status. She provided no specifics on how a Washington SLA chapter would accomplish this transformation, but her inspirational tone was sufficiently appreciated that she was elected the first president of what quickly became a large and active organization. *Special Libraries* reported, "A de-coding of Miss Hasse's Chapter report by wire in thirty-nine words yields the following record of achievement: the chapter has seven groups, each meeting monthly in addition to monthly chapter meetings; a membership of 169 members; a student loan fund; the compilation of *U.S. Government Periodicals—A Descriptive List* . . . the issuance of a Chapter *Bulletin*. All in all, the chapter is 'healthy.'"[30] Hasse kept up her work with professional organizations throughout the 1940s, continuing till past eighty as SLA's Washington monitor of government publications and a board member of the local law librarians group.

While working into old age to improve public access to government information, Hasse would have been furious to know that she had again been reported to the FBI by someone who recalled hearing of "strong evidence" that she furnished information to the enemy during World War I. After investigating Hasse throughout 1943, the bureau had only a sketchy history of her career, and it apparently never found its own file of the 1921-22 investigation. It finally concluded that there were "insufficient facts to warrant further investigation."[31]

Even the indomitable Hasse was slowed by age and arteriosclerosis, but she continued working into her ninth decade. In 1948-49, she was at the Library of Congress as a "bibliographic and political anatomist," helping William Jenkins with a project to microfilm state documents. Here Hasse had a colleague who appreciated her expertise and readily adopted what she now called "mechanized bibliography," an adaptation of her long-standing preference for organizing documents and their records by government structure. Going back to the model she had used forty years earlier in her bibliography of the original states, she planned a classed arrangement, with "the classed listings in the skeletal pattern of the structure of government . . . filled in from the supporting sources in print and in manuscript." In a monograph on collecting and using state documents, Jenkins gave many pages to praise of Hasse's insight into the special nature of government publications and her vision of a research service that would provide access to content. He credited Hasse with developing a "constructive pathway toward the development of a science of public documents."[32]

In the spring of 1949, Hasse had a health crisis, probably a stroke or heart attack, and became largely house-bound. She finally inquired about a civil service annuity for her years of government work but was told she had not accumulated enough to qualify. She apparently persisted, only to be informed that auditors had determined that she actually owed the government $150 for a double credit in January 1919. Hasse replied with an explanation of the hectic circumstances and assurances that it was either a mistake or someone's attempt to pay overtime for long hours of work on reports for the peace treaty negotiators. Despite her age and ill health, Hasse mustered the energy to reject any implication of impropriety on the part of one who had devoted her life to government information: "What I object to is the implied smear. It is well known that I am a specialist in the analysis of government documents of this and other countries and most of my work for this government has been on emergency calls to contribute this specialty. This I have done but not on a clocked-day time."[33]

Meanwhile, she worked on a personal project, accumulating thirty-nine folders of references for a bibliography on European federation, hoping to contribute to the movement that seemed to offer Europe's only hope of ending the horrors of war in the twentieth century. She also unsuccessfully sought work as indexer of the published papers of Thomas Jefferson, "to round out my career." There was a last government assignment, a bibliography on immigration law for the Immigration and Naturalization Bureau.[34]

In her homebound period, Hasse especially treasured "the nicest letter I ever had," Ellen Commons' affectionate thanks to "my Pilot" for inspiring her to remain a librarian. That and an honorary membership from the Special Libraries Association in 1952 were the consolations of her last years.[35]

Finally Hasse was no longer able to remain at home and entered a nursing home where she died on July 28, 1953. Her estate consisted of little more than her house, which she left to Elizabeth Maynard and her two children, presumably Leslie's family, and two nearby lots left to her sister Hilda and her brother's widow. The will made no mention of Leslie, not even in the list of next of kin. (According to the Social Security death index, he died in Texas in 1976.) Hasse's personal possessions were left to Tilloah Squires, her companion of many years, and her nephew George Fielding, who lived in the Washington area. Squires also was bequeathed the contents of Hasse's bank account, a small amount consumed by the estate's final expenses, and was named executor but declined to serve. Fielding observed that she seemed eager to dispose of Hasse's books and papers, understandable when she had to leave her longtime home. Why Squires was not left the house is another mystery of her relationship with Hasse; Fielding understood her to be a sort of paid companion.[36]

The Washington newspapers and the New York Times published obituaries of Hasse as an expert in government publications, variously described as a bibliographer or editorial analyst, with little or no mention of her library career. The library press marked her passing with brief notes that gave no indication that she once had been "the most famous woman in American library service." Only Special Libraries eulogized her: "Tireless in her work, her entire career was devoted to the teaching and practice of her chosen profession, and countless librarians are indebted to her for the counsel and advice she was willing to give, and for the reference tools, bibliographies and indexes she bequeathed to the world." Hasse would have appreciated that, but what she really saw as her epitaph had already appeared many years before, in her tribute to Charles McCarthy: "Optimistic, adventurous, defiant, humanly generous, in his social outlook, scornful of the petty attitudes of the complacently unquestioning, McCarthy was and ever will be a joy and an inspiration."[37]

Notes

1. AH correspondence about financial matters, AH-LC.

2. AH correspondence about bibliographic and indexing work, AH-LC.

3. AH correspondence with Alvern Sutherland, Levrett Lyons, and Harold Moulton, May-Sept. 1933, AH-LC.

4. Marian Manley, "Tessa Kelso, August 13, 1933," LJ 58 (Oct. 1933): 800; AH to Emma Baldwin, 6 Jan. 1934, AH-LC.

5. Adelaide Fielding Kerr to David Laughlin, 22 Sept., 3 Oct. 1990, in possession of the author.

6. Background on the New Deal is drawn primarily from Blanche Wiesen Cook, *Eleanor Roosevelt*, vol. 2, *1933-1938* (New York: Viking, 1999); George T. McJimsey, *Harry Hopkins: Ally of the Poor and Defender of Democracy* (Cambridge: Harvard University Press, 1987); T. H. Watkins, *The Great Depression* (Boston: Little, Brown, 1993); Dixon Wecter, *The Age of the Great Depression, 1929-1941* (New York: Macmillan, 1948).

7. AH to T. I. Crowell, 15 Aug. 1933, AH-LC.

8. L. S. Boyd to AH, 20 July 1933, AH-LC; Brookings inquiry, 28 Feb. 1934, AH-LC.

9. *Library Accessions* (weekly mimeographed list), RG 69, Works Progress Administration, U.S. National Archives; *Washington News*, 27 June 1935; Helen Moore to AH, 28 June 1935, AH-LC.

10. Watkins, *Great Depression*, 247.

11. Adelaide Hasse, "Bibliographical Notes on Housing," *Annals of the American Academy of Political and Social Science* 190 (March 1937): 226-33.

12. AH to Eleanor Roosevelt, 1 July 1936, Malvina Scheider to AH, 7 July 1936, AH to Scheider, 7 July 1936, Franklin D. Roosevelt Library, Hyde Park, NY; AH's European travel from her passport, AH-LC.

13. AH to Axel Dahlberg, 24 Feb. 1937, AH-LC; SL 30 (Jan. 1939): 25; Adelaide Hasse, *Bibliography on Urban Real Estate Appraisal* (Washington: Joint Committee on Appraisal and Mortgage Analysis, 1937); SL 28 (May-June 1937): 171.

14. Commons to AH, 14 April 1950, AH-LC.

15. Betty Schwartz, "The Role of the American Library Association in the Selection of Archibald MacLeish as Librarian of Congress," *Journal of Library History* 9 (July 1974): 241-64; LJ 63 (15 July 1939): 546.

16. AH to John C. Merriam, n.d., AH-LC.

17. Vance to AH, 27 April 1936, AH-LC; *New York Times* clipping, 16 May 1936, AH-LC; Wayne Wiegand, "This Month, 66 Years Ago," *American Libraries* 33 (Feb. 2002): 69.

18. DCLA banquet program, 1 April 1936, AH-LC.

19. Cook, *Eleanor Roosevelt*, ix.

20. *New York Times* clipping, 2 Oct. 1937, and Buffalo Public Library to AH, 14 Oct. 1937, AH-LC.

21. Cook, *Eleanor Roosevelt*, 458-60; Crane to AH, 26 Aug. 1937, and clipping of the poem, AH-LC.

22. AH to Mary Louise Alexander, 1 Sept. 1939, AH-LC; Commons to AH, 28 Sept. 1939, AH-LC.

23. *Washington Post* clipping, 9 Sept. 1935, AH-LC; John Corbin, " Strange Career of Adelaide Hasse," *Wilson Library Bulletin* (June 1981): 757.

24. Various employment forms in AH-LC and her federal employment file, U.S. National Archives and Records Administration, Civilian Personnel Records, St. Louis.

25. David Lynch, *The Concentration of Economic Power* (New York: Columbia University Press, 1946); AH to Myron Hoch, 30 June 1948, AH-LC.

26. SEC employment, AH federal employment file; Eleanor Cavanaugh to AH, 26 Dec. 1946, AH-LC.

27. Civil Service Commission appointment, AH federal employment file; Census Bureau appointment, AH-LC; Linda Morley to AH, 21 March 1945, AH-LC; Maria Brace to AH, 14 March 1945, AH-LC. Morley and Brace were active in SLA.

28. AH correspondence with Catholic University, AH-LC.

29. Adelaide Hasse, "To Be or Not to Be," in *Washington, D. C. Chapter Special Libraries Association Fiftieth Anniversary* (Washington: The Chapter, 1990).

30. SL 33 (July-Aug. 1942): 211.

31. U.S. Federal Bureau of Investigation File 100-227405 (1943).

32. William S. Jenkins, *Collecting and Using the Records of the States of the United States: Twenty-five Years in Retrospection* (Chapel Hill: Bureau of Public Records, Univ. of North Carolina, 1961), 20-27.

33. AH to Warren B. Irons, Civil Service Commission, n.d. [1951], AH-LC.

34. AH to Julian Boyd, n.d. [1950], AH-LC; *Washington Evening Star*, 29 July 1953.

35. AH to Commons, 13 June 1950, AH-LC.

36. AH's will, Orphan's Court of Montgomery County, Maryland; George Fielding's granddaughter, Ariel Fielding, to the author, 12 Sept. 2004.

37. SL 44 (Oct. 1953): 344; SL 12 (Dec. 1921): 236.

Epilogue

History of a Reputation

At the time of her death, Adelaide Hasse seemed to have been forgotten, but, in the final ironic twist of her career, there were latent forces that soon would revive her memory, so that by the turn of the century, *American Libraries* would sanctify her as one of its hundred library leaders of the twentieth century. There she was, among many of the contemporaries who figured largely in her life: the men who inspired her, Billings and Dana; men who tried to destroy her, Metcalf, Lydenberg, and Williamson; men who admired her work, Dewey, J. C. M. Hanson, Charles Martel, and the ambivalent Bowker; and the women, both friends and foes, who matched her ambition and shared her great expectations for libraries, Ahern, Hewins, Moore, Mudge, and Sears. Only thirty of the hundred leaders were women (half of them children's librarians), and many of Hasse's notable women contemporaries didn't make the list, but, in the half century since her death, the unsinkable Adelaide Hasse had risen to the status of a giant of the profession.[1]

Unfortunately, *American Libraries* didn't seem fully aware of what made Hasse a library leader. In its capsule description, there was no mention of her classification and cataloging, her bibliographies, her work for the federal government, all part of her lifelong commitment to government information, nor of her role in library education, and certainly nothing of her autobiographical pamphlet and other controversial commentary. Her achievement was the NYPL government documents collection: "Known for her acerbic personality, she nonetheless developed a model public documents collection at New York Public Library with John Shaw Billings' blessing and tutelage." The dualism that plagued Hasse in life continued to shadow her memory, as even praise for one of her achievements was tinged with negativity about her personal qualities. The reference to an "acerbic personality" was taken from a biographical dictionary entry that was entirely positive about her achievements and mentioned her "brilliance" in the same sentence as the negative reference to her personality. *American Li-*

braries said nothing about the personalities of the other leaders; there was no suggestion that Dana and Billings were acerbic or Lydenberg and Metcalf backstabbing assassins. Why Hasse was singled out as the only one of the hundred library leaders known for an unpleasant personality is unclear, as is the logic of the "nonetheless" linkage to her development of a great collection, as though lack of sweetness were a handicap that would keep a woman librarian from achieving, unless granted the "blessing and tutelage" of a distinguished male director, John Shaw Billings. In reality, Hasse's exuberantly extroverted personality was not acerbic, though her words sometimes were, and many friends and admirers found her charming. If the hundred library leaders were ranked for congeniality, she would be far from the bottom, but the Anderson network's character assassination continued to undermine her reputation, even as other factors advanced it.

On the positive side, her monumental bibliographies had always been valued by librarians, but what began the revival of her reputation was the expansion of the depository library program in the 1960s. Hasse might have been dismayed at the further growth of the program she thought too large in 1908, but the existence of over a thousand depository libraries meant a larger group of librarians specializing in government information and using her classification system (the role of William Leander Post having been forgotten). The new breed of documents librarians finally established the Government Documents Round Table that Hasse had advocated sixty years earlier and became a vocal part of ALA, sometimes labeled as zealous as Hasse had been. The larger number of depositories also created a market for the kind of indexes to content that Hasse had sought, particularly in the invaluable indexes to congressional hearings and government statistics issued by Congressional Information Service (CIS). Though much of her career remained obscure, Hasse became a sort of patron saint of government documents librarians, and the Government Printing Office named a room in her honor in 1985.

Meanwhile, feminism, deeply suppressed in the 1950s, revived in what became a new wave of change, with new interest in women's history. In librarianship, this meant an increased awareness of the women who had shaped American libraries in the early years of the century. A leader in seeking out the biographies of those women was Laurel Grotzinger, who wrote several brief accounts of Hasse's life, including her entry in the *Dictionary of American Library Biography*. Grotzinger even acknowledged that Hasse had been fired in 1918, a subject so delicate that, as late as 1973, the *Encyclopedia of Library and Information Science* said only that with the coming of a new director, "Miss Hasse, with boundless energy and specialized experience, did not adjust."[2]

Even as Grotzinger emphasized Hasse's achievements, she reinforced the Anderson version with her DALB reference to an acerbic personality and the suggestion that Hasse "is not easy to know or like" (which might be said of most of the achieving women of the past two centuries). This was supported by Metcalf's memoir, in which he showed no embarrassment in revealing his role in her dismissal, assuring his readers that, though he felt rather badly about ending Hasse's long service, "I am convinced I did the right thing." He was followed by Paul Winkler's biography of Williamson, which quoted Hasse's brusque 1912 memo as evidence of the trouble she caused but omitted any reference to the awkward fact that Williamson returned to the Economics Division because she was fired, vaguely attributing his rehiring to a "personnel crisis," the nature of which was said to be unknown. With no explanation of the circumstances in which Williamson got the job he needed, there was no occasion to quote his vicious comments about Hasse to the trustees. The book showed only Hasse's sharp assertion of her division's independence, with no indication that Williamson had been far nastier in attacking her in a secret proceeding. In a review, Edward Holley criticized the failure to explain Williamson's role in Hasse's dismissal or his later battles with Roger Howson at Columbia, but even in calling for better analysis of these conflicts, Holley conceded, "Granted Hasse was a difficult woman," with no suggestion that Williamson and Howson might have been difficult men. After all, as Winkler summed up their twelve-year war, "Howson and Williamson were both gentlemen, but both were forceful men with strong wills and convinced of their own beliefs."[3]

Though Metcalf's memoir included the text of the letter calling for action against Hasse, its implications about the atmosphere in NYPL went unanalyzed, as did the correspondence included in Hasse's pamphlet. Instead, two writers of dissertations, Catherine Shanley on the Library Employees Union and Barry Seaver on Rebecca Rankin, accepted the dubious allegations of Hasse's enemies. Shanley repeated the narrative of Anderson and the other men, including the canard that Hasse refused to provide documents reference service, while both propagated Metcalf's unproven claim that Hasse "orchestrated" an attack on the administration. Neither suggested any possible connection between Hasse's dismissal, Rankin's transfer, and Metcalf's appointment as executive assistant.[4]

While these contributions to library history reinforced the view that Hasse was a difficult woman, they at least acknowledged her existence. Other studies, in which she should have had a place, ignored her altogether. Hasse's efforts in library education were unrecognized even in a history of the Los Angeles training program and an account of women leaders of library schools, and she was barely mentioned in Vann's history of library education before 1923, which touched briefly on the LAPL program, indignantly criticized the tone of Hasse's and Dana's ALA committee report, dismissed Hasse's criticism of library school graduates as "antagonistic," and made no mention of the School for Business Librarians.[5] Hasse's development of entries for government documents found no place in a monograph on corporate entry that devoted much attention to the problems presented by governmental bodies.[6] A study of the Public Documents Committee skipped over Hasse's tenure as chair, saying nothing about her initiating the first documents round table or her frank comments about depository libraries.[7]

Strangest of all, Dee Garrison's influential study of the feminization of American librarianship discussed the Library Employees Union but made no mention of Hasse's dismissal, her autobiographical pamphlet, or her forcefully worded calls for change in 1917-19, the period Garrison identified as a crucial turning point. Hasse would seem to be a significant subject for Garrison, since she vigorously expressed Garrison's own view of the culture of public libraries and was severely punished for doing so. Garrison has been criticized for blaming the victim in attributing what she sees as the stunted development of public libraries to women librarians "who did not question their sex-typed roles." Hasse challenged sex roles at a crucial point in women's history, and her firing sent a message about what happened to women librarians who didn't know their place. That Garrison, for all her impressive research, apparently was unaware of the controversy about Hasse, shows how thoroughly memory of the events of 1918-19 had been repressed.[8]

Thus the name of Adelaide Hasse was honored by the government documents librarians who followed her career model, denigrated by Anderson, Metcalf, and Williamson and those who accepted their authority, and ignored by historical studies of library issues in which she had been involved. Essentially, her memory was trapped in the conventional metaphors of the female: the hardworking housekeeper, drudging away at the details of her bibliographies and classification; the angry, disorderly shrew who had to be purged by the male leadership; and the invisible woman, whose challenges to the status quo were forgotten. But unlike most of her contemporaries, Hasse left records that could provide a more balanced understanding of her life and work. Besides the extensive print record in periodicals and *The Compensations of Librarianship*, there were the long-submerged archival records awaiting discovery in the NYPL Archives, the Library of Congress, the National Archives, and the files of the FBI, as well as in the papers of various contemporaries. Marshaling these resources, it is possible to see her career in full and to recognize issues broader and deeper than an allegedly difficult personality. Indeed, that very emphasis on personality suggests an avoidance of questions as valid now as in Hasse's lifetime.

Though not an acerbic personality, Hasse certainly was opinionated, outspoken, and combative, as were many of her contemporaries in the Progressive Era. In her ambition and impatience, she was not always perfectly honest or consistent, but she did pursue high ideals and high standards of performance. These are the characteristics of many successful Americans. Indeed, Hasse was a prime example of the determined, self-promoting, high-energy extrovert associated with success in American culture—the go-getter, the entrepreneur, the maverick. This was the persona of the dominant national figure of her middle years, Theodore Roosevelt, and of many of the men she knew personally. The annals of business and politics abound in such temperaments, and though they may arouse resentment, stir controversy, and sometimes self-destruct, they are admired, even revered, for their risk taking, their large achievements, their ability to get things done with creativity and panache. Usually, of course, they are men, working in complex situations where conflicting policies and ambitions are understood to be normal, at least among men.

That such personalities continue to be regarded as problematic in women is widely recognized in the literature on gender. It has even been the subject of a Supreme Court case, *Price Waterhouse v. Hopkins*, about a woman similar to Hasse. Ann Hopkins brought suit against a major accounting firm, charging that she was denied a partnership that would have been routinely granted to a man with her record of bringing in business, while she was evaluated negatively for using "foul language," not wearing make-up, and generally needing to go to "charm school." The court agreed that such gender stereotypes in the workplace are a form of discrimination against women. As Justice Brennan commented, "We sit not to determine whether Ms. Hopkins is nice, but to decide whether the partners reacted negatively to her personality because she is a woman." The case was widely discussed as a historic recognition of the subtle realities of sex discrimination, but news reports indicate that such stereotyping remains a problem for ambitious women.[9]

That Hasse clashed with men considered "giants of the profession" reinforced the negative view of her personality in library history. In the status hierarchy of librarians, directors of large, prestigious libraries held the highest rank, with no suggestion of problems with their management or their personalities. Anderson, Metcalf, and Lydenberg were directors of very large libraries, while Williamson was doubly respected as director at an Ivy League university and the initiator of what was assumed to be a great advance in library education and professionalism. There is no acknowledgment that they were sometimes nasty, unscrupulous, and, yes, even difficult, nor is there any suggestion that they may have feared and hated Adelaide Hasse as much from their own ambitions and anxieties as for her behavior. Certainly the man Hasse most admired, Billings, had a fierce temper, a sharp tongue, and a brusque determination that his orders be followed, but his personality has not been treated as problematic in library history. Though descriptions of Billings and Hasse suggest similar temperaments, it doesn't seem to occur to anyone that the great man was a role model for the difficult woman. The double standard is the essence of sexism, but so deep is the deference to these men that library historians seemed unable to recognize the bias in their perception of Hasse—or, indeed, in attitudes towards the first generation of women librarians, who tend to be either ignored or presented with condescending sentimentality.

Hasse's drive, ambition, and vigorous criticism were characteristic of many of her women contemporaries, both in the library world and in the Progressive Era generally. As Jill Ker Conway has written of those crusading women, "Their language was pungent, their schedules were enough to daunt a professional athlete, and, for those who worked with them, their force of character something of primal dimensions."[10] Yet most of them were careful to present a conventionally feminine image, Conway concludes, because a woman must fit the female stereotype to win support. Conway has written of her own discomfort with evidence of egotism and selfishness in the secular saint Jane Addams, and perhaps there has been similar uneasiness with Hasse's sharp tongue and open conflict with male authority figures. Hasse certainly tried to adopt stereotypically feminine themes in her claims that she was "called" to her jobs and guided by her leaders, Kelso and Billings, her emphasis on motherhood keeping her mentally healthy, and her insistence that she sought only to follow the wishes of Billings and was motivated by love of her library. Yet, from the beginning, she feared gender roles as a trap, and over time she became increasingly androgynous, asserting her expertise in public affairs information, her challenging ideas about libraries, and her insistence that pay and working conditions be improved. In her relations with coworkers, she encountered the woman's double bind and wearily concluded, "When I am friendly and kindly and diplomatic, I am ineffectual," a feeling familiar to many, even unto the present day and generation.[11]

That Hasse's persona has been classified so negatively raises questions about the attitudes of a profession that perpetually complains about its image and pay while largely ignoring the achievements of its founding mothers and classifying as "giants" men who were no more than ordinary examples of the managerial class of their time. The firing of Adelaide Hasse was known to many of the opinion leaders of her era and probably contributed to the long-standing negative image of library administration, the factor underlying President Franklin Roosevelt's refusal to appoint a "professionally trained seal" Librarian of Congress and the perception that NYPL had declined for decades until rescued by Vartan Gregorian, a Ph.D. with no experience as a librarian but an ample supply of Hasse-like energy and enthusiasm. Gregorian's autobiography cheerfully recounts his indifference to rules, involvement in fierce academic battles, protest against demeaning treatment, and relish for fund-raising. Though an immigrant, swarthy and speaking with an accent, the exuberant Gregorian was a brilliantly successful salesman for NYPL in a way that would have delighted Hasse. His reputation is still another example of the double standard in regard to personality. Although Gregorian's success might seem to raise questions about the impact of uninspiring men like Anderson and Lydenberg, their personalities have been accepted as the norm that requires no examination in library history, while Hasse is labeled difficult and acerbic, an aberration, an unnatural woman.[12]

This is not to say that a particular personality is good or bad, but rather that Hasse's type tends to be more valued in American culture. Everyone has strengths and weaknesses, of course, and the nature of personality, its impact and interaction within organizations, is elusive, contingent, and not suited to easy generalization. As Carol Tavris wrote of the Hopkins case, personality is ultimately a mystery: "We will never know the truth about Ann Hopkins —whether she is outspoken or overbearing, confident or arrogant—because both sets of perceptions are true, from the beholder's standpoint. But by framing the problem as one of her personality, her colleagues deflected attention from the systematic practices of their company and from their own behavior."[13]

In the same way, emphasis on Hasse's personality has been a distraction from the actions of Hasse's coworkers and the management practices at NYPL, as well as the related issue of sex discrimination. With closer look at Anderson, Metcalf, and the other prominent men who demonized her, it is possible to see Hasse as a victim of a flagrant double standard and of wartime hysteria about disloyalty, which became entangled with hostility towards an ambitious woman, a union sympathizer, an outspoken critic of the culture of libraries, and a German American. This makes her an awkward subject for a profession that remains overwhelmingly female, has benefited from union membership, prides itself on devotion to intellectual freedom, and seeks greater diversity, in both its own ranks and its clientele. To a great extent, Hasse was a martyr to causes of fundamental concern to librarians, and her dismissal came at a significant point in the history of American libraries and the women who worked in them. When Garrison suggests that libraries lost momentum because women librarians preferred the role of genteel hostess, the lesson those women learned from the experience of Adelaide Hasse should be part of the analysis.

Underlying this are assumptions crucial to a feminized profession, that it was not normal for a woman librarian to claim expertise as Hasse did or vigorously express controversial opinions or dispute the decisions of men. That this history has implications for the current work environment of a predominantly female profession is suggested by one of the few observers to discuss conflict in libraries, Herbert White, who has complained of an obsession with niceness in library management. White argues that libraries too often drive out the best and brightest for not conforming to the comfortable mediocrity that is the group norm. In words that recall Adelaide Hasse, he urges administrators to seek and encourage "wild ducks" without regard for their congeniality, even if it means facing down the "lynch mob" of staff threatened by those with more ability or different ideas. "If change comes, it is usually from the shrill insistence of annoying individuals," but too many directors prefer "pleasing incompetents."[14]

The culture of niceness that worried White may also be found in library historiography, which has been described by Suzanne Hildenbrand as resembling "traditional patriotic narrative in United States history." Hildenbrand points to gender as a factor in such banality and concludes, "The narrow focus of library history, celebrating white male leadership . . . , reflects the politics of library history," which she sees as indicative of the dominance of a small male elite, clinging to power and status amidst an overwhelmingly female workforce, needing "to manage myth and memory in order to both distance itself from the nonelite and to scapegoat it."[15]

In the history of American libraries, Adelaide Hasse would not want to be remembered as either monster or victim. She sought always to live largely, and her inner narrative was of the hero's quest. Rejecting the conventional roles of madonna of the children's room or small-town Marian the Librarian, she invented a career of professional expertise that gave her a half century of intellectually challenging work in New York and Washington, contributing to both scholarship and public policy. In that career, she asserted that a woman librarian could live a public life of achievement and recognition. What she would find frustrating now is the memory hole into which her values and her ideas have fallen. Hasse spoke and wrote about issues that are as relevant today as a century ago, despite ever-changing conditions. How should librarians be recruited and educated? What is the nature of their professional expertise? How do libraries function as organizations? What services do they provide? How do they provide access to government information, or any specialized information, beyond a minimal level? What are the dynamics of a feminized profession? These are questions for continuous dialogue and debate, not tidy, correct answers. Hasse tried to stir such discussion, but her ideas were submerged in allegations that she was a difficult, disloyal woman. Ultimately, however, her place in library history has more to do with her work, her values, and her experience in a gendered system than with the enigmas of personality.

Notes

1. "100 of the Most Important Leaders We Had," *American Libraries* 30 (Dec. 1999), 38-47.

2. Laurel Grotzinger, "Adelaide Rosalie Hasse," DALB, and "Adelaide Hasse," *ALA World Encyclopedia of Library and Information Services*; James Bennett Child, "Adelaide Rosalia Hasse," *Encyclopedia of Library and Information Science*.

3. Keyes Metcalf, *Random Recollections of an Anachronism* (New York: Readex, 1980); Paul Winkler, *The Greatest of Greatness: The Life and Work of Charles C. Williamson* (Metuchen, NJ: Scarecrow Press, 1992), 209-28; Edward Holley, review of *Greatest of Greatness, Library Quarterly* 63 (Jan. 1993): 121-22.

4. Catherine Shanley, *The Library Employees' Union of Greater New York, 1917-1929* (Diss., Columbia University, 1992); Barry Seaver, *The Career of Rebecca Browning Rankin* (Diss., University of North Carolina, Chapel Hill, 1997).

5. Marion Horton, "The Los Angeles Library School," LJ 48 (15 Nov. 1923): 959-60; Martha Boaz, "And There Were Giantesses in Library Education," in *Women in the Library Profession: Leadership Roles and Contributions* (Ann Arbor: University of Michigan School of Library Science, 1971),1-10; Sarah Vann, *Training for Librarianship before 1923* (Chicago: ALA, 1961).

6. Michael Carpenter, *Corporate Authorship: Its Role in Library Cataloging* (Westport, CT: Greenwood Press, 1981).

7. Susan Lee Grabler, "Government Information Of, By, and For the People: The Changing Mission of the American Library Association's Public Documents Committee, 1876-1956," *Journal of Government Information* 22 (Jan.-Feb. 1995): 45-69.

8. Dee Garrison, *Apostles of Culture: The Public Librarian and American Society, 1876-1920* (New York: Free Press, 1979).

9. Carol Tavris, *The Mismeasure of Women* (New York: Simon & Schuster, 1992), 21-23; Kathleen Hall Jamieson, *Beyond the Double Bind: Women and Leadership* (New York: Oxford University Press, 1995), 136-41.

10. Jill Ker Conway, *True North* (New York: Knopf, 1994), 149.

11. AH to Harry Lydenberg, 16 Feb. 1916, AH-CB.

12. Gordon S. Wood, "Only in America," review of *The Road to Home: My Life and Times,* by Vartan Gregorian, *New York Review of Books* (25 Sept. 2003), 78-80.

13. Tavris, *Mismeasure,* 22.

14. Herbert S. White, "The Tyranny of the Team," LJ 114 (15 April 1989): 54-55; White, "Never Mind Being Innovative and Effective—Just Be Nice," LJ 120 (15 Sept. 1995): 47-48; White, "Smearing with a Broad Brush," LJ 120 (15 Oct. 1995): 41-42.

15. Suzanne Hildenbrand, "Women in Library History: From the Politics of Library History to the History of Library Politics," in Suzanne Hildenbrand, ed., *Reclaiming the American Library Past: Writing the Women In* (Norwood, NJ: Ablex, 1996), 2-3.

Index

About the Author

Clare Beck is emeritus professor at Eastern Michigan University, where she served as government documents librarian. She holds degrees from the University of Chicago, the University of Denver, and Eastern Michigan University. Her papers on American library history have appeared in *College and Research Libraries, Library Journal,* and *American Libraries,* and in the collections *Reclaiming the American Library Past: Writing the Women In* and *Gendering Library History.*